A LIVING HISTORY READER
VOLUME ONE

MUSEUMS

Other AASLH books by
Jay Anderson
Time Machines: The World of Living History (1984)
The Living History Sourcebook (1985)

A LIVING HISTORY READER
VOLUME ONE

MUSEUMS

Jay Anderson

American Association for State and Local History
Nashville, Tennessee

Published by the American Association for State and Local History, an international
non-profit membership organization. For membership information, please contact
Membership Services, (615) 255-2971.

96 95 94 93 92 91   7 6 5 4 3 2 1

Library of Congress Cataloging-in-Publication Data

A Living history reader / Jay Anderson . . . [et al.].
      p.   cm.
      Includes indexes.
      Contents: v. 1. Museums—v. 2. Reenactors.
      ISBN 0-942063-13-9 (v. 1).—ISBN 0-942063-18-X (v. 2)
      1. Historical museums—United States.   2. Open-air museums—United
States.   3. Historic sites—United States—Interpretative programs.
4. United States—History, Local.   I. Anderson, Jay.
E172.L58 1991
973—dc20   91-14576
                                                                         CIP

Contents

VOLUME ONE—MUSEUMS

PART V: Villages

PART VI: Experimental Programs

PART VII: Concerns

PART VIII: Afterword

Preface

A decade ago, with the encouragement of the staff of the American Association for State and Local History, I set out to write three books on living history, or historical simulation. The first, *Time Machines: The World of Living History* (1984), chronicled the living history movement from the point of view of a participant observer. Writing it was a joyful experience, an opportunity to recollect in comparitive tranquility several decades of adventurous "time travel" via outdoor museums and reenacting. My second book, *The Living History Sourcebook* (1985), was a guide to many of the best resources that make it possible for us to vicariously enter other periods of time and—with research, hard work, and not a little luck—to understand them better. Writing the sourcebook taught me how really broad and deep the living-history movement had become. This present two-volume anthology, A LIVING HISTORY READER, reacquainted me with many of the excellent articles that have been written about living history, especially by museum interpreters and enthusiasts.

The reader is not meant to be a casebook, documenting the history of the field. Nor have I tried to duplicate the fine compendia of practical skills articles such as those that have appeared in the *Book of Buckskinning* series. Rather, I wanted to compile a reader of previously published articles representing both wings of the living-history movement: outdoor museums and reenacting. I've selected articles that are thought-provoking, readable, and that collectively present a cross-section of what has been written about historical simulation. In order to keep the book reasonable in both length and price, a number of good articles have been omitted. Many of the essays I considered for inclusion in this reader came from journals and magazines no longer being published; few publications are as ephemeral as those in the living-history field.

The entries in this volume of the READER focus on living-history museums. After a brief introductory article the sections are: beginnings of the living-history museum; forts; farms; villages; experimental programs; and concerns raised by scholars both within and outside the museum field. Volume one ends with a brief afterword. The second volume of the READER deals with reenactors and follows a similar format, with sections on: the European scene, warriors, battles, voyages, treks, and the never-ending quest for authenticity.

Although I've written headnotes for each entry, the articles are reprinted exactly as they were originally published. This includes footnotes, which vary considerably in format. A few minor changes—a word or a phrase or two—were made at the request of several authors.

My thanks to each of the contributors, whose work made this collection possible, and to their publishers for their generous permission to use the material. Also I am indebted to Maryanne Andrus, George Chapman, Jim Phillips, and Mary Kay Schmidt, graduate "students" of mine at Utah State University. Their assistance was invaluable. They worked long and hard on this book, giving freely of their concern and counsel. Without their help, I quite simply never would have completed A LIVING HISTORY READER. Finally, thanks to my wife, Jan, who patiently nurtured me through the writing of the entire living-history trilogy.

Jay Anderson
Providence, Utah
March 1991

Part I
Introduction

Living History

Jay Anderson

1

Originally published in American Quarterly *(Fall 1982), this is the first article to consider all aspects of the living-history movement as a unity. Defining living history as "an attempt by people to simulate life in another time," the author suggests that historical simulation is generally used for three basic reasons: to interpret the past at outdoor museums and historic sites, as a research tool in experimental archaeology, and as an enjoyable recreational activity for history buffs interested in discovering what life in the past was really like. Numerous examples are given for each branch of the living-history movement, which the author believes has an important role to play in American culture.*

Living history is an idea well known to lay historians and museum interpreters but seldom heard of in academia. It has taken form as a serious movement in Europe and North America, especially since World War II. Its supporters are numerous and mixed: John D. Rockefeller, Jr., Thor Heyerdahl, James Deetz, and Alvin Toffler. Museums that use living history as a primary mode of interpretation number in the many hundreds, and their annual visitors number in the tens of millions. Living history has been used by archaeologists to measure the energy needed to pull a wooden moldboard plow on a 1770s Pennsylvania farm. It has helped folklorists rediscover how Pilgrims built their houses and brewed their beer in 1627 Plimoth, and it has provided historians with a method of communicating to contemporary Americans the network of social classes operating in an Indiana frontier village during the 1830s. Finally, living history has become a popular hobby for thousands of history buffs, many of whom made the long march to Yorktown in 1981 to commemorate the end of the American Revolution.

By and large, living history has found greater expression in museums, research projects, and folk festivals than in scholarly articles. Thus, this essay must be more of an introduction to the movement's people, places, and ideas than a comprehensive bibliography.[1] The first part will briefly sketch the history of the movement, and three sections on the primary functions of living history—research, interpretation, and play—will follow. In conclusion, I will evaluate the movement's potential role in the field of American studies.

Living history can be defined as an attempt by people to simulate life in another time. Generally, the other time is in the past, and a specific reason is given for making the attempt to live as other people once did. The reasons vary, but the three most common ones are: to interpret material culture more effectively, usually at a living museum; to test an archaeological thesis or generate data for historical ethnographies; and to participate in an enjoyable recreational activity that is also a learning experience. Folklorists would classify living history as an interesting form of expressive culture that can function in a variety of ways. It can be used as a research and interpretive tool for better understanding the culture of one's counterparts in other times and places. It can also serve as a medium for acting out in a socially acceptable way behavior not commonly encountered in the contemporary world; for example, dressing up in armor and fighting with swords and shields, hunting wild game with a muzzleloader, Morris dancing on May Day, or most commonly for living-history buffs, getting together for a weekend bivouac or rendezvous with fellow militiamen, regulars, voyageurs, or buckskinners.

Living history is related to other creative and symbolic forms, especially drama, ritual, pageantry, and play. It is obviously theatrical with its use of costume (period clothing), props (artifacts), sets (historic sites), role playing (identifying with historical characters), and the designation of time and space as special and somehow not part of our ordinary everyday world. Living history can be as safe and acceptable as a midwestern Madrigal supper or as unsettling as guerrilla theatre in a suburban shopping mall. Essentially, it is the intrusion of the past into our present, and it can be both a fascinating and threatening experience. (A recent cinemagraphic example is the scene in *Time Bandits* when the mounted knight crashes through the boy's closet door into his bedroom.) People seem drawn to living-history demonstrations, an attraction not overlooked by editors of heavily illustrated popular culture magazines such as *Smithsonian* and *National Geographic*. What seems to interest them is the simulation of everyday life in the past, of folklife.[2]

Serious interest in the folk and their everyday life began in Europe in the last century. This scholarship was often carried out by folklorists associated with a growing number of folk museums, government-supported institutions whose purpose was to collect, study, preserve, and interpret regional culture as it evolved in the many local provinces. J. Geriant Jenkins, keeper of the Welsh Folk Museum, clearly explained the mission of the European folk museum:

> What the student of folklife is not concerned with, except as they affect the daily life of the people, are the political crises, the diplomatic intrigues, and the prominent personages of the past that quite properly find their place in the usual history books. Our chief aim is to study ordinary people as they constitute the overwhelming proportion of every community. Our duty is to collect the tools and implements that they need and to record details of their life, their skills, their homes, their fields, their customs, their speech, and their leisure activities. The student of folklife searches for the key to the world of ordinary people; he attempts to throw light on their astonishingly ill-documented day-to-day life. It was the prophet Esdras who said, "It was not in our minds to be curious of the high things, but of such as pass by us daily." That is the theme of folklife studies.[2]

A quiet moment for Jo Daley, a graduate student at Utah State University's Ronald V. Jensen Living Historical Farm.—*Photo: Tom Allen*

In this century, European folklorists were joined in their study of regional folklore by a variety of other disciplines, especially the comprehensive work of the Annals School of Fernand Braudel, Marc Bloch, and the French social historians. Folk museums were established throughout Europe, but their energies were directed toward the collection and preservation of artifacts and the documentation of regional culture, especially traditions being altered or eliminated by the popular culture promulgated by the industrial revolution.[3] Educational programs and the interpretation of artifacts in their social and cultural contexts were not a high priority.[4] The simulation of life in the past at European museums was limited to an occasional craft demonstration or performance of folk dancing. (Some folk museums seem to go out of their way to avoid even a suggestion of historical simulation. In 1976 I saw interpreters at the English Acton Scott Working Farm Museum harrowing their fields in white laboratory coats, a popular uniform at the Welsh Folk Museum as well.) On the whole, Europeans were more interested in the material rather than the cultural aspect of material culture.

In North America, the attitude toward using folk museums and historic sites as appropriate settings for living-history programs, especially those that demonstrate how people culturally defined and used the built environment and its artifacts, was more favorable. The idea of establishing outdoor museums to preserve and interpret historically significant buildings and larger artifacts easily moved across the Atlantic. In 1926, John D. Rockefeller, Jr., agreed to provide the funds for the restoration, reconstruction, and refurnishing of Williamsburg, the Colonial capitol of Virginia. Eventually, 500 structures were rebuilt in an accurately recreated cultural landscape. As was not the case in Europe, at Williamsburg interpreters were dressed in clothing appropriate to the Colonial period, and in many of the shops regular demonstrations of colonial crafts were given. Cary Carson, director of research for the Colonial Williamsburg Foundation, has explained the reason for adopting living history and stressing realistic interpretation:

> Colonial Williamsburg had spent fifty years painstakingly re-creating an eighteenth-century town down to the last footscraper. Its first official statement of purpose, written in consultation with John D. Rockefeller, Jr., himself and unrevised until 1979, asserted that an authentic, three-dimensional environment was essential to understanding the "lives and times" of the early Americans and appreciating their contribution "to the ideals and culture of our country." Translated, "ideals" meant the concepts of self-government and individual liberty espoused by four indisputable worthies—Washington, Jefferson, Madison, and Henry—and expounded by them in the first two buildings that Rockefeller reconstructed at Williamsburg, the Capitol and the Raleigh Tavern. "Culture" they understood not as anthropologists use the word but in the sense of "high culture," the culture of pie-crust tables and upper-crust

manners. Small houses, ordinary furnishings, and such lesser folk as lived in Williamsburg were a part of the picture too. . . . The "lives and times" of ordinary people embroidered a variegated and richly detailed background that was needed to lend credibility to those few whom Rockefeller called "the great patriots."[5]

In the next three decades, scores of historic sites and outdoor museums were founded in the United States and Canada. They too were modeled on regional European folk museums but emphasized in true democratic fashion the "world of ordinary people." In this respect, Old Sturbridge Village, Mystic Seaport, the Farmer's Museum at Cooperstown, and the other new museums broke sharply in purpose with Williamsburg. However, they were inspired by the latter's use of costumed interpreters and historically accurate craft demonstrations. They sought to become "living museums of everyman's history," built on the premise that the folklife of a region is historically significant and its material culture should be collected, preserved, studied, and especially interpreted. The larger museums took the form of villages and relocated a selection of buildings in which the activities of ordinary townsfolk could be simulated, thereby preserving and presenting a variety of crafts, professions, and rural lifestyles.[6] However, it was the other primary American institution, the farm, that became most clearly identified with living history. In 1965, Marion Clawson, a foundation director in Washington, D.C., proposed that the government establish a system of twenty-five to fifty actual, operating, living-history farms representing the major regions and historic periods in American history:

> Within the limits necessarily imposed by a sampling of time and geography, the farms should be reasonably typical of the time and place each is chosen to represent. The farm size, its crops, livestock, production methods, the products sold—all these and other details of the farm should be as accurate as it is possible to make them. The critical aspect of this proposal is that each farm should be operating—a living farm and a living home. A family, or families, would actually live on them, operate them, and live as nearly as possible like the prototype. . . . Public visits to these living farms would naturally be encouraged, yet would have to be managed carefully to avoid conflicts with the actual farm operation. In addition to coming to look, visitors should have the farm "interpreted," in park managers' jargon. Some visitors would have rural backgrounds and would appreciate the exhibits; but most would be so urban as to not understand the importance of what they saw at the farm unless told about it.[7]

Clawson's idea was well received. With support from the Smithsonian and the Department of Agriculture, the Association for Living History Farms and Agricultural Museums (ALHFAM) was founded in 1970 at Old Sturbridge Village. Its founding membership represented a cross-section of the agricultural and museum community: historians from the Smithsonian, National Park Service interpretive specialists, open-air museum staff, and a number of living-history buffs who had been active in the Civil War Centennial. ALHFAM has become the umbrella organization for the living-history movement. It is based in the Smithsonian, publishes a bimonthly *Bulletin*, and holds an annual conference, generally at a living-history museum in the United States or Canada. Most of the theoretical and practical writings on living history have come from its leadership. These include John Schlebecker's master plan for a national system of farms, *Living Historical Farms: A Walk into the Past* (1968), and his basic guide, the *Living Historical Farms Handbook* (1972); Darwin Kelsey's article, "Harvests of History" (1976), still the best introduction to living-history farms; and Sharon Eubanks's comprehensive bibliography of all the 833 books, pamphlets, and films related to living history and reviewed in the ALHFAM *Bulletin* (1970-1976).[8] In 1980 the membership of ALHFAM agreed to welcome all living-history projects, not just farms, and the variety of ALHFAM's membership is an index to the breadth of the living-history movement. Besides farms, there are villages, historic houses, forts, ships, urban neighborhoods, and archaeological sites.[9] No one knows how many living museums there

Sydney Harris giving her son a Saturday afternoon bath at the Ronald V. Jensen Living Historical Farm.—*Photo: Jeannie Thomas*

Larry Miller, Ronald V. Jensen Living Historical Farm, demonstrating "a fine hand with horses."—*Photo: Jeannie Thomas*

really are in North America. A directory has never been published. My own estimate, based on figures from a variety of sources, is that there are perhaps 650 institutions that regularly present living-history programs and could be considered serious "living museums." This figure includes at least 140 farms, still the single-most common type.[10]

Students of museums have continually noted an American preoccupation with the educational responsibility of their institutions.[11] This burgeoning of living-history programs and museums in America was due largely to a belief in its interpretive potential. Living history was considered a good way to make "history come alive" at museums and historic sites often considered stuffy and dull. As G. Ellis Burcaw, chair of the museum studies program at the University of Idaho, noted:

> History on the continent is dead, beautifully embalmed, but dead. . . . Open-air museums have well-researched, accurately identified buildings but with no depiction of daily life. Their farmsteads are the empty husks of peasant culture, collected as curiosities, not as settings for the explication of social history."[12]

American living museums sought to avoid this malaise by using living history to enliven their programs and to foster a more comprehensive understanding of their sites' historical significance.

The claims of living-history enthusiasts are easier to appreciate if we consider earlier exhibit techniques. At first there were "cabinets of curiosity," random cases filled with an odd mixture of history's flotsam and jetsam, awaiting little more than the visitor's "idle inspection." This was followed by the formal exhibit, which grouped objects in categories—uniforms here, arrowheads there, and so on. Next came the interpretive exhibit with its goal of placing artifacts in context, especially the human context in which they originally functioned. The underlying questions raised by interpretive exhibits were—how did people make, obtain, use, and value these objects? The basic mode for the interpretive exhibit was a unit of bounded space, such as the diorama, period room, and later, entire blocks of historic space: a house, farm, village, or district. How did living history fit into this continuum? Preserve a western ghost town and you have an interpretive exhibit. But set it in motion with the addition of well-trained interpreters who go around doing what the townsfolk originally did—tend bar, shoe horses, file claims, ride around town, and so on and you have the living museum, a life-size diorama you can actually enter.[13] Once inside, you can use all your senses: see the horses, smell the wood smoke, touch the quilt, hear the cow bells, taste the gingerbread, and on and on. Museum curators believed they had found in living history an antidote to museum fatigue. This was the pedogogical tool that could enliven their programs and historic sites.[14]

Just as important, however, was living history's potential to communicate the humanistic themes formulated by a new generation of scholars who used a multidisciplinary approach to interpretive history. The work of James Deetz, a respected archaeologist who became assistant director of Plimoth Plantation in the 1960s, is representative. Working with historians, archaeologists, folklorists, "new" social historians, and interpretive specialists from the museum field, Deetz began to test at Plimoth the potential of living history to interpret a number of new humanistic themes. And he took time to report on the results of his efforts in a number of articulate journal articles. In 1971 he examined the most ubiquitous of American historic sites, the historic house, and asked "Can it live?" The answer was yes, if it was redefined as a "pseudo event."

> To be "live," a museum is not simply operating, with someone spinning in the corner or splitting shingles in the yard. To function properly and successfully, a live museum should convey the sense of a different reality—the reality of another time. Even the past from which we are separated by only fifty or a hundred years is of sufficiently different quality that to be thrust into it would induce culture shock. Reading the 1892 Sears Roebuck catalogue can cause this reaction if one considers the number of opium cures avail-

able to an obviously hooked public; it reveals a significant bit about life at that time.[15]

In 1969 Deetz explored "The Reality of the Pilgrim Fathers" and suggested that a step into the time capsule of re-created Plimoth evokes a living community of Pilgrims—its smoky odors, animal noises, and household clutter—and dispels our misconceptions and stereotypes. He suggested that "shrines" like Plimoth couldn't help but make political statements, and he hoped that the "story of the Pilgrims and their fellow Colonists could be told like it was." He noted that:

> It is strange, indeed, that many Americans invoke values in the name of the country's founding fathers, including the Pilgrims, that these men of the past would find somewhat peculiar. Some of the dissent that has recently disturbed much of the nation is not essentially dissimilar from that which caused our first settlers to remove themselves from familiar ways and set out into an unknown world.[16]

Recently, in two articles, "A Sense of Another World: History Museums and Cultural Change," (1980)[17] and "The Link from Object to Person to Concept" (1981), Deetz argued that living history should be taken to its logical conclusion—first person interpretation in a completely re-created cultural landscape:

> It occurred to us that the live interpreters ought to be re-creations at Plimoth too. We had them speak in period dialect, which we were able to research, in first person. At that point the visitors became the interpreters, and we started calling the interpreters informants. It was as if the visitors coming into the exhibit were anthropology fieldworkers going in to experience a community and elicit from it what they could.[18]

In short, Deetz contended that living museums should re-create, within the limits of their boundaries and resources, facsimiles of entire cultures—not just the houses, fences, fields, and other appendages of the cultural, man-made landscape, but the social context as well: people going about their everyday lives, working, playing, praying, celebrating, and so on. With museums like this, any of the popular new social history themes could be interpreted: culture ecology, enculturation, family, sex roles, function of material culture, and aging, to name a few. The requirements are money and years spent "painstakingly re-creating" an eighteenth-century (or sixteenth-, seventeenth-, or twentieth-century) town (or farm, factory, etc.) "down to the last footscraper" and a well-trained staff capable of acting the part of informants from another, dated culture.

As can be imagined, the feasibility of living-history interpretation as advanced by Deetz and others has been questioned. Iowerth Peate, curator of the Welsh Folk Museum, asked, "How far can a folk museum go in reconstructing the past?" His answer, based on "practical, financial, and all other grounds," was "not too far." He argued that the cost of staffing, organization, operations, and materials would make such projects (at least in a European folk museum whose purpose is to inter-

An interpreter enjoys a good historical smoke at Fort Snelling's Fur Trade Weekend—*Photo: Jim Phillips*

pret an entire regional culture over time) completely prohibitive.[19] Robert Ronsheim, who worked for Deetz in the education department at Plimoth and later joined the staff at Connor Prairie (a re-creation of an 1830's Indiana village), asked in another article, "Is the Past Dead?" (1974). His answer was:

> The past is dead, and cannot be brought back to life. Those beliefs and attitudes, conscious and unconscious, rational and irrational that provided a foundation for institutions, governed conduct and controlled behavior cannot mean to us what they meant to those who lived then. Some of the elements are missing; others have a different color and shape when viewed from our pattern of beliefs. So, too, with the affective life of individuals and families. Nor can any material re-creations ever be complete or authentic. Any historian, social scientist, or curator dealing with the past must tell his student, the museum visitor, that the past cannot be recovered. The message is, however, a positive one: The past has a unity and needs to be considered as a whole. This is something many historians who write books or give lectures have been able to avoid by dealing with specific portions of the past; most historical museums cannot avoid the issue.

A living-history program is important, even an essential

tool, to be used in capitalizing on that opportunity. Properly used, the interest and involvement it can generate can be used to aid the visitor to a clearer perception of the past.[20]

Most professional interpreters who use living history share both Deetz's enthusiasm and Ronsheim's realism. Given the large number of folk museums that have started in the last two decades, they also seem to have rejected Peate's projection that "practical financial considerations" would make living history projects "ludicrous." For Americans, history might be dead, but living history is alive and well.

The challenge of realistically simulating and interpreting everyday life in an accurately re-created farm or village presented special problems for the museum researcher. The research base needed for a living museum had to be nothing less than historical ethnography, and many curators adopted H. Stuart Hughes's definition of history as "retrospective cultural anthropology."[21] The major European folk museums had established a tradition of folklife research to document

Ray Allard, Senior, member of La Compagnie des Hiverants de Rivier Ste. Pierrir, taking a break at the Faribault Cabin in Shakopee, Minnesota.—*Photo: Jim Phillips*

their collections. American living museums needed to go further, since their aim was to place their artifacts in a complete social and cultural context. The best living museums mounted serious multidisciplinary research programs enlisting as consultants historical archaeologists, cultural anthropologists, geographers, "new" social historians, folklorists, and agricultural specialists. The model project was the Freeman Farm at Old Sturbridge Village headed by Darwin Kelsey, a cultural geographer. His theories of what living-history farms should be were presented in a series of thoughtful articles.[22] He pointed out that living-history farms were:

> . . . historical in the broadest sense of the word, offering a patterned coherent account of the past that is intended to be true. They are thus analogous to written history and exhibits in traditional history museums. Even though they often appear concrete and complete—that is, real—they are only accounts of the past and not the past itself. . . . LHF's represent theories—that is, generalization—about the past. As in any historical account, they are based on incomplete evidence. They are subjective, as in any "model" produced in the arts, humanities, or sciences.[23]

Kelsey went to the trouble to ensure that his farm at Old Sturbridge Village was based on the most complete body of evidence his architects, architectural historians, curators, horticulturists, and agricultural and other kinds of historians could unearth. The final product, a fully documented farm and agri-culture, was Kelsey's message.

A completely different point of view was taken at the Colonial Pennsylvania Plantation, a restored Quaker farm of the 1770s outside Philadelphia. The directors decided to use the farm as a historical laboratory, in which various types of research (archaeological digs, architectural investigations of the farm's buildings, analysis of probate inventories, studies of the surrounding cultural landscape, and living-history experiments with farming, domestic science, etc.) would be carried out before and with visitors. In short, the medium of research, finding out how ordinary people actually once lived on a farm like this one became the message. Historiography itself was the exhibit. Both staff and visitors shared the same perspective; they were people living in the present, curious about what everyday life was like for their counterparts in the past, about how modern life had developed from this earlier form-what changed, what stayed the same, why, why not—and about what research techniques had been developed by the new "hybrid" disciplines that could help answer these questions. As project director in 1974, I described a typical weekend:

> Families come and share with us our research problems and solutions: for example, our archivists discuss with visitors the inventories farmers from the period left behind and how we are deciphering these in hope of discovering what the range of material culture on a typical Chester County farm was. Our archaeologists (mainly college and high school students) share examples of actual artifacts which they are excavating here on the site. And finally, our

farm staff demonstrates how we are reproducing items of that material culture; e.g. tools, furnishings, clothing, and then put these items to work. In short, on weekends we interpret not just the content of Colonial history, but the methods of researching Colonial history.

The effect of these educational programs stressing historical methodology is startling. People are delighted with this "treasure hunt" philosophy. . . . The idea of using a living history farm as a tool to solve research problems is a new one for most people but one they can readily grasp. After all, the public had no problem in readily understanding where our "land ship" is headed. . . . The Colonial Pennsylvania Plantation is very much a people's populist project.[24]

The project became a highly visible exercise in American "ethnoarchaeology" and told its staff and visitors as much about our contemporary patterns of historical inquiry as it did about the actual content of Colonial Quaker folklife.

The Colonial Pennsylvania Plantation also became the leading American example of "experimental archaeology," or the use of living history to test an archaeological thesis or generate data for historical ethnographies. Its research director, Donald Callender, Jr., himself an archaeologist who had worked at Tikal, Guatemala, carried out a series of experiments: reconstructing and analyzing the function of a springhouse, monitoring several trash pits, and comparing the efficiency of a modern plow and a 1770s wooden replica. The results of these experiments were published[25] and communication established between the staff and other ethno- and experimental archaeologists in Europe and the United States.[26]

The use of living history as research continues at Living History Farms in Des Moines, Iowa. This 600-acre folk museum has five re-created historical sites: an 1875 rural village and four operating farms—pre-contact Native American, 1840s subsistence, 1900 horse-powered, and a futuristic demonstration exhibit. The latter is based on experimental farms set up near land-grant colleges in the days before county agents. It features an earth-covered, energy efficient, solar farmhouse, conservation fields and farming methods, and a selection of exhibits dealing with futuristic portraits of life and work in the Corn Belt. This emphasis on stewardship was one of the reasons Pope John Paul II selected the museum as the site for his visit to rural America in October 1979. The staff at the museum views the sites as a series of stops on a regional time tunnel. Visitors and staff move from one era to another, steeping themselves in the culture of that period, and then making comparisons between them. The effect is a modest "culture shock" and raises questions of what actually happens to regional traditions and lifestyles when a culture changes. Here, the staff and visitors not only question what and how we can learn about everyday life at a particular point in time, but why one historical period and culture differs from another. One staff member described the museum as a "controlled exercise in regional schizophrenia."[27]

Projects and museums that use living history as a research method have grown in popularity, in part because people seem fascinated by them. *National Geographic* and *Smithsonian* have reported on not only Kon-Tiki and Mayflower II, but Ra I and II, the Brendan, and most recently the BBC Celtic Village project.[28] In all of these, the present meets the past with a focus on the "quest," modern man using science, technology, his imagination, and adventuresome spirit to put himself in his ancestor's place and vicariously experience it. There is an underlying message of hope in these projects: if we can understand how mankind managed to travel from the past into the present, perhaps we can also imagine how we are going to move from the present into the future. It is an appropriate theme for people engulfed by Alvin Toffler's *Third Wave* (1980).[29] These projects also have the advantage of placing scholar and visitor together, sharing the same curiosity, and evaluating the answers that result when modern man tries to simulate life in another time.

While these projects are undeniably popular with the public, how do they stand up as serious research efforts? The scholarly literature evaluating living history as a valid method has grown since the publication of John Coles's *Archaeology by Experiment* (1974). A collection of reports, *Experimental Archaeology* (1977), followed three years later and included an article by John Chilott and James Deetz, "The Construction and Uses of a Laboratory Archaeological Site." In 1981 Richard Gould and Michael Schiffer edited another collection of essays, *Modern Material Culture: The Archaeology of Us,*[30] which contains a number of studies that examine the living museum as a complex late twentieth-century artifact, raising questions of the kind dealt with at the Colonial Pennsylvania Plantation and Living History Farms. The intellectual excitement generated by these essays suggests that the use of simulation as a research tool is being taken seriously.

So far this essay has dealt with the use of living history by established museums, sanctioned by what Robert Redfield called the "great tradition." There is, however, a concurrent movement quite apart from the organized scholarly projects undertaken at Williamsburg, Old Sturbridge Village, and Living History Farms. It is a "folks" living-history movement, of the people, by the people, and for the people. Its social history has not been chronicled, but its significance is obvious to any observer of the contemporary American scene.

One stream of the movement began in 1931 with the organization of the National Muzzle Loading Rifle Association. The number of members in the NMLRA has grown steadily, and its annual "shoot" in Friendship, Indiana, draws tens of thousands. A large number of members live in a "primitive" area and take part in the Mountain Man Aggregate, which requires participants to wear 1750-1840 clothing, use open, nonadjustable sights on their flintlock rifles, build fires with flint and steel, be skilled at throwing tomahawks and knives, and of course, be crack shots. With the celebration of the Civil

War Centennial and the American Revolutionary War Bi-centennial, many NMLRA members joined with others of similar interest to form military units. Battles were re-enacted and public interest grew, especially with the widespread press coverage of these massive living-history demonstrations. An example in book form is the Civil War chapter in *National Geographic's America's Historylands: Touring Our Landmarks of Liberty* (1962).[31] The spirit of these participants is captured in Hank Boughton's comments:

> In 1968, I organized a group of buckskinners to duplicate the march that George Rogers Clark made across the Illinois Territory to Fort Kaskaskia. It was a 125-mile walk. Clark and his men did it in five days, and we had to do it on the same days he did it. And it worked out fine.[33]

Another Mountain Man, Dale Black, is typical:

> I've been interested in early history all my life, ever since I was in grade school. . . . Hawk (Hank Boughton) and I, I guess, go back about ten years (1969). We wanted to follow the historic way of doing things, and dress like it, instead of just saying, "Well, I'm going to shoot a muzzle-loader." There's really more to it than just having a rifle and a pouch and shooting a few targets. You get to reading history, and you get interested in it, and the more you get into it, the more history you assimilate. Right now I've joined a Civil War outfit and that's an entirely different part of muzzle-loading. We re-enact battles, for example. It just all depends on how far the individual wants to go. . . . We're usually working on a part of our gear, like authentic-type moccasins or authentic-type belts or some ironwear for our cooking. . . . I might say "My cooking utensils are not quite right," and I'd spend a lot of time going to museums until I found a part I was really interested in and that suited me. . . and then you go home and do your best to re-create it.[34]

There have been two recent developments in the folks' living-history movement. First, it has spread to include a variety of other groups in addition to the mountain men and military units. These include the longhunter, settler, *coureur de bois* and Woodland Indian, voyageur, various western Indians, and most recently, medieval folk from every level of society—especially nobility, peerage, officers of the court, and other worthies. Simulation of life in another time need not be linked to America's wars or the frontier. It can also leap back to Old World culture hearths.[35]

The second development is a desire on the part of these history buffs for recognition and acceptance. This may take the form of a desire for organization, a regular schedule, or a home. A variety of organizations have sprung up: American Mountain Men, First North-South Brigade, Brigade of the American Revolution, Northwest Territory Alliance, and the Society for Creative Anachronism (the medieval folk). One could also add a number of Country Song and Dance Society local branches with their Morris teams. Many publish newsletters and sketch books.[36] The organizations may agree to participate in fixed schedules.[37] Homes are found in county historical societies, isolated state parks and historic sites, and sometimes private lands. The desire of the folks' movement to cooperate with the National Park Service was discussed in a recent article in *History News*, "War Games: Is History Losing the Battle?" (1981). Betty Doak Elder, the author, said that she had received more mail concerning this piece than any other in *History News*.[38]

The use of living history as an enjoyable recreational activity that is also a learning experience will continue whether or not the National Park Service, museum curators, or academic historians approve of it. Folks who are doing living history know why they do it. It provides comradeship, travel, a channel for intellectual curiosity, family fun, camping out, and opportunity to play-act, and finally, money. Most living-history festivals are also markets where there is much buying and selling of food, crafts, and reproductions.[39] The folks' movement is part revival, revitalization movement, ethnohistorical secular ritual, and nostalgic response to future shock.

Living history has a potential role to play in the field of American studies. There are four characteristics of the movement that suggest to me that it will be a valuable research and interpretive tool. First, the focus on living history has been overwhelmingly on folklife, the everyday experiences of the mass of ordinary men, women, and children. It is part of the democratizing of historiography and echoes Theodore Blegen's call:

> The pivot of history is not the uncommon, but the usual, and the makers of history are "the people, yes."

> This is the essence of grassroots history. It grapples, as history should grapple, with the need of understanding the small, everyday elements, the basic elements, in large movements. It recognizes, as maturely conceived history should recognize, the importance of the simple, however complex and subtle the problems of understanding the simple may be.[40]

At one time, critics of living-history programs, either scholarly or lay, could dismiss them as "antiquarian" or "pots and pans" history, of limited interest or value to the larger field. This elitist perspective is no longer credible. Nothing less than "total history" will do.

A second related aspect of the movement is its emphasis on the region. In Europe, folklife studies and regional ethnology are the same, and American studies is our counterpart to this cross-cultural regional view of the history of a people.[41] Most living-history programs are intensely regional; they focus on the day-to-day experiences of people with their natural environment as mediated by a cultural landscape, often a farm or rural village. The best programs at regional folk museums such as Old Sturbridge Village or Living History Farms focus on significant themes in cultural ecology. The recent writings of Avlin Toffler and Joel Garreau suggest that much of our present and future history will center on the region.[42] If this is so, living history is centrally placed to study and interpret this history.

Third, the living-history movement has been an un-

The roots of re-enacting. Joshua Phillips at the Eagle Creek Rendezvous, Shakopee, Minnesota.—*Photo: Jim Phillips*

usual meeting ground for a variety of disciplines at the academic level. Historical archaeologists, cultural geographers, social historians, and folklorists have all worked together toward a common goal, often in a neutral place, the folk museum. In addition, living-history programs have brought together university professors and laymen, representatives of the great and little traditions. The "play" aspect of simulation has often appealed to both groups and relationships have thus formed. Needless to say, this is an unusual, favorable trend.[43]

Finally, in a period of extremely rapid cultural change, with people engulfed by a tidal "third wave" and in a state of "future shock," living history may offer respite by providing "enclaves of the past and future,"[44] similar to those re-created at Living History Farms. At best, these enclaves will provide large numbers of people with the opportunity to "back sight" and identify meaningful cultural landmarks. They will function as collective exercises in ethnohistory. At worst, they will be temporary escapes for a people suffering from acute nostalgia. The potential for the popular culture to exploit living history and use it for political purposes is real. The popularity of historical theme parks is an obvious warning. One hopes that as a people we will prefer the more mature message of Fabre:

> History celebrates the battlefields whereon we meet our death, but scorns to speak of the plowed fields whereby we thrive. It knows the names of the kings' bastards but cannot tell us the origin of wheat. This is they way of human folly.[45]

Notes

1. An excellent bibliography of references up to September 1975 is Ormond Loomis, *Sources of Folk Museums and Living Historical Farms*, Folklore Forum Bibliographic and Special Series, no. 16 (1977).
2. J. Geraint Jenkins, "The Use of Artifacts and Folk Art in the Folk Museum," in *Folklore and Folklife: An Introduction*, ed. Richard M. Dorson (Chicago: University of Chicago Press, 1972), p. 498.
3. Ormond Loomis devotes an entire section to books and articles describing European folk museums in *Sources on Folk Museums*, pp. 20-29.
4. The best overview of the subject is Kenneth Hudson's *A Social History of Museums* (London: Macmillan, 1975). Alexander Fenton presents the current European attitude toward folklife in "The Scope of Regional Ethnology," *Folklife: A Journal of Ethnological Studies* 11 (1973): 5-15.
5. Cary Carson, "Living Museums of Everyman's History," *Harvard Magazine* 83 (July-August 1981): 25-26.
6. The only guides to American outdoor museums both draw attention to the village. See Nicholas Zook, *Museum Villagers USA* (Barre, Mass.: Barre, 1971); and Mitchell Alegre, *A Guide to Museum Villages* (New York: Drake, 1978).
7. Marion Clawson, "Living Historical Farms: A Proposal for Action" *Agricultural History* 39 (April 1965): 110-11.
8. John Schlebecker, *Living Historical Farms: A Walk Into the Past* (Washington, D.C.: Smithsonian Institution, 1968); Schlebecker and Gale Peterson, *Living Historical Farms Handbook* (Washington, D.C.: Smithsonian Institution, 1972); Darwin Kelsey, "Harvests of History," *Historic Preservation*, 28 (July-September 1976): 20-25; Sharon Eubanks, *A Bibliography of Books, Pamphlets, and Films Listed in the Living Historical Farms Bulletin from December 1970 through May 1976* (Washington, D.C.: Smithsonian Institution, 1977).
9. A brief history of ALHFAM was given by Wayne Rasmussen, a historian with the Department of Agriculture, in his presidential address "History on the Farm," *ALHFAM Annual* 4 (1981): 1-6.
10. Lee Kimche, "American Museums: The Vital Statistics," *Museum News* 59 (October 1980): 52-58.
11. Kenneth Hudson's *Museums for the 1980s* (New York: Holmes and Meier, 1977); and *The Directory of Museums and Living Displays* (London: Macmillan, 1985) are the best international surveys.
12. G. Ellis Burcaw, "Can History Be Too Lively?" *Museums Journal* 80 (June 1980): 5-7.
13. Holly Sitford, "Stepping Into History," *Museum News* 53 (November 1974): 28-36.
14. William T. Alderson and Shirley Payne Low's *Interpretation of Historic Sites* (Nashville: American Association for State and Local History, 1976) is the best introduction to interpretation at historic sites and outdoor museums. See also Freeman J. Tilden's *Interpreting Our Heritage*, rev. ed. (Chapel Hill, University of North Carolina Press, 1976) and Frederick Rath and Merrilyn O'Connell, *Interpretation: A Bibliography* (Nashville: American Association for State and Local History, 1978).
15. James Deetz, "The Changing Historic House Museum: Can It Live?" *Historic Preservation* 23 (January-March 1971): 50-54.
16. James Deetz, "The Reality of the Pilgrim Fathers,"*Natural History* 78 (November 1969): 44.
17. James Deetz, "A Sense of Another World: History Museums and Cultural Change," *Museum News* 59 (May-June 1980): 40-45.
18. James Deetz, "The Link from Object to Person to Concept," in *Museums, Adults and the Humanities* (Washington, D.C.: American Association of Museums, 1981), p. 18.
19. Iowerth Peate, "Reconstructing the Past," *Folk Life* 6 (1968), 113-14.

20. Robert Ronsheim, "Is the Past Dead?" *Museum News* 53 (1974): 62.

21. H. Stuart Hughes, "History, the Humanities and Anthropological Change," *Current Anthropology* 4:2 (1963): 141.

22. Darwin Kelsey, ed., "Outdoor Museums and Historical Agriculture," *Agricultural History* 44 (January 1972): 105-27; Kelsey, "Historic Farms as Models of the Past," *ALHFAM Annual* 1 (1975): 33-39; Kelsey, "Harvests of History," *Historic Preservation* 28 (July-September 1976): 20-25.

23. Kelsey, "Harvest of History," p. 22.

24. Jay Anderson, "The Colonial Pennsylvania Plantation," *ALHFAM Annual* 1 (1975): 39.

25. Donald Callender, Jr., "Reliving the Past: Experimental Archaeology in Pennsylvania," *Archaeology* 29 (9176): 173-78.

26. See Peter Reynolds, *Farming in the Iron Age* (Cambridge: Cambridge University Press, 1976); and "Experimental Archaeology and the Butser Hill Ancient Farm Project," *The Iron Age in Britain: A Review*, ed. John Collis (Sheffield: Sheffield University Press, 1977), pp. 32-41; *I Build a Stone Age House* (London: Phoenix House, 1962); and *International Study Conference on the Role of Regional Ethnology in Environmental Interpretation and Education* (Strasbourg: Council of Europe, 1976).

27. Jay Anderson, "Immaterial Culture: The Implication of Experimental Research for Folklife Museums," *Keystone Folklore* 21 (1976-1977), 1-15. This article places Living History Farms in context.

28. For an example, see Timothy Green, "Living Like Iron Age Celts," *Smithsonian* 9:3 (June 1978); 80-88.

29. Alvin Toffler, *The Third Wave* (New York: William Morrow, 1980).

30. John Coles, *Archaeology by Experiment* (New York: Scribners, 1974); Daniel Ingersol, John E. Yellen, and William MacDonald, eds., *Experimental Archaeology* (New York: Columbia University Press, 1977); Richard Gould and Michael Schiffer, eds., *Modern Material Culture* (New York: Academic Press, 1981).

31. National Geographical Society Book Service, *America's History-lands* (Washington, D.C.: National Geographic Society, 1962, 1967).

32. Reid Lewis, "Three Hundred Years Later: Reenactment of the 1673 Jolliet-Marquette Voyage," *Historic Preservation* 26, (July 1974): 4-9.

33. Elliot Wiggington, ed., *Foxfire 5* (Garden City, N.J.: Anchor, 1979), p. 412.

34. Wigginton, ed., *Foxfire 5*, pp. 407-408.

35. David Schwartz, "Morris Dancers are Coming So It Must be May," *Smithsonian* 12:2 (May 1981): 118-124.

36. William H. Scurlock, *The Book of Buckskinning* (Texarkana, Ark.: Rebel, 1981); Robert Klinger and Richard Wilder, *Sketch Book 76* (Union City, Tenn.: Pioneer Press, 1967, 1974); any of the eight books by James Hanson or Charles H. Hanson published by The Fur Press in Chadron, Nebraska; a good example is James Hanson, *Voyageur's Sketchbook* (1981); Society for Creative Anachronism, *The Known World Handbook* (Media, Pa.: South Carolina Anachronism, 1979).

37. Ronald Akin and Bruce Fingerhut, eds., *Book of Festivals in the Midwest 1980 and 1981* (South Bend, Ind.: Icarus Press, 1980).

38. Betty Doak Elder, "War Games: Is History Losing the Battle?" *History News* 36 (August 1981): 8-13.

39. An example is the Feast of the Hunter's Moon, a two-day reenactment of the arrival of voyageurs to Fort Quiatenon near Lafayette, Indiana. The festival draws 50,000 people, 4,500 participants, and leases 144 booths where a considerable amount of money is exchanged. The Feast is sponsored by the Tippecanoe County Historical Association and is representative of the folks' living-history movement.

40. Theodore Blegen, *Grass Roots History* (Minneapolis: University of Minnesota Press, 1947).

41. Don Yoder, "Folklife Studies in American Scholarship" in *American Folklife*, ed. Yoder (Austin: University of Texas Press, 1976), pp. 3-19.

42. Toffler, *The Third Wave*; Joel Garreau, *The Nine Nations of North America* (Boston: Houghton Mifflin, 1981).

43. A fine example of this is found in Roger Welsch, "Very Didactic Stimulation," *History Teacher* 7:3 (May 1974): 356-64.

44. Alvin Toffler, *Future Shock* (New York: Random House, 1970), chapter 17.

45. Cited in John Schlebecker, *Whereby We Thrive*, (Ames: Iowa State University Press, 1975).

Part II
Beginnings

The Changing Historic House Museum

Can It Live?

James Deetz

In 1967 Jim Deetz joined the staff of Plimoth Plantation in Plymouth, Massachusetts, and began to put forward a new theory for interpreting historic sites. Drawing from historical archaeology, folklore, the "new" social history, and communications, he shaped living history into a powerful mode of interpretation. This article appeared in the January-March issue of Historic Preservation *and quickly became required reading for anyone concerned with historical simulation. Using Daniel Boorstin's concept of the "pseudo event," Deetz argued, "Every functioning historic house museum that addresses a point in time past is, in fact, a pseudo event and should aim at making the experience the best pseudo event possible.... To be "live," a museum is not simply operating, with someone spinning in the corner or splitting shingles in the yard. To function properly and successfully, a live museum should convey the sense of a different reality—the reality of another time." A decade and a half later, Deetz's challenge commands our attention and provides the measure by which we evaluate our efforts at making the past "live."*

In his book, *The Image,* Daniel Boorstin develops the concept of the "pseudo event," meaning the re-creation of reality to the extent that the image becomes the standard by which reality is judged. As in a world of shadows, man is evaluating the accuracy and reliability of real things in terms of the characteristics of the images he has created about them.

Every functioning historic house museum that addresses a point in time past is, in fact, a pseudo event and should aim at making the experience the best pseudo event possible within the limits that can be commanded.

To be "live," a museum is not simply operating, with someone spinning in the corner, or splitting shingles in the yard. To function properly and successfully, a live museum should convey the sense of a different reality— the reality of another time. Even the past from which we are separated by only fifty or a hundred years is of a sufficiently different quality that to be thrust into it would induce culture shock. Reading the 1902 Sears, Roebuck catalogue can cause this reaction if one considers the number of opium cures available to an obviously hooked public; it reveals a significant bit about life at that time.

Over the past two years an attempt has been made to make Plimoth Plantation in Plymouth, Massachusetts, an honest and hopefully true segment of the living past by making a statement about a particular point in time. The specific date is 1627; what is being re-created is Plymouth Colony, a community of 300 people living in a fortified village. There is totally open access to all exhibits: visitors may crawl into bed or sit on a chair. They may chase the chickens or use the implements in the house. Nothing is labeled because people did not have explanatory signs in their houses in the seventeenth century. It has been discovered that the public, once liberated from a strictly visual response to the exhibits, responds to an appeal to all the senses.

The smells at Plimoth are rich, varied, and not always nice. There is an abundance of sounds since the livestock often wanders around free, in many instances going in and out of the houses.

Plimoth interpreters undergo an intensive training course every spring, prior to opening in April, including seminars, discussions and role-playing in experimental situations, reminiscent of group encounter sessions. The aim is nonprogrammatic interpretation, immersion into total understanding of seventeenth-century village life, to foster the ability to converse with visitors naturally while putting in a hard day's work running the community as a person of the time, in fact, would. Unanticipated events occur regularly, and flexibility of response is encouraged.

Concentration on a specific point in time demands rigorous attention to period detail to re-create the material world of Plimoth Plantation. This explicit effort to combine fragments of an earlier period is antithetical to the period-room concept. Handmade reproduction furniture in Jacobean style is ordered from England, with the request that it appear c. 1620 and show evidence of at least seven years of use and trans-Atlantic transport. Some pieces are given further treatment upon receipt to provide greater variation in degree of apparent wear. However, none of these artifacts shows the patina and wear that three centuries would have produced.

In the introduction to his book, *A Guide to the Artifacts of Colonial America*, Ivor Noel Hume takes a swipe at the period-room concept by pointing out that rooms assembled in this fashion are moribund, erased of the presence of past occupants. At Plimoth the attempt to create past presences and the imprints of past behavior is believed to be an effective way of communicating to the public an impression of a living reality.

The actual use of a historic house exhibit in as real a situation as possible is important to give reality to clutter and debris in a behavioral context. The interpreters have on occasion moved into the houses for periods of several weeks to accustom themselves to the foodstuffs and furnishings, selected according to a block of

History very much alive at Plimoth Plantation.—*Photo: Victoria Fisher*

seventeenth-century inventories, that would have been available. It is an educational experience and demonstrates what can happen to a house given this particular combination. While it is realized that there is a limit to the extent to which one can project himself 300 years backward, it makes a good pseudo event.

This approach requires a healthy tolerance for dirt and discomfort. The fact that exhibits become rather flyblown at the peak of the season may shock some visitors. But it adds a vital dimension since seventeenth-century farmhouses were fly-ridden.

The only requirement regarding interpreters' seventeenth-century dress is that they appear each morning in clean clothes. They go away at night fairly dirty, having scoured pots, dug in gardens, and prepared meals. They look natural and convincing. In summer they may go barefoot, and since a number of college students are employed, there is a lot of hair in evidence. Incidentally, a thorough and extensive monograph on seventeenth-century hair styles has been prepared by staff researchers to support the presence in the village of these styles.

Even on the hottest days a fire remains burning on the hearth. It speaks in implicit ways to visitors that the fire had to be at least a bed of coals in the seventeenth-century because it was not simply for huddling around at night for good cheer and a drink. Indeed it was a necessary and central part of existence.

While giving these living presentations, Plimoth is aware that other valuable interpretive areas are being overlooked. A living museum is probably the last place to communicate understanding of material objects per se—for example, the nuances of early seventeenth-century carved oak furniture. Nor should it be expected in a functioning household, where the artifacts are, after all, the props and the scenery. In terms of the accuracy of the furniture, Plimoth has high standards, although the architecture admittedly needs to be more stringently authentic. Efforts are being made in this direction.

A program like this places great physical strain on artifacts, far above their limit to withstand. Reproductions are used entirely in furnishing the houses since valuable artifacts should not be exposed to this treatment. However, it is comforting that pilferage has been low after the exhibit barriers were removed.

Many of the artifacts are based on measured drawings of archaeologically recovered prototypes. Others are based on contemporary graphic materials, such as prints and paintings. Often two or three hundred pictures are examined before the drawings for a single object are commissioned. After a two-year search, a blacksmith was found willing, capable, and skilled in making the countless tools required. In addition to the costly quality furniture reproductions, seventeenth-century ceramics, pewter, textiles, and pottery are also copied.

As extreme as it may sound, the full re-creation of buildings for the purpose of living displays ought to be considered, from the sill right on up. This expensive pursuit should be part of long-range planning because in preserving an original historic structure as an end unto itself, it is actually being subjected to potential destruction. In fact, its success might be said to be measured in the amount of destruction that ensues.

In the multiple-object sets such as Plimoth Plantation, the emphasis is on the gestalt created rather than on the individual piece. It has been observed over the two years of this experiment that the interpreters, without a word being said, are beginning to shift the whole presentation from third person, past, to first person, present. Guides are frequently saying, "We do," not "They did." The value of this approach is that they are really beginning to communicate something of the total experience of Pilgrim life to the visiting public.

Preparing to bring home the harvest at Plimoth Plantation.—*Photo: George Chapman*

Thoughts on the Re-creation and Interpretation of Historical Environments

John Fortier

3

Drawing on his experience as superintendent of the Fortress of Louisbourg, John Fortier presents a clearly reasoned, delightfully expressed essay on the potential of living history as a "personal approach to understanding the past." He introduces the concept of role-playing: "If the goal of a museum village is to re-create a real place, it follows that the lives of the original people, as well as the landscapes and furnishings they knew, are relevant and deserve to be recalled." But Fortier also counts the costs and cites Louisbourg as a case study in what to do and what not to do when undertaking a serious living-history program. "Historical reality," he notes, is "elusive and momentary. It may exist in its ideal form only for as long as the swing of a door, or the moment it takes for a costumed figure to disappear around a street corner. Yet that moment can bring a sense of timelessness, a realization of the humanity we share with our ancestors, that will not be like anything else you can experience." These thoughts were published in the Schedule and Papers of the Third International Congress of Maritime Museums *(1978).*

I present this paper to you, a conference of maritime museums, fully conscious that my own institution has neither ships nor crews to sail them, nor even a working waterfront. All these lie in the future, when Louisbourg is completed.

Given the variety of delegates to this conference, and such a broad topic as interpretation, I have to stake out some ground and make some assumptions.

First, what we have in common are collections and the challenge of presenting them to the public. I will speak in the context of outdoor museums because, in my opinion, they have all the problems of the traditional museum, and more. They also have more opportunities to attract and inform the public.

Second, "interpretation" is the variety of methods by which we communicate. At any rate, that seems to be a working definition in North America. The key word is "communicate."

Third, you could tell me more about most methods of interpretation than I could tell you, so I will dwell on the area in which Louisbourg has had its most significant experience—what is often called "animation" or "living history."

I can think of nothing about interpretation that is unique to maritime museums. All museums share the re-sponsibility to collect, preserve, study, and display. The philosophy and methods behind the interpretation programs of a maritime museum are no different from those of its landlocked counterparts. As an interpretive device, the re-creation and animation of a historical environment represents one of the fullest and most peculiar forms of development of historical properties. If you make the attempt, I think you will find that the problems, opportunities, excesses, and triumphs of outdoor museums and museum villages anywhere are much the same.

I am getting to a point where I seldom describe this as "living history." On the basis of too little achievement, such as getting some visiting adolescents to sweep the porch with a folksy broom or putting on a checkered apron while they dangle some string in a vat of candle wax, some of our colleagues in outdoor museums have rushed into print proclaiming the joys of self-discovery. And they usually call it "living history."

I have seriously considered writing an article entitled "Is Living History Dying, And If So Did We Kill It?" But I am still trying to take its pulse. Meanwhile, I think the concept should be de-mystified from the awe with which it seems to be regarded, or at least rescued from the educators and restored to the keepers of tradition. To be valid in a museum context, this activity has to begin with the premise that those involved are custodians, not merely actors in a loosely scripted play.

Living history is not an end in itself. It is a way to communicate. Allowing for the private enthusiasts who stage craft demonstrations, military drills, and re-enactments primarily for their own edification, a museum's first concern must be whether this activity supports or subverts its interpretation program. In the sheltered and—as we have so often been told—the too-tidy world of museum villages, let us consider the stages by which we have escalated to this phenomenon.

It began in the nineteenth century with historical pageants, which sprang from theatricals. Much of this had a pietistic and patriotic tinge we have never outgrown; indeed, we are often not even conscious of it.

This led to demonstrations of historical activities, customarily the basic crafts, usually derived from frontier life chronicles that portrayed our history with a broad and often careless approach during the first half of the twentieth century.

By the time Williamsburg was restored, it was a logical step to present the historic buildings along with appropriate activities, furnishings, and dress in a context that was delightfully complete. We reacted enthusiastically to the idea of a total historical environment—see how often it has been emulated—and it raised the stakes in the game of historical re-creation. We began to think we could, and should, extend this method from tangible objects to express the intangible moods and concepts of life long ago. Our standards and our expectations were now considerably higher.

In other parts of the world, where history began earlier and the physical remains of the past are more common, this need to re-create seems not to be felt as strongly. Europeans appear to be more comfortable with their past; in any case, their use of historic properties and their methods of showing them to the public are not as extravagant. They are less concerned with getting a good show from their historic buildings and are more appreciative of the continuity that comes from keeping them in use for any reasonable purpose.

We tend to use the same term—"animation"—as Europeans do, to describe the activities that take place in historic areas. But there we part company. In North America our concept of animation is based on demonstrations or special events staged for the public. Europeans, even in their museum villages, consider animation to be almost anything oriented toward culture; they are much less concerned with making it fit the epoch of the buildings' style and are generally more relaxed about the whole process. From this distance, I think they are more confident about their place in the continuum of history and therefore feel less compelled to dissect it into segments of neatly defined age, locale, and character the way we do with our museum villages on this side of the Atlantic.

"Living history" has added a new dimension to our approach toward historical animation. In some cases the public is secondary; the individual is seeking an experience and insight primarily for himself. In other cases the public is invited to participate in the activity. The key word in all cases is "participate." In all its permutations, living history offers a much more personal approach to understanding the past; not surprisingly these activities have led out of the structural confines of our museum villages and forts, away from the museum's preoccupation with fine arts and conservation, and toward the imperative: "Do your own thing."

The next step was acting a role, to represent one's self as a historical character, even refusing to acknowledge to spectators that the present exists. That brings us almost full circle back to the pageants of the last century, albeit with greater fidelity of detail.

Given a willing suspension of disbelief by those who view it, the characterization of specific people through role-playing may be desirable as a further means to understand and communicate. If the goal of a museum village is to re-create a real place, it follows that the lives of the original people, as well as the landscapes and furnishings they knew, are relevant and deserve to be recalled. This can be presented to the public as our own experience in re-experiencing and understanding the past, quite apart from any dramatic impact it may have. It helps focus the application of research in social history, and it can lead the animator toward a sympathy for the person represented much like that of a biographer for his subject. But there are many pitfalls, and to progress beyond this kind of representation to acting a role, in the face of all incredulity, in a device that may be appropriate and possible—given the knowledge and skills required—only in special circumstances and not on an everyday basis.

For reasons that we found compelling, Louisbourg has experimented with all these methods of interpretation.

First, the reconstruction is synthetic. The original structures were demolished and only fragments have survived in the fabric of the town that is presented to the public. So we felt a need to augment the effect of the reconstructed buildings by putting our guides and custodians in appropriate clothing to help portray the history of the place.

Second, Louisbourg offered an extraordinarily complete context, almost entirely free from modern intrusions. We felt that if a re-creation of life in the past could succeed anywhere, it would be on this townsite, which already was remarkable for its mood of isolation and timelessness.

Third, the reconstruction shows a specific and very brief period of time, the early 1740s, because construction of the fortress and town was not finished until then and in 1745 there occurred the first of two sieges in which Louisbourg was heavily damaged and its French inhabitants were sent back to Europe. The reconstruction may be unique in its focus on such a brief time span. Our presentation is very specific to Louisbourg and avoids what is traditional or cultural in a more general sense. The historical setting, inhabitants, even the conceptual framework we encourage among our animators are set in the year 1744, when war had been declared between England and France, but life went on much the same in what the visitor knows is a town doomed to destruction.

The rigorous application of this concept has prevented our showing much that is interesting from earlier and later periods. But we feel that in view of Louisbourg's dramatic history the interpretive device of focusing on this "moment in time" compensates for what we lose in being so specific by creating greater interest and realism for visitors. Also, by avoiding the generalities of culture and tradition we are able to realize and show more of the complexities of life.

The appropriateness and cost-effectiveness of these methods of interpretation can be questioned, as can the reconstruction itself. The answer depends on whether the message we feel is important can be communicated better this way or some other way.

Unfortunately, we in the museum business have no adequate means to measure the impact of what we do. We know the average visitor will absorb only a very small part of the information available. But are static exhibits more effective than animation? Are audio-visual displays more effective than publications? I have yet to see a survey that could measure appreciation, or knowledge applied, or insight, much less quantify the extent of knowledge the public may acquire on a visit. My own methods of judging effectiveness are very informal: eavesdrop on visitors, ask the guides what questions people ask and where they seem to find things of interest,

talk to staff in the local restaurants and travel bureaus, read the letters and complaints that visitors send us, and follow the articles written about the reconstruction in the newspapers and travel guides. Since interpretation is basically the application of intellect and imagination in the first place, I doubt we can become very scientific in evaluating its effect on the other end.

In my opinion, animation has a valid role in the interpretation of historic sites and buildings, particularly to a North American audience. I also feel strongly that if it is attempted, it should be done with a serious commitment of resources and very careful attention to detail. It is, after all, a portrayal of other people's lives.

Those who get involved in animation should soon find that doing it well is more of an effort than they imagined. If we lead people to believe that in our historical environments they really can discover the past, then we owe them the whole thing; if our presentation to visitors is any less complete than life itself, we will merely substitute our own cloudy view of the past for the one they had before.

It will be expensive. Even when volunteers reduce the cost or simply help field a convincing number of people in costume on special occasions, the cost of researching, clothing, and providing props for this type of presentation is considerable.

It requires extensive training. No one can ever learn enough to really represent someone from another century, and the greater the gulf in time the less we can hope to overcome it. With a large staff it will be a constant concern to keep or replace key personnel. People with sufficient motivation to rise to the challenge of being good animators are rare.

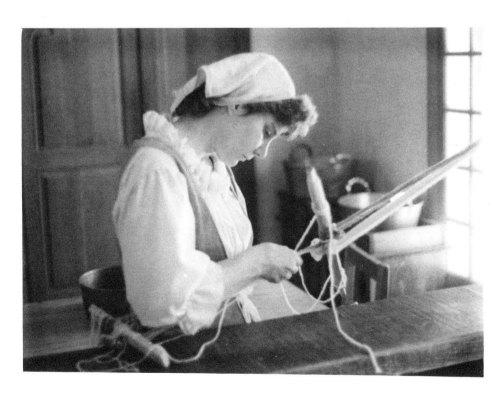

Interpreting domestic weaving at Fort Michilimackinac, Michigan.—*Photo: Tom Allen*

It also requires a historical environment that can be very difficult to achieve. Apart from carefully staged presentations, I do not favor animation among ruins or anywhere except in an accurate and complete historical setting. Small things, such as correct tableware or accoutrements, can be as difficult to achieve as the buildings themselves.

Having created a historical environment, you will have the ongoing problem of preserving it from modern intrusion—the sights, sounds, and obvious signs of vehicles, service facilities, maintenance crews, or the neighbors if they live close by. Very few people voluntarily approach this environment with the respect or concern for detail that is needed to keep from being compromised to the point of absurdity. Much effort is required to ensure that the historical setting can operate with dignity.

Animation can be hard on the very objects the museum wishes to display. Antiques will not survive the use, or lack of attention, that results from ongoing animation. Sooner, rather than later, they will have to be replaced by reproductions, and the breakage rate can be alarming. Our contemporaries, especially students, simply do not know how to use or care for historical implements. This legacy of the age of obsolescence is an interesting lesson in itself, but it can cost you dearly.

Even more than the other forms of interpretation, animation is continually prone to being garbled. It can become a game the public plays with your staff, and the staff will constantly be forgetting the information it should know and inventing some vivid substitutes. Between the inaccurate things animators say and the inappropriate things they do, much planning and effort will be required merely to ensure that the animation program avoids being absurd.

Animation can become an excuse for animators to ignore visitors by busying themselves with routines and avoiding personal contact. If animators begin taking refuge in busywork, they undermine their personal effectiveness as well as the credibility of the program. The foundation of a realistic animation program is activity, purposeful and relevant to the historical environment, rather than footloose posturing in costume.

If animators are acting a role, they have to be responsive enough to their audience to know when to step out of the role. We find that role-playing may be most effective between the animators themselves rather than between animator and visitor. The public is not prepared to respond directly to role-playing, and could immediately destroy its authenticity if they did. Role-playing can easily be carried too far and become clownish. Finally, the very success of animation or role-playing can draw attention away from everything else in the museum. It is a powerful magnet for the crowd, many of whom readily give up the exercise of their intellect and imagination merely to enjoy the show.

On the other hand, the animation of a historic site or building offers some unique opportunities. It has an enormous capacity to demonstrate. Craft activities and kitchens lend themselves especially well to this method, because in many cases the animator is doing something already familiar. Animation can be used to demonstrate through clothing and deportment the subtle differences between social classes. It can show in an instant complex information that would require paragraphs to describe by the traditional methods of labels and pictures. Consider the difference in appeal between showing visitors a soldier's drill manual and showing them a line of infantry marching and firing their muskets. What didactic exhibit could hold a visitor's attention long enough to explain all the procedures required to get a sailing ship under way? Yet, who could avoid watching the same thing as a living demonstration? A perspiring animator, or a furnished room that is grubby from real use rather than contrived by a curator, adds a personal dimension to history. Here we can forcibly make the point that our ancestors were people much like ourselves, and since we are not the first to have the problem of getting through life, perhaps we might learn more from them than we thought.

Animation is immediate and can be one of the most effective ways to involve people in experiencing the past. If people learn most easily when all their senses are involved, the outdoor museum has a significant advantage in the variety of ways it can stimulate a visitor's interest, involvement, and understanding. Louisbourg has applied this principle to its dining places, based on a cabaret and auberge that operated in the original buildings and which provide only the food and drink available during the eighteenth century. The furnishings and service reflect the social status of the original proprietors, and both places observe the laws of fast and abstinence prescribed during that time by the Catholic Church. We feel this experience is far more meaningful for a visitor than looking at the bedroom of some historical character. Complaints about the lack of amenities at dinner are offset by the challenge of a realistic, if unexpected, historical experience. Yet visitors would probably not accept the same level of realism if it were not presented as an integral part of an animation program.

Animation also has a great potential for use in films and still photographs, or for expressing the mood of a historic environment without having the public come near or speak to the animators. Animation at a distance can be surprisingly evocative, even in daylight, and is the least susceptible to errors. Museums have been so dedicated to the maximum transmission of facts that many animation programs have never moved beyond the concept of costumed lecturers. Yet Louisbourg has had its greatest response from events such as its Candlelight Tours, in which the activities of a garrison town at evening are acted out by animators who entirely ignore the visitors, and visitors are forbidden to speak to the animators. Tour leaders provided all the information on what is experienced, in the detached and omniscient style of the stage manager in Thornton Wilder's play "Our Town."

In distinguishing between visitors and a public audience who has not yet come to us as visitors, I think we have an obligation to speak to everyone—particularly if our institutions are tax-supported. Animation and its interpretive by-products such as films and school kits are very effective ways to extend a museum's message to the non-visiting public. A great deal could be said about problems with film makers and news crews who may get involved, which only reinforces the need for the museum to control animation very carefully and control anyone who would interpose their interpretation of history between the museum and the public.

Animation can be a powerful learning experience for the person in costume. When volunteers are involved, at all ages from the very young to the very old, their study and insights really amount to an extension program, which benefits the volunteer as well as the public.

In spite of the ways that animation can distort the message, an animator who is a good communicator can clarify information for visitors and build on their interest to lead them away from simple nostalgia into a deeper and more personal appreciation of history. Animation is also an excellent device for the outdoor museum to highlight areas, draw visitors through (or out of) buildings, and attract them to go where you want them to go.

The irony is that if animation is approached seriously, its very success in establishing a historical milieu will bewilder and discomfit visitors. As it happens, many things keep us from reaching such a level. Few museums are prepared to study the historical dialects that should be spoken by their animators, or substitute replica coinage for modern currency, or set their clocks by the sun, or adopt the religious observances of the historical culture they would re-create. Not many are prepared to give up all interpretive signs outside their buildings. Even a modest reduction in modern lighting, heating, seating, paving, toilets, and safety precautions is a thankless job, which leaves no doubt that in any choice between realism and personal comfort, our visitors, and our staff, would gladly not get too realistic. If we give visitors the orientation and inconvenience that they would experience if they really stepped into the past, they complain; if we don't, our critics deride us for sugar-coating history.

Recognizing that Louisbourg would have to escape from the self-imposed limitations of its "moment in time" approach, we have found that a serious animation program almost demands that the rest of the interpretation effort be adapted to support it.

Instead of interpreting a wide sweep of history and culture in our exhibits, as we had planned to do in our early enthusiasm, we found we must tailor our interpretation to the reconstruction, specifically to those lessons and insights that the work has made evident. When we perceived that much relevant information was not getting through to visitors, we reduced everything that could be said about Louisbourg's history to six themes: Louisbourg as a fortress, naval base, fishing port, entrepot, capital, and community. Then we began to correlate all our efforts and projects toward reinforcing these basic themes.

Because the fortress is usually cold and windy, while the buildings offer little comfort and visitors are often confused by their surroundings, Louisbourg has devised a "theme lounge" where people can relax and have their questions answered and problems looked after. Here the discomforts and disorientation of the visit are relieved by a haven where the "moment in time," rigorously applied elsewhere, does not apply. The biggest consideration is comfort. The interpretation approach is soft sell. The buildings have been chosen carefully so that the view of the reconstruction outside reinforces the historical theme explained inside. While visitors rest, they can browse through the staff reports and historical sources relevant to the theme, see a variety of films, listen to records, or meet our staff to learn more about this particular aspect of Louisbourg's history.

Because many of our historical buildings contain exhibits rather than furnishings, we have reversed our original approach to exhibit design; instead of flashy modern exhibits, which contrasted with the historical setting and threatened to overwhelm it, our exhibit style attempts to complement and reinforce the historical atmosphere. We respect the floor plan and divisions of rooms as if the building were an original structure, and we try very hard to avoid letting any lights or labels be seen from outside. In a panel near the door we will describe the original occupants and hope that, in spite of the exhibit, the ambience of the time and the presence of the people who lived there will still be felt. Our exhibits staff is less than enthusiastic about the numerous restrictions they must accept under this policy, but we feel there is no choice if we are seriously to portray a historical town.

Our exhibits themselves can no longer speak about any subject we choose, or be based necessarily on objects. Because the historical experience is amply confusing, our first concern in the didactic exhibits is to explain what visitors see around them. The exhibits become labels for the reconstruction and activities outside. The subjects are chosen, and the content is heavily influenced, by the need to explain the historical milieu rather than merely to present the prize objects in the collection. There are times when our exhibits come closer to being pages of books mounted on the walls because we do not have objects appropriate to the subject that must be covered.

Finally, we have had to relegate complex subjects, such as the development of fortifications or the history of the sieges, to other formats including publications, films, and guided walks rather than present them through exhibits inside the historical buildings. This is probably a good idea anyway, but had we attempted otherwise we know that any detailed presentation, which ordinarily has a sedate museum atmosphere to encourage visitor attention, would have to compete on losing terms with the sounds and sights and smells of the animation program around it. Almost no one would bother to finish seeing the exhibit.

I dwell on these problems and opportunities because it helps point out some basic questions about a museum's entire program of interpretation.

First, what is the message? Every museum should have a brief statement of purpose for its interpretation program, in which it describes the basic knowledge it wishes to communicate and explains why people should spend their time visiting in the first place. In writing such a statement for Louisbourg, I asked myself what I would say if I met some people at the airport, during the few minutes before their flight left, and I wanted to persuade them to cancel their trip to come and see the place where I worked. Building on this brief statement of purpose, I feel we also need a more detailed plan of the ways and places in which our museums will use all the available methods of interpretation, including animation, guided or self-guided tours, formal exhibits, audio-visual installations, and publications, to convey the message we have decided is important. This all seems basic and obvious, but I am surprised at the number of museums in which it has not been done; their interpretation planning is rudimentary at best; it tends to be *ad hoc* and opportunistic rather than systematic, and the staff does not have the same goals or a common set of assumptions about how to achieve them.

Second, we need at least a hypothetical visitor to aim at. We need to identify our audience and respond to specific types of visitors. In addition to the quantifiable characteristic of age, origin, length of visit, and so on, we need to assume a level of interest, involvement, and intelligence on the part of our audience; we should gear our interpretation to these assumptions, then watch to see whether we succeed. And we need much more comparison among museums of visitor characteristics.

Third, we must continually be measuring which interpretive methods appear to be most effective in expressing the museum's resources and programs. How you assess this will be your problem.

Fourth, are the methods by which we communicate still in support of the basic purposes of a museum—to collect, study, preserve, and display? Have the methods begun to undermine the purpose? Were the basic purposes clearly recognized in the first place? I have seen some new museums and museum villages develop with great enthusiasm toward the single objective of display. The popularity of animation is partly responsible for this because, following the lures of modern advertising techniques, some museums are rushing to become display centers to the neglect of their long-term responsibilities. Communication is the goal of interpretation, but interpretation is certainly not the only function of a museum. I sense that North American museums are beginning to realize how far they have gone in pursuit of public approval, partly in response to accusations during the 1960s that they were islands of irrelevance. If we are drawing back from a communications binge, we may evolve toward more emphasis on conservation and study.

Our colleagues who were late in starting to overhaul their interpretation programs can learn by our experience and avoid the excesses. In the last decade we have seen the continued development of theme parks—the "Gay 90's" villages, African Kingdoms, Santa Claus workshops, Frontier Towns, and so on. We can only admire the planning, logistical base, and operational so-

Don Dickerson, "du Bois," and Gerald White "le Blanc" arm wrestling in old Fort Niagra.—*Photo: Tom Allen*

phistication of Disney World; it and its imitators are a great success at their stated purpose, which is entertainment. But we should know we cannot compete on that basis, even when, as with outdoor museums and parks, our interpretive technique mingles education with re-creation.

If you go to all the trouble I have described in order to launch an animation program, you can still expect historical reality to be elusive and momentary. It may exist in its ideal form only for as long as the swing of a door, or the moment it takes for a costumed figure to disappear around a street corner. Yet that moment can bring a sense of timelessness, a realization of the humanity we share with our ancestors, that will not be like anything else you can experience.

The rest of the time you will be striving for the impossible, knowing you really cannot re-create or re-experience someone else's life. Yet the effort itself is significant and interesting, and so are the insights that result. I find that we get out of it in the same measure as we put into it. It is possible to play it out on a superficial level, and it is possible for animation to be much more meaningful.

Good animation comes close to realizing the reasons why we preserve and study the past. In the words of the historian Julian Boyd: "Our historic shrines, our parks, our restorations, our pageants, and our monuments constitute a vast textbook across the land, wherein millions of people may deepen their experience, renew their acquaintance with the roots of their institutions, and occasionally encounter those rare moments of understanding and insight that regenerate our strength."

Complete success may not be possible, but is anything less than a total effort a worthy goal?

Living Museums of Everyman's History

Cary Carson

As the director of research for the Colonial Williamsburg Foundation, Cary Carson sees living museums as a way of taking "history directly to the people." And the "history" that Carson has in mind is the "new social history." He argues in this essay, first published in the summer 1981 issue of Harvard Magazine, *that living museums, "collections of ordinary, everyday activities re-create the basic life experiences that serve as focal points for the new social history—birth, education, work, marriage, diet, disease, and the provision of clothing, housing, and material possessions." Carson concludes: "Like it or not, museums are forums, not attics. Their visitors' enthusiasm for thoughtful history has gone far to assuage the misgivings of attic-loving professionals."*

For graduate students at Harvard in the late sixties, it was easy to believe we had cornered the best of two sublime worlds. What the formal curriculum didn't offer inside the Yard, we heard for free outside in Harvard Square. Nowhere else, we told ourselves, was it so convenient to read history in the morning and watch it happen after lunch. Imagine our surprise, then, when one day a colleague over in the American Civ. department chucked his studies and announced that he was moving out to central Massachusetts to usher in the revolution at Old Sturbridge Village. Those who knew his mind assured us that he meant the revolution, the same one that seemed forever in rehearsal on the Cambridge Common. His manifesto caught the sansculottes with their sangfroid down. Not only were they unprepared to hear apocalypse preached by a defector from the common-room presidium, but that he should seek asylum in a museum of early-American rural life was—what was the word they used—unreal, to say the very least.

Looking back, I can see that events turned out differently than any of us expected. But to give this fellow his due, he was more nearly right than we were. True, Sturbridge Village never became his Finland Station. Nevertheless, he perceived something that few other professional historians were seeing in 1969 (those I knew, at least). Even now, more than ten years later, the role he was one of the first to envision for popular-history museums, a role many are now trying to fill, is still little understood by the public that flocks through their gates.

Like many breakthroughs, the connection he made seemed elementary afterwards. Ours was the first crop of American graduate students to get caught up in the enthusiasm for the so-called "new social history." We were attracted to its egalitarianism and to its "scientific" dedication to finding out how past societies were structured and how their parts worked together to form organic communities. At heart, I suppose, there was an even more basic appeal. To a generation of political activists and sidewalk superintendents, here was history writing that played down the importance of studying the past for its own sake and played up the notion that all history was a laboratory where historians with social-scientific bents could discover long-term changes in patterns of human behavior. We prided ourselves on being too professional to misrepresent the past for the purpose of promoting social change. Yet we were confident, in an unspecific sort of way, that the new social historians' penetrating insights would eventually raise the consciousness of our students and of the readers of the books and articles we would soon be writing.

Our Sturbridge dissident saw through this little fiction. He knew—and in our bones, we knew too—that scholars lose control over the use of their ideas as they trickle down from learned articles to monographs to textbooks to lesson plans. By going to Sturbridge, he was cutting out the middlemen. He was taking the new brand of history directly to the people, to the body politic. That was the essence of his originality; for, while back in Cambridge, conventional wisdom had it that "the people" were the readers of the *New Republic* and the *Saturday Review*, he saw the tremendous possibilities latent in museum villages. Their collections of ordinary, everyday activities re-created the basic life experiences that serve as focal points for the new social history—birth, education, work, marriage, death, diet, disease, and the provision of clothing, housing, and material possessions.

Their assemblages of buildings in town- and farm-like settings reconstructed the physical contexts and spatial dimensions that families, households, and whole communities once occupied. Not least of all, outdoor history museums already commanded a loyal following of ordinary, everyday visitors numbering millions every year.

They were a ready audience, too, anxious about widespread social change and consequently eager to find out what made human communities tick. From the mid-sixties onwards, museum interpreters—the listening kind—detected a shift in the tenor of the questions their visitors asked. "It's a populist spirit we notice here," said Jay Anderson about the Colonial Pennsylvania Plantation, a historical farm outside Philadelphia of which he was formerly director. "People who come are showing that they're not interested in seeing only how the rich lived. They want to see how their own counterparts lived, the dirt farmer, the working man." So ultimately it was not a handful of renegades from university history departments who set museum villages on their new course; credit for that really belongs to the visiting public and to those few perceptive institutions that trimmed their sails to catch the shifting wind.

Paying them that compliment is not to deny that the many historians, anthropologists, and folklorists who have since joined history museum staffs have not made a significant difference. They have. From them has come an intellectual coherence and a sense of purpose that museums seldom had before. Old Sturbridge Village still has not sparked a proletarian uprising, but it and other "living-history museums," as they call themselves, have recently begun advancing ideas about the past that have serious—and deliberate—implications for the present and the future. Change is a hallmark of history, they say. Preparing people to cope with change is, therefore, the business that history museums ought to be engaged in. Where educational institutions, of whatever ilk, profess objectives like those, it behooves their clientele to take a little time beforehand to find out more about them.

The new history has several characteristics that adapt it well to the museum village milieu. Invented in France a generation ago, the approach was taken over by English and American historians but did not lose the distinguishing trait of French historiography, its comprehensiveness. All human behavior—the thoughts, actions, and conditions of all peoples from all cultures—falls within its purview. That alone ought to fit it neatly

Black history replayed at Colonial Williamsburg.—*Photo: Colonial Williamsburg Foundation*

into the working philosophies of such museums as Colonial Williamsburg, Plimoth Plantation, Upper Canada Village, Old World Wisconsin, and many similar restorations and reconstructions that try (with varying degrees of candor) to portray all the past that's fit to show.

The "total history" is, therefore, inherently a demographic history. It rejects the traditional notion that rulers are more important than the ruled, that might confers the right to be remembered, or that money does all the talking historians need listen to. By reordering priorities to elevate the lowborn to equal prominence with presidents and prime ministers, the new history makes itself singularly attractive to those historical places whose misfortune it has always been that George Washington slept someplace else. Total history gives rhyme and reason to everyone in a historical community, the nobodies no less than the somebodies.

It sounds only fair and reasonable. Yet an egalitarian approach to studying the past runs against deeply ingrained assumptions that many historians still cherish. I found that out the hard way, some years ago. I was courting a national philanthropic foundation at the time, in hopes of getting grant money for archaeological excavations at a new history museum on the site of Maryland's earliest colonial capital, St. Mary's City. An eminent historian on the foundation's research committee, a gentleman of the old school, scoffed at our proposal. "Nobody I ever heard of came from St. Mary's City," he objected, and brushed aside our suggestion that nowadays some of a historian's best friends are anonymous. Fortunately we had a champion on the committee, an old Park Service hand, whose summation of our case stands out in my mind as a classic defense of the new historians' position. "Members of this committee," he chided them, "will spend thousands to find out what a dinosaur ate for breakfast, but not a penny to rediscover the daily habits of their own ancestors." We got the grant.

Old ways of thinking are naturally hardest to uproot at museums and historic sites that really can lay claim to having been born in, slept in, died in, or fought over by bonafide history book celebrities. I know, because I work for one. Colonial Williamsburg has spent fifty years painstakingly re-creating an eighteenth-century town down to the last footscraper. Its first official statement of purpose, written in consultation with John D. Rockefeller, Jr., himself and unrevised until 1979, asserted that an authentic, three-dimensional environment was essential to understanding the "lives and times" of early Americans and appreciating their contribution "to the ideals and culture of our country." Translated, "ideals" meant the concepts of self-government and individual liberty espoused by four indisputable worthies—Washington, Jefferson, Mason, and Henry—and expounded by them in the first two buildings that Rockefeller reconstructed at Williamsburg, the Capitol and the Raleigh Tavern. "Culture" they understood not as anthropologists use the word but in the sense of "high culture," the culture of pie-crust tables and upper-crust

manners. Small houses, ordinary furnishings, and such lesser folk as lived in Williamsburg were part of the picture too, but not in the same way that social historians consider them important today. At Colonial Williamsburg the small fry were a supporting cast in a drama starring John Fry, a fictitious upper-class planter who plays the title role in "The Story of a Patriot," Williamsburg's celebrated orientation film, which has now been seen by more than twenty million visitors. There and throughout the historic area, social history was a backdrop, a stage set, to the real story, the story of 1776, the struggle for freedom, liberty, justice, and representative government. The "lives and times" of ordinary people embroidered a variegated and richly detailed background that was needed to lend credibility to those few whom Rockefeller called "the great patriots." (Even today we refer to them in shoptalk shorthand as "the first string" or "the all-stars.")

Little by little, though, history museums, ours included, are finding another meaning for democracy. Social history, in its newer sense as the history of society, emancipates everyone who left traces of himself in the records or underground. Inevitably, where so many are served by such fragmentary information, emphasis shifts from individuals to groups. That raises new questions, which sooner or later someone turns round and asks of the same prominent, well-recorded personalities whom historians thought they knew quite well already. Hence, even museums that have legitimate reasons to commemorate history's best and brightest feel increasingly obligated not just to extol their immortal achievements, but to explain where and how they fit into the life of their communities. Visitors to George Washington's birthplace at Wakefield, Virginia, see a film, for example, that depicts a Colonial plantation as seen through the eye—indeed, from the eye level—of a six-year-old child. It tells a lot about perceptions of childhood in the eighteenth century, and only what little is worth knowing about Baby George. Likewise, Lincoln's boyhood home in Spencer County, Indiana, is presented now less as a shrine to the sixteenth president and more as a living-history farm community. What Abe's legendary exploits as a railsplitter, cabin builder, and flatboat deckhand lose in heroic proportions, they gain back in the realistic portrayal of him as a plain frontiersman. As the myths of physical prowess are dispelled, due consideration can be given to those remarkable habits of mind that truly set him apart from his neighbors.

History writing that puts people into groups, whether families, households, or neighborhoods, concentrates on shared experiences. An emphasis on the basic conditions of everyday life is a second characteristic of the new history scholarship that takes advantage of the resources and aptitudes of open-air museums. No one knows who first had the bright idea of putting collections of farm tools, cooking utensils, and spinning and weaving equipment back into active service, but it is now the rare historic house or farm museum where someone isn't dipping candles, carding wool, or theorem-painting. Such activities are most certainly not history in and of themselves, least of all the new history. But interpreters engaged in such activities are in fact going through motions that once were full of meaning, some of it explicit, much of it deeply cultural. Working, playing, growing up, getting married, bearing children, getting old and sick, and finally dying are life experiences that every society plays by different rules; usually artifacts are involved. By collecting them and putting them to their original uses again, museums can run a time machine backwards, as it were, using artifacts to re-create activities, and activities to recall the underlying framework of beliefs that gave meaning to both the routine and the extraordinary in people's lives.

This third attribute of the new history, its interest in a society's "collective consciousness," forces new historians and their museum counterparts to go beyond merely enumerating who was who in the past and describing what life was like for them. Real history describes in order to explain. Living history, to deserve the name, must harness its tremendous descriptive powers to the ultimate goal of explaining to museum visitors something worth knowing about the past. If wool carding does not lead to a discussion of farm economics and work roles in pre-industrial communities, or theorem-painting to an explanation of attitudes toward leisure and women's education, then the museum that demonstrates these activities has merely polished up old-fashioned pots-and-pans history and nothing more.

It is not an easy kind of teaching to do. Summer heat, crowds, and weary tourists are but three of a thousand extenuating circumstances that will tempt museum teachers to keep their interpretations short, sweet, and superficial. Lapses by individual interpreters can be excused as human nature; museum-goers should be much less forgiving of that growing number of living-history museums that base their whole method of operation on the assumption that a re-created past speaks for itself, that a meticulously accurate portrayal of historical events or activities provides its own adequate explanation.

That assumption was carried to a logical and interesting extreme a few years ago at one of the earliest innovating museums in the country, Plimoth Plantation, a "living folk museum" of Pilgrim history located outside Plymouth, Massachusetts. After twenty years in the business of ancestor worship, it was born again in 1967 when Jim Deetz, a Harvard anthropologist, became its associate director. He set about investigating the Pilgrim Fathers (and the Pilgrim Mothers and Pilgrim Offspring, too) in the same way that his academic colleagues studied Australian aborigines or groups of gorillas. He took the viewpoint that William Bradford's colonists had more in common with late sixteenth-century peasant farmers and artisans than with their latter-day Mayflower descendants—a view that took the descendants some getting used to. Research proceeded along those lines, and soon after, so did interpretation in the replicated Pilgrim village. Interpreters stopped lecturing about the early settlers and started doing the things they thought the colonists had done. Visitors were invited to play anthropologist-for-a-day. If they came to the museum when the "villagers" were cutting hay, they learned all about haying. When the staff was cleaning eel, eel-gutting topped the agenda. In effect Plimoth was saying to the public: Take us as you find us and make whatever sense of things you can.

As I see it, that is often the problem with living-history interpretation. Many people bother to make no sense of it at all. They get caught up in the excitement, but receiving little or no help in organizing their impressions so they can draw some meaningful generalizations from them, they go away full perhaps, but not nourished.

The most conscientious of the new museums, Plimoth Plantation among them, acknowledge this problem and are experimenting with solutions. So far, Old Sturbridge Village has had the most success. It has organized its whole museum around three groups of ideas: work, family, and community. Although visitors are free to roam at will, everywhere they go they encounter the central themes in one form or another. For example, they find family life explained in many of the restored houses. Interpreters at a parsonage discuss religion and reform to call attention to one family's ties with others in the village community. The schoolhouse and the meeting house are used to teach about the community itself, its mores, and its conduct of public business. A restored and restocked general store reminds visitors that a village must have relations with the world outside. And so it goes, through dozens of exhibits, craft shops, farms, and activities that are no less enthralling than those to be found at museums where these are ends in themselves. Indeed they are more so, because a visitor comes away from Sturbridge with his head full of ideas that have been carefully planted and encouraged to grow into a knowledge of the past sufficiently well developed to be called out later and used again. In short, learning worth keeping.

Yet even at Sturbridge I feel something is missing. The ten-year-old promise that history museums could popularize a new kind of social history, a history of society, still is not fulfilled. Even the best new museums fail to infuse their time-capsule restorations with a sense of process, a sense of change. How did the historical communities they portray get to be that way? What dynamic forces were at work to transform them from what they had been to what they became? If there is truth in the claim that museums ought to give people practice in understanding the nature of change, then they must cultivate still another area of interest to historians, new and old—namely, the influence of population and economic growth on the structure of society.

I know no museum currently open to the public that takes as its principle mission the interpretation of the evolution of economic and social life. I know three that have something of the sort on their drawing boards. Sturbridge Village wants to build a mill town adjacent to its farming community. Side-by-side, they would be used to tell how agricultural New England was gradually industrialized. At Colonial Williamsburg we are looking at ways to use several early seventeenth-century fort and farmstead sites, recently discovered at Carter's Grove Plantation, to explain how demographic conditions and economic forces transformed two immigrant peoples—one European, the other African—into the settled, indigenous cultures represented by the surviving mid-eighteenth-century plantation house and a slave village to be reconstructed nearby.

The third institution goes even further. It actually uses the term "process museum" to describe its genus and species. This is brand-new Historic St. Mary's City, a remarkably well-preserved archaeological village site in southern Maryland that the state is excavating in partnership with the Smithsonian Institution, the University of Maryland, and George Washington University, through their respective American studies programs. Al-

though the site is best remembered as the Jamestown of Maryland, the colony's seventeenth-century seat of government, the open-air museum being built there today will span 350 years of Chesapeake history. Its outdoor exhibits will deliberately juxtapose the history of the seventeenth century against later periods, up to and eventually including the present day.

A sneak preview shows how. Visitors to a broad headland overlooking the St. Mary's River will eventually view parts of a reconstructed Yeocomico Indian village that occupied the site in 1634, the palisaded fort that the original settlers built on top of it, Governor Leonard Calvert's mid-century plantation, bits of the late seventeenth-century capital, and a surviving nineteenth-century industrialized farm, each layered one upon another. Here and elsewhere, stratigraphy will give shape not only to what people see, but to what they learn. "Our whole purpose in serving up the past like a Dagwood sandwich is to teach the people about the process of change," explains one of the historians working in the project. "Here in the village center we want to raise ques-

Worker's history recreated by Dan Stebbins, master wheelwright.—*Photo: Colonial Williamsburg Foundation*

tions about the physical forms that communities take. How often have they been a matter of conscious choice? How far can they ever be?

As at Sturbridge, historians and planners at St. Mary's City talk about offering visitors something they will have the pleasure to learn by putting their minds to work. "We want them to take away something they can ponder afterwards." To do that, they are organizing the entire eight-hundred-acre museum into several coordinated groups of exhibits. The Indian village, fort, and later settlements will make one cluster. Another they call "Man on the Land." Its point of entry will be a natural history center in a woodland setting, where visitors will step back into a Chesapeake landscape that looks as it did to the earliest explorers. They will learn how a virgin world kept itself timed and balanced before the Indians, and then the colonists, cleared the forests. The notion of wilderness as a closed, self-regulating ecosystem is intended to draw a deliberate contrast between the natural world and four restored or reconstructed farms that will follow in chronological sequence after the nature center. First will come a middle-sized tobacco plantation, its economy meticulously re-created from a unique set of farm accounts kept by a St. Mary's County planter from 1662 to 1672. From there, visitors will proceed to two eighteenth-century farmsteads practicing a mixed tobacco and cereal agriculture, and finally to a mechanized, horsepowered farm conglomerate, which bought out its older, smaller neighbors after 1851. Each will re-create the setting, the cast of characters and critters, and the round of seasonal activities appropriate to its period. More important, each will give a different slant on the cluster's organizing idea—that farming, by its very nature, skews the natural balance in favor of the crops that farmers grow to make a living. Inevitably there are consequences, seen and unforseen in real life; but in the artificial worlds that history museums concoct, hindsight deepens insight. Alert visitors, proceeding from one farmstead to the next, will observe tended fields and neglected orchards, fences and outbuildings in repair and disrepair, healthy and scrawny livestock, free and unfree labor forces, and contrasting standards of living in farmhouses and slave quarters. These are the visual cues that interpreters will use to make their point that farmers' deliberate manipulation of the environment left indelible marks on the people, on the land they worked, and ultimately even on the character of their communities.

Exhibit clusters are the device that Historic St. Mary's City has invented to create time-lapse history. There are other ways to condense centuries into single afternoons. Improvising on an old National Park standby, the exhibit-filled interpretive center, the Minnesota Historical Society has written a master plan that organizes the themes of an entire state's history into a network of semi-autonomous regional centers. An Iron Range Center, a Forest History Center, and an interpretive facility, still on the drawing boards, devoted to the story of farming in the upper Midwest, have an opportunity to deal candidly with the state's natural and human resources, industries' use and misuse of them, and the paradoxes of "progress."

At Colonial Williamsburg we have a different problem and a different solution. Rockefeller's restoration turned the town's historical clock back to the space of a few years between 1750 and the Revolution. That does not stop us now from considering a proposal to organize the town into distinctive neighborhoods and combine the craft shops and exhibition buildings into several compact learning centers. At each, interpreters would develop one or two aspects of Williamsburg's central theme: becoming Americans. The restored town's abbreviated chronology may only be one moment frozen in time, but visitors can still explore the all-important process of change if interpreters deliberately bring them in on the middle of uncompleted, long-range historical events—the ripening of American and Afro-American culture, for instance, or the evolution of everyday self-government into a revolution in political philosophy and action.

When historians and teachers take their calling in public education so seriously, their "students"—75 million visitors to history museums and historic sites every year—ought to pause at the turnstiles long enough to ask what they are letting themselves in for. What are the ultimate lessons of history that these beguiling museum teachers camouflage so charmingly with costumes, carriage rides, and craft demonstrations?

My predecessors at Colonial Williamsburg gave that question long, hard thought, and over the years they came up with answers that precisely fit the temper of their times. In 1950 it was to "stimulate such thinking on the American heritage as will lead to constructive action on the part of our audience." They had in mind constructive civic action, of course, a citizen's commitment to defend the principles of liberty "whatever and whenever they may be under challenge." Those were the words that for years introduced "The Story of a Patriot," which premiered five months after Soviet tanks crushed the Hungarian revolution.

Rockefeller himself was more philosophical. His purpose in restoring the town, he explained many years later, was to immortalize "those great patriots whose voices once resounded" in the House of Burgesses as "an inspiration to noble living." Even today, the notion of history as hornbook has staunch advocates at Colonial Williamsburg and throughout the museum community. Author and archaeologist Ivor Noel Hume argues forcefully that history teachers might possibly forestall the decline and fall of the American republic if they could just rekindle "a new willingness to return to the Spartan and self-sacrificing values that led Englishmen to build new lives and a new nation in America." The tradition is a hardy perennial, with deep roots in Americans' anxiousness about their country's future.

Yet I for one am bothered by history used as catechism. I recall James Agee's observation after visiting

Williamsburg just before his death, in 1955, at which time he met some of the very people who were putting into practice the "constructive action" philosophy of education. They were "good scholars," he wrote to a friend; all the same, he detected "a little of the sadness of faculty people (my age and younger) without a great enough subject to involve their best energies." His remark hinted at the fallacy and futility inherent in putting history on a pedestal. Noble living and Spartan values are praiseworthy personal goals, just as preservation of a democracy is a laudable aim for a people that has chosen—and knows why it has chosen—that government rather than another. But teachers generally, and museums in particular, must not confuse ends and means or forget which they are about. It is not a teacher's business to choose sides and then instruct others in the rightness of those choices. History teaching turned to those purposes is at heart coercive. It puts the answers before the questions and rewards obedience before honest inquiry.

Real history teaching is a liberal art, a liberating art. It frees men from slavery to those who would do their thinking for them. It schools their choices, not only by giving practice in the skills needed to make independent decisions, but by concentrating the mind on those matters that are truly subject to free will. Everything else—all those forces over which men and nations have little or no control—these the study of history dissects and lays bare. That, too, is knowledge worth having. We are powerless to work our will on many things, but knowing how they work on us is an educated person's best defense against futile undertakings and unreasonable expectations.

The great sway that the new social history—this history of society—now holds in some of the leading museums in the country is owning to its fitness to this task. Its emphasis on the basic conditions of everyday life demarcates the barriers that set limits on human experience and, so doing, challenges the modern notion that freedom is the absence of restraint. Within very real limits, museums are saying to their audiences, everyone makes conscious and unconscious choices that steer their lives this way or that. Communities are the contrivances man makes to gain a little control over the intractable world around him. Museums that re-create historical communities do so more and more nowadays in ways that deliberately call attention to the relationships that individuals have formed with their fellows to enlarge their freedom of action and thereby achieve more than they could have alone.

Like it or not, museums are forums, not attics. Their visitors' enthusiasm for thoughtful history has gone far to assuage the misgivings of attic-loving professionals. Ten years ago, just about the time my Harvard acquaintance began proselytizing Sturbridge Village, students at the College of William and Mary petitioned Colonial Williamsburg for permission to march down the Duke of Gloucester Street and stand in silent vigil around the Capitol to protest the war in Vietnam. The foundation, which could hardly say no to these latter-day sons and daughters of liberty, complied. It also took certain precautions. A phalanx of troopers escorted the marchers along the parade route. At the Capitol, a picked company of vice presidents kept watch from the dormer windows. Yet no one was prepared for what actually happened. The students, brushed up and on their best behavior, had no sooner taken up their vigil than ordinary tourists—the everyman and everywoman kind—began leaving the buildings. Some, true to form, snapped pictures of the marchers. Others hesitated for a moment, then walked across the forecourt and silently, solemnly joined hands with the protesters. The anxious faces at the upstairs windows were at first disbelieving, then slowly perceiving, and finally exultant. Here, wonder of wonders, were three hundred people bearing witness to Williamsburg's oft-repeated motto, That the Future May Learn from the Past.

The old words rang fresh and true that October morning—and still do, because once again the past seems nigh and the future close at hand.

Part III
Forts

Louisbourg
Managing a Moment in Time

5

John Fortier

Awesome in scale, the Fortress of Louisbourg lies isolated at the end of Nova Scotia's stunningly beautiful Cape Breton Island. Focusing on the year 1744, interpretation varies from historical simulation to static exhibits and films telling the fascinating story of Louisbourg's restoration. The number and variety of the interpretive modes at Louisbourg is daunting—the fortress was, after all, once a small city, made up of soldiers, sailors, fishermen, merchants, and craftsmen of all kinds. John Fortier, who directed this Parks Canada project for over a decade, gives us a truly-in-depth analysis of the fortress's interpretive efforts. Few evaluations of a living-history museum's program match Fortier's thought-provoking essay. It was originally published in 1981 in the National Museum of Canada's "Mercury Series."

An "Elevation of Mind and Spirit"

Few historic sites in Canada can trace their development to a Royal commission; yet that was the point of departure for the spectacular renaissance of the Fortress of Louisbourg and the official sanction for its emphasis on interpretation. In the late 1950s, the gloomy future of Cape Breton's coal mines was the subject of an investigation by a Royal commission, headed by the Hon. I. C. Rand. One of the Rand Report's most perceptive observations was that a viable way of life on the island was a matter not only of economic alternatives but of cultural ones:

> A single extractive industry, by its nature, is not a desirable economic base for a community. . . . For the Sydney-Glace Bay-Louisbourg District, alternative and supporting economic and cultural activities must be considered, a scheme adequate to introduce new wealth into Cape Breton and bring fresh and heightened scenes and an elevation of mind and spirit to its people.

What could be more stimulating to the imagination or instructive to the public, the report concluded, than a reconstruction of the ruined fortress that would give "a comprehensive representation of the material and cultural community, set up in a strange land inviting settlement."[1]

The fundamentally interpretive nature of the reconstruction was further expressed in the approval given by the federal cabinet:

> The Fortress of Louisbourg is to be restored partially so that future generations can thereby see and understand the role of the fortress as a hinge of History. The restoration is to be carried out so that the lessons of History can be animated.[2]

That brief comment remains our best statement of direction. Our greatest problem was that the sponsors of the project had little idea how difficult it would be to achieve what they wanted. Since its beginning, the reconstruction has had to cope with the exigencies of massive development while at the same time defining what forms that development should take.

It is clear from reading early publicity that many people wanted a "Williamsburg of the North"— extensive reconstruction, period environments, animation in costume, local spinoffs benefitting tourism, culture, and crafts, and a major expression of Canadian identity. Yet Louisbourg was a political response to an economic situation; while social and cultural gains were foreseen from the beginning, they were left in outline form for later development.

Heritage or Kitsch?

From the beginning some of the methods of the reconstruction, if not the aims themselves, were controversial. There is no denying that the project was launched under less than ideal circumstances. Research, planning, and design were rushed. The reconstruction preserved some original archaeological features such as wells and drains and foundation walls, but inevitably destroyed others. The Engineer's residence, the Ice House, and the King's bastion guardhouse have been rebuilt on their original, stabilized foundations; fragments of walls in other buildings, such as the Carrerot House, and several cobblestone floors and sidewalks associated with such buildings as the Bakery, De la Valliere Storehouses, and King's Storehouse, have been left intact. In other cases, where old walls were declared to be structurally unsound, they were dug out and replaced by concrete footings; nothing survives of the Barracks except a cobblestone floor and one "holy door" in the basement, preserved *in situ* at considerable expense.

The incorporation of various, and sometimes extensive, pieces of structural fabric into the reconstruction is more than a gesture. It provides a continuity between past and present, which some people feel is impossible in a reconstruction. We don't agree with this objection, and one basic premise at Louisbourg is that because this town has been rebuilt on the site itself, for purposes we feel are legitimate even if different from the intentions of the founders, it has an intangible validity more like historical preservation than the "synthetic" reconstructions with which it has been categorized. This debate has continued since work began, and the answers often depend on one's point of view.

When such reconstruction becomes a parallel to historic preservation, we should examine the uneasy relationship between the two endeavors, since the professional standards and values of one inevitably begin to influence the other. The quality of the work at Louisbourg—indeed, the feasibility of trying to re-create the structural and conceptual milieu of an earlier epoch—have been questioned by preservationists. Some have argued that the spending of millions of dollars on reconstruction at Louisbourg was a distraction from more urgent and valid work that needed to be done to preserve existing structures in the rest of the country. Douglas Richardson, of the Department of Fine Arts at the University of Toronto, had this to say in an article entitled "Politics and Priorities in Architectural Preservation":

> It is ludicrous in the light of other more pressing problems. . . that the Federal Government pours twenty-three millions of dollars into the fabrication of Louisbourg. . . . No matter what pains are taken, so-called living museums in this country—based upon the relatively slender evidence (from an art historian's point of view) of the best archaeological excavations and historical research—are, comparatively, as dead as any artificially animated rubber dodo. . . .[3]

Well, that misses at least one point. The fortress was rebuilt to create jobs, attract tourists, and expand the cultural horizons of a region long afflicted by a company-town mentality. The money that went into Louisbourg would very likely not have been available to save old buildings somewhere else, and much as some people in the big cities may resent the flow of money to the hinterland, Louisbourg's reconstruction got started because there were politicians who wanted exactly that to happen.

The preservation movement in England, the United States, and most recently in Canada, is concerned mainly with old buildings. In general it includes outdoor museums because of their obvious architectural content. But among outdoor museums, whether they are primarily surviving old buildings or reconstructions, whether they have been created on an original site or not,

the buildings and streetscapes tend to be a point of departure from which to exhibit and explain the lives of people.

The group who consider themselves "preservationists" tend to be more absorbed in architecture or urban renewal and a little slow to extend their concern to artifacts, crafts, or the kinds of displays that are found in outdoor museums. And often they don't have much patience with reconstructions.

A case can be made, however, that by its ambitiousness and popularity the reconstruction of the fortress has encouraged public interest in, and acceptance for, the broader field of historic preservation, both in Ottawa and in the provinces. Whether the example is the Citadel in Halifax, the Historic Waterfront Properties, or some of the restorations and outdoor museums that have flourished since the 1960s, a common theme when work begins is that the towns are catching up with their history, and the Fortress of Louisbourg is often their point of comparison. In this era of "vastly expanding public interest in and concern for heritage,"[4] it is easy to forget that when the reconstruction of the fortress was launched, it stood virtually alone as an example of government action on the heritage scene. For a decade it was by far the major, and almost the only, effort by the federal government to develop and interpret its historic sites. As the work progressed, those who approved were encouraged. Those who disagreed voiced their opinion that somebody had to get in charge of heritage, survey the national resources, and chart directions. In 1973, with a grant of $12 million, Parks Canada created Heritage Canada as a counterpoint and a complement to government action. Here was an open admission that big government could not, and would not, do everything; here was an invitation to private citizens to organize, influence legislation, and take over more of the custody of their heritage. Louisbourg had a distinct role in this, somewhat like the grain of sand in an oyster that irritates until it produces a pearl.[5]

Heritage Canada began with the preservationists' bias toward structures over other forms of historical resources. In the words of one disgruntled staffer, its idea of heritage amounted to "mostly town planning and how to turn old buildings into boutiques and apartments." But it is gratifying to see that the organization is now broadening its view. Pierre Berton, now chair of its board of governors, has listed three criteria for preserving a building or site. These are:

- The memory of a historical person or event
- Social significance
- Texture—in other words, variety and "character."[6]

If they look at Louisbourg, people could find all these conditions met in the reconstruction of the fortress. And they could find in the reconstruction a pretty good object lesson to support two of their basic concerns: a reappraisal of the throw-away society and a search for alternatives to the urban lifestyle of North America. In each of these areas the reconstruction of Louisbourg, like other outdoor museums, has something to say to those who will accept it as a work of scholarly inquiry.

It is still easy to start a vigorous debate over the merit of "replic" structures and objects as opposed to preserving the real thing. Often the dialogue is full of loaded words and implied tradeoffs, such as "elitism," "artificiality," "synthetic," "imitative," and "kitsch." The arguments on both sides can be persuasive,[7] but there is room for all concerned to be less defensive about their roles. The strong points and the limitations of each are obvious: preservation aims at a continuing use from the fabric of the old; museums attempt to show the old as it was. We need both.

One can hope, based on the trends of the last few years, that the complementary endeavors of outdoor museums ("museum villages") and architectural preservation will each continue to enlarge its focus, and that a common concern with heritage and lifestyle will enhance the state of the art in both areas. Such a logical outcome, in Canada, is rather overdue.

One of the best observations, to put this in perspective, comes from a meeting of architectural historians:

> The preservation movement rests ultimately upon the conviction that material objects from the past are subject to historical explanation, and that the quality of our lives is enhanced if we live with these objects and understand them.[8]

In the end Louisbourg may not be preserving old buildings, but it is preserving a heritage and a way of life—to the extent that such a thing can be done in the face of many practical difficulties.

Public History, Living History

If Louisbourg is not in the mainstream of the preservation movement, it is near the forefront of "public history." By that is meant the work done by publicly funded agencies such as museums, archives, historians working in various federal departments, resource surveys, and historic parks. As it has progressed, the reconstruction has expanded the cultural horizons—and the heritage consciousness—of people who experience it. It has spun off several local museums through the voluntary involvement of park staff in historical societies and restorations of old buildings. It has begun to project its historical image through a variety of filmed and printed media. And it has given all of us some insights that would not have been possible without a reconstruction that focused on the past and involved us in it with all our senses.

The preservation of objects, the use of objects and processes to teach, and the presentation of historical lifestyles in an environmental text are well within the mainstream of museum endeavor. The potential for outdoor museums to attract and involve visitors gives them an advantage in communications that many institutions envy. Yet if the methods and objectives of the reconstruc-

tion clearly find a more congenial peer group among outdoor museums, that hardly settles its identity. That formative field has yet to find its own level professionally.

Reconstructions and outdoor museums face criticism not only because of what they have not done but also because of what they do. There is a school of thought that their most characteristic form of interpretation—having people inhabit period buildings in period clothing—somehow makes the past trivial. Marcella Sherfy, a historian with the U.S. National Park Service, has summarized the case against living history as it is presented by many outdoor museums, including Louisbourg:

> It has become a form of communication used more to attract interest and applause than to translate park values into understandable terms. Its use as a vehicle for transmitting contemporary social and political beliefs abuses historical people and the sense of the past. Its sweeping claims to broad portrayal of the past blur visitor perception and appreciation of historic resources. . . .
>
> Our claims to presenting a total re-creation of the past are misleading and destructive. Our certainty that we can "know" earlier generations denies essential human complexity. More important, that claim distorts our visitors' understanding of history and its value to the present.[9]

Well, that depends on how one views an exercise that is highly subjective. It puzzles me how people, many of whom realize the limitations of other forms of communication, expect so much from living history and complain in such decisive terms when they fail to find it. I concede that living-history programs have often been launched with a lot of hype, which has made them sound like some kind of communications breakthrough. On the other hand, these expansive claims are often not made by museum workers but by the media, feature writers, or tourism promoters. The same kind of hype and nostalgia gets applied to every facet of history including historic buildings, urban renewal projects, even static exhibits, but there seems to be no comparable debate whether the imperfections and exaggerations invalidate activity in those areas as well. There is, after all, no perfect medium in which to communicate—no book, no file, no lecture, no work of art. . . .

It is particularly unhelpful to come across criticism that outdoor museums should "tell it like it was," a phrase that usually implies dirt, illness, and nasty dealings with the neighbors. Yes, these elements remain largely unportrayed by costumed animators, though not necessarily when films are being made at our sites. And it is undoubtedly useful for the staff of outdoor museums to be reminded that there are limitations to their interpretive medium and that they should not promise more than they can deliver even if it means deflating the expectations of some of their visitors. On the other hand, the critics of period demonstrations and re-enactments ought, in fairness, to be held accountable for their own distortions of the past. One example comes to mind:

At the gates of Louisbourg, in 1745, there were not well-garbed ticket takers, but syphilitic whores ready to give happy but brief surcease to the agonies of licentious soldiery whose lives were poor, nasty, brutish, and certainly short.[10]

In reality, at the gates of Louisbourg, there are and were neither of these, and our research has put us in a position to discuss the actual operation of a fortress at considerable length with anyone who wants to take the time. It happens that most vacationers do not, and we will hardly hold their attention further by striving to be offensive. Nor can anyone express the past more honestly by harping on the unpleasant aspects. In general, I think outdoor museums are not falling short of their obligations in this regard much more than any other medium, including those of writers, teachers, and film-makers. At the same time, we do not consciously dismiss or avoid the unpleasant aspects of life in animation, exhibits, publications, or any other medium. One of our most popular events has been a "gossip's tour," which retells, from the historical documents, some of the venal and scandalous happenings in eighteenth-century Louisbourg. The very idea of showing a town doomed to war and destruction ought to be grim enough to appease most realists.

The Limits of Reproduction

"Interpretation" is the variety of methods by which we communicate, and costumed animation at Louisbourg or at many other outdoor museums is not the only approach to understanding and explaining the past. As a result of our experience with visitors and of self-examination as to what we could do best, we have been moving away from the "show biz" approach of some outdoor museums and closer to the European style of historic site interpretation. We all can think of costumed demonstrations or re-enactments in which the spectacle seemed somewhat larger than life. Extremely well staged and photogenic, they were not valid as history of the place. These events receive much encouragement from spectators and tourism promoters to grow until they resemble Buffalo Bill's Wild West Show or the goings-on at some of the "theme parks" in Upstate New York. Unfortunately, many of our visitors have these images firmly in mind and are looking for more when they arrive at our gates.

Given the temptations toward that kind of distortion and the public appetite for it, Louisbourg has consciously adopted a low-key approach to the portrayal of its historical scene. The soldiers seldom drill or fire any guns, and their uniforms are rumpled and worn. The civilian animators demonstrate workaday routines. Some of the most evocative depictions of the past are staged only for films and photographs, then edited for presentation to the public.

At the same time, we have tried to make room among the animation for personal discovery and more reflective uses of the site. Visitors can study; small organizations can hold private meetings; specialized training and dramatic presentations can be accommodated inside some of the reconstructed buildings even while the period environment is interpreted around them. We found that to head in the other direction, avoiding any use that was not "period immersion," was a bit sterile. It was also impossible to find anyone sufficiently trained to stage a meaningful immersion, and the average visitor certainly wasn't up to it. To keep a sense of perspective we find there is room for limited contemporary use of the site as long as it respects the history of the original inhabitants.

At Louisbourg we don't wish to be known simply as a reconstruction. We manage a park full of historical resources, and we want people to regard Louisbourg as more than a pleasant spectacle. After all, the fortress and town have been only partially reconstructed in one corner, and one corner only, of a historic site that would be tremendously significant in Canada's history with or without a reconstruction. It is clear that conservation and interpretation of the archaeological site and of the artifacts and antiques in our care will require more attention than they have been getting. The archives and research collections at Louisbourg are unique, and we are unique as a national park for the staff and effort we are devoting to making them accessible. We are trying to maintain a level of scholarly activity that is extraordinary among parks and unusual even in the more scholarly world of museums and historic preservation.

Many of those who question the reconstruction have a great deal of respect for the research and attention to detail that have saved it from being just another make-work project. That has probably been Louisbourg's most significant contribution to the rest of Parks Canada, and through it to the general level of professionalism with which historic sites and buildings in Canada are preserved and interpreted. The new Parks Canada policy is laced with references to upholding authenticity and integrity in historic environments—a welcome development to those who are familiar with the rudimentary level of interpretation in many parks.

Museum Perspectives

There is a problem with parks such as Louisbourg and with outdoor museums in general. Whenever history is presented in a more dynamic fashion than the usual static exhibits or gallery talks, the methods do not fit conveniently into the norms of traditional education or the traditional museum. It is a mistake either to force outdoor museums into the same mold or to ignore them because they are different. In fact the resources, management problems, visitor expectations, and interpretive parameters of outdoor museums and historic parks are so different from those of the traditional museum that one wonders how the common bonds have not long ago been overwhelmed by the differences.

Some of the differences are quite pronounced. What traditional, big-city museum has to worry about land and wildlife management, for example, or herds of "period" animals, or traffic circulation and signage, or highway maintenance, or recreational amenities such as picnic areas and campgrounds, or combinations of natural and man-made disasters such as forest fires, coastal oil spills, and environmental pollution? All this comes in addition to the intricate logistical and supervisory problems inherent in costumed animation. It is rare that the staff of a traditional museum is involved in such problems, yet the staff members at outdoor museums and national or provincial historic parks and sites contend with these and many other problems as well as the customary museum preoccupations involved with administration, curatorship, and exhibits. Outdoor museums are a broader field and require work beyond the narrow bounds of their own disciplines. It is high time that outdoor museums and historic parks got an association, or greater recognition within the existing associations, to grapple with their unique problems.

Some of the bonds between traditional museums and outdoor museums are weakening perceptibly. Parks Canada, for example, feels that its objectives are so different from those of the museums operated by other federal agencies that a common front is not feasible even in such mutual endeavors as research, the acquisition and care of collections, or the representation of themes in Canada's history. It is a matter of policy that national historic parks and sites will collect only the objects that are related to their specific interpretive message, and that they will not maintain collections as research centers in parks. In a "park context," it is sometimes difficult even to relate to the concerns of the museum world within Parks Canada. The high-profile, national park issues of conservation, land use, and visitor management often overshadow the problems of the scattered, mostly small-scale historic buildings and sites in our national system. While historic sites and national parks share a common concern with conservation, the problems and skills involved may be quite different. And the recreational imperative of parks is not always compatible with the educational or cultural imperative of historic places. At another level it becomes difficult for "site-specific" historic specialists to justify a continuing involvement with traditional museums, their methods, and standards. This body of problems, which has serious implications for both parks and museums, has yet to be addressed as a professional issue.

More Than Just Buildings

Against this background, the Fortress of Louisbourg has continued to evolve from the role first envisioned for it. As the current reconstruction phases down to completion in the early 1980s, the continuing operation of the fortress and surrounding park will begin fully to pay for itself as a cultural investment. On an annual budget of roughly $3 million per year, Louisbourg's measurements of performance will not be all intangible. But to a large extent its success will continue to depend on how well it manages the less quantifiable areas of conservation and

interpretation. Particularly in the way it interprets the past, the fortress has already begun to learn from its own experience.

While adhering to the original concept, some of the changes are important. First of all, Louisbourg's interpretation has changed to take into account the extensive research findings, which have been accumulating since the project began. We no longer view Louisbourg primarily as a fortress (even the word "fortress" is not entirely appropriate, in English or in French), although the sieges remain as critical episodes in its history. Instead, we have based the interpretation on six themes: Louisbourg as a fortress, as a naval base, as a fishing port, as an entrepot, as a capital, and as a community. This much fuller framework leads to some significant departures from the way Canadian history is usually taught. For years, if people knew anything about Louisbourg, it was the myth of the mighty fortress and the story of the two sieges usually told from the English side.

As the thought processes of the reconstruction forced a new perspective on us—one from inside the walls of the fortress—-we saw that the story of Louisbourg could never be told only from a military point of view. The fortress was like the frame for a picture in which the broad image of the commercial and social subject matter has been only vaguely perceived. The economic importance of the Atlantic fisheries, the colony of Ile Royale's unique social life that made it different from the rest of North America, the realization that research for the reconstruction has had to break new ground because many historians have been preoccupied with a "Laurentianized" perspective on New France—these have become working assumptions among the research staff at Louisbourg. They have begun to influence the interpretation that visitors encounter at the fortress, and as the message spreads, they will alter the way Canadians understand the early history of the continent. In spite of delays and backlogs for publication, a growing selection of the dozens of Louisbourg research reports are being made available by Parks Canada in three formats. *Manuscript Reports*, on topics of limited interest, are filed in the national and provincial archives; *History and Archaeology*, on topics of general scholarly interest, are sold in a typed format; *Occasional Papers*, on topics of scholarly and popular interest, are sold in a glossy and well-illustrated format.

Since its beginning, the reconstruction has assembled an enormous data base of documents, artifacts, antiques, and secondary sources. Although researchers from outside the project have been slow to use these collections, their value is reinforced when studied in the context of the historic site itself, and many opportunities remain to do original research in this neglected field of Canadian history. Louisbourg's approach to the detailed design of furnishings for reproduction, and its establishment of an overview mechanism for training and historical authentication through what we call "Period Presentation" are meticulous endeavors, which support interpretation for visitors and also enhance the base for future research. The reconstruction has also in the process taken a major role in providing information on the material culture and lifestyle of the French to other museums, to schools, journalists, and film-makers. This ripple effect has spread an awareness of the French, and a more precise knowledge of the way they lived, far beyond the walls of the fortress itself.

In light of this research and our own experience in operating the reconstruction, as well as public comment whether favorable or adverse, we have reconsidered the ways in which we interpret the past. We have tried to become more rigorous by defining historical authenticity beyond structural terms and developing methods by which it can be achieved.

A Moment in Time

We have shifted the period of time shown by the reconstruction from the year 1745, when the fortress was first besieged and conquered, to the year before. As it happened, the choice of the early 1740s was practically made for us. On the eve of the first siege the fortifications were just being completed but had not yet suffered the effects of the war, after which they were in a continual state of repair and modification. The choice of the year 1745 presented an absurdity because midway through what is now our visitor season the fortress had been bombarded into surrender and occupied by the New England forces. This was obviously a difficult series of events to portray by animation. So we moved back to the previous year. Any period much earlier was impossible because significant portions of the quay front and the Porte Frederic had not been completed until the 1740s. At that point in Louisbourg's history, war had been declared, but the domestic rhythms of life talk about both peace and war; it helps explain the scarcity of soldiers and ships, because most of the garrison spent the summer of 1744 on expeditions against British forts, and it introduces some sympathetic parallels between the tensions that beset eighteenth-century Louisbourg and those of our own time. In all, the narrow focus of the reconstruction on a single year is a valuable, possibly unique, interpretive device that allows us to evolve the life of a real town, which visitors know was doomed, through what has been called "the last of the good years."

We call this interpretive focus "A Moment in Time," although not without reservations that we are promising too much. So we are moving to clarify what that experience should mean for ourselves and for visitors. It is not a "time trip." It is a framework to re-experience, however dimly, a critical period in the lives of real people who lived in Louisbourg and to examine the insights that we ourselves can gain from occupying specific households and going about the same activities. Because the reconstructed buildings, yards, and streets are so specific and the period in which they are portrayed is so specific, Louisbourg's animators bear the added burden of

representing someone who really lived there in the eighteenth century. Costumed animation is not only a form of demonstration for visitors; it becomes a process by which the animators themselves can try to understand their role and describe it as a learning experience. Not surprisingly, this had led at times to a crisis of identity—our own identity.

We have suspended role-playing between costumed staff and visitors except in certain, carefully orchestrated situations. It was leading to confusion and, worse, to the message being distorted. We still allow role-playing among animators but encourage it to be done by deportment and gestures rather than by speaking. If we do return to role-playing with visitors, it will be in the style developed at Colonial Williamsburg, using trained actors with prepared scripts, in high-profile situations that visitors can take or leave. It will not be forced on visitors as part of an experience. Meanwhile, Louisbourg's costumed staff is now told that there should be no doubt in anyone's mind that they are twentieth-century employees of Parks Canada who are representing historical people and are not passing themselves off as living, eighteenth-century people in spite of all incredulity.

In most reconstructions there would be no compelling reason to be so specific, or to highlight a specific year. Louisbourg is different. The fortress site, and the fifty-seven square kilometres of park land that surrounds it, offer a setting almost entirely free from modern intrusions. We felt that if an evocation of life in the past could succeed anywhere, it would be on this site, which already was remarkable for its historic significance, isolation, and atmosphere of timelessness. And if we were to show a fortress and town that were not severely damaged by war or under extensive repair, it would have to be a thin slice of time in the early 1740s. The rigorous application of this concept has indeed prevented our showing interesting structures and activities from other periods. But we feel that Louisbourg's dramatic history deserves this kind of emphasis, with its concomitant reminder of the cataclysm that awaited the town.

In place of whatever interpretive impact we may lose by being so specific, we can achieve greater realism and interest for visitors. By avoiding generalities of culture and tradition, we are able to show more of the complexities of real life. We would not recommend such a trade-off for museum villages that do not have an episodic history comparable to Louisbourg's, but for the fortress we feel the disadvantage of a very thin slice is offset by the advantage of providing a very good look. One result of the Moment in Time is that it forces both researchers and interpreters to be more exact. They cannot stop with concepts and generalizations. They must verify the smallest details of architecture, furnishing, and activities, preferably by analyzing processes in much the same way as the "experimental archaeology" practiced in Britain. While the research problems are greater this way, so are the rewards.

To those who think reconstructions should reflect continuity or the process of change between past and present,[11] we can only reply that Louisbourg, as a Colonial town, is remarkable for the abrupt ending it reached in the 1760s. There has been virtually no carry-over of language, culture, traditions, or even human occupation of the site. Louisbourg's interpretive strongpoint is contrast, not continuity. We do, in fact, interpret the ruins and the subsequent history of the fortress; we also encourage architectural styles, signage, and symbols in the modern Town of Louisbourg, which represents the area's nineteenth-century heritage and reflects continuity where it is more appropriate.

Period Presentation

We define "Period Presentation" as everything done or shown in a period environment. In order to defend and to enhance the rigorous authenticity we feel is essential to a serious evocation of the past, we have confined period interpretation almost exclusively to the reconstructed fortress. Furthermore, the only events that will be presented to the public in that environment are those which have a basis in the original town and in the experiences of the original people who lived there. We feel that anything less would be absurd and disrespectful toward the people whose lives are being interpreted.

Exceptions to this policy are few and carefully considered: we allow small meetings by visitors inside period buildings, but as private functions rather than as public events and definitely not as part of the period presentation. We allow our costumed people out of the fortress only if the focus remains on the past and its people. The most popular event of this type is a fashion show, which describes behavior and social customs as well as clothing styles, presented in the park's Visitor Reception Centre or in carefully selected settings outside of the park. We will not send costumed people to participate in parades, festivals, and similar occasions except in rare cases when we feel their representation of the past can be sustained with dignity among the other activities. We do not loan costumes or animators to add "color" to other events. We feel such publicity is counterproductive to our main interpretive purpose. We insist that getting into costume at all is a privilege to be earned; anyone who does must first pass basic training in what they are to represent. Just as we seldom appear outside the fortress, we do not welcome visitors in costume since they compete with and confuse our own presentation. We do not welcome the filming of commercials or similar presentations that merely use the reconstruction as a stage to promote their own message. We do not agree to the fortress being filmed as a substitute for some other place, such as Quebec or France. If these uses do not respect and portray the history of the fortress and its people, they are not, in our opinion, compatible with serious interpretation. This policy has been unpopular at times, but it has saved the historic site and the heritage it represents from exploitation, both commercial and cultural.

As for publicity, we find that nothing promotes the image we want better than scrupulous integrity in our interpretation.

To support the period environment, we have written detailed guidelines for period food services (the only kind allowed inside the fortress), for the forms of cultural activities and special events that are acceptable within the reconstruction, and for the display techniques that we consider appropriate in period buildings. On a preliminary basis we have planned in some detail the allocations and activities of staff in costume, the interpretive focus of each major period environment, and the period context in which animators should place themselves.

Because the environs of the fortress are sacrosanct, we have opened up the area of the visitor center and its hillside overlooking Louisbourg harbor for nonhistorical events: commemorations, pageants, flag-raisings, and so forth by other organizations. Our own costumed people do not get involved in these, and such events do not spread to the fortress. We continually insist that if we are going to evoke the past to the extent that we do inside the fortress, we must keep every incompatible activity at arm's length. Fortunately, the park has an extraordinary amount of natural area surrounding the reconstruction. Also, the individuals and agencies we have encountered almost unanimously come to respect the policy, even if they don't always agree with it.

Alternatives

It must not be assumed that reconstructions and museum villages need to rely exclusively, or even primarily, on costumed animation. They can and should have a more varied interpretive repertoire. Louisbourg's experience suggests a clear need to define complementary forms of interpretation.

In its interpretive plan the reconstruction seeks to present a representative cross-section of architecture, social classes, and activities. An early scheme to reconstruct individual structures throughout the town was soon changed to concentrate the effort in one quarter. By rebuilding the entire quay front as well as part of the fortifications, the reconstruction mustered sufficient concentration and depth to give visitors a sense of being in a real town. With a growing appreciation of the importance of the fisheries, this area has been extended into the Faubourg outside the fortress walls. A combined fisherman's house and cabaret is now the first thing to greet visitors when they leave the bus that has brought them from the visitor center.

The reconstruction of a complete corner of the town left us with some buildings about which too little was known to present them in period. Although we have since changed the planned use of a half-dozen buildings from exhibits to period environments (since that is what visitors really want to see), we were left with a number of houses and storehouses in which formal exhibits seemed desirable. The ground rules for these exhibits are rather different from those of the traditional museum. First, they must respect the layout and space limitations of the period buildings in which they are installed just as though that building were an original structure. Second, exhibits should not be visible from the street, a rule that means further restrictions on the placement of lights, cases, and labels. Third, these exhibits must supplement the period milieu by dealing with themes and subjects too complex to be explained by way of animation. As it happens, these often do not correspond with the objects in our collections, so the exhibit suffers from a lack of three-dimensional artifacts and antiques. Fourth, the exhibit style has evolved from modern/Expo in our early efforts to a conscious application of eighteenth-century styles. An exhibit now presents, in its own unique way, another aesthetic dimension on the period. All these constraints make our formal exhibits extremely difficult to bring off satisfactorily, yet in spite of the limitations I believe we are on the right track, and when formal exhibits are installed in historic buildings, no other approach can be as appropriate.

Although we once had very ambitious concepts for our exhibits (2,000 years of architecture, for example), we have learned that visitors really want most to know what is around them, so our approach has become more specific to the site itself. One exhibit describes how the reconstruction was carried out; another presents basic types of artifacts that have been excavated. In the latter, which occupies several barracks rooms, the cases have been designed to resemble soldiers' bunk beds and thus remind viewers of the original use of the area. One exhibit describes how the French constructed their buildings. It features a corner of the house left open for viewing from its basement, built on original masonry walls, to its attic. Another exhibit tells visitors how the French built and garrisoned a fortress, since the original scale of operation can never be guessed from the limited animation that is possible. Our most recent exhibit debunks the myths that have grown up about Louisbourg since the eighteenth century: that it was a mighty fortress, that it was a bottomless pit for the French treasury, that King Louis XV expected to see its towers rising in the west, that Cape Breton was a fog-bound place of exile. In this exhibit we begin with the myth, then refute it using quotes from the eighteenth century. In the principal residences we are combining period rooms, a storehouse converted to serve as a theatre, and a gallery of the handful of furnishings that survive from the original town. In all our recent exhibits it is still possible to look beyond the exhibit to the period building itself and to study, if one wishes, its architecture and use of space. To further recall the original inhabitants of such nonanimated buildings, we plan to summarize their histories on panels near the doorway.

Creature Comforts

When we planned a period environment that would surround visitors, we assumed they would welcome the experience and the challenge of discovery. After several years of operation we are less optimistic that most visitors desire anything remotely like the discomfort and disorientation that would result from a real periodenvironment. The limitations of living history were already becoming evident to us from the point of view of accuracy; now some visitors had begun to complain that the period people were unfriendly, uncommunicative, not at all like good public servants.

We had a new visitor center and a new transit system, but we found that neither helped prepare visitors for the period environment as well as we had hoped. The average visit in the late 1970s was only about two and a half hours in duration, when two days would hardly be long enough.

Concluding that we must either take account of our audience or lose them, we began to reconsider interpretation from a visitor's point of view. Guided tours and public toilets are now more available. There are more benches to rest on, even though we have no evidence for such amenities in the eighteenth century. When the weather is bad, the buses run inside the fortress so people won't have to walk so far. We provide wheelchairs for visitors who get tired and are devising a special tour route for people confined to wheelchairs. We realize that, even making a visit less rigorous than it would have been in the eighteenth century, there is a need for some places where visitors could rest and reorient themselves from the fatigue of a period environment that is unfamiliar and uncomfortable.

Theme Lounges

In order not to lose an opportunity to reinforce interpretation while visitors rested, we have developed several small lounges, each to reflect one of the six historical themes presented in the visitor center. With some searching we found six buildings where the view of the reconstruction is complementary to the subject theme of the lounge inside. As far as we know, the concept of a theme lounge as a museological embellishment of a rest area is unique to Louisbourg. It gives us a chance to take some discomfort out of the period experience and to provide information of a different kind from that which is appropriate in a period environment. A theme lounge is neither a period room nor an exhibit but something midway between. It allows us to make available the kinds of printed information, films, and recordings that are out of place in a period environment, and it allows us to discuss a far broader range of topics and activities than would ever be possible through animation. Theme lounges should encourage in visitors a sense of what it would really be like to live in our period buildings instead of merely to look at them. For that reason we gladly provide such amenities as a small room where children can take naps or mothers can nurse their infants. And the theme lounge should provide a "home base" of reorientation from which to resume a visit to the fortress. While we can lead people to the information and make it inviting if possible, we should not despair if they decide not to follow up on it. Our staff in a theme lounge are hosts first of all and teachers only secondarily.

In our own debates, theme lounges have been seen by their critics as either pseudo-historical rooms that ought to be properly presented in period or as a multimedia distraction that cannot avoid being hopelessly at odds with the historical environment. This dilemma points up the difficulty of adapting period rooms for modern purposes. Theme lounges in fact are not some kind of unfulfilled exhibit in an unvalidated period setting; they are an exception to the Moment in Time, necessary because the period environment is restrictive and inflexible. One challenge is to blend them into the historic buildings they occupy in the same way as we try to blend formal exhibits into being a reinforcement of period aesthetics without confusing people that such facilities originally occupied the buildings into which we have had to put them. Another challenge is to operate facilities like theme lounges with such confidence that they no longer seem to be intrusions and we no longer feel obliged to apologize for them as something less desirable than a period environment.

It can be difficult to know when theme lounges are succeeding but easier to know when they are not. Theme lounges fail if they are not operated with concern for the comfort and interests of our visitors. They fail if they merely become waiting rooms for an audio-visual show. They fail if visitors do not feel that here they can relax in one of our period buildings. Theme lounges fail if they do not offer alternative experiences and sources of information to those normally found in period buildings. And theme lounges fail if they do not reorient visitors.

This raises an important point: until we discover why and how well visitors are oriented in the first place and how they become disoriented on site, we cannot reorient them properly. It is clear that many of them experience confusion somewhere along the process. We are assuming for now that theme lounges are the best way to deal with this problem, but much more study of our visitors is necessary before we can best know how to introduce them to our site. Like visitor fatigue, visitor orientation is one of the greatest practical problems facing outdoor museums.

Some of our experiments with theme lounges have not been unqualified successes. In our desire to make the most of period environments, we outfitted one theme lounge to appear virtually the same as an animated building. The result had little distinction between what should be two very different types of operation, and even our own staff became confused. It remains to be seen how closely an adaptation like a theme lounge can resemble a period environment without losing its effectiveness as a rest area and change of pace. It may be too optimistic to hope that visitors can relate to a highly period theme lounge as a focus for their own activities and inquiry: the truth may be that visitors merely see it as another kind of animation, toward which they can remain passive. In drawing a line between the two environments, one rule of thumb is that a theme lounge should respect the period building as though it were a genuine old structure and only allow minor structural modifications that would be generally acceptable as historic preservation. Another general rule is to "go to period" in a theme lounge only if we are prepared to work at maintaining the distinction through other means, such as an introduction to the house, and even then to go period only with furnishings and not with costumed staff.

We cannot yet define all the period-related activities that may or may not be appropriate for a theme lounge; that can only come from more experimentation. At the moment, the trend is toward yet another category of visitor facility operated as Activity Centres. One of our most popular services to visitors has been a children's interpretive center, where parents can leave their children with interpreters for their own special tours and activities. This has been so well received that the same thing is being established for adults. We find that visitors are more likely to get involved with staff in contemporary uniforms rather than with animators in costume—and as with the theme lounges, the activity centers allow us to cover a much broader range of subjects than animation alone.

While exhibits, theme lounges, and activity centers should reflect a period ambiance, and two or even three may work together in the same building, we can only sort out their purpose and their impact on visitors by leaving a certain amount of breathing room between each type and the way they are operated.

Tours and Trails and Popular Tales

Exhibits and theme lounges at Louisbourg are the most developed forms of complementary interpretation to period environments, but other forms are planned. Prominent ruins around the town, siege works, and smaller sites throughout the park, as well as the Atlantic coastline itself, will be interpreted by self-guiding trails. A variety of cassette recordings may someday be available to rent for special tours. Publications for visitors are still in their infancy, our first priority being an adequate guidebook, and the second being a comprehensive report on the research and reproduction of Louisbourg's period clothing. Meanwhile, to encourage a flow of popular articles and an easily read, comprehensive history of the fortress, we contributed toward bringing Silver Donald Cameron to the College of Cape Breton as writer-in-residence. His work has already produced the kind of popular writing that goes beyond our own "corporate mold."

In response to complaints from native people that their story was not represented in the reconstruction, the park has added three Micmac Indians to its animation staff. Each is able to speak the Micmac language and is expected to represent and explain his native culture.

The history of the fortress and its reconstruction are being interpreted off the site through contemporary drama in the visitor center and, in schools throughout Nova Scotia, by the Mermaid Theatre group based in Acadia University. Another drama company is being formed by a group at St. Francis Xavier University to sponsor period plays and develop role-playing in the fortress. Both organizations, along with the staff of the Army Museum in the Halifax Citadel, help provide specialized training for park staff.

Training has a high priority. Over 10 percent of the budget for guide staff is devoted to training time, and a similar effort will be made to teach historical trades to the artisans who are now establishing the park's period maintenance unit. From a basic course required of everyone who appears in costume, the training grows progressively more specialized. Our main challenge in this area is to provide a better balance of practical information and history, to refine our teaching methods, and to develop refresher courses and mid-season training for guides so that the learning effort is not limited to the beginning of each summer.

Oiling the Hinge of History

In a time of dwindling finances, several new programs involve the community and support the park. A Volunteer Association, one of the first in Parks Canada, has attracted local people of all ages. The group has expanded animation in the fortress and developed new interpretive programs, including businesses, that were beyond the means of Parks Canada. A Louisbourg Institute, established with the cooperation of the College of Cape Breton, will encourage academic programs including seminars, publications, research and teaching, and an undergraduate course in museum studies. The Cape Breton Development Corporation, as a Crown Corporation concerned with the local economy, has funded the development of several period food services in the fortress and the nascent effort to make and market reproductions of artifacts. A new craft center, funded by DREE and the Nova Scotia Department of Tourism in the present-day Town of Louisbourg, will build on the skills and resources of the reconstruction to develop crafts that are not appropriate as animation in the fortress but which provide an extension of the fortress interpretation in terms of reproductions and quality theme-related souvenirs.

With experience in operating the reconstruction, we find ourselves more realistic in accepting certain limitations. The fortress is not, and probably never can be, a microcosm of French culture. Surrounded by a population that is almost entirely English-speaking, whose second language is more likely to be Gaelic than French, the reconstruction will have to achieve its Moment in Time using a core of local people whose culture and language are vastly different from the historical characters they represent. What saves this from being absurd is the interest of the modern people themselves and the experiment in understanding that engages them. Our local artisans and guides are legitimately proud of their fortress as something remarkable that Cape Bretoners have done. As interpreters they are at their best not as surrogate Frenchmen but as Maritimers bringing the fortress and Atlantic Canada—then and now—into better perspective in the regional mosaic of their country. At such a personal level of communication, which is what interpretation is all about regardless of the technique, the differences between the original inhabitants of the for-

French marines on the outskirts of the French Colonial Empire, Fort des Chartres, Illinois.—*Photo: Tom Allen*

tress and their present-day representatives are no more significant than the similarities. The insights flow from both. The public response to most of our techniques has been overwhelmingly favorable, but then the French left us a visually magnificent fortress to reconstruct and a story of compelling interest. Given such assets to begin with, interpretation is easier no matter what technique is used.

One major, continuing difference between Louisbourg and most other outdoor museums is the historic site itself. Most museum villages have been installed on artificially created sites. Most have admirable interpretive programs, but they can never interpret the real history or the sense of immediacy of the past that Louisbourg enjoys. Doing it all on the original site has made our work far more difficult but also more rewarding. And I believe it has made us think more about interpretation, not only to make the most of the reconstruction, which after all is a synthetic product of our interpretation of the evidence, but also to put it in perspective against the fascinating story and enduring attractiveness of the historic site itself.

Tastes change. Budgets change. Our view of the past changes, and with it changes the interpretation of history that we give to our public. The reconstruction, the park, and the presentation of history at Louisbourg are still finding their level. That is all to be expected, and we are probably better at our job when we are continually challenged to explain ourselves. This process will continue although the rebuilding has ended. The tension of self-examination, the search to improve, the challenge to communicate, the management dilemma of preserving while using may well be the most remarkable things about Louisbourg as a national historic park in the years ahead.

Notes

1. I.C. Rand, et. al., *Report of Royal Commission on Coal* (Ottawa: Queen's Printer, 1960), pp. 46-47.
2. Cabinet Minute, 1961, quoted in John Lunn, "Fortress of Louisbourg Interpretive Plan" (Louisbourg: Fortress of Louisbourg National Historic Park, 1970), synopsis.
3. Douglas Richardson, "Politics and Priorities in Architectural Preservation," *Heritage Canada* 2:1 (Winter/*hiver* 1976): 28-31.
4. John Lunn, quoted in "Opinion," *Heritage Canada* 1:6 (December/*decembre* 1978): 40.
5. See, for example, R.A.J. Phillips, "How We Started," *Heritage Canada* 5:3 (June/*juin* 1978): 40.
6. Pierre Berton, "Why Preserve?" *Heritage Canada* 4:3 (June/*juin* 1978): 19-21.
7. See, for example, A. Horace Herchmer, "Disneyland Defended," and M. C. Lorignal, "Conservation *vs.* Kitsch," *Heritage Conversation* 2:4 (Autumn 1976): 23-27.
   While Herchmer's article defends architectural controls to maintain the appearance of a historic district, as opposed to allowing evolution in response to everyday needs, I could not help being impressed by the similarity of the arguments for and against "synthetic" structures.
8. Osmund Overby, in abstract of papers for the Society of Architectural Historians 1975 meeting, entitled "Historic Buildings Rendered: Documentation and Preservation," *Journal of the Society of Architectural Historians* 34:4 (December 1975): 287.
9. Marcella Sherfy, "Honesty in Interpreting the Cultural Past," *Parks* 3:4 (January-March 1979): 13-14.
10. R.A.J. Phillips, quoted in *Heritage Conversations* 3:1 (Winter 1977): 23-23.
    Not all critics are so glib. See Thomas J. Schlereth, "It Wasn't that Simple," *Museum News* (January/February 1978): 36-44. Also Marcella Sherfy, "Interpreting History," *Trends* (January, February, March, 1977): 36-37. Both provide positive suggestions on achieving historical honesty. For my own opinions on the pitfalls and potential of costumed animation, see "Thoughts on the Recreation and Interpretation of Historical Environments," in *Proceedings of the Third International Conference of Maritime Museums* (Mystic, Connecticut: Mystic Seaport Museum, 1979), pp. 251-262. I won't attempt to categorize a thought-provoking article by David Lowenthal, "Past Time, Present Place: Landscape and Memory," *The Geographical Review* 1 LXV:1 (January 1975): 1-36.
11. Edward P. Alexander, *Museums in Motion* (Nashville: American Association for State and Local History, 1979), pp. 93-95.

Fort Wayne
Soldiers Return to the 1816 Frontier Outpost

6

Rod King

Throughout its early history, Living History Magazine *ran a series of "profiles" describing forts in Canada, the United States, and Australia and their living-history programs. Rod King's article about Historic Fort Wayne, a reconstructed frontier fort in northeastern Indiana, appeared in spring 1984. He quickly gets to his main point: "What makes Historic Fort Wayne different from many walled forts is its unique first-person character interpretations by the more than 130 volunteers and paid staff members. They engage guests in conversations and activities. . . There is no tape recorded historical spiel or walk-through tour." The purpose of living-history interpretation, he notes, is "to give the public a first-hand look at fort life, impart some history about 1816, and bring life to what would otherwise be a sterile wooden fortification." The results of this program, King concludes, reach beyond the fort's walls: "Historic Fort Wayne is more than just a well-done tourist attraction. It is considered a symbol of the city; one that the entire community is proud of."*

Visitors to Historic Fort Wayne, a reconstructed 1800's frontier outpost in downtown Fort Wayne, Indiana, find themselves in an 1816 time capsule. Once inside the solid oak palisades, they're totally immersed in a carefully choreographed living-history program.

The aroma of the daily stew rations being prepared in the enlisted men's kitchen, of corn bread baking in a reflector oven, of game hens and apples cooking in other fireplaces fill the air. Spinning, weaving, sewing, sweeping, and candle-making are being done simultaneously in the various buildings, while planting and weeding vegetable gardens, splitting and stacking wood, and sharpening tools are carried out outside the walls.

Soldiers drill in full dress uniform within the walled parade ground, practice firing muskets and cannon, load ammunition, and clean weapons. When their work is done, checkers is a favorite pastime. Or they might be engaged in a full-scale re-enactment of a War of 1812 skirmish complete with the deafening noise of musket and cannon fire, the distinct odor of gun smoke, and dramatic hand-to-hand combat.

What makes Historic Fort Wayne different from many walled forts is its unique first-person character interpretations by the more than 130 volunteers and paid staff members. They engage guests in conversations and activities that highlight events of that historical period and make their visit an enjoyable experience. There is no tape recorded historical spiel or walk-through tour. Even

though volunteers play the roles of documented individuals who actually lived at the fort in 1816, Executive Director Loretta Glenn is emphatic that "they are not actors." She says, "The job of our people playing character roles is to give the public a firsthand look at fort life, impart some history about 1816, and bring life to what would otherwise be a sterile wooden fortification."

A sentry greets visitors at the gate and explains that interpreters only discuss events that happened prior to the summer of 1816. The guard, in his authentic uniform, is careful to tell guests that he is their last contact with contemporary society and that questions on modern events, products, and people will either be ignored or receive blank, befuddled stares from interpreters. He gives them a brief history of the fort, its commander, and the buildings and suggests they begin their visit by going through the museum area.

No matter how busy interpreters may seem at their day-to-day activities, they always have time to talk with visitors. Characters banter with guests about the weather, the pesky insects, how tired they are, and the general conditions of life in the fort. Real emotions are part of each interpretation. Visitors are sometimes asked to participate by stirring the stew, turning the spit, joining in a game, or being part of a mock wedding, funeral, or court martial.

Women let guests in on choice pieces of gossip about the commanding officer's daughters and other fort women. Visitors also find themselves being sounding boards for the age-old soldiers' complaints of poor pay, terrible food, skimpy whiskey rations, and, of course, unreasonably hard work. The blacksmith, baker, and carpenter explain their trades and spice their interpretations with tidbits about how they make extra cash working for the civilians on the side.

An occasional spat between enlisted men might erupt into a pushing and shouting match that has to be broken up by officers. An on-the-spot court martial is sometimes performed with the offending soldier sentenced to walk the compound locked in stocks or spend time on the punishment horse with an eight-pound cannon ball chained to each leg.

These spontaneous vignettes give the fort its unique flavor. The byplay between characters humanizes the history lesson and allows visitors to realize that people like themselves had a hand in shaping the destiny of the country.

Some visitors delight in trying to get fort interpreters to break character. An occasional modern slang expression might be heard to slip out, but characters have become adept at blocking out the present. In addition, it is a matter of pride among the interpreters to remain in character.

If a police car or EMS vehicle should race past the fort with siren screaming, a standard comment to a visitor who might ask about the noise would be that the "Indians or soldiers are particularly rambunctious today." To answer a third-grader's question about why the fur buyer didn't use a motor on his boat on trips from Detroit, the interpreter played ignorant and asked the boy to explain the contraption. When asked if Major Whistler, commander and fort designer, is related to the famous artist, interpreters say that they "don't know about any such painter, but there is a hint of some artistic talent in the family."

The fort blacksmith, on the other hand, has a different

Peace in the midst of war. Interpreting women's work at Fort Wayne.—*Photo: Historic Fort Wayne*

problem. His shop is located outside the fort walls. Visitors are attracted by the sound of his hammer on the anvil as they cross the St. Mary's River from the visitor's center and go directly there without knowing that interpreters only discuss 1816 happenings. He has, on occasion, had to abandon his character role to smooth the feathers of a ruffled guest who expected present-day answers to his questions.

Detailed military records made by fort commanders, now filed in the National Archives in Washington, D.C., have enabled researchers to learn about the soldiers and even many of the civilians who were associated with the outpost in 1816 as traders, Indians, craftsmen and their families, and even visiting relatives. More is known, of course, about some characters than others. Records are sketchy, for instance, on wives, children, traders, and merchants. Individuals interpreting those roles generally discuss their specialty such as a craft or cooking. Women, for example, would know little about politics and the military, so they talk about their husbands' work, their family heritage, and their children.

Volunteers are encouraged to do additional research on their characters beyond what is provided by the fort staff. One woman spent a vacation in New Hampshire cemeteries and libraries learning more about her character's background. The Irish renegade and chicken thief has developed a plausible brogue and a fair repertoire of ballads he sings to the accompaniment of a dulcimer. Touches like these make living history even more real for visitors.

Just knowing one's own character background is not always enough, however. Women must also know about their husbands' family roots, their occupations, black pot cooking, or spinning, weaving, or quilting. The woman who portrays the role of the fort commander's daughter and housekeeper must always be familiar with all the herbs in her small garden and know their uses. Many visitors are interested in herb cooking and question her at length.

The fort itself is a faithful reproduction of the third and last American fort built in Fort Wayne. It was started in 1815 and completed in 1816 to command the junction of the St. Mary's, St. Joseph, and Maumee rivers and allow easy water transportation between the Great Lakes and the Mississippi River. Major John Whistler, who was the grandfather of the famous painter, designed the fort to be the strongest in the West and last a hundred years.

It was abandoned in 1819 when the frontier moved farther west. Some of the buildings, however, lasted until 1852 and served as the nucleus of what has become the modern city of Fort Wayne.

In addition to the daily living-history program, mid-April through the end of October, the fort is also the site of special activities. For a weekend in May, the fort's regular inhabitants give up their posts to members of The Brigade of the American Revolution who take over the outpost. Special emphasis is given in August to a War of 1812 weekend for a re-enactment of the seige of Fort Wayne by the British. The "trappers rendezvous" is the last big weekend activity in October and brings buckskin-clad trappers and traders from throughout the Midwest. Christmas at the fort is an annual event held November 25 and 26 to celebrate Christmas customs of the Old World and Colonial America.

The Glorious Fourth of July celebration is of special significance to Historic Fort Wayne since it was the only holiday observed on the frontier and it was carefully documented by individuals who attended the ceremonies in 1816. Interspersed with these activities are folk-craft weekends at which early American crafts are demonstrated and sold. The fort is also the focal point of the city's annual Three Rivers Festival held in early July.

After normal interpretation hours, the fort is used for overnight encampments of elementary school youngsters who come with their classes to learn about area history by living it for a few hours. In addition, a yearly Music Fest featuring a fife and drum corps, folk music groups, and the Fort Wayne Area Community Band brings in a large audience for an evening of music. Of particular interest is the conclusion of the program, which features the 1812 Festival Overture complete with the fort soldier's firing muskets and cannon.

Probably the most unique feature of this re-enactment facility is that it is entirely supported locally through its gate receipts, sales of items in its gift shop, overnight program, special events, and gifts from local individuals, businesses, and foundations. It has an operating budget of $230,000, of which 46 percent is provided by gate receipts. The gift shop provides 15 percent, 37 percent comes from gifts and grants, and 2 percent from special events.

Historic Fort Wayne is more than just a well-done tourist attraction. It is considered a symbol of the city; one that the entire community is proud of.

Fort Ross
From Russia with Love

Diane Spencer Pritchard

In 1985, Diane Spencer Pritchard and her husband Bill were honored by the American Association for State and Local History with an Award of Merit for their work at Fort Ross Historic Park, in northern California. In this excellent article, first published in the fall 1984 issue of Living History Magazine, *Pritchard shares with us the hectic, challenging, successful living-history program, which once a year re-created the year 1836 when the Russian American Fur Company was in its heyday and Fort Ross was a vital marketing center for Russians, Pomo, Spanish, and American traders. She takes us behind the scenes and discusses the organization necessary to develop and operate a realistic historical event, which uses both professional museum interpreters and re-enactors. It is her point of view that makes this article especially valuable to us today.*

Most Americans are aware of Alaska's rich and varied Russian heritage, but few know that in the early nineteenth century Russia's imperialistic hopes extended into California as well. In fact, in 1812 officials of the Russian American Fur Company actually established a colony, Fort Ross, on northern California's Sonoma coast.

Construction of this colony carried serious international consequences, for the site was not selected by chance—the audacious Russians purposely chose to build their outpost on land long claimed by Spain. Using the native Kashaya Pomo Indians as pawns, the Russians asserted that the Indians—not the Spanish—actually owned the land. To support further their claims to sanction the building of the colony, the crafty Russian officials executed the only known treaty with a California Indian group, by whose terms the Kashaya actually ceded to the Russians the land on which the fort stood. Faced with a *fait accompli* and militarily too weak to forcibly eject their unwelcome neighbors, the Spanish soon learned that their severe frontier existence could be considerably softened by the items purchased or traded from the Russians. Thus, throughout the life of the little colony, peace existed not only between the Russians and the Pomo, but between the Russians and their Spanish— and later, Mexican—neighbors as well.

Fort Ross was not the military outpost it seemed, but rather a hunting and trading establishment. As the southern-most colony of the Russia American Fur Company, a commercial organization much like the Hudson's Bay Company, the major purpose of the settlement was to provide a profit for the stockholders each year. Initially, the seal and sea otter skins, grains, fruits, and

Another visitor from beyond: a Hudson's Bay Company trapper at Fort Ross.—*Photo: Lincoln Spencer*

other agricultural products the colonists hunted, produced, or traded kept the settlement afloat commercially. But as the years passed, overhunting of the otter and the opening of California ports to free traders of all nations sharply reduced the colony's never-munificent profitability. By 1839 company officials were awash in a sea of red ink, and to cut their losses the decision to sell Fort Ross was made.

Yet, under Russian occupation, Fort Ross was a veritable crossroad of culture on the bleak California frontier. During the tenure of the last commandant of the colony, Alexander Gavrilovich Rotchev, and his cultured wife, Elena Pavlovna Gagarina, many amenities of civilization such as French wines, fine crystal, a piano, and an exceptional rose garden could be enjoyed by the many travelers who visited the colony each year from around the world.

Life at the fort was undoubtedly colorful and probably even occasionally exciting. The prattle of many languages—Russian, Aleut, Kashaya, and the German, English, French, and other Indian dialects of the numerous traders and visitors surely combined with the vivid costumes of inhabitants and guests to lend a truly unique ambience to the settlement.

In 1841, Fort Ross was sold to John Sutter of the Sacramento Valley and subsequently passed through the hands of several Americans. In 1906, owner George Call deeded the fort itself to the State of California, and it became one of the first historical units in California's now-gigantic state park system.

Through the years, the original Russian structures had been modified to suit the purposes of a working ranch or allowed to sink into ruin. Early in its guardianship, however, the State of California committed its resources toward eventual restoration of the site to its appearance in 1836—the heyday of Russian occupation. To achieve that end, numerous difficult circumstances have been surmounted, including the fact that for many years California Highway 1 ran directly through the fort, bisecting its north and south walls, to restore the site to its original Russian appearance. Despite the state's care, however, only one original structure has survived the ravages of time and the elements. Yet several other buildings have been reconstructed, and thus far all completed structures reflect the highest degree of historical and archaeological research. The result is breath-taking—and a little mystical—for to step inside Fort Ross is truly to travel back in time.

Inaccessibility, of course, contributes greatly to this heady atmosphere. The fort lies ninety miles north of San Francisco and can be reached from north or south only by narrow, twisting Highway 1. Yet despite this problem, the park is visited by an astonishing number of visitors each year. It thus seemed both proper and logical that a living-history program be presented as an adjunct to the usual interpretive program of the park.

The first living-history program at Fort Ross was presented over the Labor Day weekend in 1981, and it immediately became apparent that both the uniqueness of the site and its near-inaccessibility would challenge and reward organizers and visitors alike.

Groundswell for organization of the program came, appropriately enough, from California Department of Parks and Recreation employees who had been involved in planning and interpreting the site. Bill Pritchard, supervisor of the interpretive planning unit in Sacramento, was awarded the position of chief guru and *quid pro quo* of the loosely formed committee because of his long association with and extensive knowledge of the park. Mike Tucker, Rob Wood, and Dave Vincent, all of inter-

Spanish cavalry "visiting" the Russian settlement from their base at San Francisco Presidio.—*Photo: Jack Dunham*

pretive services as well, joined Pitchard in blocking out major concepts to be interpreted by the scenarios, historical activities to be presented, and other such substantive needs, while Glen Burch of Parks and Recreation's Santa Rosa Area Office worked on providing personnel, doing costume research, and training participants. Others, like myself, whose responsibilities included publicity and media liaison, attached themselves to the project with the tenacity of leeches, and planning began in earnest early in the summer of 1981. All of us on this organizational committee had been involved in planning and participating in living-history activities in other California state parks, and we felt it important for the ideological success of the Ross program to generally agree on a working definition of living history. Thus our program goal—what we optimally hoped to achieve—was not simply re-enactment or a series of theatrical costumed scenarios, but a quality historical experience for the visitor containing elements of both re-enactment and theatre, yet adding a third, crucial element: audience participation.

With a good working knowledge of many of the historical events that occurred at the fort during the 1836 time period selected by the program organizers, it was not difficult to construct scenarios that would involve both participants and the visitor audience. But because of the distance involved, arranging for props, artifacts, and other historical items related to these scenarios demanded close attention. Pritchard, Tucker, Wood, and Vincent dissected each activity and scenario, itemizing needs literally down to the last hairpin. Their lists eventually resulted in two entire truckloads of material traveling Highway 1. The most difficult item to supply was Elena Pavlovna's piano. As I had volunteered to take that role, coming up with an appropriate instrument fell to

me when committee efforts to rent something suitable in towns closer to the park than Sacramento came to naught. In a fit of desperation, I rented a piano myself with the excuse that I needed it for a party—not entirely a fabrication! Had the victim business known the rented piano would be moved from my living room five minutes after it was delivered, loaded onto a truck, and driven by a participant not possessing the necessary truck license down one of the most hair-raising highways in the United States—and back again—it would have sued me blind.

The list of participants in the event mushroomed rapidly as news of the developing program spread in historical circles. While the committee welcomed all who wished to participate, they determined that attendance at Burch's training sessions would be mandatory. This sort of "quality control" helped ensure against walk-on participants who had detracted from living-history programs in other parks.

Two groups who worked with us in the Ross program contributed greatly to our success. The New Helvetia Brigade of Mountain Men, a spectacularly authentic group devoted to re-creation of the 1830's fur trade era, early in 1981 took the plunge from re-enactment to living history by participating in the Sutter's Fort program. They accepted our invitation to portray a Hudson's Bay brigade trading and visiting at Fort Ross, and their encampment on the point outside the stockade walls added an exciting dimension to the activities of the program. Since that first Fort Ross living-history program, the beauty and serenity of the site has captured the group's imagination and caused its members to become deeply involved with interpretation at the park; they have attended all subsequent living-history programs and in 1983 initiated a volunteer program of armament and exhibit maintenance. Indeed, several brigade members

Enjoying a Russian folktalk at Fort Ross's living-history weekend.—*Photo: Diane Spencer Pritchard*

have taken the unprecedented step of turning in their buckskins for the boots and tunic of Russian promyslenikki (fur trappers).

The Slavyanka Chorus, a professional men's choir based in San Francisco whose entire repertoire is devoted to authentic Russian and eastern European liturgical and folk music, attended and performed Russian melodies in appropriate areas of the Fort. Their music and costume provided a moving counterpart to the more mundane activities and crafts of the Russian colonists portrayed in the program. Slavyanka has also become a "regular" in the continuing program.

It was clear, even before actual program planning began, that the Russian ethnic history and culture to be interpreted at Ross would be a difficult aspect of the project. Although a good deal of information exists on the early California Hispanic culture, California's Russian heritage has generally been ignored. Additionally,

perhaps the best sources for information lie in books written in Russian and not yet translated into English. As a result, intensive participant training was needed in order for our volunteers to have a basic understanding of why Fort Ross existed, what was done there, and by whom. Without these basic tools, participants would be unable to respond adequately to remarks and questions from visitors or initiate appropriate conversation, and the particular directive we hoped to achieve in our program—quality visitor experience—would be lost.

The training sessions provided our people more than just help in history and costuming; they also led participants through the maze of character research. Characterization in this program was complicated by the fact that while some information exists on several major characters such as commandants of the fort, other Russian American Company officials stationed there, and some foreign visitors, there is a relative dearth of useful

The Kuskov store in the heart of Fort Ross..—*Photo:* Santa Rosa Democrat

research on the activities of ordinary Russian pro-myslenikki. An unusual number of participants were thus required to create composite characters, both male and female, from the known parameters of the site's history. This sort of creative effort was not everybody's cup of tea: many participants, particularly first-timers, were far more comfortable portraying a personality who actually existed than in coping with the multitude of options open in creating a believable historical character.

In my role of Elena Rotcheva, I unfortunately found just the opposite to be true. The parameters of this character's history precluded random interpretation of events afforded to the composite characters, and I felt additionally handicapped by the relative lack of information on the social, cultural, and ethnic attitudes that would have been typical of an upper-class Russian lady of the period and undoubtedly reflected in her behavior within the multicultural milieu of Fort Ross society. In addition, the decision to provide a piano on which this character could play period music—intended to create a better understanding of the cultural life at Fort Ross in 1836—in actuality removed the role from living-history characterization and placed it in the category of performance. No one on the committee realized this would happen at the time the decision was made to use the piano scenario, and the end result clearly was not within the scope or goals of the program. In later program evaluation, it was decided to interpret the period amenities in other ways, and the piano scene has been dropped from subsequent programs with no noticeable decrease in overall quality or visitor interest.

Ultimately, some sixty-five individuals participated in the first living-history program at Fort Ross, enough to populate the site and make the dream of turning back the clock in this magic place seem plausible. The visitor count was nearly triple the usual, even for a holiday weekend and suggested that the all-out publicity effort, particularly crucial to the success of a program held in such an isolated location, had helped carry the day. Although no Bay area television stations took up the challenge to travel the grueling ninety-mile road, a number of radio and newspaper personnel did, resulting in resoundingly good publicity for the program. And in the end, most participants committed themselves to holding a living-history program at least once a year at Fort Ross.

Since that time, living-history programs have been held here on a yearly basis. Although each program has had a different flavor as research expands character possibilities and individual participants change, each has

The blockhouse and chapel within the palisade of Fort Ross.—*Photo: Jim Phillips*

been equally successful—to such an extent that in 1984 the program has, with the blessings of the Department of Parks and Recreation, been expanded to two, two-day programs. Several groups in addition to the New Helvetia Brigade and the Slavyanka Chorus have queued up to join the participants, bringing with them both knowledge and enthusiasm.

Hectic? Yes. Challenging? Always! But the beauty and serenity of the location and the professionalism and enthusiasm of the participants have combined to produce one of the most colorful and exciting programs in the United States, one whose future is unlimited and whose depths have only begun to be tapped. Nasdrovya, Krepost Rossiia!

Living History Along the Santa Fe Trail

Mark L. Gardner

The interpretive program at Bent's Old Fort in La Junta, Colorado, has long been a model for historic sites interested in working cooperatively with experienced re-enactors. Mark L. Gardner's in-depth analysis of the 1846 fort's history and programs describes how to develop a really first-rate program. This article first appeared in the Fall 1983 issue of Living History Magazine *and it still remains one of the few descriptions of a western historic site that uses historical simulation to its greatest advantage. Gardner ends his essay with an interesting statement: "Bent's Old Fort, as well as other historic sites, should always seek to better its interpretive program; not just for the sake of living history or the visitor, but for the sake of history itself." He quotes Nancy Jane Cushing, the fort's chief of interpretation, "People think that history is of famous people, that's not true. It's the ones behind the scenes—history is of common folk. We hope that when people leave Bent's Old Fort National Historic Site they will have a greater appreciation of their forefathers—where they are today—and that history is made up of people just like you and I."*

"**I** visited the fort and found it situated a hundred yards from the river in a dry, sandy, and gravelly soil, on a small rise, or swell, in the prairie. . . At a distance it presents a handsome appearance, being castle-like with towers at its angles, or, as we call them, bastions, with portholes, and only one *porta*, or entrance, protected by a massive gate. . . It is of mud brick or adobe, quite convenient and capacious, affording all kinds of accommodations to travelers, such as repairing teams (for which they have a blacksmith shop), provisions, repairing guns (for which they are provided), procuring ammunition, horses, or mules, or articles from the store, which is filled with articles for the Indian Trade. . . At present it is crowded with all kinds of persons: citizens, soldiers, traders to Santa Fe, Indians, Negroes, etc. . ."

George R. Gibson, a soldier under Kearny and Doniphan during the Mexican War, wrote the above description of Bent's Old Fort in 1846. A lot of changes have transpired in the 130 odd years since, but if Gibson were alive today and able to visit Bent's Old Fort National Historic Site, located six miles east of La Junta, Colorado, he would probably describe much the same scene. The reconstructed trading post lies on the foundations of the original and appears as that fort did in 1846. Inside, a living-history program interprets the story of Bent's Old Fort by portraying some of the characters Gibson saw. Today, trappers, soldiers, traders, and Indians can still be seen.

Between 1830 and 1833, the Bent-St. Vrain Company (composed of two brothers, William and Charles Bent, and Ceran St. Vrain) employed about a hundred Mexican laborers from Taos and Santa Fe to construct a fort on the north bank of the Arkansas River (then the boundary between Mexican and United States Territory) near the crossing of the mountain branch of the Santa Fe Trail. Ceran St. Vrain and Charles Bent were already making a successful business out of trade over the trail with Mexico, and it was hoped that with the new fort, under the management of William Bent, they could capitalize on the lucrative Indian trade as well.

And this they did. Located near the bison country and close to the hunting grounds of the Cheyenne, Arapahoe, Comanche, and Kiowa, the Bent-St. Vrain Company did a massive business (some sources say as high as $100,000 a year) and eventually came to dominate the fur and robe trade in the Southwest. The fort was also close enough to the mountains to encourage beaver trappers to come in and trade their pelts for supplies or credit at the fort's store. It was the trade for buffalo robes from the Indians, however, that proved the most profitable by the 1840s. Since beaver prices had fallen so sharply, few trappers were making a living from that sole occupation. Some trappers, such as Kit Carson and Dick Wooten, hired on at the fort as hunters and Indian traders.

Being located on the mountain branch of the Santa Fe Trail, Bent's Old Fort also became a way station for travelers, soldiers, traders and adventurers. A list of some of the more famous western personalities to visit the fort includes John C. Fremont, Col. Henry Dodge, George Frederick Ruxton and Francis Parkman. However, as powerful as the Bent-St. Vrain Company had become, Bent's Old Fort was destined to last only about fifteen years.

The year 1846 saw the Bent-St. Vrain Company at its peak. It also was a year of war with Mexico and, consequently, heavy military traffic over the trail to Bent's Old Fort. General Kearny used the fort as a supply base; government cattle overgrazed the nearby pastures, and military stores flooded the fort. Immigrants and gold seekers were to follow. Indians claimed that all the activity of the trail was scaring the buffalo herds and ruining their hunting. Indian wars broke out in 1847, and Charles Bent, the newly appointed territorial governor of New Mexico, was killed and scalped at his home in Taos. The Bent-St. Vrain Company broke up with St. Vrain taking the retail stores in Taos and Santa Fe and William, the fort.

The Indian trade was suffering by this time, but it wasn't until an outbreak of cholera among the Indian tribes in 1849 that William realized the trade at Bent's Old Fort was finished. William and his family abandoned the fort and headed thirty-eight miles down the Arkansas where he later built what was to be called Bent's New Fort.

Some sources say that William set fire to the Old Fort's storerooms and powder magazine before leaving. Although there was evidence of a fire in the archaeological report on Bent's Old Fort, there is no way of knowing whether William or the Indians perpetrated the act. Nevertheless, there was enough of the fort remaining to be used as a stage station by the Barlow and Sanderson Stage Company in the 1860s, and the walls even served as cattle corrals as late as the 1880s. In 1921, though, all that was remaining of the fort above the ground was washed away by a flood of the Arkansas River.

In 1963, after passing through the hands of the Daughters of the American Revolution and the State Historical Society of Colorado, the fort site was acquired by the National Park Service. After an extensive archaeological excavation of the fort's ruins between 1963 and 1966, the Park Service drew up plans to reconstruct Bent's Old Fort. Construction began in 1975 and in 1976, the year of the Bicentennial and Colorado's Centennial, the fort was completed. Constructed and furnished to appear as it did at its peak (1846), Bent's Old Fort National Historic Site was to tell the story of economic imperialism and westward expansion.

The original master plan in 1975 called for six audio-visual programs (dealing with the different historic aspects of the Bent-St. Vrain Company) in six of the fort's rooms and a sound system in the fort's plaza "over which tape recorded snatches of authentic period music and background sounds of voices and work can be played sporadically." Fortunately for the historical integrity of the site, common sense prevailed and only two programs were installed (there is now only one), and the period music and sounds of voices and work were left up to the living-history staff to provide.

When visitors arrive at Bent's Old Fort today, they are first greeted by a ranger at the fort's contact station and then must walk a quarter-mile trail into the past to the fort. The parking lot is hidden by a small rise, and it is hoped that visitors will leave their modern thoughts and worries on the prairies behind them. Upon entering the gateway and emerging into the fort's plaza, visitors may see any or all of the following characters: trader, blacksmith, carpenter, trapper, clerk, dragoon, Indian, and Mexican laborer.

The trader, which I portray, is responsible for explaining the reason for Bent's Old Fort and the trading operations of the Bent-St. Vrain Company. Frequently taking a "first person" approach when a visitor steps into the trade room, I offer to buy the visitor's buffalo robes for two dollars apiece. The trade room is one of the highlights of the fort and the only one of its kind in the Southwest. The immense variety of goods contained behind the counter (all found in the original trade ledgers of the Bent-St. Vrain Company) range from "Chemical Opodeldoc" to trade beads to dried apples. The wide selection of goods emphasizes the point that the fort was not only a trading post for Indians, but a supply post for trappers, traders, and adventurers as well.

The trapper, Dan Muldoon, can be found almost anywhere in or outside the fort. If he is not riding his mule, Dan is either explaining the workings of a beaver trap or his flintlock Leman trade rifle. He tells the story of the beaver trapper who has brought his furs in to trade at Bent's Old Fort and to get re-outfitted for another year in the mountains.

The dragoon, Jim Stewart, portrays a soldier in Kearny's "Army of the West." Although at Bent's Old Fort only a short time, the army's story is important in relation to the park's theme of westward expansion and manifest destiny.

Allen Addison, an Arapaho Indian, represents the plains tribes that once traded at Bent's Old Fort.

The blacksmith and carpenter, George Ainslie and Dave Marshall, portray two very important characters at Bent's Old Fort. Historically, they would have been constantly making repairs and items for use at the fort. And, being located on a major trail, there were always horses, mules, and oxen to be shod and wagons to be fixed. George is very skilled in nineteenth-century blacksmithing (it's his professional occupation). He forges such things as period trade axes and knives in the fort's working blacksmith shop and is currently replacing a lot of the fort's hardware that he found to be inaccurate.

Dave is also busy, making furniture reproductions for the use of the living history staff. When Bent's Old Fort National Historic Site was furnished, pressure to do it quickly and a lack of readily available reproductions forced the Park Service to furnish the fort with a lot of antiques. Consequently, because of the rules regarding historical preservation, those antiques cannot be used by the fort's staff. Dave is slowly but surely solving this problem by making historic reproductions of those pieces in the fort's carpenter shop.

Both Dave and George took part in the construction of a period Conestoga freighter which, when it's not being pulled in parades or used in educational programs, is parked in front of the fort.

The Mexican laborers (portrayed by Richard Medina and Alexandra Aldred, the supervisory park technician) take care of the livestock and prepare period meals for the living-history staff. They tell the story of the laborer who stayed on with the Bent-St. Vrain Company after the fort was completed to maintain the adobe structure.

"People believe what they see," says Nancy Jane Cushing, chief of interpretation, "and if we can portray these characters, it's more believable. Through historical accuracy and integrity, our living history program strives to draw the "big picture" of those events and types of people who influenced the trade and expansion of the Southwest.

All of the positions except blacksmith and Mexican laborer are seasonal. Seasonal positions with the Park Service are filled each year for the period of May through September. While it is common for many parks to fill these positions with college students, Bent's Old Fort tries to hire people with a strong background in living history. Some of the interpetive staff, like Dan Muldoon and myself, belong to living-history units not associated with the Park Service. Dan is a member of the American Mountain Men, probably the most authentic among the countless "buckskinning" groups, and I belong to the 1st Regiment Missouri Militia at Arrow Rock State Historic Site and the Missouri Civil War Reenactors Association.

To help round out the interpretive program, Bent's Old Fort has a large volunteer pool to draw from in the local area. All volunteers must, however, pass a Bent's Old Fort history course (given at the local junior college by park staff) before becoming active in the living-history program.

Bent's Old Fort not only stresses living history in its every day interpretation but in special events as well. Each 4th of July there is an old-fashioned patriotic celebration with speech making, period music, and games. In September more than 300 mountain men gather at Bent's Old Fort to re-create a historic fur trade rendezvous. This is by far the fort's largest event. Trader's blankets fill the fort's plaza, and the hustle and bustle of the original fort is reborn. Bent's Old Fort's quest for accuracy and integrity in living history, however, was best achieved in an event called "Winter Quarters," which was held in March of 1983.

"Our objective with Winter Quarters," said Cushing, "was to provide an 1846 environment to people who are involved in history—teachers, historians, curators—so that they could take back with them an enthusiasm and realistic understanding of fur-trade history to interpret to others."

Fifteen people were selected to participate in this four-day "in-depth living-history experience." Upon arriving at the fort, the participants were immersed in a "first person," role playing situation. They were required to wear period clothing and do period tasks (all twentieth century clothing and baggage were locked away). Through the medium of living history, the participants experienced such frontier skills as trapping, mule packing, blacksmithing, carpentry, cooking, and others associated with every day life at a trading post. Participants were even given "credit" at the fort's trade room so that authentic items such as tobacco, whiskey, and playing cards could be purchased in a historical manner. Because of the enthusiasm shown for Winter Quarters, it is planned to be an annual seminar.

Bent's Old Fort, as well as other historic sites, should always seek to better its interpretive program; not just for the sake of living history or the visitor, but for the sake of history itself.

"People think that history is of famous people," commented Nancy Jane Cushing, "that's not true. It's the ones behind the scenes—history is of common folk. We hope that when people leave Bent's Old Fort National Historic Site they will have a greater appreciation of their forefathers—where they are today—and that history is made up of people just like you and I."

For more information about Bent's Old Fort National Historic Site and its living-history program, write to the following address: Bent's Old Fort National Historic Site, 35110 Highway 194 East, La Junta, Colorado 80151.

The Fort Yellowstone Walk

9

Paul Schullery

Paul Schullery became a naturalist in Yellowstone in 1972. In this unusually helpful article, which appeared in the spring 1981 issue of The Interpreter: A Journal for Environmental Communicators, *he provides the living-history movement—in both its professional and amateur sides—a model for a tour using historical simulation. In a decade that has seen the gradual decline in attempts to found and develop large, complex "total historical environment" sorts of outdoors museums, Schullery's description of a comparatively inexpensive living-history program is significant. It will, I suspect, provide the model for most historical simulation programs of the future. In essence, it is a one actor play (like "Mark Twain Tonight" or "Give 'em Hell, Harry") performed for a limited audience in a historical environment. It requires visitors to suspend disbelief and filter out obvious modern intrusions, feats of imagination, which most visitors are eager to do. "The Fort Yellowstone Walk" may well be the harbinger of living history's future.*

The Historical Setting

The involvement of the United States Army in the early management of America's national parks is one of the most unusual chapters in American military history. From the late 1880s well into the 1900s, the War Department played an important role in the protection and development of several parks. Yellowstone and the early California parks were routinely patrolled by cavalry troops for many years, in some cases even after the establishment of the National Park Service in 1916. Of these parks, Yellowstone's experience was the most involved and lengthy and was probably also the most important in terms of the effects of military management on the future of the national park system. The army developed many policies and originated some important management directions that were carried on by the park service.

Only in Yellowstone was a permanent year-round post established. From 1872 to 1886, Yellowstone struggled under an inadequate civilian administration. In 1886, for a variety of political reasons, the Secretary of the Interior invited the Secretary of War to post soldiers in the park to protect it from poachers, vandals, and thoughtless tourists. The military presence was viewed all along as a "temporary expedient," but the army stayed in Yellowstone until 1918, even after the National Park Service was created. The army provided the endangered young park with order and protection through its most vulnerable years. Until recently, the significance of the army administration was not widely appreciated, but we now know that Yellowstone was literally saved from destruction by the troops. Besides their major contribution in protection and management of the park, the army left us a visible legacy in Yellowstone in the form of Fort Yellowstone. The fort buildings, which now house park service offices and personnel, were constructed between 1890 and 1915, and have since been classified as an important historical site. It was this site that became the subject of the park's first major living-history program in 1973.

The Challenges of the Walk

Our mission on the Fort Yellowstone Walk was to give the visitors a feel for the life of the army days, and an appreciation for the army's contribution to the park of today. We had an interesting and generally unknown story to tell. The army's mission in Yellowstone was peculiar—the protection of a civilian area (administered by the Secretary of the Interior, from whom the commanding officer at Fort Yellowstone actually took orders!) in peacetime. It was a lot like martial law. Fort Yellowstone, now Park Headquarters, was an intriguing artifact of a strange experiment in interdepartmental cooperation, an experiment that worked surprisingly well.

When I became a naturalist in Yellowstone in 1972, a Fort Yellowstone Walk was being conducted several times a week by naturalists in their regular uniforms. It was a leisurely one-hour tour of the four rows of buildings that compose the fort. It was standard tourist fare, with routine stops at key points to discuss such things as stables (now garages), barracks (now administration building), and other structures. At the close of the 1972 season, we were informed that the following year the walk would become living history; that we take the visitor back to army days (1915 was chosen as the year) and give them a tour from the viewpoint of a noncommissioned officer.

At that time there were three of us giving the walk. We had no special inclination toward, or interest in, what seemed to us to be a very difficult assignment in role-playing. We had very little of the kind of information that would be needed to succeed. Moreover, besides our replica army uniforms and sidearms, the only real props we had were the buildings themselves. All the buildings were in use as residences, offices, and so on, and it was not possible to enter any of them. The fort fronts on a major park intersection, and there is a steady and noisy flow of modern traffic to be dealt with. We were leading groups of people through a residential area, across the back yards of park employees. Almost all the time it would be up to the naturalist—the soldier—to provide the mood and setting needed to make visitors feel as if they were in 1915. Giving people a taste of the old days under these circumstances seemed almost impossible.

Preparations

With so few effective props, and with such totally modern surroundings, we found it necessary to concentrate attention on ourselves. It seemed very important to project a very strong character. We became soldiers of many opinions, and we talked about what we thought as much as about what we did. Most of the color and excitement of the walk had to come from us.

We all developed characters to portray, usually just extensions of our regular personalities (if they could be called regular). None of us were trained actors, and so we knew that our best bet would be to rely on our own sense of judgment rather than try to act as if we had some other set of values and ideas. At first, suffering from a shortage of background information on the fort, the walk was much like it had been as a naturalist walk except that we used present tense ("Here's our jail; it was built five years ago, in 1910. Private Flannagan is in there drying out from a long weekend in town.") We were hesitant to encourage visitor involvement because we would quickly start to get questions we couldn't answer.

Our research was undertaken out of desperation. A few excellent publications appeared that covered the subject, but they were not detailed enough for us. We contacted the National Archives and purchased photocopies of certain record groups, such as Fort Yellowstone orders of the day for 1915 (we chose 1915 because it permitted us to talk about almost the entire army stay in Yellowstone and because it was the first year cars were allowed to enter the park), quartermaster reports, duty rosters, and the like. We searched out transcripts of interviews with old-timers. We checked 1915 "current events" so that we could speak casually about the news ("the Lusitania was sunk yesterday, and I think it's about time we show them Germans who's boss.")

As our research deepened, we discovered the kind of gems we really needed. We located surviving copies of the park's "little red book," a slim pocket-sized volume carried by the soldiers. It contained the park regulations, and many copies were slightly curved to hip-contour from all those years in pants pockets. From the book we sternly read instructions to the proper tourists and the less-respected "sagebrushers" (people who

camped wherever they liked along the park road.) We told them not to bathe without suitable bathing attire, to keep their firearms sealed, not to drink alcoholic beverages in the park, and we singled out the sagebrushers, insisting that they "don't hang your laundry where it will flap in the breeze—scares the devil out of the horses." We discovered that at one time a special board of inquiry was held in Yellowstone to investigate Fort Yellowstone's incredibly high desertion rate. These and many other tidbits helped us piece together the life of a soldier.

Good reference material was only part of the preparation. Cooperation from the community was equally important. We had no difficulty convincing our supervisors that we had to keep modern distractions to a minimum, but sometimes relations between naturalists and neighbors were strained. One of the largest residences in "Officer's Row" now serves as a dormitory for young seasonal employees, who immediately took a fancy to our full-dress blue uniform with gold braids. As we marched past this building, we had just pointed out as Lieutenant So-and-So's house, we were frequently met with a full-volume stereo performance of the Beatles' "Sergeant Pepper's Lonely Hearts Club Band." We had to admit, there was a resemblance. Less amusing were numerous close calls when employees' children, playing in their own back yards, came within inches of smacking some unwary visitor on the walk in the head with a line drive. Eventually, as adult employees came along on the walk, they learned what we were up to and made an effort to keep things quiet those few hours each week when we were out.

Possibly the single most useful preparation we made was observing another living-history program. We traveled to Wyoming for a quick look at a well-established program at Fort Laramie. The remains of the fort were being restored, and the entire area was potentially living history material. There were usually two or three historical "characters," including a storekeeper and soldiers on duty. They gave us a good lesson, by example, in how to approach absolute strangers and start talking as if it were many years ago (the fort also had a few rangers who occasionally walked the area answering other questions.) We learned many things from the Fort Laramie staff, including the importance of a strong presentation (if a family of visitors had a dog with them, one soldier invariably tried to buy it for the meat) and the necessity of knowing one's personal story very well (these soldiers, who dealt with individuals and small groups all day, had complete life stories ready to tell).

Refinement

Each of us eventually went his or her own way in developing the walk. One carried large (20 x 30 inch) photographs of the fort as it appeared in army days and used them as reinforcement (a neat trick, considering that he used them without breaking his 1915 character). When a female naturalist began giving the walk from the viewpoint of an officer's wife, she had virtually no information about what wives did at the fort. Hers was the most difficult challenge and was met successfully by great amounts of research.

But we diverged beyond the styles of our presentation, and I had the good fortune and opportunity to diverge most totally. In the fall of 1974 I began the first of three winters of working at Yellowstone as a historian. I managed the park's archives, those being the complete administrative records of the park since the first records were kept in the early 1880s. I sorted, indexed, microfilmed, and generally played around with a wealth of original material. In the process, I wrote my M.A. thesis, an archival study of the Yellowstone collection, and gathered, without even trying, an embarrassing wealth of obscure information.

My walk changed radically after I spent a winter in the archives. I was able to become, much more completely than had been possible before, a real soldier. And, I reasoned, a real soldier would probably not be as programmed about what he said or did as would a ranger. A real soldier would have no training in leading a walk, and so I just led the people around, stopping here and there, responding to the needs of the moment. I cajoled the group into involvement. Often, at the very beginning, I would almost dare them to catch me with a tough question. I knew the hotel rates (with or without bath), my monthly pay, the cost of freighting grain for the horses clear from Livingston, Montana, my commanding officer's company, the cost of a dozen eggs, and an appalling amount of equally trivial stuff that fascinated visitors.

The additional information made the walk far more realistic, and I think, it was probably a lot more fun. My own confidence (not to say arrogance) about my facts seemed to give the group added confidence as well. Conversations developed, about President Wilson, Indian policy, the war in Europe, shooting bears, where to get a drink in a "dry" park. . . whatever seemed interesting. As well as I could, I added new material to the "Fort Walkers File" that we maintained, so that others could benefit from my vast trivia load, but a lot of my information was so fragmented that I simply couldn't organize it in a file. It just came out when I needed it. I had an unfair advantage over the others who have the walk, and to some extent we just had to accept that.

Observations and Lessons

If there are any lessons to be learned from our experience, they will have to come from our individual responses to the challenge. Each of us dealt with the mechanics of the walk differently. Getting started posed problems because the walk necessarily originated in front of the busy Mammoth Hot Springs Visitor Center. One of us chose simply to appear at the scheduled hour (usually 7:00 p.m.) and start talking to the waiting group as if it were 1915; his bravado was sufficient to get them into the idea very quickly (a tape-recorded bugle call immediately preceded his arrival). Shouting orders and announcing his impatience with stragglers and sagebrushers, he quickly led the group off to a quiet spot on a nearby lawn, sat them down, and lectured them on the history of the fort. Another of us appeared well before the walk began, talking to visitors as they arrived and explaining what would happen when the walk began. At the hour, he told the group that for the next hour it would be 1915, asked them to save all modern questions until the end of the walk, and asked them to clue in any late arrivers so that they wouldn't break the mood of the walk by asking questions that didn't fit.

Once the walk began we had some cardinal rules: for anything short of an emergency we would not break character; we would not let the visitors lure us back to the present; and we would accept all intrusions in that same spirit. Our salvation, again and again, was humor. We were all reasonably glib and were prepared to ad-lib our way out of a jam. We warned the group of the approach of a bus with "Watch out for that dang stagecoach; those drivers drive crookeder than they talk." Once the visitors saw the fun of such fantasies they played along and often improvised their own. Annoying employee children, who often tagged along and made a nuisance of themselves, were a big problem. They were noisy, rude, and often impossible to control without completely disrupting the walk. I could turn them to some advantage by explaining to the group that children of officers outranked me and muttering something under my breath about army brats. Most problems of this kind could be neutralized. A noisy car roaring by gave the opportunity to editorialize about the wisdom of letting horseless carriages into the park. A remark such as "You folks mark my words, someday this park will have more of those blasted things than it will know what to do with!" would bring a few smiles and might even prompt some questions about park travel. A parking lot full of snowmoving equipment became "that empty lot over there where the barracks burned down a few years ago." Buildings built after 1915 we simply refused to see— "What buildings over there; you must be seeing things. You know there's a rule against drinking in the park?"

On rare occasions character would be broken—to give a foreign visitor a better explanation of what was going on, or on one occasion, to discuss legal issues with a large leather-clad person on an even larger motorcycle, who happened to be driving by, saw the group, and drove across the lawn to get a better look.

For me, the most important lessons came when I found myself so overloaded with information that I could genuinely talk like a soldier. I had a rare luxury of being able to behave as I thought a soldier would. The result was in some ways a total break from the training we get in formal presentations.

I knew that a real soldier wouldn't concern himself with thematic continuity; none of that "we'll learn more about that at the next stop; please follow me," sort of teacher-pupil exchange. A real soldier might even dislike the assignment. He would be so accustomed to certain information and sights that he would ignore them. Sometimes I ignored the most imposing landmarks, just to goad the group in asking about them. I rambled. I complained about silly policies. I criticized my supervisors. I acted as much like a real soldier as I could. I acted as if the walk had no purpose, beyond my need to obey my captain's orders and show people around. No two walks were alike (though, if I was not really fired up for a walk, I was as capable as anyone of returning to a formula presentation and turning off about 80 percent of my mind).

This new approach had obvious risks. The impromptu unscheduled stop to answer a question might turn into a rousing fifteen-minute debate on whether or not we should keep shooting cougars in the park. It might take me a while to "read" my group and discover if it contained anyone game enough to quarrel with me. There were, naturally, a few important ideas I always hoped to get across during the hours. And it was supposed to be only an hour. I often ran over, sometimes even going an hour and a half. In my own defense, I would say several things. First, the critiques I received from my supervisors were quite positive. They didn't always like my loose approach, but they had to admit that the group was getting an exceptionally vivid taste of the past. Second, the approach was much more fun for everybody than a canned presentation with memorized remarks at each stop. I had more fun, and I projected more enthusiasm, and I'm certain the group had more fun. Of all the activities I led in Yellowstone, this was the only one at which I thought I really excelled, and at which I felt most regularly the rewards of enthusiastic audience response.

Third, it is true that the informality and looseness of the presentation didn't yield uniform results in each walk, but it is also true (and I think more important) that even the worst walks I gave were more lively than a canned talk, and that the best ones were a real thrill. The risk of an occasional off night, of a failed effort, was more than justified by the rewards of a "good" night.

It's tempting to generalize from this experience and suggest that we could use less formality in many kinds of activities. I know that I found myself loosening up in nature walks, and during my last summer in the park, when I was a supervisor, I was pretty tolerant of informality and spontaneity that other supervisors frowned on. In the Fort Yellowstone Walk, however, the circumstances were unusual. I was overqualified for the walk, and any lessons taken from my experience would have to be applied to other circumstances with caution.

We took each other's Fort Yellowstone Walks when we could, and we all learned from each other. That interchange shouldn't be underestimated. My fellow fort "walkers" didn't have my background in the subject matter, but they were my superiors as gifted educators, and I learned many things from them about the teaching process. It was also useful to have a "plant" in the crowd on such a walk, someone who could ask a few questions and maybe help get the group involved. None of us gave memorized speeches, so there was always something new in the walk. It was that newness, that opportunity to experiment, that enabled someone with my limited patience and attention span to keep giving and enjoying the Fort Yellowstone Walk for six seasons.

Part IV
Farms

Agricultural Museums
A New Frontier for the Social Sciences

10

R. Douglas Hurt

This brief article first published in History Teacher *(1980), relates the North American living historical farm to its European antecedents and counterparts. Hurt not only discusses the historic European open-air museums with their essentially static displays of farm buildings and implements, but also examines the experimental work being done at centers like Denmark's Lejre. "Experiments that enable modern man to recapture specific agricultural skills and methods increase understanding of the past." He sees the fully operating living historical farm as both a potential experimental research center and an institution capable of more fully interpreting the whole of agricultural life rather than just the domestic arts usually demonstrated in outdoor museums. "By growing plants, tending animals, and tilling fields, these museums can serve, in part, as experimental laboratories and functioning farms and thus encourage the rediscovery and preservation of a nation's agricultural heritage."*

Museums, for the most part, are show places for revered artifacts and symbols of the past. They serve as depositories, research centers, and educational institutions, which enable the public to interpret the past through sight, touch, and inquiry. Agricultural museums, in particular, which display farm tools and implements and collections of agrarian documents, give the visitor a better understanding of some aspect of life than he had before his visit. In the western world, agricultural museums or agricultural sections in more general museums have become especially popular in urban areas. General interest in our agricultural past is increasing perhaps for reasons of curiosity or nostalgia or because of recent concerns about crop failures and food shortages.[1]

Generally, agricultural exhibits are limited to a single aspect of production, such as viticulture, tobacco culture, or horticulture, and to a specific time span. Few museums illustrate completely one branch of agriculture from its origin to the present; the better centers specialize in both subject and time. In Europe, the United States, and Canada, agricultural museums have tended to concentrate in three areas—ethnology, technology, and living historical farms. Although the purpose and function of one type may overlap with another, each museum tends to have a focus that is unique.[2]

European agricultural museums, for example, emphasize different aspects of rural life than do agricultural museums in the United States and Canada. The difference is particularly evident in the Scandinavian countries where the concept of "open air" museums originated. The theme of an open-air museum is the re-creation of village farming settlements emphasizing folk culture and its architecture.[3]

An open-air museum was first proposed in the 1790s by Charles de Bonstetten, a Swiss scientist. The numerous statues of peasants in regional costumes on Fredemborg's Royal Castle park grounds in Nordsjaeland, Denmark, reportedly had prompted his suggestion. Bonstetten had urged that peasant farm homes be erected and furnished with the appropriate tools and furniture. The first open-air museums, however, did not come into being until 1867 when a wealthy Norwegian moved some old farm buildings onto his land near Christiana (Oslo) for their preservation and viewing. This action, in turn, inspired Swedish-Norwegian King Oscar II to transfer several farm buildings onto his estate, also near Christiana, thus forming the nucleus for what has become the present-day Norwegian Folk Museum. A few years later in Sweden, Arthur Hazelius, a language teacher interested in ethnology, was instrumental in founding an open air museum—the Nordiska Museet—in Stockholm. Like Bonstetten, Hazelius stressed the importance of preserving the rural tradition in the face of an increasingly industrialized society.[4]

As enthusiasm for the Norwegian Folk Museum and

the Nordiska Museet grew, displays of the interiors of farm homes began to appear in the more traditional Scandinavian museums as well. Rooms from original farmhouses were reassembled in the galleries, and farm buildings were transferred to common sites for public visitation. Many university students, convinced that industrialization was destroying the cultural heritage of the pre-industrial age, pitched in to aid scholars and museologists in preserving farmsteads in central locations for exhibit and study.[5]

The first elaborate open-air museum was established in 1891 at Skansen, a branch of the Nordiska Museet. Hazelius again played an important role in securing farm buildings from various parts of Sweden and later acquiring entire farmsteads arranged in the traditional quadrangle pattern. Other features of authenticity included interpretations in folk costumes, the keeping of live animals, the revival of folk music, and ready demonstrations of craft and cooking procedures. The net effect was the re-creation of a rural past, which linked north Europeans to their cultural heritage.[6]

Skansen became the prototype of agriculturally oriented open-air museums; others quickly followed in Norway, Finland, Russia, Rumania, Germany, Belgium, Wales, and the Netherlands. Though small, these museums today number in the hundreds and have been responsible for saving thousands of farm buildings from destruction. Generally, the oldest of these open-air museums have emphasized peasant culture on the assumption that the preservation of rural life provides important information for ethnological research.[7]

To ensure authenticity when moving farm buildings to centralized locations, many open-air museums have used painstaking measures to re-create the original setting. Some have gone as far as to map the cobblestones in the dooryard to ensure that each would be reset in its proper location or to transplant the original grasses, weeds, and flowers to the museum site. In this way many museums maintained their integrity as centers for primary research.[8]

Several European agricultural museums have gone beyond merely preserving a specific cultural heritage and

Herding sheep on the Common at Old Sturbridge Village.—*Photo: Robert S. Arnold, Old Sturbridge Village*

are actively engaged in researching early farming methods. The Czeckosloveske Zemedlske Museum in Prague, for example, has experimented with eighteenth-century ards and plows, and the Museum of English Rural Life in Reading has experimented with the Donnerupland-ard from the pre-Roman iron age in Denmark.[9]

The most extensive research in this regard is taking place at Lejre, Denmark. The Lejre Research Center, founded in 1864, tests historical theories about technology, archaeology, and house construction of the past. Its purpose is to run a permanent series of "imitative experiences," which provide explicit portrayal of Danish ancestral life.[10]

The existing as well as proposed facilities at Lejre are designed to study prehistoric times to the early nineteenth century. Accordingly, the museum has single dwellings and village groupings from the Neolitihic, Bronze, and Iron Ages, and the Viking and Migration periods. It has, in addition, two complete farm sites—one from the seventeenth century and one from the nineteenth—which are supplemented with workshops that demonstrate crafts closely related to agricultural society, such as weaving, pottery, carpentry, and ironsmithing.[11]

Lejre strives to discover and preserve pre-industrial agricultural technology and the skills and production methods peculiar to a self-sufficient society. With such knowledge, it is thought possible to contribute to agricultural development in countries where modern mechanization has not occurred either due to economic difficulties or educational deficiencies. Be that as it may, Lejre's preservation of craftsmanship relating to the production of food, tools, and domestic goods provides important information about Danish culture.[12]

At Lejre specialists conduct experiments in such areas as the climate of the living environment, the factors involved in quartering livestock in the house, and the normal daily wear on the farm home. Testing is particularly complicated since it involves the reproduction of implements, the use of livestock for draft power, a supply of skilled workers, an area available for experimental fields, and a knowledge of soil characteristics and plant types from a specific time in the past. The center's experimental work with the Hendriksmose-ard, which dates to 300 B.C., is an example of the agricultural research conducted at this museum. By observing the ard's efficiency and wear, its marks on the subsoil, and the harnessing of oxen to it, specialists have been able to learn a great deal about ancient agricultural practices in Europe.[13]

For example, because the original Hendriksmose-ard was too precious to risk damage in the field, researchers were forced to make their own. After several of the copies broke during use, they discovered that tillers probably made more suitable ards than did carpenters. The center's own tillers soon learned from experience how to select wood and shape it without weakening it, while carpenters tended to be overly concerned with making the implement attractive and gave little consideration to the practical requirements of plowing.[14]

The experimenters also discovered that the Hendriksmose-ard could be changed to a ristle-ard by fitting it with a wooden arrow-shaped share. Since the Hendrikmose-ard and the ristle-ard existed at the same time, ancient European farmers were, no doubt, able to adapt their implements to meet various agricultural conditions. By converting the Hendriksmose-ard to a ristle-ard, the farmer could more efficiently break or loosen sandy loam soil. Experiments with the Hendriksmose-ard revealed that plowing furrows close together was difficult, because the ard share easily moved into the furrow that had just been plowed. When a sole was added to the ard, however, the problem was solved. Tests also showed that the ard's foreshare quickly became dull during plowing and needed periodic sharpening with an ax.[15]

Experiments that enable modern man to recapture specific agricultural skills and methods increase understanding of the past. The Hendriksmose-ard studies suggest a number of significant conclusions. First, selecting a tree and crafting the wood into a serviceable implement required a good deal of skill; the ard was probably made by the farmer himself, particularly if he had the same difficulty with carpenters that his modern counterpart experienced. Second, a good deal of time was required to train the oxen to pull the ard; farmers did not simply purchase a two-ox team (which the Hendriksmose-ard required), hitch them up, and begin plowing. The oxen had to be trained to obey commands, pull the ard, follow the furrow, and turn at the end of the field. Third, and most important, the experiments indicated that a man could plow 3.6 to 4.6 kilometers per hour. Thus, by rough calculation, one can determine the approximate amount of land that could be tilled in a day and, by considering other factors such as civilization, labor supply, and soil fertility, estimate farm size in northern Europe during Roman times. Finally, because the Roman-age farmer knew how to convert his implements to meet different soil types and conditions, he was probably as practical-minded as farmers are today.[16]

The Lejre Center has also studied the influence of different animal breeds on the vegetation changes and has taken steps to raise the nearly extinct Gothland sheep. The open-air musems on the European continent and Great Britain, however, have been only minimally concerned with preserving declining breeds of domestic animals; in Great Britain the scientific community has been more interested in the project than have the agricultural museums.[17]

In general, the open-air museums in Europe and Great Britain have not shown much interest in making their farmsteads fully operational. At the Nordiska Museet in Stockholm the effort had to be discontinued in the 1930s because the museum could not afford the needed security in safeguarding the tools and implements from the public. The Butser Ancient Farm near Petersfield,

England, however, is currently growing two species of primitive wheat (Emmer and Spelt) dating approximately from 300 B.C., as well as other early cereals and plants, in an attempt to learn more about the Iron Age economy.[18]

The European approach to open-air museums has been followed in Canada and the United States. Upper Canada Village near Morrisburg, for example, re-creates an eastern Ontario village of the mid-nineteenth century. There, as at many European open-air museums, the visitor can observe a host of activities that relate to rural life, such as cheesemaking, spinning, weaving, and quilting. The collection includes a wide variety of hand tools and early horse-drawn machinery—hay rakes, reapers, threshers, and rollers. Upper Canada Village never existed in reality. The buildings, furnishings, and machinery were moved to this location to save them from destruction or dispersal when the St. Lawrence Seaway was expanded. But the agricultural exhibits and other village activities successfully portray Ontario's rural life prior to Canada's Confederation in 1867. In the United States, open-air museums with rural orientation are typified by Old Sturbridge Village near Sturbridge, Massachusetts, Plimoth Plantation at Plymouth, Massachusetts, Colonial Williamsburg near Williamsburg, Virginia, and the Farmers' Museum near Cooperstown, New York.[19]

Until recently American and Canadian agricultural collections in museums have been almost solely concerned with technological displays of tools and implements in locations such as the Smithsonian Institution's National Museum of History and Technology in Washington, D.C., the Agricultural Hall of Fame and National Center near Bonner Springs, Kansas, and the National Museum of Science and Technology in Ottawa, Canada. Certainly, exhibiting agricultural tools and implements is valuable as a supplement to written sources and prevents faulty inference concerning their use. Still, technological change is difficult to portray, and mere museum displays show little about the process of farming. Agricultural exhibits are seldom fully described, and labels or displays are often insufficient in explaining farming and farm life. Since people often have great difficulty imagining how man lived prior to the invention of television and a host of electrical kitchen appliances, the traditional ethnological and technological museums, accordingly, fail to provide the visitor with an adequate understanding of agricultural life.[20]

To remedy this deficiency in agricultural museums, a group of historians and museologists have created a new type of museum—a living historical farm. Herbert A. Kellar, curator of the McCormick Collection and Library, first proposed the idea in 1945, but real interest did not develop until twenty years later. At present, a number of living historical farms exist in the United States and Canada. In order to give some unity to this development and encourage the founding of other such farms, the Association for Living Historical Farms and Agricultural Museums was founded on September 17, 1970.[21]

Living historical farms are natural extensions of the open-air museums at Colonial Williamsburg and Old Sturbridge Village; as such, they constitute a unique type of agricultural museum, doing what indoor museums cannot and what most open-air museums do not do: they show what has always been most important about agriculture—the actual tending of living plants and animals. Living historical farms illustrate the husbandry of some specific time in the past, demonstrating the tools and implements, animal breeds and plant varieties characteristic of the age. Some living historical farms, such as George Washington's birthplace near Fredericksburg, Virginia, and Lincoln's boyhood home near Rockport, Indiana, portray life at the time and place of a notable person. Others, such as Colonial Pennsylvania Plantation near Edgemont, Pennsylvania, the Iowa Living History Farms near Des Moines, and Old Cienega Village near Santa Fe, New Mexico, depict agriculture as it was at a general period and place. Some living historical farms exist separately, but others are joined with traditional open-air museums.[22]

The emphasis at living historical farms is on the farming process itself. These museums help correct misconceptions about agriculture that one often receives at ethnological and technological museums, where agriculture is romantically portrayed or where the struggle for survival is overly emphasized. Living historical farms simply acknowledge the problems farmers faced and re-create the past as accurately as possible.[23]

Living historical farms have also been the first agricultural museums to collect animals and plants with the intent of exhibiting them along with tools and implements in a functional setting. This activity is important, for although only about 4 percent of the American population live on farms, most Americans still retain an interest in agriculture and are eager to learn about their nation's agrarian tradition. Living historical farms uniquely portray farm life, which even in its most recent form is already outside the personal experience of most Americans.[24]

Besides functioning as public educational centers, some living historical farms, such as the National Colonial Farm at Accokeek, Maryland, and the Freeman Farm at Old Sturbridge Village, have begun developing plant varieties and breeding animals representative of a specific time in the past. Such efforts have been limited. Ideally, it is best left to seed companies or the United States Department of Agriculture, for they have the funds and expertise to undertake a broad program for the storage of germ plasm. Still, living historical farms can aid the program by serving as limited depositories for plant and animal germ plasm.[25]

These various forms of agricultural museums enable visitors to reflect on their rural past. By viewing objects, demonstrations, and farm settings, one can more fully understand one's ethnological background, one's nation's technological development, and the agricultural practices of one's forefathers. And as a result, one can

Spring plowing on the Pliney Freeman farm, Old Sturbridge Village.—*Photo: Robert S. Arnold, Old Sturbridge Village*

better comprehend the process of agricultural development and the nature of farm life today. But agricultural museums in the western world also offer scholars a broad field for inter-disciplinary research. Social, economic, cultural, and environmental historians should find ethnological or technological agricultural museums and living historical farms natural provinces. Folklorists, sociologists, and anthropologists, too, will find many avenues for research at these institutions.

Agricultural museums, then, are multifaceted institutions. Traditionally, they have provided not only interesting places to spend a leisurely afternoon, but have also served as research centers for the scholarly study of agrarian documents and objects. Although such museum functions will not disappear, agricultural museums have the unique capability of doing much more and thereby becoming increasingly relevant to both visitors and scholars. By growing plants, tending animals, and tilling fields, these museums can serve, in part, as experimental laboratories and functioning farms and thus encourage the rediscovery and preservation of a nation's agricultural heritage.

Notes

1. Alma S. Wittlin, *Museums: In Search of a Usable Future*(Cambridge, Mass.: MIT Press, 1970), pp. xi, 1-2.
2. Ivan Balassa, "The Agricultural Museum, Budapest," *Museum* 22 (1969): 44.
3. Richard W. E. Perrin, *Outdoor Museums*, Milwaukee Public Museum Publication in Museology No. 4 (Milwaukee: Milwaukee Public Museum, 1975), p.9.
4. Kai Uldall, "Open Air Museums," *Museums* 10 (1957), 68-69; *Skansen: Buildings and Animals* (Stockholm: n p., 1966), p.4; Mats Rehneberg, *The Nordiska Museet and Skansen* (Stockholm: n p., 1957), pp.7, 14, 20-22.
5. Uldall, "Open Air Museums," p.68; Darwin P. Kelsey, "Outdoor Museums and Historical Agriculture," *Agricultural History,* 46 (January 1972): 111-112.
6. Rehnberg, *The Nordiska Museet and Skansen*, p.7; Perrin, *Outdoor Museums*, p.11; *Skansen: Buildings and Animals*, p.5; Kelsey, "Oudoor Museums and Historical Agriculture," p.114.
7. Uldall, "Open Air Museums," pp.69-70; Josef Weyns, "Bokryk: The First Open-Air Museum in Belgium," *Museums* 12 (1959): 18-20; Vladimir Ivanov, "The Open-Air Museum, Kizhi, Karelian A.S.S.R.," *Museums* 22 (1969): 60.
8. Kelsey, "Outdoor Museums and Historical Agriculture," p.113.
9. Hans-Ole-Hanson, *Reports from Experiments in Lejre, 1968: 1* (Lejre, Denmark: Historical Archeological Research Center, 1969), p.3.
10. "Some Main Trends in the Development of the Lejre-Center," undated manuscript (mimeographed), Division of Agriculture, Na-

tional Museum of History and Technology, Smithsonian Institution.

11. "Lejre Center," *Living Historical Farms Bulletin* 2 (March 1973), p.2.

12. "Some Main Trends in the Development of the Lejre-Center," Smithsonian Institution.

13. Ibid.

14. Hans-Ole-Hanson, *Reports from Experiments in Lejre*, pp.3, 11.

15. Ibid., pp.25, 29, 34.

16. Ibid., p.40.

17. "Some Main Trends in the Development of the Lejre-Center," Smithsonian Institution; Darwin Kelsey, "Why Preserve Declining Breeds of Livestock?" *Living Historical Farms Bulletin* 1 (September 1971): 3.

18. John T. Schlebecker, *The Past in Action: Living Historical Farms* (Washington, D.C.: Smithsonian Institution Press, 1967), p.3; Peter J. Reynolds, *The Iron Age Farm Demonstration Area* (Winchester, England: County Recreation Department, 1976).

19. Upper Canada Village (N.p.: n.p., n.d.); W. J. Patterson, Superintendent of Historical Sites, Upper Canada Village, to the author, February 4, 1977.

20. Russell H. Anderson, "Agriculture in the Museum of Science and Industry Founded by Julius Rosenwald," *Agricultural History* 3 (October 1929), p.183; John T. Schlebecker, *Agricultural Implements and Machines in the Collection of the National Museum of History and Technology*, Smithsonian Studies in History and Technology No. 17 (Washington, D.C.: Smithsonian Institution Press, 1972), pp.1-2; T. A. Brown, Curator, Agricultural Technology, National Museum of Science and Technology, Ottawa, Canada, to the author, March 7, 1977; Kelsey, "Outdoor Museums and Historical Agriculture," p.122; Schlebecker, *The Past in Action: Living Historical Farms*, pp.1, 3; John T. Schlebecker, "Living Historical Farms Tell It Like It Was," *Contours of Change*, United States Department of Agriculture Yearbook, 1970 (Washington, D.C.: Government Printing Office, 1971), p.230.

21. Herbert A. Kellar, "Living Agricultural Museums," *Agricultural History* 19 (July 1945): 188; Marion Clawson, "Living Historical Farms: A Proposal for Action," *Agricultural History* 39 (April 1965): 110; John T. Schlebecker, *Living Historical Farms: A Walk into the Past* (Washington, D.C.: Smithsonian Institution Press, 1968), p.5; John T. Schlebecker and Gale E. Peterson, *Living Historical Farms Handbook* (Washington, D.C.: Smithsonian Institution Press, 1972), p.2.

22. Schlebecker, *Living Historical Farms: A Walk into the Past*, p.10; G.T. Sharrier, "The Holt Hall of Agriculture," *Living Historical Farms Bulletin* 3 (March 1974): 2; Schlebecker and Peterson, *Living Historical Farms Handbook*, p.1; Wayne D. Rasmussen, "Living Historical Farms and Maryland Agriculture," *Associates NAL Today* 1 (October 1976): 43; Charles E. Hatch, *Chapters in History of Popes Creek Plantation* (Washington, D.C.: United States Department of the Interior, 1968); Edwin C. Bearass, *Lincoln Boyhood as a Living Historical Farm* (Washington, D.C.: United States Department of the Interior, 1967); "Plimoth Plantation Training Manual," unpublished manuscript, n.d.; *Plimoth Plantation Annual Report, 1975*; Invadel Huff, Iowa Living History Farms, to the author, February 4, 1977; G. T. Sharrer, "Old Cienega Village Museum," *Living Historical Farms Bulletin* 4 (December 1974): 4.

23. Roger Welsch, "Sowbelly and Seedbanks: The Living History Museum as a Process Repository," in Virginia Briscoe and Jay Anderson (eds.), *Proceedings of the Annual Meeting of the Association for Living Historical Farms and Agricultural Museums*, June 16-18, 1974, University of California, Davis (Washington, D.C.: Smithsonian Institution Press, 1975), p.23; Rasmussen, "Living Historical Farms and Maryland Agriculture," p.43; Clifford Lord, "The Farmers' Museum: The Museum of the New York State Historical Association at Cooperstown," *Agricultural History* 17 (July 1943): p.171; *An Informal Guide to the New York State Historical Association* (New York: New York State Historical Association, 1975), pp.17-18.

24. Rasmussen, "Living Historical Farms and Maryland Agriculture," p.43; Schlebecker, "Living Historic Farms Tell It Like It Was," pp.229, 231.

25. Rasmussen, "Living Historical Farms and Maryland Agriculture," pp.43, 45.

Harvests of History

11

Darwin P. Kelsey

Darwin P. Kelsey, a cultural geographer and former director of museum administration at Old Sturbridge Village, argues in this essay, which appeared in July-September 1976 issue of Historic Preservation 28 (1976) *that the living historical farm is a new hybrid of historic site that seeks to preserve material and nonmaterial culture in context and in process. The simulated environments of living historical farms are not only unique institutions for preserving cultural intangibles but also effective experimental laboratories for teaching subjects that previous scholars had written off as "best left to the imagination." Living historical farms provide, Kelsey argues, "in addition to strict intellection and cognition, experimental modes of knowing—knowing through sight, sound, smell, touch, taste."*

In the past ten years, a new variety of historic site has taken root and begun to blossom in the field of historic preservation. It is being called the "living historical farm" (LHF). This new variety has many strains. In them can be seen, in different combinations, mutant characteristics of some older varieties, including the historic house, history museum, folk-life museum, outdoor museum and agricultural museum.

Since the variety has many strains, the definition of living historical farms must be broad enough to describe all of them, yet concrete enough to be meaningful. Just such a definition is available in John T. Schlebecker and Gale E. Peterson's *Living Historical Farms Handbook* (Smithsonian Institution Press, 1972): "On living historical farms men farm as they once did during some specific time in the past. The farms have tools and equipment like those once used, and they raise the same types of livestock and plants used during the specified era. The operations are carried on in the presence of visitors."

LHFs have been started in more than two dozen states, and there are a few in Canada as well. Most are privately sponsored, although a few receive their primary support from one or more government agencies. Among the more widely known are the Loyalist Farm at Upper Canada Village, Morrisburg, Ontario; Joslin's Farm at King's Landing, New Brunswick, Canada; Pliny Freeman Farm at Old Sturbridge Village, Sturbridge, Massachusetts; Lippitt Homestead at the Farmers' Museum in Cooperstown, New York; Powell Farm at Old Bethpage Village Restoration, Old Bethpage, New York; Living History Farms, Des Moines, Iowa; National Colonial Farm, Accokeek, Maryland; Turkey Run Farm, a National Park Service site in Virginia near Washington, D.C.; Georgia Agrirama at Tifton, Georgia; and Quiet Valley Farm Museum in Stroudsburg, Pennsylvania.

Historical farming operations are in development at many other locations, including the Colonial Pennsylvania Plantation, Edgemont, Pennsylvania; Skinner Settlement, Corinth, Maine; Oliver H. Kelley Farm, Elk River, Minnesota; C. Nelson Hackett Ranch, Woodland, California; Jensen Farm, Logan, Utah; Conner Prairie Pioneer Settlement, Noblesville, Indiana; and several National Park Service sites, among them the Lincoln Boyhood National Memorial, Lincoln City, Indiana, and George Washington Birthplace, Fredericksburg, Virginia.

All LHFs exhibit agriculture and farm life, but they do so in different ways. A few are somewhat like traditional agricultural museums, displaying collections of plows or farm vehicles from different periods or demonstrating a greater variety of processes and activities than would have been found on a single farm at one period. Other LHFs may represent the way of life not only of a particular time and place but also of a particular farmer or type of farmer, social class, ecosystem, or market economy. Historical farms of this kind usually have it as their goal to create a total period environment. Some are more successful than others, but most LHFs go further in this direction than do other museums or preservation projects concerned primarily with architecture.

Schlebecker and Peterson categorized LHFs as either memorial or typical. Memorial farms might more logically be termed "unique" or "particular". For example, some farms have been preserved as memorials, and even developed as LHFs, because they are associated with a famous person (Washington, Lincoln, Roosevelt) or someone of local prominence. Similarly, there are farms that are being developed as LHFs because they happened to be sites of major Revolutionary or Civil War battles. Many other factors, including ownership by the founder of a rural institution (the Grange), possession of distinctive architectural features (round or hexagonal barns) and rare ecological characteristics have served as stimuli to preservation. The characteristic that leads to the use of each of these farms as an LHF is that each is particular, unique. The opposite kind of historical farm is the typical one, which is valued less for its own sake than for characteristics it shares with many other farms that were in the area at a given time.

An LHF is historical in the broadest sense of the word, offering a patterned, coherent account of the past that is intended to be true. They are thus analogous to written history and exhibits in traditional history museums. Even though they often appear concrete and complete— that is, real—they are only accounts of the past and not the past itself. Even an LHF that attempts to replicate what it was at an earlier period is now only an account of the original. The complex web of interrelationships that once existed between parts of the farm and its milieu is now largely gone, leaving only traces (an interesting point for reflection by architectural preservationists and museum curators, some of whom tend to confuse the artifacts produced by a living system with the living system itself). LHFs represent theories—that is, generalizations—about the past. As is any historical account, they are based on incomplete evidence. They are subjective, as is any "model" produced in the arts, humanities, or sciences. As is true of any history or model, they also are bound to contain some inaccuracies, irrelevancies, distortions, or "noise." In short, one cannot expect everything of LHFs that might be expected of the empirical world. But if one knows how to "read" these accounts of the past, they can tell a great deal.

If a living historical farm is only an account of the past, can it be viewed as preservation? LHFs tend not to place primary emphasis on architectural artifacts, even of the folk or vernacular sort. Some are total reconstructions. Those that use period buildings usually subject them to as much alteration and wear as would occur in most nonmuseum uses. Nor do tools and implements, by themselves, occupy center stage. They are in active use on LHFs and are thus subject to wear and damage unless reproductions are substituted. On most LHFs, old seed varieties and other plant materials are as important as architecture and equipment. So, too, are "rare" breeds of domestic livestock. Work processes, such as spinning, weaving, cheesemaking, meat curing, plowing, scything, timber hewing, fence building, irrigating, gardening and maple sugaring, receive as much preservation effort as do material artifacts. Music, games, festivals, and other rural customs are practiced and perpetuated.

What manner of preservation is this? It is holistic preservation: preservation of material and nonmaterial culture in context and in process.

All this is a great deal of work. It requires great investments of time and money for research, planning, development, and interpretive programming. Are some of these things of only peripheral interest? Would it be better to leave some things to the imagination? What interests one LHF visitor may not be what interests another.

As for leaving things to the imagination, one need only reflect on conversations about "how it was in the old days" to realize that most historical imaginings are either insipid or wild.

Roger Welsch, writing in the May 1974 *The History Teacher,* found LHFs and similar projects very instructive. He pointed out that it is "very difficult to re-create a mental attitude by unlearning [our modern knowledge and] experience but given an appropriate environment. . . a willing mind can approach the ideal far closer than it might by purely intellectual effort." The simulated environment becomes not only a tool for teaching what is already known but also an experimental laboratory in which to seek information about aspects of the past not told by archival, archaeological, and other material data. It also provides a laboratory for testing some of the conclusions of previous scholars who touched on "subjects best left to the imagination," as, for example, how buildings "must" have been used.

There is also another side of LHFs. Behind the scenes at many of these sites, architects, architectural historians, curators, horticulturists, agricultural and other kinds of historians ply their trades. Traditional building research and conservation procedures are much in evidence as are similar procedures for tools and implements. Agricultural and horticultural historians are busy identifying old varieties of field crops, vegetables, and fruit. Considerable time is devoted to tracking down surviving examples and establishing programs to ensure their continued survival. Old Sturbridge Village, for example, now maintains a "preservation orchard" with more than 100 apple varieties whose origins predate the mid-nineteenth century. The orchard, which is analogous to a storehouse of artifacts, supplies scions for Old Sturbridge Village as well as other museums and interested individuals.

LHFs are thus beginning to play a significant role in preserving genetically diverse plant material, lack of which could easily lead to national and international disaster. One need only think back to the corn leaf blight of 1970 to recognize the danger. Nearly 15 percent of the United States corn crop was lost, and in some southern states more than half of the year's crop could not be harvested. The problem was that most United States corn farmers were growing a modern hybrid strain that turned out to be highly susceptible to a particular fungus disease. Evaluation of that epidemic has demonstrated that nearly all commercial crops in the United States are similarly vulnerable. Often, the only defense is to turn to plant varieties that are naturally resistant to the disease—if they still exist. The so-called Green Revolution, while producing higher crop yields, has resulted in a dramatic discarding of "inferior" varieties. While these varieties may not yield as highly under certain conditions, they may well contain the genetic diversity necessary for survival as circumstances change. Many LHFs, therefore, take very seriously their function of preserving plant materials.

The situation is similar in regard to livestock. LHFs need farm animals that are appropriate to their region and period. It is not simply a matter of "looking right," although that is important. Oxen and horses working the land, cattle and sheep grazing, chickens scratching around the barnyard, all are integral elements of historical farm environments. They are powerfully evocative visual elements of the landscape, and LHFs have as much responsibility for accuracy here as elsewhere. But livestock now, as in the past, are selected for their ability to adapt to and efficiently utilize particular environments. Livestock breeds differ significantly in their ability to subsist on low-quality forage, resist disease and parasites, maintain high levels of fertility, or give birth to young without assistance. Historical evidence and modern observation suggest that some prize modern livestock would fare rather poorly in certain environmental situations that so-called commercially uncompetitive breeds utilize quite efficiently. Devon cattle in the East and Longhorn cattle in the Southwest are prime examples. Although they cannot do as well as some modern breeds in high-energy-input farming systems, they may well be superior in such low-energy-input farming systems as existed in the past and may be needed again to supplement current systems. These "living relics" were once leading commercial breeds. Many people in the LHF movement believe that by studying them in environmental settings similar to those in which they once were widely used, it will be possible not only to gain insights about the past but also to discover possibilities for the future.

In general, American agricultural scientists and livestock breeders have not recognized the need to preserve older breeds for their genetic potential. This seems a peculiar form of myopia, given the growing awareness of need of genetic diversity in plant material and the widespread efforts in Europe to ensure the survival of now rare breeds of domestic livestock. LHFs perhaps can be vehicles for raising the level of consciousness of American livestock scientists and breeders.

Turning to a brief account of the development of the concept of living historical farms, one finds it described in the journal *Agricultural History* as long ago as 1945. Historical farming demonstrations were begun at Old Sturbridge Village and the Farmers' Museum in Cooperstown, New York, by the early 1950s, and in 1961 Upper Canada Village opened with farming demonstrations comparable to those at Sturbridge and Cooperstown. By the mid-1960s, expansion of these early farming exhibits was being planned, and the idea of LHFs was given a boost in 1965 by another proposal published in *Agricultural History*, advocating establishment of a network of twenty-five to fifty historical farms in carefully selected parts of the country to "portray some of the main elements of U.S. agricultural history." This was written by Marion Clawson, of Resources for the Future, Inc. He emphasized two things—that the farms should be operating, and that they should together make up a coordinated system under federal sponsorship and direction.

The proposal led to a feasibility study jointly undertaken by the U.S. Department of the Interior, National Park Service, the Smithsonian Institution, and the U.S. Department of Agriculture. This, in turn, resulted in a rather grand plan to establish a federally funded and administered program of operating historical farms. Included in the scheme were an extension service to provide a corps of experts in various fields to help start new LHFs, an experiment station to undertake the mechanical and biological experiments necessary to develop crops, livestock, and implements, and an accreditation service to guarantee high standards of operation on LHFs. The estimated cost for the first three years of this program was nearly $700,000, and Congress did not choose to fund it. The Clawson proposal did,

Harvesting hay in turn-of-the-century Iowa.—*Photo: Miriam Dunlap, Living History Farms*

however, arouse much interest and continuing support in the federal agencies that undertook the feasibility study, and it also encouraged a few new private projects.

Interest in the concept grew during the late 1960s, and staff members at various projects began informally to organize an information-sharing network. By 1970, the need for a more formal and systematic way of assisting one another was recognized. In September of that year, a number of people attending an agricultural symposium at Old Sturbridge Village joined together to found the Association of Living Historical Farms and Agricultural Museums (ALHFAM). Subsequently the association was formally organized, a constitution prepared, an annual meeting established, and publication begun of a quarterly *Bulletin* and *Annual* yearbook. ALHFAM has be-

come a focus of interest in living history. (For information, write Secretary-Treasurer, ALHFAM, Smithsonian Institution, Washington, D.C. 20560.)

Individual LHFs represent different mutations of the old varieties of historic preservation. Collectively, however, they seem to be developing into a new and vigorous hybrid. As they progress, they may help us make sense of that often used but inadequately explained phrase, "getting a sense of the past." They provide, in addition to strict intellection and cognition, experimental modes of knowing—knowing directly through sight, sound, smell, touch, taste. The "sense" we get is only an account of the past, to be sure. But it is a holistic sense constructed from holistic preservation.

Historical Farms as Models of the Past

12

Darwin P. Kelsey

I was in the audience when Darwin P. Kelsey delivered this keynote address to the Association for Living History Farms and Agricultural Museums 1975 conference at the University of California in Davis. He was president emeritus. His words were eye-openers then and still are. The address, published in the 1975 ALHFAM Annual, *is still a valuable yardstick for measuring the degree to which a living historical farm has realized its statement of purpose, objectives, and goals—in short, its reason for being. Year after year its ideas have challenged those of us working at living historical farms. It has become a classic.*

First of all I must say that I am frequently struck by the great improbability that I should ever be, or have been, president of such an august national association as ALHFAM. And to be emeritus—from anything, at my tender age—seems even more unlikely. Still, the increasing grayness of my pate begins to raise doubts in my mind as to how tender my age really is.

Presidents or presidents emeriti, it seems, are often expected to give what is called an "address" (whether they are really able to or not, for reasons, say, of feeble mindedness, a ridiculously busy schedule, or some other infirmity). I gather that such occasions are largely ceremonial, that one can give such an address relatively free from bodily pummeling and other forms of critique. At the close of these discourses, the speaker is normally given a short polite bit of applause and then allowed to just go away. This is called "executive privilege." Not being kindly disposed toward most executives or most privilege, I would normally waive this customary right—but I have some foreknowledge of what is about to follow.

Some presidential addresses present the new and exciting results of the speaker's most current research. I considered doing that. But my boss pointed out, recently, that I hadn't done anything along those lines for many months and so that didn't seem especially promising. Another approach that has class, or at least is commonly resorted to, is to undertake reflections on a lifetime of scholarship: to grapple with fundamental philosophical and methodological conundrums. Now here, I perceived, was my opportunity, since my scholarly life has been so short and limited, not much could really be expected of me. And I was further encouraged to pursue this type of address by a statement said to have been made in "one of the better historical journals by an acute and hard-nose critic of historical writing."[1] In trying to put his finger on just what it is that makes for good historical writing he concluded that "each point about it has just that air of obviousness which everyone can agree to, but which no previous writer seems to have attained."[2] So I began to cast about for something really obvious in regard to historical farms that everyone had overlooked.

Well, it was a snap; I stumbled onto something right off. I noticed that in the growing body of literature relating to historical farms there is seldom any attempt to define them or say anything fundamental or basic about their nature. In fact, John Schlebecker and Gale Peterson may be the only persons to have published what might reasonably be construed as a definition. In the opening paragraph of the *Living Historical Farms Handbook* they say:

> On living historical farms men farm as they once did during some specific time in the past. The farms have tools and equipment like those once used, and theyraise the same types of livestock and plants used during the specified era. The operations are carried on in the presence of visitors.[3]

As a definition, their statement has certain characteristics to recommend it: concreteness, simplicity, flexibility, and breadth. Alternative definitions could certainly be developed, although producing one equally concise and actually superior might not be easy. And even if we were to discover a short formal definition, somehow superior, it would still exhibit a type of inadequacy inherent in all short formal definitions. It would be too abstract and general to give a very full understanding of the phenomena to which it related; so specific examples would necessarily have to follow, to make comprehensible the general relationships identified in the definition. They suggested that historical farms may be grouped into two general categories, which they termed the "memorial" and the "typical," and described what they believed to be their essential characteristics and subtypes. The term "memorial" does seem appropriate for describing the stimulus for preserving or developing certain historical farms. But the terms "unique" or "particular" might be better suited to a discussion of the basic nature of historical farms since they are ordinarily considered logical opposites to the term "typical."

Farms uniquely or particularly associated with a famous person such as Washington, Lincoln, Roosevelt, or even someone of only local prominence are sometimes thought especially worthy of making into a historical farm. Others are similarly designated because they are associated with a great event such as a Revolutionary or Civil War battle; and still others because they were once outstandingly successful farms. Or they may have been the site of origin, or influential in the development of something: an institution such as the Grange, a crop variety or a livestock breed. An unusual feature of a farm occasionally becomes a stimulus for preservation: a round or hexagonal barn, an ecological complex, or something that is somehow a distinctive contrast with the surrounding area. Whatever the reason, the essential point to bear in mind is that the farm is to be made a historical farm because it is that particular farm and no other.

The logical opposite is the so-called "typical" farm—that is, a farm not valued primarily for its own sake but because it can be used to describe or study farm characteristics that are more general, that exist beyond that particular, unique farm. There is an occasionally expressed view in the living historical farm movement that there is no such thing as a typical farm, that every farm differs in some way from every other farm. I would not deny that ultimately, every farm is a unique combination of soil, slope, drainage, buildings, crops, livestock, markets, managerial abilities, and goals. But the logical conclusion of the uniqueness argument is solipsism. Furthermore, merely to say "farm" is to admit a general category of phenomena based on certain similarities. And even without a formal definition of what a farm is, it is possible to refine the notion of farm by specifying some of these similarities: dairy farm, wheat farm, general mixed farming. Or we can refine the notion of farm and the typicality of a farm quantitatively, if need be, in regard to some characteristic, such as size, organization, efficiency or production, and energy flow. Simply by definition the typical farm can be said to refer to the average, median, or mode in a frequency distribution of farms taken from the same universe or sample. The essential point is that a typical historical farm is an attempt to represent phenomena existing generally in an area at a given time.

In addition to the categories particularizing and typifying, there exists something which, for want of a good term, I shall call the "not quite farm." Sidestepping once again any effort to give a formal definition of farm, I simply wish to note that there are institutions that have been called "historical farms" that do not fit what I intuitively understand as constituting a farm. One British example, I intuitively categorize as a zoo, albeit for domestic animals, while another example from the United States, I intuitively think of as a park, a garden, an arboretum, or possibly an experiment station. In short, a "not quite farm" leaves me with the uneasy sense that somehow something is wrong, that it is not a "real" farm. It seems to have a credibility problem.

But one doesn't have to look very long or critically at the particularizing or typifying types either to experience the same uneasiness about their credibility as real farms. People predisposed to favor the particularizing type are prone to ask, "Was this farm ever once a real farm or is it just somebody's idea of what a farm was like?" Conversely advocates of typifying farms, when visiting the particularizing type, often make sly inquiries like, "What is to be done about those four of the original seven buildings on the farmstead, now gone with hardly a trace of evidence as to appearance, construction details, function, etc.?" They might also affect a certain sympathy over loss of the south half of the farm, now cut off by a modern interstate highway or lack of documentary evidence as to precisely how that farm was managed. Thus, one may leave even the particularizing farm with the uneasy sense that it differs in quite a few particulars from its original.

Occuring on all types of historical farms, certain other problems detract from their credibility, from one's sense that they really are re-creations of the past. For example, a tour of various institutions that are said to be, or to have, a historical farm reveals such things as roads on what purports to be an early nineteenth-century farm, constructed of soil cement. What are meant to pass for eighteenth-century or nineteenth-century dirt roads are well marked with rubber tire tracks. Horse or tractor drawn wagons or "carry-alls" cruise about with loads of visitors. A modern drinking fountain rears up in the middle of an early nineteenth-century barnyard. House painters or carpenters in modern garb and wielding screeching sanders and saws are observed making repairs or "restorations." Holstein oxen parade through an eighteenth-century village. Spray residues linger on apple trees. Several plows are seen in a farm barn—ostensibly to show various regional and period types. And so the list of anachronisms grows, or could grow, to several score items. We sense that they somehow detract from or taint the recreated historical environment. It becomes something that never really existed in the past; or if it did, it is now subtly or even grossly altered.

In part, these credibility problems represent a failure of various farm museums to specify clearly their institutional identity and purposes, or some inability to pursue them with rigor and diligence. But equally important, I believe, are the seeming inadequacies that stem from the way we think about historical farms, for that can lead to unrealistic expectations about what they are and what they can achieve.

The problem is symbolized rather nicely in John Schlebecker's booklet *Living Historical Farms: A Walk Into the Past*, which was intended to publicize and build popular enthusiasm for the living historical farm movement. The title, *Living Historical Farms: A Walk Into the Past*, we recognize as a metaphor. That is, living historical farms are the same as "the past." At least, that's what the title says. Yet in the text of the booklet, Schlebecker describes historical farms in terms of simile, not metaphor. He argued they are like or similar to the past in certain ways and quite unlike it in others. The metaphoric title utilizes hyperbole or overstatement, a common, and not necessarily sinful, literary device. Its strongly evocative language does attract attention (not a bad thing for a title to do). And the essay itself clearly shows the author to understand the relationship of a historical farm to the past to be only one of simile. Probably everyone who has thought about historical farms would agree; it is elementary. Yet sometimes I think we forget that fact, or ignore it, or fail to take full account of its implications; I often have, I am embarrassed to admit. And I continually hear statements by museum visitors and workers alike that reveal, at the very least, a short-term confusion of this logical relationship. As a result, we expect too much and not enough from historical farms.

Part of the remedy may lie in a conscious effort to be more precise about what we mean when we use terms that, though fundamental, are ambiguous. What makes a farm "historical"? The fact that George Washington was born or slept there? That a Civil War battle was fought there? That it existed as the home and business of someone years before anyone dreamed of making it a museum? That it represents an attempt to typify or generalize about farming somewhere at some past time? We casually assign all of these meanings to the term "historical" in this context. And the closely related term "history" can be even more ambiguous. Some use it to mean "the past" as such; or the past, present, and future, i.e., the total flow of time. Others contend that the word should stand not for the past as such or even the records, the documentation, the traces of the past which remain to us in the present. Rather, they assert, history should mean a statement of "facts" or better yet generalized "interpretations" based on such evidence. Still others use it to refer to an academic discipline. James Hexter observes, correctly no doubt, in the *History Primer* that it would be futile to try to "legislate about what history 'really' is";[4] but surely any historian (including those of us concerned with historical farms) can encourage clearer thinking by indicating what he or she means by the term when using it. Taking my own advice, I should say that I use the term "history" in a particular way because I find that, for me at least, at the present time, that way is conceptually most rewarding. My usage, with some modification, is taken from Hexter. Like him, I prefer to avoid most of the usages just mentioned, not because they are necessarily illegitimate but because it

reduces my confusion to say "the past" when I meant that, or "the total flow of time" when I meant that, and to confine my use of the term "history" to a more restricted meaning. That way I usually know what I mean by the term; I can usually explain what I mean to others; and as a further aid to clarity it usually forces me to seek the relationship of their meaning to my own.

In Hexter's usage, history means "any patterned, coherent account, intended to be true, of any past happenings involving human intention or doing or suffering."[5] While not including all of the meanings mentioned a moment ago, this is nevertheless a broad definition. Notice, however, that among its restrictions is a limitation to the human past, a widely held convention in regard to history. That is probably not an overly burdensome restriction since humans have in some way dabbled with nearly everything in the empirical world. But if I should someday find my interests unduly obstructed by that limitation, I would no doubt disavow any need to limit myself to doing history.

History, in this very broad generic sense, includes the types of accounts we all construct every day, in relating all manner of lived experience: a son's explanation of why he fell in a mud puddle on his way home from school, Hexter notes, would qualify. History of the sort professional historians produce (as professional historians) may be considered a special case of this broader generic type; as such it has certain distinguishing characteristics. The patterned coherent accounts of the past produced by all of us (hereafter referred to as Everyman) usually employ the rhetorical structure of common spoken language. Everyman expects and receives credence on the general credibility of his account and his own reputation for honesty and good recall. The accounts produced by the professional, Hexter says, usually are distinguished by a rhetorical structure of formal written prose. The grounds on which he expects and receives credence depends partly, like Everyman's, on the general credibility of his account; but a reputation for honesty and good recall isn't sufficient to establish fully the professional's credence. It rests, instead, most heavily upon the evidence he put forward to support his account. He is expected to make systematic use of the surviving record of the past, and having done so to register it in the public domain, as it were, by giving ample directions on where to find the sources for his inference so that all who care to may check the evidence for themselves. History, defined in these two senses, I believe, has considerable applicability to the concept of living historical farms.

Historical farms may be thought of as patterned, coherent accounts of the past, intended to be true, which involve human intention, doing, or suffering. They are not the past, as such, regardless of whether they are of the typifying or particularizing type. Even a historical farm that attempts to replicate what it once was, say a century earlier, is now only an account of its original. The complex web of inter-relationships that then existed between parts of the farm and between the farm and its milieu, are now largely gone, leaving only traces. How much we can infer about those relationships, how good an account we can produce in speech, in writing, in three dimensions, depends on the quantity and quality of the surviving traces of the past.

Any account of the empirical world, whether that world be past, present, or future represents an abstraction and simplification. It may take many forms. People trained in the humanities usually have a strong bias for accounts constructed from "common language," spoken or written. Those trained in the modern sciences often prefer accounts or representations of the empirical world constructed in the language of graphics or the language of mathematics. These latter are frequently referred to as "models," as indeed the former may be. A writer in the *American Scientist* a decade ago argued that "a model can be a theory, or a law, or a relation, or a hypothesis, or an equation, or a rule."[6] His view, to be sure, has been criticized as so broad as to be meaningless; mathematicians and logicians always require a far more rigorously defined set of relationships between a model and whatever it represents. But their problems often bear no close relationship to the empirical world, and my purpose, at the present, is to suggest that the idea or concept of "model" can be applied in a fruitful way to thinking about one aspect of the empirical world: farms and historical accounts of them.

The debate over what a model is frequently seems more abstruse and convoluted than the debate over what history is. For the most part, I intend to avoid that quagmire, assuming that everyone is already familiar with it, and that having used what are called "models" in their own work, my audience already considers the concept of models a useful one. Those unfamiliar with the ways in which models are used in the sciences, though, may

think them rather trivial, construing the word "model" only as a noun, meaning for example, a representation of a train or airplane. Or they may perhaps give it another common usage as an adjective, for example as "model husband," meaning an exemplar of his type. It is also widely used as a verb, as in to model or demonstrate new clothes. But these common usages provide a very limited view of the attributes of what are called "models" today.

As already noted, any account of the empirical world is a simplification and abstraction. The mind always decomposes the infinitely complex empirical world and reorders it in a simplified and therefore intelligible way, providing an overview of its essential characteristics or at least the characteristics that the person constructing the account considers essential for his purposes. Obscuring details, for those purposes, are eliminated, and the system of objects and relationships of interest stand out more clearly or separately than they actually do in the empirical world. This type of account, in the sciences, is commonly called a "model."

> A model is thus a simplified structuring of reality which presents supposedly significant features or relationships in a generalized form. Models are highly subjective approximations in that they do not include all associated observations or measurements, but as such they are valuable in obscuring incidental detail and in allowing fundamental aspects of reality to appear.[7]

And this is precisely what I believe historical farms do, and why I believe it useful to think about them as models.

Models perform certain general functions. One is psychological in that it allows some group of phenomena to be "visualized and comprehended that otherwise could not have been because of its magnitude and complexity."

The past coming to life for school children visiting Plimoth Plantation.—*Photo: George Chapman*

Two other functions have been termed acquisitive and organizational—that is, a model provides a framework for defining, collecting, and ordering significant information. They are also said to have a fertility function, meaning that by systematically ordering and associating significant phenomena, models possess special properties of intellectual stimulation, wringing the maximum information from the phenomena and suggesting generalizations and hypotheses about them. Additionally, models possess a cognitive or heuristic function serving as a device to communicate and disseminate ideas and understandings. Although not taking time to give examples, I wish to note that these general functions are as characteristic of historical farms as of other model types and subtypes.

Nor shall I take time to review the many schemes of classifying these types and subtypes. It is well to remember, however, that every model has its own peculiar built-in set of biases and assumptions that affect its manner of operation, its range of applicability, and the conclusions which it represents or which may be drawn from it. For the time being, I tend to favor a classification developed by Russell Ackoff,[9] for although it lacks some of the abstract subtleties of other typologies, it seems most closely geared. . . to model-functions that relate directly to reality.[10] Historical farms are, to be sure, abstract generalizations about the past, but compared to a mathematical model, for example, their level of abstraction is relatively low. They therefore seem amenable to analysis in terms of Ackoff's typology. And this classification scheme, I believe, should seem more amenable than most to persons who, like myself, have a strong preference for studies minimally removed from lived experience in the empirical world.

Ackoff argues that representations of the real world can be grouped into three general and somewhat overlapping categories: iconic models, analog models, and symbolic models. Each represents a different level of abstraction ranging from relatively unabstract iconic models (photographs, for example) to highly abstract symbolic models (such as a mathematical equation). Iconic models are sometimes called "scale" models. As such, the icon may or may not be composed of the same material as its original. A model barn may be constructed of oak and pine as was its original, but it could be of plastic, and a photograph of a barn is clearly not composed of the same materials. The essential feature of the iconic model is the maintenance of relative proportions among those features of the empirical world deemed relevant for inclusion in model. The scale of the features has been changed to make them more manipulable. But manipulation for purposes other than those suited to iconic models often calls for a transformation to a more abstract medium. Questions of scale may not enter into manipulations of a model where the characteristic of importance is faithful reproduction of the web or structure of relationships found in the original, as in, for example, directions of energy flow between the sub-

systems of a farm. The symbolic model is a transformation of the empirical world for manipulation of even higher abstraction. A model, however, may fit more than one category given the way they have been defined here. The point is that the empirical world needs to be transformed into various generalized and idealized forms to be comprehended; Ackoff's schema is one way to effect that transformation.

Historical farms exhibit many of the strengths and weaknesses of other models. Like any iconic model they exhibit a great richness of detail and complexity of relationships. They embody many of the features of the biophysical and cultural environment of their original and to a degree provide much the same sort of aesthetic and intellectual stimulation available from the original. But, of course, inaccuracies and distortions do limit such stimulation. Take, for example, the question of scale. Scale is important in any model:

> Change of scale must introduce irrelevance and distortion. We are forced to replace living tissue by some inadequate substitute, and sheer change of size may upset the balance of factors in the original. Too small a model of a uranium bomb will fail to explode, too large a reproduction of a housefly will never get off the ground, and the solar system cannot be expected to look like its planetarium model. Inferences from scale model to original are intrinsically precarious and in need of supplementary validation and correction.[11]

A historical farm with 10 x 10 foot demonstration plots for crops critically distorts the processes of planting and harvesting, to say nothing of the existential experience of confronting two acres of rye with a sickle. One of the practices of historical farms and outdoor museums generally, to date, has been to ignore distortions of scale or to assert their lack of significance. But to consider them in terms of iconic models is both revealing and startling. By definition, an accurate iconic model maintains a proportional relationship between all significant magnitudes within the model. If one element is scaled up or down, all other elements must be scaled up or down in the same ratio. In the hypothetical case of a historical farm with a two-acre rye field scaled down to a 10 x 10 foot plot, the farmhouse would become less than a foot square. Surely inaccurate inferences will be drawn from historical farms grossly distorted in scale.

Iconic models are always "likenesses of material objects, systems, or processes, whether real or imaginary, that preserve relative proportions."[12] But physical attributes other than magnitude are of interest as well. We not only want to know the dimensions of a farm wagon, we want to know what kind of metal and wood it was constructed of, their resistance to shock, aesion, moisture, and so on. When we "put a historical farm together" and see it in operation, we may or may not choose to use an original object such as a wagon. But even in the former instance, before long wheels, pole, floor boards, or something else will need replacement. Here, if not sooner, we must face the question of what to replace it with—that is, what sort of model will we make of the original? Will a new wheel hub be of elm, pine, or plastic? This is a question of analogy or analog—the change of medium from original to model. The answer no doubt lies in the purpose for which the model is being made. If the wagon is just to sit around, pine hubs may suffice; but if it is to be worked, pine hubs will lead to inferences like "wagons must have spent a lot of time in the repair shop" or "maybe we chose the wrong material for our model." The number of analogs or ways of representing an original are infinite, but each way has its own peculiar appropriateness or range of applicability.

Analog models are also useful for describing and analyzing the whole array of non-material aspects of any farm, such as family organization and sex roles, religious beliefs, energy flows, and so on. However, I am going to resist talking about those because to do so would add several more pages to a paper already long enough for oral presentation. Nor dare I venture into the abstruse and slippery question of symbolic models in this context, partly for the same reason but also because my thoughts on this topic are still extremely random and nebulous. I do want to close, though, with a few general observations on how thinking about historical farms as models can clarify our understanding of them.

I hope I have established the point that historical farms, whether of the particularizing or typifying type, are approximations of their originals, or more accurately, our generalizations, our hypotheses, and theories about them. Like any model they present "selected" data and are therefore subjective. They must always reflect, to some extent, the particular interests and biases of those constructing them. An economic historian will probably emphasize "making a living," a social historian will be likely to give more emphasis to the question of "lifestyle," and an environmental historian may want to emphasize "landscape transformation."

Like any model they contain "noise"—that is, irrelevancies and distortions. It is some comfort, to me at least, to be able to retort to a super-critic who gleefully uncovers an inaccuracy, "Show me any academician's model of the empirical world that does not contain similar problems!" Not that that relieves me of any responsibility to remove the "noise," to continually "tune up" the

model, as it were. On the contrary, I probably have more responsibility to do so since to think of the historical farm as a model actually makes the job easier. In part this is so because in reading any model one has to observe certain rules or conventions of interpretation. We cannot expect everything of the model that we would of its original. And as more information about a model's original becomes available, the model will need revision. We need not feel troubled by the fact that we didn't get it "just right" the first time; models never are. Nor need we be confused by those who have lived and worked with the first version of the model for a decade or two and have come to treat it as sacrosanct, indeed to consider it the living past. It is only an account of the past, the same as the next model.

Presidential addresses often need revision too, and this one is an exemplar, a model, so to speak, of one with that sort of need. So if you all will excuse me, I should get at it.

Old Sturbridge Village
Sturbridge, Massachusetts

Notes

1. J. H. Hexter, The History Primer (New York: Basic Books, 1971), p. 50. This along with Robert F. Berkhofer, Jr. *A Behavioral Approach to Historical Analysis* (New York: Free Press, 1969). I regard as the two most profound books on historical method to appear in recent decades.
2. Quoted in Hexter, *Primer*, p. 50.
3. John T. Schlebecker and Gale B. Peterson, *Living Historical Farms Handbook* (Washington: Smithsonian Institution Press, 1972), p. 1.
4. Hexter, *Primer*, p. 4.
5. *Ibid*, p. 5.
6. Hugh Skilling, 'An Operational View,' *American Scientist*, 52 (Dec. 1964), p. 388 A.
7. Richard J. Chorley and Peter Haggett, Eds., *Socio-Economic Models in Geography* (London: Methuen: University Paperbacks, 1968), p. 22.
8. *Ibid*., pp. 24-25. The remaining descriptive terms for model functions in this paragraph are adapted from the same source.
9. Russell L. Ackoff, with Shiv K. Gupta and J. Sayer Minas, *Scientific Method: Optimizing Applied Research Decisions* (New York: John Wiley & Sons, 1962), pp. 108-140.
10. David Harvey, *Explanation in Geography* (London: Edward Arnold, 1969), p. 155.
11. Max Black, *Models and Metaphors: Studies in Language and Philosophy* (Ithaca, N.Y.: Cornell University Press, 1962), p. 221.
12. *Ibid*., p. 220.

The Living Historical Farm in North America

New Directions in Research and Interpretation

13

Edward L. Hawes

A professor of history at Sangamon State University in Springfield, Illinois, Edward L. Hawes wrote the first full-scale academic analysis of the living historical farm in this essay published in ALHFAM'S 1976 Annual. His audience was the international open-air museum community, and this paper was later delivered at a congress of agricultural museum officials held in Prague. In it Hawes examines the history and theory underlying living historical farms and discusses their research and their educational, interpretive, and preservation functions. He examines the problems that living historical farms are facing and predicts the directions they may take in the future.

A new phenomenon has appeared in the museum world in North America during the past ten years. It may with some justice be termed a movement, the living historical farm movement. It is quite self-conscious, has various senses of mission, internal disagreements about goals, philosophy, and methods, and differing institutional manifestations. Here and there around North America historical farms representing certain times, places, and cultures are being put into operation with authentic or historically accurate seed and plant stock, livestock, tools, and implements.[1] Researchers and curators are dealing with new problems presented by this type of museum. Interpreters and teachers are using them in innovative ways for conveying comprehensive understandings of the past. Participation is a key element in living museum operations. Tourists, school children, and even researchers are taking part in the processes of the past in order to comprehend rural life more fully. Some farms are independent operations. Some are outgrowths of older open-air or historic house museums. In turn, they have influenced their parent museums in a living-history direction, leading to a replacement of the static, artifact preservation orientation.

This movement is very much a product of the sixties with its emphasis on understanding social and environmental realities, upon participation and innovative education, just as were the sit-ins, the free schools, the calls for participatory democracy, and the community museum. Yet the movement is a very natural out-growth of

the older and very Establishment historic house and open-air museum movements.[2] In this decade the movement might be regarded in part as a manifestation of the nostalgia impulse and the return to various forms of non-political, but still ideological conservatism. Where the movement will go in the future is unclear.

It is time, after ten years of existence, to take a good hard look at the movement. This paper represents an effort to think through what contributions it has made, to consider where the concepts of living history have led and what might be expected in the future. The problem of why few farms have been planned to represent one or another type of agriculture in an industrialized society will be considered at various points.[3] First, there is a brief review of the movement as a whole, its North American organization and its contributions through publication. Then the very fruitful model conceptions, which are being discussed and used, will be appraised and some suggestions offered for future thought. Each of the major functions of museums will be considered—research, curation, interpretation, and education—in turn. Finally, some problem areas will be discussed and promising directions for the future indicated.

Part I: The Living History Farm Movement

Living history may be defined as the re-creation of as much as possible of the totality of the past to give people a deeper sense of historical environmental realities. The traditional museum, indoor or outdoor, is concerned with collections of artifacts and structures. Education and interpretation are secondary to the preserving function. Exhibitions and media are the means of communication.[4] The living museum is more concerned with processes than collections. Interpretation becomes the primary concern and the collection of processes the secondary but very vital function. At best the aim is to involve visitors whether they be tourists, school children, or university students in a "re-creation" of a piece of a whole society in its natural and physical setting. The farm or historic site is a model or a representation of the past, not a literal "re-creation," although the latter word is often used. Rural settings are more amenable to such aims, for there the modern world can be more effectively screened out than it can at the urban site. During working hours, the bounty or paucity of nature, the treatment of the land and of humans living on it, the function of social class and traditional or popular, modernizing culture can become apparent.

It was in the mid-sixties that discussion of the idea of living-history farming began on a serious basis. Marion Clawson of Resources for the Future wrote a brief article for *Agricultural History* in 1965 outlining the possibilities. An informal group in Washington, including John Schlebecker at the Smithsonian Institution, Ernst Christensen at the National Park Service, and Wayne Rasmussen at the Department of Agriculture began moves to give some direction. Schlebecker received support to do a survey of existing resources and the needs for the longer range. The results appeared in a 1967 paper entitled, "The Past in Action: Living Historical Farms." He recommended a national system of farms representing key periods and regions in agricultural development from the beginnings to the present, to be supported by a national association that could offer extension service-type assistance. Embodying the agricultural historians' approach to the past, this survey remains one of the most significant documents of the movement.[5]

This was not just a Washington idea, however. In various localities in North America, people began organizing living historical farms and open-air museums. At Old Sturbridge Village, the Pliny Freeman Farm began its transformation into what remains one of the most historically sound and well-conceived operations in the country. In Des Moines, Iowa, a group began developing three historical farms, one portraying pioneer life, a second, that of the late nineteenth century and a third, the farm of the future.

A symposium on "American Agriculture, 1790-1840," planned by Darwin Kelsey and Wayne Rasmussen at Old Sturbridge Village in eastern Massachusetts in September 1970, was the organizing focus for the North American association. Two papers were presented that have become basic reading for anyone interested in historic farming. Schlebecker covered some of the kinds of thinking necessary to initiate and develop living historical farms. Kelsey reviewed the history and concepts of open-air museums, the conceptual problems involved in farm

museums, and the scholarly resources available to assist the researcher. It was at this symposium that the Association for Living Historical Farms and Agricultural Museums was founded. The first issue of its *Bulletin* was published in December of that year.[6]

The first annual conference of ALHFAM, as it has become known, was at Cooperstown, New York, in June of 1972. From all over North America people came to tell of their projects. Some represented agricultural museums, others, folk-life museums, and some, living historical farms, which were at that time mostly in the planning stages. The next year's conference was in Iowa, with sessions in conjunction with the Agricultural History Society meeting in Ames. There was a visit to Des Moines where the group led by William G. Murray had begun the pioneer farm operation. Several papers of use to practical farm development were presented, including one on siting from the perspective of a historical geographer.[7] By this time two additional operations that are focused upon in this paper had begun. The Colonial Pennsylvania Plantation moved from the planning stages into operation with major funding from the state Bicentennial Commission. The Clayville Rural Life Center in Illinois began a slow transition from a historical house museum and craft center toward a living-history community of the 1850s by means of living-history education and research programs carried out by university students and community residents.[8]

In 1974 the association met in Davis, California. The papers presented there appeared in the first Annual Proceedings. One of the most important articles was by Darwin Kelsey in the form of his presidential address in which he analyzed the conception of the living historical farm as a model of the past. Jay Anderson and Roger Welsch presented interrelated papers discussing foodways and other operation programs. Their concern was to show how such programs could get at three themes: historical realities, the cultural ecology of the family, and alternative technologies. Peter Cousins did a groundbreaking work on collection research and development.[9]

The membership in ALHFAM still represents that healthy diversity apparent at the 1972 Cooperstown meeting. Among the individual members are museum professionals from indoor and outdoor museums and from living historical farms. There are academic people including professors of social and environmental history, folklife, botany, agricultural history, and even classical studies. Museum amateurs form another group with a range of backgrounds and interests.[10] The institutional membership represents the configuration of the movement as a whole. A recent survey of living-history farms and open-air museums as resources for scholars and students of environmental history indicates that there are four types of institutions involved in presenting and re-creating rural life: the traditional museums of agriculture or folklife, the open-air museums, the living history farms, and the community re-creations.[11]

1. The traditional museums of agriculture or folk culture collect, preserve, and exhibit the artifacts of rural life, indoors. In all likelihood there are more agricultural than folklife museums in North America. Those with an interest in folklife have drawn their inspiration from the Scandinavian open-air museums rather than the more traditional indoor ethnological museums of southern and central Europe. There are major collections of agricultural tools and implements at the Canadian National Museum in Ottawa, the Smithsonian Institution in Washington, D.C., and the Greenfield Village and Henry Ford Museum in Dearborn, Michigan. Most outdoor museums have collections of artifacts used in their locality or region. And there is that host of private collectors, ordinary people, who are nostalgic about the rural past and gather at countless auctions the machines and tools that industrialization brought to American and Canadian farms from the 1870s on. These include the steam threshing "buffs," as they are called, who carefully restore and maintain the equipment that began to bring the factory, with its division of labor and high capitalization, to the field. Through their work the boundary of the static and the living-history collection is crossed. This illustrates one of the points that will be returned to below, that static and living-history collections are not mutually exclusive categories.

2. Open-air museums collect historic structures, household implements and furniture, and farm and craft equipment and attempt to create a context in which the objects make sense together. Most embody the folklife concept and seek to preserve the physical remnants of regional or ethnic cultures and to demonstrate the processes of production in a pre-industrialized society. Some open-air museums are based on rural or agricultural concepts. The "pioneer period" is the one often chosen, the museum consisting of log cabin, log barn, and a few outbuildings with some of the necessary implements. Often the selection of the items in the collections, including the buildings, was not done on the basis of scholarly research. Rather, it was the enthusiasm of local collectors or of a single individual, sometimes (but not always) men and women of wealth, who wanted to preserve the elements of ordinary life. Some open-air museums have living-history demonstrations of farm operations or household tasks, or maintain small demonstration plots of crops of some livestock. But there is no attempt to represent a farming system or to give a comprehensive sense of the processes of rural life.[12]

3. At living historical farms, artifacts, reproductions, living things, and farm and household processes form the collections. Many are based on well-conceived research programs, which form a sound basis for development. Carefully thought through interpretive and educational programs bring them to life. The Pliny Freeman Farm at Old Sturbridge Village in Massachusetts is one of the best examples, and at the Colonial Pennsylvania Plantation near Philadelphia, the concept of experimental history is being developed. The people there have found that little is known about the realities of eighteenth-century farming, gardening, food preparation, and preservation. They are working out methods to test what is written in the sources, and to recover, at least hypothetically, what has been lost.

4. Community re-creations are efforts to bring alive rural social environments, be they embodied in hamlet, village or dispersed settlement. They employ a variety of living-history techniques to give the sense of the ongoing lives of rural people. One of the best is Old Sturbridge Village itself.

Part II: Museums as Models

Some of the most useful and important concepts to emerge in the movement cluster around the farm and the open-air museum as models. In an effort to bring greater clarity to discussions of what living historical farms were and ought to be, Darwin Kelsey introduced the central concept in his presidential address in 1974. He defined farms as "patterned, coherent accounts of the past, intended to be true, which involve human intention, doing, and suffering. They are not the past as such."[13] They are simplified and generalized. To put this in the historian's terms, living-history museums are four dimensional interpretations of the past in which time, space, and culture are represented. Thus they can be "read" and critiqued as any historical interpretation can be.

In planning and constructing the model, a selection of what are commonly termed "facts" and a synthesizing of information to give the most accurate account of the past is necessary. Hypotheses may be formed about missing elements, such as the forms of harrows and their use, the handling of livestock or the economic impact of market changes on the farm. This may lead to a definition of the museum as a place for replicative archaeology and history. Through experiment, those aspects of life that are not adequately detailed in the sources may be "recovered" or, at least, informed estimates of their natures may be made. Revisions in the model should be possible as new knowledge is uncovered. To use Richard Candee's word, "editing" of the site and its programs is possible if the museum is properly designed.[14] Indeed, it is necessary if the museum is going to be a valid historical synthesis.

These remarks give some hints of the functions of the model conceptions that will be discussed below. They have very tangible applications in all areas of museum development and operation. Basically there are two model schemes which are of use. The first relates directly to the actual historical house, farmstead, operating historical farm, or open-air museum as a model of the past. It assists in the definition and redefinition of the facilities and the programs and in establishing and holding onto the overall identity of the museum. The concepts are becoming part of the vocabulary of the museum people in the living-history movement, but the specific model scheme presented here is my own. In this scheme there are two sets of alternative possibilities for representation of the past. The museum may be a model of a particular farm or way of life of a historical figure deemed noteworthy, or, on the other hand, it may be a model of what was typical in the locality at a given time or in a certain period. In the other set, the museum, on the other hand, may be a full-scale representation or one with some parts accurately scaled to each other, an iconic model or one with significant iconic elements. On the other hand, the model may symbolize aspects of the past. This conceptual scheme may be best understood if the two sets of terms are pictured at the ends of two intersecting continua. On the horizontal axis at the left is the particular model, at the right, the pure typical model. On the vertical axis at the top is the pure iconic model, at the bottom, the symbolizing one.

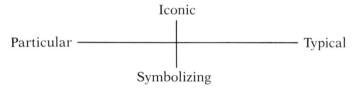

For example, the farm planned on land once owned by Oliver Kelley in Minnesota, the founder of the Grange, is an example of a particular farm. Kelsey, in his address, gave his own examples and concluded that "the farm is to be made a historical farm because it is that particular farm and no other."[15] The typical farm represents the life of a family or other social unit in a certain time and place in its natural and socio-cultural setting. Discovering the typical requires collaboration of folklife scholars, historical geographers, social, agricultural and environmental historians, and others using agreed-upon methodologies and analytical frameworks. In my opinion, the Pliny Freeman Farm at Old Sturbridge is an excellent example, attempting "to give an accounting," as Kelsey says in conversations, of the life of a tradition-oriented New England family on a small farm in the 1830s after the children have grown up and left. Most farms will fall some place along the continuum. Colonial Pennsylvania Plantation represents a particular farm in the 1770s, but it is one that was probably typical of others in the region.

Then there is the other axis with a continuum ranging from an iconic model to a symbolizing one. Here is where I definitely depart from Kelsey's scheme presented in his presidential address in 1974. Iconic models directly represent material, tangible reality on different scales. "The essential feature of the iconic model is the maintenance of the relative proportions among those features of the empirical world deemed relevant for inclusion in the model," declared Kelsey.[16] This much is agreed. So, too, is the fact that several interrelated iconic models may be involved on a single historical farm or open-air museum. The livestock and fields may be on one scale, the garden and foodways program on another, and finally the natural environment and the needs for fuel, food, and building material on another. It is important to keep this in mind in planning and operating facilities and in developing interpretive and educational programs.

At the other end of the axis is the "symbolizing" model. The term "symbolic" will be reserved for the second model scheme and will have much less wide applicability than Kelsey suggests. Webster's Collegiate Dictionary defines *symbol* as, "That which suggests something else by reason of relationship, association, convention, etc., especially a visible sign of something invisible, as an idea, a quality." To these invisibles could be added social class, a pattern in the use of land, a whole folk culture, or an ecosystem. The farm as a symbolizing model suggests intangibles; but as a physical space cannot represent them in scale or even necessarily in clear relationship. Technological progress can be suggested as it is at the Des Moines, Iowa, Living History Farms. Patriotism can be symbolized at George Washington's Birthplace in Virginia or Abraham Lincoln's Boyhood Home in southern Indiana. Yet these farms are typical of those of certain social classes and regional cultures. Their prime purpose, however, is to sanctify national myths. Farms may be suggestive in other ways, too. So they are primarily symbolizing models of reality. Elements of farms may symbolize functional or economic interrelationships that cannot be done in scale. Fields may not be in scale, and the farm understocked for various reasons. Limitations of land, labor, and financial resources may prevent this. The farming system may be said to symbolize the realities, rather than represent them with a scale model.

The second model scheme uses the categories suggested by Kelsey, the iconic, analogic and symbolic, but more in the original context of meaning from which the terms were derived, from systems analysis and operations research. This scheme is useful for site and program planning, for research design and interpretive goal setting. Each of these categories represents a completely different order of abstraction. Each has different functions. There is no continuum here.

In the true iconically modeled farm, the land area sown to different crops and the livestock will be in relative proportion. The garden will be designed to yield enough to feed the hypothetical family living on the farm. The grains produced will be adequate for what is decided to be typical in terms of the amount needed for fodder, food and marketing. The farm will have crops and livestock which have the appropriate scale to provide food, fuel, and building material. The farming systems and the environmental systems are accurately scaled. As such the farm setting can be used for serious research purposes. Experimental history becomes possible. At present there is no farm in North America that has reached this point, but the Colonial Pennsylvania Plantation is on the way.

The next model category is the analogic. Some dimensions of life are better presented in a more abstract fashion. "Questions of scale may not enter into manipulations of a model where the characteristic of importance is faithful reproduction of the web or structure of relationships found in the original, as in for example, the directions of energy flow between the subsystems of a farm." Kelsey, in saying this, seemingly implied that the farm itself could be an analogic model.[17] Not so, for there must be a transformation of properties to a higher level of abstraction in this model. Other purposes are served than physical representation of properties. Social class, traditional culture, a value system, and an ecosystem may be symbolized on a farm in some tangible way. Social class may have a material embodiment as it does at Sturbridge in the contrast of Salem Towne's house and farmstead with the Pliny Freeman farm. The life and culture of the innovative gentleman farmer and the traditional small farmer are symbolized. But the houses and barns do not serve as analogic models, rather as physically symbolizing models.

The analogic model is one in which the properties are transformed, but the essential relationships are portrayed. The two dimensional chart or graph can indicate the structure of relationships in social class, the assemblage of a folk, popular, or elite culture, or the elements of an ecosystem. Museum exhibits may be used to convey these models. So may interpretive programs, and for the living historical farm, these are the most important mode. The building system, the farming system, and the ecosystem do not communicate themselves to the ordinary visitor. The spoken act is necessary to convey the meaning. The designed interpretive programs are the analogic models of reality. There is a transformation of properties, an abstraction from the real world of the improver and lower class farmer, to a planned event. It is through the interpretive or educational programs that the essential structure of relationships making up social class, traditional culture, and value systems and ecosystems can be represented.

Finally, there is the level of abstraction represented in a symbolic model, as the operations researchers and systems analysts use the term. The farm itself can never be such, nor can the interpretive programs. "Mathematical

Old Sturbridge Village's meetinghouse Common. Recreating historic space in an outdoor agricultural museum.—*Photo: Robert S. Arnold, Old Sturbridge Village*

equations are symbolic models," says Ackoff, one of Kelsey's sources of inspiration.[8] It is easily manipulated, for it is a model in which the properties of the thing represented are expressed symbolically. This kind of model is never seen by the public. It is a research model and serves to study farm inputs and outputs, energy flows, market relationships, structural relationships in elements of material culture, and other abstracts. Base line data produced at the farm from the elements that are iconically modeled can be put into the symbolic model, and variations introduced to see what might occur under various conditions. Conceivably a computer simulation game could be prepared to involve the participant in analysis of farming systems, ecosystems, social systems, and cultural change. Such would be useful to students for learning quantitative historical and environmental analysis, to interpreters for training, and might be of some interest to the traveling public.

Part III: Research and the Model Concepts

The two most creative concepts in terms of actual impact on research and planning at this point are those of the typical farm and iconic scale model. These provide standards for evaluation and constitute challenges to most living museums, which have created symbolizing models without being aware that they were doing so. I want to examine the work at the three institutions already mentioned where these concepts are very much discussed and are leading research plans in clear directions, Sturbridge, Colonial Pennsylvania, and Clayville. These are institutions where the search for the typical and the scale models, the questions of what are the appropriate farm structures, the proper amounts of land, crops, and livestocks, and the typical inventory of farm tools and implements and household goods are seen as vital. They are also places where values, social class, traditional and popular culture, and the natural environment are all concerns. These outdoor museums will be considered chronologically to give an idea of how living-history farms give an accounting of the coming of industrialized society and the effect on farming.

The first to be considered from this standpoint is Colonial Pennsylvania Plantation. The parent organization is the Bishop Mill Historical Institute, which started with some basic givens in the terms of structures on site. There is the house built by the Pratt family over a one-hundred-year period from 1720 on, a typical stone traditional structure built in a folk form that goes back to Yorkshire. A stone cabin, perhaps the first structure on the site, a spring house with nineteenth-century modifications, a wagon barn, and the remains of a modern barn constituted the rest of the physical givens. The decade of winning national independence for what became the United States, the 1770s was chosen as the period for representation. Aside from Bicentennial considerations, it is a time that people in eastern Pennsylvania regard as most significant for so many of the remembered Revolutionary events took place in the area. However, the story is usually told only in terms either of Great Men, or, if ordinary people are focused upon, of their connection with Great Events such as the winter at Valley Forge. The organizers of the plantation wanted to "present to the public the point of view that human history is made up of the daily lives of people and that the so-called great men, great ideas, and great events are significant only to the degree to which they affect the every day," as Ross Fullam put it.[19] Thus the concept of the typical is approached directly and consciously.

It was around these physical structures that the developers have shaped their efforts. The post-1820 additions to the house were removed and archaeological work was done concurrently. A well, hidden by a porch, was excavated. A reconstructed kitchen of the 1770s was set up in the 1820 portion, using the great walk-in fireplace and the slate floor, which had been uncovered. The spring house and the stone cabin were taken back to the appearance it was assumed they had in the Revolutionary decade. The wagon shed is now in the process of restoration and reconstruction. As these developments proceeded, a garden was planted and the first steps taken toward implementing the concept of experimental history. The plantation was and is seen as an experimental station.[20] The kitchen and the garden have been tied together in an interpretive program that emphasizes that the details of ordinary life have to be recaptured by cumulative research in the field since the written sources are not sufficient.

The concept of the typical and of scale models as interrelating elements are central in the minds of researchers and interpreters. The tax list of the local township, Edgemont, in 1774, is serving as one of the key archival resources. The middle third of the farms listed, twelve in all, has been chosen as the determinant. The farm sizes in this group ranged from one hundred to one hundred and fifty acres. These farms each had two or three horses and three or four cows.[21] Using this data, the intention is to move toward an accurately scaled farm in which the inputs and outputs of kitchen, garden, livestock, and field will be accurately interrelated, so that hypotheses and eventually perhaps some conclusions can be drawn about life in the late eighteenth century in Pennsylvania.

Our second example, moving into the early phases of industrialization, is Old Sturbridge Village. It started with some farm buildings moved in from various parts of New England. In 1968, Darwin Kelsey proposed setting up an operating farm of the first decade of the nineteenth century. At first, it was seen as only indirectly relating to the village, which portrayed a fifty-year period from 1790 to 1840. The research carried out for this farm as a functioning unit was thorough. Out of it came decisions to obtain a pair of Durham oxen and to back-breed both to common "dunghill fowl," and to sheep yielding two pounds of wool per year. The fields were organized on the basis of research, which showed the relationships of land, crop, and livestock. Rye and oats were found to have been commonly undersown with clover and timothy. Potatoes and corn were determined to be included also in the usual rotation. In setting up the operating farm, there was an effort to maintain the correct scale of these elements of the farming system, including permanent meadow and pasture.[22]

Despite the fact that the village is one of the oldest open-air museums in the country, it has not stood still. The impact of the research for the farm and the impact of the unit itself as an operating entity reached to the village proper. Research led to changes in the conception of the village "green" to one of a functioning commons, which was also the nodule of a transport network. A survey of commons in paintings and in printed descriptions showed them to be irregularly shaped and cut by roads connecting the chief institutions, the bank and general store with the outside world. The staff began to think about representing a single decade, the 1830s, rather than the whole fifty-year period. This in turn had an effect on the researchers involved with the farm.

It was in this context that Caroline Sloat of the Research Department did work, which is of particular interest methodologically. She started with several givens. The Freeman Farm was to typify an ordinary small unit in the 1830s on which lived a man and woman whose children had grown up and moved elsewhere. The farm was about a hundred acres. For the children to have gone meant that the marriage had to have taken place between 1795 and 1805. These assumptions constituted the basic profile. The goal was to find inventories of farms and household of people who fit this profile. The method was as follows: Published vital statistics on births, deaths, and marriages in the county in which the village is located and two neighboring ones were searched. From these, a list of heads of households who died from 1830 to 1835 and who conformed to the profile was drawn up. Then the County Probate Registries were searched to determine for which of these typical people probate records were available. The estates of twenty-six farmers were found and transcribed. Lists to enable comparisons category by category were set up. If 60 percent of the estates listed an item, it was assumed to be typical.

The results were fascinating. It was apparent that people in the profile were not innovators, but trusted more traditional tools and methods. This general conclusion and the analysis of the occurrence of certain items had consequences. The interior of the farmhouse was drastically simplified. The pewter went out and so did the curtains. The variety of lighting devices was reduced considerably. The Bible was removed, for only five of the farms had them. Looms were not important in the farm economy of the 1830s yet they were found in 56 percent of the inventories. These were assumed to have been items stored in the attics by this time. Spinning wheels were apparently still common since 84 percent of the households had them, and cards were often found. But it is thought that, given the extent of the industrialization of carding and spinning, these also were attic items. The

furniture chosen was largely of the period when the couple was married. The message was to be that these people had to work hard to keep going, that they were not burdened down with superfluous things. Today the Freeman farmhouse represents the "publication" of this research. The farm inventory established earlier from printed sources was found through the research to have been reasonably accurate. Few of these farmers had any of the modern implements. The inventories contain only one "cast iron" plow and one "patent" plow.[23]

Old Sturbridge is engaged presently in research and planning for a second community, a textile mill village of the early nineteenth century. This will have a farm associated with a tavern, a common pattern. A field and archive research project to determine what were typical barn forms in the area is underway as part of this effort. In the light of this work, the Freeman Barn is now felt to be somewhat inaccurate. Tax records of the town of Brookfield for 1778 and 1816 have been consulted. They reveal ground dimensions of buildings and brief descriptions of the farms. No locations or assessments were included, unfortunately. The data on dimensions will be compared with the results from field work in the form of measured drawings and photographs. The work is being carried out by Frank White of the curatorial department and John Mott of the research department. They have found that the end-opening barn occurred in a much wider area than it was thought to by Henry Glassie, the major folklife scholar interested in comparative structural forms. Most of the barns, they discovered to their surprise, had full-length manure cellars. The popular culture of agricultural innovation in the early nineteenth century encouraged the construction of such barns, but the origins were folk. This research work has led the town men to question the appropriateness of the Freeman barn. It may be too rectangular. Further it has no manure cellar, is made of sawn timbers, and was framed for a tracked door.[24] Thus, some more editing of the Freeman farm is likely in the future.

Colonial Pennsylvania Plantation is "a farm in the making," as its staff very creatively puts it. Old Sturbridge is a living museum in the process of editing itself on the basis of research. The 1850 community at the Clayville Rural Life Center in Illinois with which I am associated is in the planning stage. But the research directed toward discovering the typical has already produced some significant evidence. The questions being raised and the methods under development for answering them are important. The basic aim is to re-create the lives of people who came to central Illinois in the three cultural streams, one from New England, a second from Pennsylvania and New Jersey, and a third from the South. The only original on-site structure is an inn built in the 1820s by a family from New Jersey. Thus, the search for the typical and the proper scales is not bound by many existing structures or assumptions. The inn will be the conceptual center of the operation, for it was the economic and social link with the outside world. To convey the essential givens reviewed below, the natural environment, the traditional cultures brought by people who settled the central Midwest, the new popular culture of agricultural innovation, and the character of change, two farms and some rural services like churches and schools are planned. One farm will show the life of people from the Northern regions: the other, the life of those with Southern backgrounds. On each, the research now indicates that a mix of traditional and innovative ways should be represented.

The inn of the 1820s is one physical given. The topography of the area is another, and research has revealed that it provides the range of typical land forms of central Illinois. It provides the perfect foundation for reconstructing the natural environment of woodland and prairie, which were both so important to early settlers. It is possible to reconstruct an analogic model of the boundaries of the two and of the varieties of trees in the woods and their density. The federal surveyors who laid out the grid pattern on the Midwest land were required to keep notebooks recording where they found the prairie-woodland border, what kinds of trees they saw on the section lines and their location. These records make it possible to reconstruct on paper the environment at the time of settlement anywhere in Illinois.[25]

The second major given, which research reveals, is the traditional or folk culture. Systematic research in the federal manuscript population census of 1850 verifies the origins and supports the common idea that the earliest settlers came from the South. However, the work has raised questions about how many of these people really bore the Southern culture patterns. The parents of some came from the Mid-Atlantic area, probably carrying with them Pennsylvania-German or Scots-Irish patterns. The field study of house and farm building forms has not proceeded far enough to permit sound hypothesizing.

The third given is the popular culture of agricultural innovation, which in the Midwest blossomed forth in the 1840s and 1850s. This is the time when the beginnings of industrialization of agricultural implements made themselves felt. Journals such as the *Prairie Farmer*, which began in 1841 and is still published and regarded as a progressive farm publication, the *Transactions of the State Agricultural Society*, which appeared first in 1853, and local newspapers all indicate that new ideas about crops, implements, and livestock breeding were being discussed. Advertisements for drills, reapers, and threshers and articles reporting on field trials are to be found. So are numerous ones on implements and tools requiring less capital to purchase or which could be made on the farm. Other articles tell how to improve cattle and sheep, how to best raise corn and wheat, the proper way to garden and to run the household. This popular culture will be represented in various ways at the center, both in the collections and in the interpretive program.

The fourth given is social and natural environmental change that resulted from the interaction of these factors. A common idea historians had was that the Southerners settled first and occupied the woodlands for which they had a natural affinity, and that the Northerners, from New England in particular, settled the prairies, which they had the energy and ability to bring into agricultural use.[26] The research indicates that the settlement of the Clayville area first occurred along the prairie-woodlands along the streams. Finally, there were the latecomers who had to settle the prairies, in part, because nothing else was left. Plenty of Southerners used the prairies as natural pasture, men like James Brown, an early cattleman from Kentucky who was famed locally for introducing Shorthorns.[27] The old idea that Southerners were less inclined toward innovation than the Northerners is very suspect. There were plenty of Southerners among the premium winners at the state and county fairs and among the writers of articles on innovation.

To bring all of these givens into focus, the decade of the 1850s has been chosen. The traditional cultures were still very much present, but the popular culture of agricultural innovation had begun to interact with and transform them. It was a time of transition, for the pioneer days of the 1820s and 1830s were over, but farming was not yet the fully commercial activity it became by the 1870s. The search for the typical and the scaled relationship is underway. There was a wide range of farm sizes and ways of organizing production. Utilizing the manuscript population and agricultural censuses, research is in progress to investigate the size of livestock holdings, amounts of crops, areas of origin, and the relationships existing between these. These sources are being used also to investigate how common it was to have indwelling farm laborers or domestics, either related to the family or not, the incidence of literacy, the relationship of these patterns to region of origin, and to other questions.

Here further attention is necessary to experimental history as a research mode at living historical farms. At Colonial Pennsylvania, it is an operating and interpretive mode, while it is an idea discussed by staff people at Old Sturbridge and a planned-for eventuality at Clayville. As yet there are no agreed-upon methodologies, primary questions to consider, or hypotheses entertained. No farm yet exists that is a pure iconic model, and no researchers have begun to use the concepts of the analogic or symbolic model. There is a long way to go before there is material for a publishable collection of the sort presented in John Coles' book *Archeology by Experiment*.[28]

But there is great promise in this area. At Colonial Pennsylvania experimental work is going on in the areas of food production and preservation and in farming. This will be useful largely in yielding the questions that should be asked and as a basis for developing methodologies. A recording system to permit study of the relationship of foods, their preservation, and conditions in the springhouse is in the early stages of development. An effort is being made to keep track of food cooked, preserved, and consumed by the hypothetical farm family and the actual interpreters. It is expected that the garden will be developed to the point where it can supply both the hypothetical and the real needs. The historical farmers are experimenting with plowing and cultivation times to solve the problem of weeds, which come at different seasons and with the changing soil conditions related to the weather.[29] At both the plantation and Clayville it is hoped that methods will be developed to keep close track of farm and household inputs and outputs, productivity, and energy flows. At the latter, experimental programs will hopefully be set up to yield base line data on low-energy farming and the impact of 1850 land use.

It remains to be seen how many of these intentions and plans will be realized. Even if they are, serious problems will have to be faced. The basic procedural rules in Cole's book will need revision for living-history experiments. The character of the environment at the period and place will have to be carefully determined, and the appropriate allowances made for it in analogic and symbolic modeling. Many food resources from the wild will have been lost. Soil conditions and the character of crops and livestock even phenotypically accurate may have changed so much that nutritional studies will suffer. The ways in which researchers show results will have to be explored. Modern skills, both physical and mental, which the people of the period and place did not have must be allowed for, as well as the historical manual skills, which the modern researcher can only acquire with time and practice.[30]

Part IV: Living History Collections

Just as development of a living-history farm requires the enlargement of the scope, methods, and resources in research, so does it necessitate different approaches to collection formation than those of the traditional museum. The concept of what is included in the collections has widened significantly. New methods of control and registration have to be worked out. The design of the collections and the assembling of them require close work with researchers and interpreters, maintenance people, and historic farmers. Collection development itself is becoming a process of some scientific importance for the future.

People involved in living museum work generally, and farm development specifically, are finding that distinctions need to be made between two types of collections: the static and the living. The former consists of artifacts such as authentic tools, implements, and machines used in production and living, hand-made and machine-made objects such as textiles, ceramics, and furniture. These are, of course, the standard concerns of the indoor museum. Then there are also the historic structures, houses, barns, stables, outhouses, factories, and craft shops, which are the concern of the traditional open-air museum. All of these objects must be preserved or conserved, so that original examples survive for the future.

The other type of collection, the living one, includes the historically validated seed and plant stock, the old breeds of livestock, the raw materials for home and industrial craft production, and for factory production. Reproductions of tools, implements, machines, and structures come within this type of collection. These may be freely used, for they can be replaced.

In the living museum, the processes that are often used to produce food, shelter, warmth, light, places to sit, sleep, work, and play are themselves parts of the collections. Insofar as they are recorded by various media on film, tape, or the printed page from traditional or popular culture contexts, they form part of the static collections. As they are carried out either by people who learned the processes in the social context in which they were done, or by specially trained interpreters, they belong to the living-history collections. The skills, knowledge, and behaviors of the reproducers become an important resource. This may lead to a shift upward in the status of interpreters and perhaps their pay, for they are living process repositories themselves.

I suspect that before this happens there may be an even more thorough-going shift in the concept of what is in the province of the living museum to collect and reproduce. Among professionals involved in designing and operating historical farms, signs of this are emerging. The farm as a whole is seen as a collection. The next step is easy to make conceptually, but difficult to make practically—that is, to make the historic landscape part of the collection. In addition, the more intangible, but pressingly real, even at times oppressively real, aspects of traditional culture, social class, and culture, values, and behavior patterns common to whole groups are being thought of by a few as part of the "collection" of the museum.

It may be found useful to distinguish between three categories of artifacts. Micro-artifacts are the tools, machines, and produced goods usually included under the term "artifacts." Single rural or urban structures could be included, also. The next level, that of macro-artifacts, includes whole farms, urban neighborhoods, and insofar as they have been shaped by humans, ecosystems and landscapes. Finally, the intangible folk and elite traditional cultures, social class, and culture may be regarded as meta-artifacts.[31] The advantage of this scheme is that it leads to thinking about collections in the broad terms necessary if living-history museums are to make serious scholarly contributions. Holistic thinking and planning is rendered much more likely. The phrases become rather awkward when the concept of reproductions is brought in. The question then arises of whether we should speak of micro-artifactual reproductions and so on.

It is important not to become lost in definitional games. Living-history museums have to deal with additional and very different sorts of collections than the traditional museum. Neither type, the static nor the living, can be ignored. The micro-artifact collections serve as the models, the bases for the reproductions used in process re-creation. Either the living museum must have access to a good collection of artifacts or it must assemble its own. At least it should form a collection on paper; that is, on the basis of various sources, a written and pictorial collection of the common types of tools or implements should be put together by researchers. This will provide guidelines for artifact acquisition, and should there be no examples discovered, it will give a basis for accurate reproductions.

During the period of industrialized production of agricultural tools and implements, these tasks are relatively easy—that is for the years since 1840. In the Midwest for instance, a prototype collection of factory-made horse drawn equipment for the later nineteenth century can be assembled by attending farm auctions. Implements of the 1850s are next to impossible to find, but the published record is very complete, so a paper collection can be put together to guide the reproduction process. A collection of traditional tools and implements is much harder to assemble either in the form of artifacts or of a paper collection. Wooden parts rot away; pictures are few and far between, and not necessarily accurate; estate inventories contain only vague descriptions. Traditional forms used today may have evolved considerably from their character in the period and place chosen for the farm or community re-creation.[32]

Resources in terms of money and skilled craftspeople are limited, so that even the best farms have not done what they should do in these areas. Sturbridge has a collection of agricultural implements made or used before 1840. It dates back to the early days of the museum in the late 1940s and has not been significantly augmented since then. Very few factory-made implements are included. Colonial Pennsylvania Plantation has not yet produced an implement and tool profile on paper for the 1770s. It has no type agricultural or household collections but only the artifacts and reproductions used on the farm, in the garden or the household.[33]

Seed and plant stock constitute collections that the living museum must assemble also. Effort is underway at several museums to recover and preserve historic varieties of vegetables, field crops, and fruit trees. Old Sturbridge started a living archive of apple trees common in the early nineteenth century, taking over one of the functions of the Worcester County Historical Society that was threatened by urbanization. At the National Colonial Farm in Maryland important work has been done in recovery and preservation of old varieties of corn. At Clayville, researchers went through three mid-nineteenth century sources to assemble a list of vegetables that are still available by name from seed companies. There is no systematic effort in North America to coordinate the preservation and recovery efforts. The National Seed Storage Laboratory in Fort Collins, Colorado, maintains a seed bank, which contains old varieties. A data retrieval system to enable quick determination of holdings is in the design stage, but going along

with this must be the assembling of a complete listing of historic varieties used in North America as a guideline for acquisition. The laboratory is a passive archive; it does not undertake collection on its own. There is no policy formulated as to the varieties it needs to collect. Moreover, it does not preserve plant stock.[34]

At present in the area of livestock collections, there is nothing comparable to the Rare Breeds Farm Parks in Britain. At Sturbridge, however, very significant work in backbreeding chickens and sheep is going on. Through research in paintings and written sources, it was discovered the "common dunghill fowl" of the early nineteenth century had characteristics similar to several recognized modern breeds. These included Dominiques, a breed that appeared in New England in the early nineteenth century and evolved into the Barred Plymouth Rocks; the Dorkings, both Red and Silver Grey types identifiable in Roman sources; and the Speckled Sussex. These have been allowed to cross breed indiscriminantly, and the result, Darwin Kelsey believes, is a generalized type of chicken that appears like those of the early part of the last century.[35]

The work on sheep is of potentially greater significance. The sources give weights of average fleeces and carcasses and describe other characteristics, giving rise to an image of a common sheep yielding only two to three pounds of wool per year plus meat. Kelsey decided that Wiltshires and Dorsets were the modern breeds that most clearly carried the characteristics sought. Careful breeding, he thought, would lead to a more generalized low yield sheep. The village was able to obtain three Wiltshires, one ram and two ewes, from Australia, and several Dorsets from New England and New York. The breeding has been controlled, so that now the lambs closely approach the desired phenotype. Some research is being done to determine just how accurate the "reproduction" sheep are. Wool samples are being analyzed and compared with samples from historic textiles. Skeletons will be compared with a type collection obtained through archaeological work in New England.[36]

These efforts toward recovery and preservation of historic seed and plant stock and livestock may be of great significance for the future. With the development and introduction of high yield hybrids and specialized livestock, genetic variability is being lost. Older varieties, well-adapted to local environments, are being replaced or have utterly disappeared except as relics in a few out-of-the-way areas. The hybrids require high fertilizer inputs and relatively stable climatic conditions. The specialized breeds cannot thrive on poor pasturage and fodder. Modern farming with chemical fertilizers and fossil-fuel-driven machines requires high inputs of technological energy, which is based on non-replaceable sources. As these are limited either by being exhausted or rendered less accessible by political changes, or as shifts in the climate occur, productivity under modern farming would suffer. Older forms of stock, plant or animal, would therefore be boons since they do not need the inputs on a large scale, if at all. The Sturbridge sheep can subsist on poor pasture without feed supplements. The older Devons are multipurpose meat and milk stock and also do not require the costly inputs of technologized farming. Older open-pollinated varieties of maize do well under a variety of conditions. North Americans may well find the resources of living historical farms of importance in survival in the future.

Part V: Interpretation in Living Museums

Enlarging the conception of what constitutes the collections is not the end of the redefinition of the museum that comes with living history. The word "collections" still implies a fragmented approach to historic realities, even if one thinks of macro-artifacts and re-creations of historic farms and landscapes. It is in the operating and interpretive programs that the past comes to life. The iconic and analogic models attain their greatest rele-

vance in this area. Here is where the historic whole comes together. The past meets present and transactions of tremendous significance can be expected if programs are properly designed. There is a need to examine some of the implications of the living-history conceptions for operations, interpretation, and education.

First of all, the boundary between operations and interpretation tends to be erased in the living-history museum. Interpretation is not simply carried out by the spoken word. The interpreter is the key person in bringing the past alive. He or she does activities common in a particular time, place, and culture. The interpreter as farmer drives the team and manipulates the plow. The housewife for the day cooks typical meals, does the food preservation tasks appropriate to season, and works for a time in the garden. At most farms there is not a separate group of operations people who create the illusion of the past and another group who talk about it. These

The Pliney Freeman Farm at Old Sturbridge Village: the first successful living history farm in the United States.—*Photo: Robert S. Arnold, Old Sturbridge Village*

facts are what make interpretation so central in living history. On the historical farm, the people working are part of the museum. They know the processes and how to communicate them to the public. Without them the museum would die.

Since the interpreter is so vital, training programs are recognized as of great importance. At Sturbridge, much time and effort is devoted to preparation of materials and methods to give initial training to interpreters and then to improve continually their knowledge and skills. There is a three-day orientation for all new people. Part of the time is spent talking with researchers, curators, and the major assistants in the interpretation department. Then whether they will be placed eventually on the farm, in the village, or in one of the craft shops, they all spend several days at the Freeman place, working in an apprenticeship capacity. Familiarity with farm life is recognized as necessary for all. To provide on-going training, a system of "lead interpreters" has been set up for the farm and other sites. Four days a week, these full-time people do costumed interpretation. The fifth day they are expected to do research, interpretive planning, and training of other interpreters who are working full- or part-time in their area.[37]

The living-history museum gives the opportunity for new interpretive techniques. The traditional museum depends upon guides who describe objects and activities or upon demonstrators who show craft processes and household activities. The sense of the interrelationships between these and other aspects of life is missing. There are only fragments of reality, often presented as if there was great certainty about their nature. The living historical farm or community goes beyond these modes of interpretation. It is fair to say the three basic modes of living-history interpretation have been developed in the past ten years.

The first mode gives the greatest illusion of the past, role-playing. In this mode, interpreters become specific fictional or real historic characters, members for instance of a farm family, owner and workers in a store, or craftspeople in a shop. This mode not only requires interpreters with special talents; it also requires researchers who can go deeply into the materials of social and cultural history and interpretive planners who can take the material and translate it into something approximating a script, but without that fixed immutable quality. Those who favor the other two modes of interpretation are often suspicious of role-playing. Either they fear that the visitor will be alienated by clumsy efforts at verisimilitude or will be so swept into the illusion so as to have no critical distance. Either way, they suggest that the efforts of the museum to present models of reality will be hampered. An excellent example of successful "first-person" interpretation, as it is also called, is the program at the Conner Prairie Historic Settlement near Indianapolis, Indiana.

The other modes, "point of view" interpretation and experimental history interpretation, bring greater critical distance into the process. Although it may not be termed "point of view" or "hypothetical" interpretation, this is probably the most common mode.[38] The interpreter who is costumed accurately carries out various tasks as best he or she can, given degree of skill and the state of research. In talking with visitors, the interpreter does not pretend to be part of the past. Rather, he or she is a person carrying out historical activities to give a visually accurate approximation of the past. If preparing the corn field, the interpreter might say, "I am doing what a New England farmer did in 1820 by plowing with this reproduction plow." Implied is the statement that "I am not that farmer, but if I were, here is what I would probably be doing." This is essentially the perspective from which interpretation is carried out at Sturbridge.

The third mode is the least common, experimental history interpretation. In this there is the greatest distancing of the interpreter and the visitor from the past as illusion, but probably the closest approach to the past as reality. In this mode, the interpreter wears what is explicitly termed "historic clothing," not costume. Part of the experiment is to know what it felt like to work at various activities in different seasons in the clothing people of that status and class, occupation and background, wore.[39] In preparing the corn field, this interpreter might say, "We have found out about planting corn from travel accounts and early agricultural journals. But there is much we do not find in the sources. We are trying to find these things out experimentally, to test out what the primary and secondary sources tell us." There may or may not be a research program closely tied in with this mode. The intent could be to gain experience that may lead to development of such a program. At least there is the aim of making it clear to the visitor that the museum is not a repository of "givens." Colonial Pennsylvania Plantation is still largely at this point, but it is moving to take the next step of developing a closely allied research program. When this mode is combined with research, interpretation becomes a serious, scholarly activity. This may lead to that revaluing of the function and status of interpreters mentioned above.

Part VI: Education in the Living Museum

Education and entertainment are commonly regarded as the two aims of interpretive programs.[40] Most living-history museums have other programs in which education is the sole aim, or at least, clearly the primary one. The facilities offer advantages over those of the traditional indoor or outdoor museum. Reproduction tools, implements, and furniture can be touched and used. Crops may be seen, smelled, and touched. The person taking advantage of an education program is given the opportunity to participate in re-creating the past, in either the sense of experiment, hypothesizing or role-playing. Those who have planned and developed education programs at the three institutions examined in this paper are well aware of the power of the living-history experience in education.

At the Clayville Center, even though the historical community is in the planning stage, a living-history program, Mornings at Clayville, has been developed. One class of fifth graders, from twenty to forty in number, comes to the site for five hours. They are divided into Northerners and Southerners and then further broken up into groups of four to six who work with interpreters and learn by doing. One group for instance will work in the kitchen of the Northern inn preparing bread and Yankee stew for the noonday dinner, another in the Northern kitchen garden, planting vegetables and cultivating, and a third in the upstairs of the inn where they learn basic steps in making a patch-work quilt. Interpreters are mostly volunteers from the area or students at Sangamon State University. A training handbook has been prepared for them, plus, for each of the activity areas, a notebook containing research reports and copies of important primary sources such as farming journals, travel accounts, and cookbooks. Practical training is accomplished through working with an experienced interpreter. Everyone is encouraged to work in several activity areas during the season.[41]

The most well-developed programs of the three institutions are found at Old Sturbridge. All three interpretive modes are used for elementary and secondary schools. There is a visitation program in which classes come for a good portion of the school day and are divided up into groups of ten to twelve to explore a theme such as "textiles" in New England. The whole village plus the excellent facilities in the new education building, a dramatic structure designed to be an all-weather laboratory for doing key activities in the community, are used. For instance, the children go to one of the learning areas in the education building and learn about the raising of sheep and preparation of wool on the farm, go out to the carding mill to talk with the interpreter, and then return to a craft studio where they try working with a drop spindle and a simple loom. After lunch they go to the Freeman Farm to find out all they can by talking with the interpreters on site. The interconnections of farm, mill, and town are stressed, as are the social conditions under which textile production went on. Both the experimental and hypothesizing modes are used. For secondary school students, aged thirteen to eighteen, and for older groups, role-playing programs have been designed. Each participant is given basic information about a historic personage and then assigned the task of discovering what those facts meant in practical terms in the community.

Training is an important activity, both in the preparation of escorts who work with the children and of teachers. The former learn how to "read" the Freeman Farm, to understand the processes going on there, and how to make children and older people aware of them. They learn to read contemporary rural and urban landscapes and to relate these to the past represented at the village. They have sessions on how children learn, how they think about time and relate to objects. Escorts learn about the processes that take farm-produced materials

to the finished form in mills, and the social forms through which these transformations occur. For the teacher there are training sessions ranging in length from one-day voluntary workshops to two-week summer workshops in curriculum development before which the participants are selected competitively. In all of these programs, the farm and the village are seen as learning resources in which inquiry processes are fostered. The teachers and escorts are thought of as resource people, as "organizers of experience," not as final determiners of reality.[42]

The three institutions focused on in the paper are all used for university-level teaching, and are among the few at which that is the case. Colonial Pennsylvania is used by classes in folklife at Villanova University and the University of Pennsylvania. Sturbridge has a one-year internship program for those going into museum work. The program has been funded by the National Endowment for the Humanities and represents Sturbridge's determination of the best way it can proceed in museum training. The Clayville Center functions in close association with Sangamon State University, a new institution mandated for innovation in education, concern with public affairs, and the liberal arts. Courses in Midwest rural life and its American regional and European backgrounds combine methods of social history, ethnology, and cultural/historical geography. The aim is to understand the cultures of people who make up the population of the countryside and how they have shaped the environment. There are also courses in American decorative arts, the history of architecture and of crafts, and workshops in living history.[43]

Part VII: Problems to be Faced

At a number of points potential problem areas have been touched upon. It is appropriate at this point to consider them and then, in the last section, to move to an evaluation of the directions of the living historical farm movement. The problem areas will be examined in the same order as above, that is, by focusing upon research, curation, interpretation, and education, in that order. The problems that transcend these functional areas will be looked at, especially the representativeness of farms of the history of agriculture and rural life generally and the dangers of the messages they communicate in facilities and programs.

Lack of money for research and lack of awareness that sophisticated techniques of analysis need to be used are the chief problems in the first functional area. The model concepts are adequate to guide and clarify the goals of research. Methods are being developed that promise to provide planners with the foundations upon which to design and operate typical or particular farms. But in North America, open-air museums and living historical farms do not always see themselves as research institutions. The three examined here do so very clearly, but there are others where the need just to keep open to the public with provision of minimal interpretive and educational programs absorbs their resources. At governmentally operated farms and outdoor museums, the assumption often is that the research is done at the outset, once and for all time. On-going research is not regarded as necessary.

Curation in the living-history museum suffers from lack of money and awareness also, but there are two additional problems, the want of people with skills to make reproductions and a consequent opportunism that lessens historical accuracy. It is obviously difficult to locate older types of livestock, seed, and plant stock. Back-breeding is costly, and so is tool and implement reproduction. Skilled craftspeople who can fashion the older historical tools and implements, whether hand-produced or machine-made, are very hard to locate. Sometimes in place of the proper traditional plow, a later factory-made one is used because it is available and works. A harrow of traditional design is constructed and used even though researchers and curators are uncertain as to whether it is really appropriate for the period and place. A scythe or sickle made in Denmark or Austria possessing some design similarities with ones used in the late eighteenth or early nineteenth centuries in North America is employed. One cannot be overly critical of the opportunism as long as the staff is fully aware of what it is doing and is honest about this in the interpretive and educational programs. Visual accuracy can suffer, as many professionals are recognizing. If all living historical farms go to the same sources for equipment, seed, and livestock, whether that be to Sturbridge for "dunghill fowl" or to an Austrian supplier for sickles, the regional differences will not be represented. Likewise, using early twentieth-century horse-drawn equipment on a farm that is to represent the 1870s is incorrect. These are serious problems, and it has led some museum professionals to wonder if they should share their sources of supply.[44]

The solving of these problems will require not only an investment of money in field, library, and archival research and then in artifact reproductions and stock-locating programs. There is also a need to encourage people to enter traditional crafts or to learn older machine production processes. They will have to be taught to seek out older craftspeople and learn bygone methods and be trained to recover—through experimental research—that which has been lost. The "back to the land" and the craft movements in North America can serve as sources of people. But both of these movements have a very eclectic sense of history. There must be opportunities and encouragement for training in the scholarly skills and standards of the technological historian and ethnologist.

In interpretation and education, there are three problems: The first is fairly easily solved, that of stimulating and maintaining the interest and enthusiasm of the interpreters. One way to do this is to vary the tasks assigned to them. On the living-history farm this is simple enough, for so many activities are seasonal. Where edu-

cational and interpretive programs are closely linked, interpreters can be drawn into the teaching process. This not only enhances their self-esteem, but contributes to their growth as educational problems are faced and dealt with. Sturbridge is trying out this idea. Even where experimental history is not the principal interpretive mode, the findings of interpreters are valuable. Setting up a formal feedback and evaluative function for them to relate to researchers and curators increases their effectiveness and preserves information that would otherwise never be communicated. In a fully experimental history research program, they would become full partners in the never-ending process of defining historical realities. Thus, the living-history concepts may be applied to solve the old problems of keeping the interpretive program fresh and interesting for interpreters and the public.

The second problem is not easily solved, that of obtaining visual accuracy, given the values and rewards in North American society and the fact that farms are only operated eight or nine hours a day. The visual demographic profile is usually inaccurate. Pliny Freeman did not have a half dozen young men working on his farm. The household work was not done by three or four women in their twenties or their sixties. There was Freeman himself and his wife, in their early fifties, and a younger hired man. But, given the eight-hour day, even with reduced scale farming, all the work cannot be carried out by two men. There is a need to interpret, and time is "lost" in an operations sense to the performance of this function. If the household was interpreted with a full lifeways program in which all essential tasks would be fully carried out, a similar problem deriving from this situation would exist.

The problem of lack of visual accuracy does not arise simply from the necessity of the shortened work day. People who are willing to do interpretation fall into two age ranges. At Sturbridge, most interpreters fall into either the twenty-one- to thirty-five-year age group or the over sixty group. The older people work part-time only, for if they did more, they would lose Social Security benefits. The young people are drawn by the possibility of learning how to live a "simpler" life. The pay is low, but the learning experience makes up for it. People in the years in between are generally unwilling to work for the low wages museums offer interpreters.

The third problem is closely related, that of holding onto a skilled staff. It takes several years to acquire the skills of manual farm operations, such as plowing and scything, and to be fit to carry them out for long periods. Just at the time when these are fairly fixed, the recognition comes that there is no place to go upwards in the museum and to utilize the skills.[45] North American society does not reward manual skills with either money or status. There are all sorts of subtle and not so subtle pressures to move onward and upward in socially defined terms. This will be a particularly acute problem at any institution that seeks to carry on an experimental research and interpretive program. To solve it, more pay will have to be offered interpreters, particularly those who take up research functions. The revision upward of the status of interpreters mentioned above would help in this too.

The social context in which the living-history farm movement operates intrudes again and again. It is appropriate, therefore, to turn to several problem areas steming from this context and transcending the specific museum functions. They are interrelated problems and ultimately touch upon the fundamental problem of the role of the museum in society. They raise important questions that must be faced. How close can the individual farm come to social and environmental reality even if it wants to? How close can the movement itself come to it? These questions relate to social and value limitations. But there is another that arises from the very nature of living history itself. If it is consciously decided to represent reality, how can the delicate balance between the inevitable quality of illusion and the interpretive realities be struck and restruck to communicate the historical realities? The questions suggest strongly that society imposes limitations, and the very concepts of living history have their own flaws. These must now be examined.

The national system of farms representing different periods and systems of farming proposed by John Schlebecker has not come about. That federal funding was not forthcoming was only indicative of the real problems. There was no way to coordinate the various private and public efforts that have resulted in the planning and development of at least thirty-five farms including fully operating ones and others that are essentially grossly underscaled demonstration areas. The Association for Living Historical Farms and Agricultural Museums has not been in a position to provide such coordination.

To a degree what Schlebecker feared has come about. Many farms fall into the "particular" category, representative not of what was typical in the area, but an operation of a wealthy or famous man. Some are typical, but of a generalized "pioneer" period. These serve to reinforce the national myth of Canada and the United States of the humble beginnings of people in lands of opportunity where all started equal and were able to climb without hindrance to the level of their ability. This is the essence of the liberal origin myth. The word "liberal" is used here in the sense of that ideology that goes back to the eighteenth century and has various manifestations in Europe and North America, which may or may not, in the current political vocabulary, be termed "liberal." The word "myth" is not used here as equivalent to "lie." Rather it denotes an operant belief and value system, a way of viewing the world that drives people with a complex mixture of truth and untruth, reality and unreality.

Another myth related to this one is re-created on at least one operating historical farm, and several others planned—the myth of the unmitigated blessings of technological progress. The 1900 farm at Des Moines, Iowa, is being developed to indicate the advances since the pioneer period. Labor-saving mechanical devices are stressed. Originally, there were plans for a third farm—one of the future—with cybernated operations carried out by complex machines under the control of a few men. The vision has been reduced somewhat to that of a future more within grasp, a farm extrapolated slightly from the present. This is the sort beloved by the Department of Agricultural and Farm Bureau where one farmer is seen as feeding forty people. The complex interrelations and dependencies of the farmer with a host of other people who make that possible may be lost sight of. Social and environmental costs could be ignored.

Several farms around the country now or will represent the 1850s: Old Bethpage on Long Island in New York State, Old Westville in Lumpkin, Georgia, and Clayville in Illinois. In part, probably, this decade was chosen because of the difficulty of obtaining reproductions of the factory-made complex horse-drawn or tractor-pulled equipment of the later years. The basic tools and implements of the period can be reproduced without too much difficulty, although the reapers and drills would present serious problems in terms of cost and the skills needed for reproduction. More historically and educationally valid reasons also exist. This was a transition era during which the traditional and the modern were mixed, a time when it is easy to look backwards and forwards. The interpretive and educational program possibilities are significantly enhanced by the choice of this time. But it is not easy to communicate these realities to the various publics served by living farms and communities. There is a desire to see the "old fashioned," not to come to grips with traditional or modern cultural realities, with the facts of social class and unequal opportunity. There is an inevitable tendency to project the myth of "the good old days" on the living museum.

It is clear that the agriculture of the industrialized era has not been adequately represented. Its earliest stages are re-created at Colonial Pennsylvania and Sturbridge and elsewhere, and the take-off years are or will be shown at several institutions. The second agricultural revolution from 1750 to 1880 is incompletely shown. We need more than just the Des Moines operation for the later years. The third agricultural revolution, which is going on before our eyes, is not the subject of any static or living museum, at least in ways that will give a comprehensive understanding of its character and meaning. Completely industrialized agriculture, the sort that has appeared under the social form of agribusiness, is both too much with us and too little understood to be represented in the living museum. It does not validate the national origin myths since it is of a period far removed from the pioneer times. The social and economic forms, which have appeared, create real problems for the liberal myth of the open society with equal opportunity. The living-history farm is probably not the place to try to communicate the realities. The indoor museum, where the analogic models can be explored to uncover the underlying realities, would be more appropriate.

Social myths and social realities shape long-range choices about what periods to represent and what messages to give through program facilities. On a more immediate basis, they act to limit the extent to which historical realities can be represented. Open-air and living-history museums often present "sanitized versions of the past," as Richard Candee put it.[46] They go beyond the limitations that considerations of public safety and health impose. Governing boards and the public want the farms and the communities to be clean, neat, comfortable, and even odorless. Some visitors are bothered by the uneven grass kept down by the sheep and cattle, and by the pigs in their pen on the farm. The fear of the sensual and the unwillingness to consider another complex of realities prevent the public from accepting the past. Thus, planners are hesitant to re-create elements of life that will offend the modern sense of taste and order. It took some time to convince the trustees and the maintenance department at Sturbridge that the early nineteenth century village commons was not a neat, rectangular mown "green" serving aesthetic purposes, but was shaped by its economic functions. These changes have made the village more historically accurate. Yet they may cause the simplified view of "progress" to be verified in the mind of the casual tourist. The problem of the projection of myths, tastes, and assumptions of the public upon the living museum has yet to be dealt with adequately. And there is no simple answer to the problem of how to balance illusion and reality so as to avoid reinforcing those myths, tastes, and assumptions.

Yet researchers, curators, planners, interpreters, and educators all have heavy obligations to portray reality as best they can. This is a scholarly obligation at the very least. From the larger social and environmental perspective, it is a humanitarian one, as well. By way of summarizing some of the points made above and bringing several ideas into focus, the two intersecting continua pictured and discussed earlier in the paper will be returned to. As the model concepts are used in research and development, they will bring out some dangers, which should be faced and dealt with if possible. To reduce the analysis to a two-dimensional one, any farm or community will fall primarily into one of the quadrants formed by the intersecting lines. Each one of these quadrants has its own dangers.

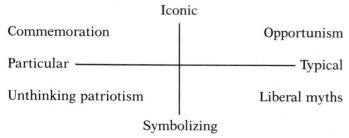

The emphasis on the iconic and the typical can lead to the opportunism of representing what works and can be done easily, toward an avoidance of the deeper social and environmental realities. The emphasis on the iconic and the particular may lead to simple commemoration of a person and what is known about him or her. Going on around leads to the blend of the particular and the symbolizing model where unthinking patriotism is encouraged. Finally, the focus on the typical and the symbolizing model verifies liberal myths of pioneer and technological progress.

Part VIII: Possible Directions in the Future

It is clear that living historical farms and communities must be careful about the conscious and unconscious messages they communicate. There are signs that people involved in the various functions connected with research, development, and operations are aware in one way or another of the dangers. The intrinsic nature of the living-history concepts with their reality seeking and process orientation leads to this. There are three directions being taken that are unquestionably positive. First, the museum is being conceived as a place in which a process of reality recovery proceeds; second, contemporary issues are being considered in their relations with museum objections; and third, significant efforts are underway to re-create environmental realities.

First of all, viewing the museum as much a collection of processes as of objects has several important consequences. Processes never have quite the absolute quality about them that artifacts and structures do. It is easier to see the historical model as imperfect, incomplete, as an approximation of reality. Research becomes necessarily an on-going process as does collection development and refinement. Other analogies operate also. The farm is a place of recurrence, yet change. Biological processes are repetitive, yet slight variations bring altered relationships of livestock, crops, and land use. The same is true of social processes. Market conditions change. Wages increase. The cost of land rises. One person's abilities, values, and background may offer advantages which were not there before, under prior conditions. It becomes natural to think of editing the museum. New findings in research are embodied in changes in the physical aspects and in the interpetive and educational programs.[47]

The museum is seen as continually in the process of development. The "farm in the making" is spoken of at Colonial Pennsylvania. The "community in the making" is discussed at Clayville. The realities of social and environmental change can be presented in the development of the museum itself. But a further step can also be taken. Education and interpretive programs can be designed to raise questions about versions of history learned at school. The establishment of ordained givens and a sanitized past can be avoided. The past can be used to illuminate the present, and the drawbacks and the benefits of progress.

This takes us to one of the most sensitive areas in museum work, whether the institution be a living historical farm or a traditional outdoor museum: the relationship to contemporary issues. Women's liberation is an important concern in contemporary North American society. There are implications for living-history museums. Put one way, the question is, "To what extent does the requirement of visual accuracy and the iconic model require that sex roles, if research establishes what they really were, be filled by interpreters of the appropriate sex?" Put in another way, the question becomes, "Do women have the right to learn and demonstrate historical crafts and farm activities that were not carried out by members of their sex regularly in earlier times?" Administrators are asking whether equal opportunity legislation requires that women be able to become historical farmers, agricultural laborers, and blacksmiths. If so, what do they wear, historic clothing of men, or some version of working women's dress that is safe and permits the range of motions needed?

These questions are being asked at Old Sturbridge. At conferences or seminars of museum professionals they are sure to give rise to passionate discussion and even heated anger. Other related questions have been treated only abstractly. Should the Southern plantation use black labor, and under what conditions? Should a historic farm in the American Southwest use Mexican labor if that was done in the period and place represented? Should the demographic profile be striven for at all costs? No one seems to have asked about men playing what are commonly regarded as women's roles, cooking, dairying, raising infants. The implications of experimental history for answering these questions have not been explored. It is possible by pushing the questioning to the extreme to lessen the sensitive character of the "women issue," but it is also possible to ignore it, which is dangerous for the institution and unjust for society.

This striving for representation of realities takes us finally to areas that are less controversial, at least on the surface. Living-history farms and communities are aiming at preserving, recovering, and portraying the larger realities of the natural and social environment. As to the former, a recent survey by the resource committee of AL-HFAM indicates that three approaches are common.[48] First, there are those institutions that re-create historical environments or are planning to in the future. Sturbridge has very consciously moved to do this, both at the farm and in the village area. The woodland is being pushed back to give the impression of the deforested New England of the 1830s. Exotics of later times are being removed. A similar process is going on at Colonial Pennsylvania. At Clayville, actual reconstruction of prairie and woodland will have to take place. In the second category are historical farms that are preserving the natural environmental features that have survived relatively unchanged from the period chosen. Finally, there are the other farms that must deal with the natural environment, at least by implication. In North America, just as in Europe, the landscape is a human artifact. Farming always involves the maintenance of an immature ecosystem, and this is there for those given the eyes to see.

Social and cultural realities are being represented at

many farms. Sturbridge's tradition-oriented Freeman is compared with Salem Towne, the upper-class innovator. The Colonial Pennsylvania farm is explicitly one of middle-level family, ambivalent about the American Revolution, but alert to economic opportunity arising from the conditions it introduced. At Clayville the givens of traditional culture, a popular culture of agricultural innovation, and social class and change will be represented. At each of these institutions there are dangers built into these choices. The facilities and programs at a living museum have a tyranny just as a textbook does. They say, "Here is reality!" For instance, the visitor might walk away with the notion that lower level farmers were traditional, and it was only the rich who were innovative. The typical farmer in southeastern Pennsylvania was ambivalent toward the Revolution. The Southerner was as inclined to be innovative as the Northerner, but in different areas of life and with a different style and "set of values." All of these messages may be true, but then again, they are oversimplifications, which will lead the uncritical public to incorrect views of the past.

Clearly the living historical farm and community are important phenomena in the museum world. Products of the interaction of a number of cultural currents in the sixties, they mean many things to many people. At the outset they represented attempts to get at various realities of the social and natural environment not included in museums before. In the seventies, they may become institutions of escape, places for indulging in nostalgia. It is likely that they may survive this particular cultural current. For the concepts of living-history have a quality leading to self-correction, to re-editing the models of the past and using them for a process approach to interpretation and education. Thus, fundamentally I am optimistic in regard to the future.

Notes

1. There are two current descriptive lists of farms and open air museums. One is entitled *Selected Living Historical Farms, Villages and Agricultural Museums* by Daryl Chase (Washington, D.C., 1975), a popular guide. The other is by this author, "Directory of Living Historical Farms and Open Air Museums," *Environmental History Newsletter* (Pittsburgh, Pa.: Duquesne University) 3:1 (1976): 18-40. It is intended for museum people and scholars primarily. See also the list in John Schlebecker and Gail Peterson, *Living Historical Farms Handbook* (Washington, D.C.: Smithsonian Institution Press, 1972), pp. 43-59. When this article went to press, the handbook was still available from the U.S. Government Printing Office, #4700-0185, for $1.70.

2. Darwin Kelsey, "Outdoor Museums and Historical Agriculture," *Agricultural History* 46 (1972): 111-113; Richard Candee, "Saving the Unsavable: Second Thoughts on Museum Villages as Preservation" (unpublished manuscript), pp. 2-7. The National Trust for Historic Preservation, based in Washington, D.C., is moving away from this orientation as perusal of its publications will reveal: *Historic Preservation* 1 (1952) to date (now quarterly); *Preservation News* 1 (1960) to date (now monthly).

3. This paper was presented in one of the five plenary sessions of the Fouth International Congress of Agricultural Museums in Reading, England, April 5-10, 1976. The theme of the conference was "Industrialization in Agriculture".

4. See the definition of a museum in Marilyn Hicks Fitzgerald's *Museum Accreditation: Professional Standards* (Washington; D.C.: American Association of Museums, 1973), p. 8.

5. Marion Clawson, "Living Historical Farms: A Proposal for Action," *Agricultural History* vol. 39, no. 2 pp. 110-11 (1965). Schlebecker's study was published as an offset typescript by the Smithsonian Institution. It is unfortunately out of print. His booklet, *Living Historical Farms, A Walk Into the Past* (Washington D.C.: Smithsonian Institution Press, 1968) contains some of the information.

6. "American Agriculture, 1778-1848; A Symposium," edited by Darwin Kelsey. *Agricultural History* 46 (1972): 1-258; Schlebecker, "Curatorial Agriculture," pp. 95-103; Kelsey, "Outdoor Museums and Historical Agriculture," pp. 105-127; and the commentary by James R. Short is also quite valuable, pp. 129-134. These three papers have been published as *Farming in the New Nation* (Washington D.C.: Agricultural History Society, 1972). *Bulletin* of the Association of Living Historical Farms and Agricultural Museums, 1 (1972)–4 (1975), quarterly; 5 (1975), bimonthly.

7. "Farming in the Midwest, 1840-1900: A Symposium," *Agricultural History* 48 (1974); Paul B. Frederic, "Geography and Living Historical Farm Sites" pp. 5-10; Robert E. Ankli, "Farmmaking Costs in the 1850's," pp. 51-74; Fred Bateman and James D. Foust, "A Sample of Rural Households Selected from the 1860 Manuscript Census," pp. 75-93; Raymond Baker, "Indian Corn and Its Culture," pp. 94-97. No presentations at the first ALHFAM conference in Cooperstown were written up and published.

8. The first plan for Clayville was embodied in the offset printed "A Proposal; A Rural Life Center at the Clayville Stagecoach Stop," November 1972.

9. *ALHFAM Annual* (1975), Kelsey; pp. 33-38, Anderson; pp. 21-22. Published by the Association for Living Historical Farms and Agricultural Museums, Smithsonian Institution, Washington, D.C.

10. See the early "Directory of Persons Interested in Living Historical Farms" in the *Handbook* by Schlebecker and Peterson, pp. 59-79.

11. This four category scheme was briefly sketched out in the article, "Living Historical Farms and the Environmental Historian," pp. 20-21, which preceded the Directory in the *Environmental History Newsletter* 3:1 (1976)

12. The Farmer's Museum at Cooperstown, New York, is one example. Another is the Clayville Rural Life Center as it presently functions.

13. *ALHFAM Annual* 1 (1956), p. 36.

14. Replicative and experimental history are discussed below. See footnote 29. Candee, "Saving the Unsavable," pp. 10-12.

15. *ALHFAM Annual* 1 (1975), p. 34. This scheme, which deals with the farm or open air museum as physical entity, allows determination of the boundaries in time, space and culture. This may meet the concerns of Iowerth C. Peate, who in a brief essay in *Folklife* 6 (1968), p. 113, raised questions of just how far the folk museum should go in re-creating the past. He asked, "Even supposing that we could produce a full historically accurate reconstruction of 15th, 16th, 17th, 18th, and 19th century farms at work in a folk museum, . . . where do we stop? Do we also reconstruct period markets and fairs to illustrate the marketing of produce and the hiring of laborers?"

16. *Annual*, p. 37. Kelsey presented two schemes also. His first one was the particular/typical model, following the suggestions of Schlebecker and Peterson in their *Handbook*, pp. 6-8, where they discussed "memorial" and "typical" farms. His other scheme involved the concepts of iconic, analogic, and symbolic. The first two categories he applied to actual farms. He was unsure how to use the term "symbolic." *Annual* (1975), pp. 37-38. As will be seen, I believe it is necessary to return to the meanings of these terms as they came from systems analysis. This restricts the use of the categories analogic and symbolic considerably. To Sonia Siebert, one of my best graduate students at Sangamon State, I owe a debt of gratitude. She forced me to do some careful rethinking through an unpublished paper in which she critically analyzed Kelsey's article, raising questions about the meanings and examples given for the three levels of abstraction. The reformulation into two model schemes, however, is my responsibility.

17. *ALHFAM Annual* 1 (1975), p. 37.

18. *Ibid*.

19. "What is the Colonial Pennsylvania Plantation? A Working Definition." Unpublished/ms., 1975, p. 2.

20. Jay Anderson, "On the Horns of a Dilemma: Identity, Museum Funding, and Administration at the Colonial Pennsylvania Plantation, " in *ALHFAM Annual* 3 (1977) pp. 18-19.

21. The figures come from the tax list at the end of Ross Fullam's report, "What is the Colonial Pennsylvania Plantation?" The bottom third includes four farms of 100 acres that exhibit the characteristic patterns. Thus the plantation is "more typical" than its developers imagine.

22. The information here is based on visits to the Freeman Farm at Old Sturbridge and conversations with Darwin Kelsey since 1972.

23. Interview with Caroline Sloat, January 5, 1976, and a letter of June 15, 1976.

24. Interview with Richard Candee, January 5, 1976, and Frank White, January 7, 1976. Glassie, *Pattern in the Material Folk Culture of the Eastern United States* (Philadelphia: University of Pennsylvania Press 1968), pp. 160-61.

25. See article by Elizabeth Weir and Edward Hawes in *ALHFAM Annual* 3 (1977). pp. 25-31.

26. Richard Lyle Power, *Planting Corn Belt Culture* (Indianapolis: Indiana Historical Society 1953), and Douglas McManis, *The Initial Evaluation and Utilization of the Illinois Prairie, 1815-1840* (Chicago: McManis University of Chicago, Dept. of Geography, Research paper #94 1964).

27. Hawes and Weir in *ALHFAM Annual* 3 (1977). James N. Brown, "The Best Mode of Raising and Managing Cattle on the Prairies of Illinois," *Transactions, Illinois State Agricultural Society* (Springfield) 2 (1856-57), pp. 372-76.

28. John Coles, *Archaeology by Experiment* (New York: Scribner's, 1973).

29. Interviews with Don Callender, research director, January 11, 1976, and Ross Fullam, farm manager, January 9, 1976. See also Callender's article, "Reliving the Past, Experimental Archeology in Pennsylvania," in *Archeology* 29 (1976), pp. 173-77.

30. Coles, *Experimental Archeology*, pp. 15-17. These comments derive from the discussion in the session on "Experimental Archeology" at the annual meeting of the Society for Historical Archeology, January 10, 1976. An unpublished transcript of the session's discussion is available at the Colonial Pennsylvania Plantation. Two observations by Henry Glassie in his presentation should be mentioned here. He suggested that twentieth-century people are much more facile at problem solving than the people whose culture is represented in the re-creation of seventeenth-century Plymouth in Massachusetts where he worked for a summer. More important, and perhaps less debatable, was his thought that in experimental history we run a great danger of making a "white hole," a culture composed of skills, behaviors, and beliefs attributed to people of earlier times by the experimenter who finds them useful in the work of imitative or replicative research, and who assumes their historicity.

31. This is the author's scheme. Duncan S. Cameron suggested the word "kinetifacts" to cover processes demonstrated in science museums. "Viewpoint: The Museum as Communications System" *Curator* 11 (1968), pp. 33-40. The word might well be used in outdoor history and folklife museums also.

32. See Peter Cousin's article, which is invaluable in this area: "Defining the Typical: Documenting Tool and Implement Program," *ALHFAM Annual* 1 (1975), pp. 15-20.

33. Interview, Frank White, January 7, 1976; Don Callender, January 12, 1976.

34. At Clayville, researchers went through three mid-nineteenth-century sources to assemble a list of vegetables, then consulted present catalogs to see what is still available. The next step will be to compare period descriptions with present crops. On the Seed Storage Laboratory see the author's "Historic Seed Sources and the Future," in *ALHFAM Annual* 1 (1975), pp. 28-32.

35. Interview, Darwin Kelsey, January 8, 1976.

36. *Ibid*. Tina Bielenburg is working on wool and weaving characteristics; Joanne Bowen on skeletal remains.

37. Interviews with Tim Wheeler, January 7 and March 8, 1976.

38. It was Joan Seidl, then master teacher in the Education Department at Old Sturbridge, who first brought these terms to my attention. She uses them with slightly different meanings, however.

39. Interview with Daphne Wilcox, manager of interpretation at Colonial Pennsylvania Plantation, January 11, 1976.

40. Freeman Tilden, *Interpreting Our Heritage*, (Chapel Hill: University of North Carolina Press 1967).

41. *Two Year Report, Clayville Rural Life Center* (1975), pp. 9-11. A very perceptive article on the program by Victoria Pope, "Clayville Returns to the 1850's," appeared in the *Illinois Times*, a seri-

ous weekly news journal. Colonial Pennsylvania Plantation has a small-scale education program. Teachers are encouraged to come with classes if they undertake preparation and guide functions. Children learn about history as a process of discovery through experiment. Interview with Daphne Wilcox, January 11, 1976.

42. Interview with Joan Seidl, January 6, 1976. The author has observed this particular thematic tour. The special issue of *Social Education* 39 (1975), pp. 454-481, contains valuable material on using museums and communities to learn about the past and present. The section was edited by Alberta P. Sebolt, director of museum education at Old Sturbridge.

43. The author's article, "Living Historical Farms and the Environmental Historian" in the *Environmental History Newsletter* 3:1 (1976), p. 23, footnote 1, indicates some other museums with such connections to universities and colleges. The Sturbridge program is highly competitive. In 1975-76, the second year of operation, five interns were chosen out of 180 applicants.

44. Some of these points came out in the seminar on "The Living Historical Farm as a Museum" at Old Sturbridge Village, June 8-13, 1975, sponsored by the American Association for State and Local History.

45. The information on Sturbridge comes from Timothy Wheeler to whom I owe a debt of gratitude for his provocative ideas on interpretive programming and organizing.

46. Interview, January 5, 1976. See his "Saving the Unsavable," p. 8 (unpublished/ ms.).

47. Candee suggests reasonably enough that some museums should not change. "Saving the Unsavable," p. 11.

48. See Hawes, "Living Historical Farms," *Environmental History Newsletter* 3:1 (1976), pp. 21-22.

Part V
Villages

The Reality of the Pilgrim Fathers

James Deetz

The former director of research at Plimoth Plantation, archaeologist James Deetz contends that "a step into the time capsule of re-created Plimoth evokes a living community of Pilgrims—its smoky odors, animal noises, and household clutter—and dispels our misconceptions about colony life." His article describes the research base and mode of interpretation that make Plimoth Plantation a powerful experiment in the presentation of history to the general public. This article first appeared in the November 1969 issue of Natural History.

A step into the time capsule of re-created Plymouth evokes a living community of Pilgrims—its smoky odors, animal noises, and household clutter—and dispels our misconceptions about colony life.

We present William Randall, and Elizabeth, his wife, of Scituate, for abusing the constable, Walter Hatch, in word and action, as by threat, and refusing to give surety according to the warrant, and that when he strained for the magistrate's table, his wife tore the distress out of his hand, and hurt his hand so that blood was shed.

We present Alice, the wife of Richard Berry, of Yarmouth, for going into the house of Benjamin Hammond, when nobody was home, and feloniously took away a woman's shift, that was new made, but without sleeves, and a piece of pork.

We present Joane, the wife of Obadiah Miller, of Taunton, for beating and reviling her husband, and egging her children to help her, biding them knock him in the head, and wishing his victuals might soak him.

We present Thomas Clark, of Plymouth, for taking of six pounds for the bare loan of twenty pounds for one year, which we conceive is great extortion, contrary to the laws of God and man.

We present John Peck, of Rehoboth, for lascivious carriages and unchaste in attempting the chastity of his father's maid servant, to satisfy his fleshy beastly lust, and that many times for some years space, without any intent to marry her, but was always resisted by the maid, as he confessed.

October the 1, 1661. Whereas I, Abraham Pierce, Jr., have foolishly and unadvisedly reported to Ruth Sprague and Bethiah Tubbs, at the house of Francis Sprague, that Rebecca Alden and Hester Delaney were with child, and that thereupon we should have young troopers within three quarters of a year, I do freely and from my heart own my fault herein, and am heartily sorry that I have so spoken, to their great reproach and wrong and the defamation of their relations, which I earnestly desire may be passed by of them all; and I hope I shall forever after take heed what I do speak and report of at any time.

Those, having viewed the dead body of the said Robert Allen, and heard the relations of those that were in the house of the said John Allen, where he, the said Robert Allen died, at the time of his death, do with one consent declare, that he came by his death by laying violent hands upon himself.

Mistress Lydia Garrett, of Scituate, to have liberty to sell strong liquors, in regard that sundry in that town are oft times in necessity. . . .

The total number of people who lived in Plymouth Colony during its independent existence—1620 through 1692, when it merged with Massachusetts Bay Colony—was probably not in excess of 10,000. The simple rural life was free of the complex social network of classes and occupational specialties characteristic of later urban centers. For this small colony, a wealth of documentary material, including church records, court records, probate data, tax lists, laws, and vital records, allows for controlled consideration of the many variables of social change. Unlike any of the other colonies of the time, the study of Plymouth is manageable. Furthermore, in researching its history and culture in depth, it is possible to set straight a host of misconceptions that most people hold of the "Pilgrims" and their seventeenth-century descendants.

By the nineteenth century the term "Pilgrim" had come to evoke a romantic image of these people. Genuine understanding of them was buried beneath a thick layer of idealized portrayals in prose, poetry, and painting. Even today, the Pilgrims are usually thought of as a rather cheerless lot, wearing somber dress and living in crude log cabins.

The Pilgrim fathers were, in fact, a people typical of their time, with a culture as different from that of Americans today as are many cultures of modern Africa or Latin America. From routine land dispositions through all manner of deviant behavior, the trials and troubles of the Pilgrim colonists were entered at court in thousands of cases, from 1633 through the end of Plymouth Colony's existence. Not that the Pilgrims were more rowdy or disorderly than any other group of early seventeenth-century colonists. They were simply human. Recently uprooted from relatively stable European societies, they faced in this fresh environment a whole new set of problems.

Perry Miller, the historian, aptly describes the small earnest group who settled in the new land:

> The persons who made up the "Pilgrim" company were homespun, hard-working farmers from Nottinghamshire and Lincolnshire; their minister, John Robinson, was a university man, and Elder Brewster had spent a couple of years at Cambridge, but otherwise they were men instructed only in the Bible and simplicity of spirit. They had openly broken with the Church of England, and ,proceeded to set up a completely "separate" body. No government in Europe at that epoch would have tolerated the existence of such a society, outside and independent of the established institution, and it is no wonder that the bishops and the sheriffs of England got after this congregation with vehemence.

There is little doubt that these dissenters from the Establishment were a difficult people for their fellow Englishmen to adjust to, and England was probably more than happy to see them leave. Coming to America after a twelve-year stay in Holland, the Pilgrim congregation, joined by others whose motives for leaving were quite different, established a foothold on the New England coast in what is today Plymouth, Massachusetts. In the first years of the colony, the events for which they are remembered by all took place—the first thanksgiving, the Indian Squanto teaching them how to plant corn using herring fertilizer, Myles Standish's courtship of Priscilla Mullins, and John Alden's reluctance to speak on his behalf. Familiar paintings call to mind a band of people walking through the snow to church, blunderbusses on their backs, buckles on their shoes and hats, peering fearfully into the wilderness for some untold danger. But after the dramatic events of the colony's first few years, it is as if Plymouth had vanished from the face of the earth. For with the arrival of multitudes of Puritan immigrants into the Massachusetts Bay Colony during the 1630s, the attention of most historians shifts to events in that colony, while Plymouth to the south continues its way of seeming serenity, a cultural and historical backwater with little of interest to justify research. Yet it is this very attribute of calm, orderly cultural change in a small, rural population that makes Plymouth Colony a unique stage on which to see in microcosm many of the processes through which English culture became a very different thing, ultimately to be called American.

Today it is possible to visit the little community of Plymouth, re-created in full scale two miles south of its original site. The re-created settlement looks much as the original did to the Dutch trader Isaac de Rasieres in 1627, seven years after the arrival of the Mayflower. Shortly before the community broke out of its fortified isolation and spread over the surrounding coast and countryside, de Rasieres recorded one of only three eyewitness accounts now in existence:

> New Plymouth lies on the slope of a hill stretching east towards the sea coast, with a broad street about a cannon shot of 800 feet long leading down the hill; with a street crossing in the middle, northwards toward the rivulet and southwards toward the land. The houses are constructed of clapboards, with gardens also enclosed behind and at the sides with clapboards,so that their houses and courtyards are arranged in very good order, with a stockade against sudden attack; and at the ends of the streets there are three wooden gates. In the center, on the cross street, stands the governor's house, before which is a square stockade upon which four patereros are mounted, so as to enfilade the streets. Upon the hill they have a large square house, with a flat roof, built of thick sawn planks stayed with oak beams, upon the top of which they have six cannons, which shoot iron balls . . . and command the surrounding country.

The original "broad street about a cannon shot of 800 feet long" is now Leyden Street in modern Plymouth, and the cross street where once stood the governor's house and the square stockade is the location of a drug store, hardware store, electric company, and post office. But on virtually identical terrain on the Eel River to the south, the Plymouth of 1627 is now being re-created as an outdoor museum by Plimoth Plantation (the spelling was used by William Bradford in his classic history of the colony), a non-profit, educational organization. After one walks through a cool pine woods where logs are being cut and dressed as they were when the Pilgrims built their village, the "large square house, with a flat roof" appears, and stretching below it toward the sea, a narrow dirt street with small frame houses and thatched roofs gives the visitor the impression of stepping into another century.

Plimoth Plantation was founded twenty years ago to create an understanding of the Pilgrims and seventeenth-century America through exhibits, publications, films, and educational programs. In addition to the village exhibit, it also operates *Mayflower II*, a reproduction of the type of vessel that brought the settlers to America, as well as a typical northeastern Algonquian Indian summer encampment. But it is with the re-created village that it seeks to communicate an understanding of the way of life in Plymouth during the colony's first ten years.

The village is presented as a living community, where people perform the routine tasks involved in the life of the time. Two very important considerations underlie everything in the village exhibit. One relates to the way people tend to overinterpret the labels applied to historical periods. If the question is asked: "Is 1620, the year of the *Mayflower's* arrival in Plymouth, closer in time to Columbus or to the American Revolution?" most people would link the Pilgrims closer to 1775, unless they actually calculated the difference. In reality, the Pilgrims are slightly closer in time to Columbus. The result of this mental distortion of time is that the 155 years between 1620 and 1775 are lumped together indiscriminately and collectively labeled American Colonial. True, the Pilgrims did create a colony in America, but American Colonial suggests candle dipping, spinning wheels, diamond-pane windows, horn books, and a host of other things that did not exist in Plymouth during the first ten years of its existence, and in some cases now for decades to follow. Another similarly vague and overgeneralized label is medieval, and while it suggests King Arthur, serfs, knights, and castles to many people, the truth is that the culture of the earliest settlers in North America owed as much to its medieval heritage as it presaged the culture of Colonial America a century later. The way of life brought to these shores by seventeenth-century Englishmen was one that represented a long, slow adjustment to a relatively stable natural and social environment. But once implanted in the New World, it underwent rapid change for the next century in response to the dramatically new conditions. The 1627 village exhibit attempts to convey an awareness that these people were different in many ways from their American descendants of a century later. Sometime in the course of the eighteenth century, a watershed was reached beyond which the lifestyle became one that modern Americans can identify with on the basis of their own experience in twentieth-century America.

The second consideration in the presentation of a living 1627 village is based on current thought concerning media. Marshall MacLuhan tells us that media in modern America are changing from "hot"—very structured and linear, with a high information content—to "cool"—non-linear, with little structure and low information content and requiring the involvement of more than one of the senses to fill in the picture. In MacLuhan's terms, print is hot; television, cool. The village is also cool in media. All senses are appealed to, and structured information content is relatively low. Signs, labels, and other written information are almost nonexistent. Nothing is displayed or demonstrated simply for the sake of display or demonstration, yet by inquiring and conversing with any of the many interpreters in the village, information is easily obtained. There is no area within the village that the visitor cannot touch, handle, and experience. Live animals are present among the houses; it is not unusual to pass a chicken in a doorway or to encounter a sheep in a backyard lot. Fires are burning in all the houses, even on the hottest days, since the fireplace is the sole source of cooking heat, hot water, warmth on cool days, and frequently, light at night. It is important for a visitor to experience the discomfort of the hearth on a hot day to appreciate the problems of life in the absence of an electric or gas range, not to mention air conditioning. The smoke from the fires, the clucking and crowing of the chickens, the smell of foods cooking and of a nearby sheep pen combine to create a continuing impression of reality based on an appeal to sight, smell, touch, and hearing.

Naturalness is the key to the dress of the interpreters

Signing the Mayflower Compact.—*Photo: Plimoth Plantation*

in the village, who wear costumes typical of the period. The plantation's personnel can go barefoot if they desire, as have farming folk of all ages in warm weather. They might get soiled from cleaning the great iron cooking pots, carrying water, or preparing and cooking foods in the fireplaces. Visitors are somewhat surprised by the appearance of the village and its inhabitants, since it is so different from most other outdoor re-creations of the past. Yet, to create a neat, apple-pie orderly community is simply not in accord with known historical fact. The problem of completeness and accuracy is a subtle and difficult one. It will never be possible to re-create everything, and were the level of realism stricter, appearances would be even more cluttered; the task is to produce reality to the point where a different lifestyle is suggested, one quite unlike our own.

The houses are equipped with simple furniture typical of the period. Many of them do not contain bedsteads, but rather, simple pallets laid directly on the floor. There is a clutter of all the necessary equipment for survival—cooking gear, hoes, axes, bags of grain, drying vegetables and herbs, weapons, and clothing. The general impressions is one of activity and life. As Marshall Davidson writes in *The American Heritage Book of Antiques:*

> At a time when, as in Plymouth and other seventeenth-century communities, the average household consisted of nine or ten people, the hall [main downstairs room] must have presented a cluttered and untidy appearance, hard to imagine from the decoratively arranged examples of such interiors . . . in most museums and other historical restorations.

Not so at Plimoth Plantation, where the clutter is both apparent and a direct result of the kinds of tasks being done. Smelling the wood smoke, walking the dusty street, standing in a cluttered household, all contribute to the impression of entering another world—a full-size, populated, seventeenth-century time capsule.

While the physical exhibits give an impression of the intangibles of early Colonial life, the all-important aspects of the culture that are not directly visible—law and government, religion, economics, social structure—are presented by the interpreters in the village. The rack of matchlock muskets in the Myles Standish house provides an excellent point from which to develop an explanation of the military practices of the time. A box of surgical instruments in the house of Samuel Fuller, the village physician, leads to the broader questions of what a doctor did, both as healer and farmer, in a simple agrarian community. The piles of clapboards, skins, and bags of corn in the common storehouse illustrate the trade that was so critical to the colony's economy during those first years.

The complexity of research that makes such a re-creation possible involves a staff of professisonal anthropologists, historians, and museum specialists in a varied, cross-disciplinary program. Whether data are being gathered on domesticated animals of the period to support the selection of the correct breed of cattle for the exhibits or on ceramics of seventeenth-century Plymouth for a monograph to be published by the plantation, a broad-scale approach is taken, incorporating the analysis of contemporary documentary materials such as wills and estate inventories, of archaeological assemblages from seventeenth-century house sites in the area, or of Dutch and English paintings and prints of the period for comparative information from Europe. In this way, the plantation's research accomplishes two different, but related, purposes: the authentication of the exhibits and research aimed at publishing a wide variety of material on Plymouth Colony.

The year 1627 was chosen as a re-creation date for a number of reasons. It was in that year that the first land grants were made to individuals beyond the immediate environs of the fortified village. For the first seven years, the Pilgrims were tightly grouped within their palisade, gaining a foothold on the land, and being augmented in their numbers by other immigrants who arrived from England on at least a half-dozen ships that put in at Plymouth. These ships also brought livestock and quantities of consumable goods. Although a precise population figure is almost impossible to obtain, the total number of people in the community after seven years was between two and three hundred. Of this total, relatively few represented the original *Mayflower* voyagers, since half of the original 100 passengers died during the first winter. The Pilgrims had financed their movement to the New World through a joint economic venture with a group of London merchants, and until 1627, all property was held in common, and the colony benefited corporately from the fruits of its labor. This procedure has often been referred to as a form of communism. In fact, as a recent historian has appropriately remarked, the system might better be termed "exploitative capitalism," since the colony's products were shipped to England for a profit through which the colony was to be supported. The joint stock company was liquidated in 1627, with the Pilgrims assuming the debt; as a result, property, including land and livestock, was divided among the various households in that year, and a census was taken, which provides the information regarding the number of families and houses at that time. De Rasieres' description of the early village also dates to 1627. Any later date would make it impossible to show a complete social community in one place, since outlying farms developed in the following years. Earlier dates from the intervening seven years have even less specific data on which to base a reasonable re-creation.

Using such information, the general demographic and physical form of the village can be approximated. However, the problem of just what kinds of houses should be built is a very complex one. Research on the subject of early Plymouth architecture must rely on data that are essentially comparative. The oldest documented house in the colony area postdates the mid-seventeenth century, and the earliest house in New England, the Fair-

The reality of men's work: pit sawing lumber.—*Photo: Plimoth Plantation*

banks house in Dedham, Massachusetts, dates to 1636. To determine the appearance of Plymouth's earliest homes, it has been necessary to use contemporary English data from southern and eastern England, the area from which most of Plymouth's earliest settlers came; mentions of the village and houses in various records; and a comparative study of somewhat later seventeenth-century houses in the immediate area. From the composite, a prototype early Pilgrim dwelling has been designed, which can be varied in size and form to a certain degree. But the houses of 1627 Plymouth probably shared a number of basic features. They were all of frame construction, with small paper-covered windows. Chimneys were of wood, covered with wattle and daub, a wickerwork of flexible small branches amply plastered with mud. Roofs were mostly of thatch, though some could have been covered with shingles. In 1627 legislation was passed in Plymouth prohibiting the further use of thatch because of fire hazard, although the main danger seems to have been from fires that started in poorly daubed wooden chimneys and spread to the roof. Floors were dirt or wood. Floor plans were either of the single-room type, with the chimney at one end, or a two-room type with central chimney. A loft served as a storage and sleeping area.

Turning to the problem of furnishing the houses, the colony's estate inventories provide a valuable source for research. Then, as now, when an individual died, his estate was inventoried by an agent of the court and a value placed on his property, item by item. The plantation has transcribed several hundred of these inventories from the crabbed Elizabethan script of the originals, which are still located in the Plymouth Registry of Deeds. Inventory recording did not begin until 1633, but it still offers a reliable idea of what a house of the period contained. The most striking thing about these inventories is the relative scarcity of major pieces of furniture: bedsteads, tables, chairs, cupboards are rare. The most common item of interior furniture is the chest, and it must have served many purposes—as a storage container, a seat, a worktable on which to prepare food or do any other small task, and a place from which to eat. Contemporary paintings and prints from northern Europe show chests serving in precisely the same capacity. Fireplace and cooking gear, tools, weapons, farming implements, and raw materials—leather, cloth, and food—loom large in the inventories, and it is reasonable to suggest that the most important items of property in the first ten years were those essential to provide food and shelter.

Among the earliest house inventories, that of one William Wright has been used to re-create precisely the material culture as a whole. This inventory was taken room by room, so that we not only know what Mr. Wright owned, but also in what room it was located at the time of his death. Re-created in the Winslow house, this inventory is complete to the linens in the chest in the sleeping chamber and the shoes beneath the canopied bedstead.

Wright was exceptional in owning, not one, but two bedsteads, although one was located in the loft, presumably unused, while the bedding that might have gone with it was located in the room below.

The inventories, however, do not tell us anything about the physical appearance of the various items of furniture, tools, and implements. For this information it becomes necessary to rely on paintings and prints of the period. The plantation maintains a large punch card file of such pictorial material, coded according to sixty-six material culture categories. It is thus relatively easy to sort out as many examples of any type of object as are needed to determine its appearance, as well as its physical placement within a room. Archaeological investigations in the colony area are also of some use in this connection, although most sites thus far excavated by the plantation date to a somewhat later time.

Having created a village of simple frame houses, and furnished them according to the best research data available, it remains to populate the village with trained interpreters who give the appearance of seventeenth-century Pilgrims. Dress is the most conspicuous difference between the interpreter and the twentieth-century visitor, and the clothing worn is based on research into English styles of the period. The Pilgrims were a simple folk, not of the highest socio-economic class of England. Regrettably, little study has been done on the dress of the plainer people of England of the time, so the plantation had to commission special research projects to obtain adequate information, thus ensuring proper attire for its personnel. Many people are greatly surprised by the colorful costumes. Unlike the stereotype so long associated with the Pilgrims, of people somberly clad in gray and black, they, in fact, dressed in quite bright and varying colors. In this case, the inventories again become useful, since in listing clothing, color is often mentioned. And while one does find an occasional, rather ambiguous reference to a sad-colored cloak, brighter colors generally prevail.

The material culture of the Pilgrims reflects the means by which they met the challenges of their environment. But there are also technological, social, and ideological dimensions that must be considered in presenting a full picture of early Plymouth. Within the past five years the plantation has done intensive research on such subjects as the development of farming practices in the colony, the effect on Pilgrim culture of the years spent in Holland, relationships between the Pilgrims and Indians, deviant behavior and the courts, social structure and family life in the colony, the culture of the Wampanoag Indians of the area, the financing of the colony and its economic practices, the books in the colonists' libraries (titles are listed in the inventories), and a number of other subjects. These studies are done either by the research staff or by consulting scholars, and all have resulted in formal reports and publications. The plantation's archaeological program is typical in many ways of this kind of research. There are numerous seventeenth-century homesites still in existence, and they are being systematically investigated. A typical "Pilgrim site" is the remains of a farmhouse. There is usually some evidence on the surface of a collapsed brick chimney, and a slight depression marking location of the cellar. These sites are very rich, and it is not unusual to recover as many as 10,000 artifacts from a single house, as well as some indication of its size and shape. The cluttered aspect of the Plymouth homesteads, for example, is amply supported by archaeology. Scattered around the house, for a distance of several yards, is a thick deposit of trash—broken pottery, animal bone, shells, nails and other structural hardware, and broken implements. One can easily imagine the state of such a house at the time—it must have been indeed a pungent and unsanitary situation. But the colonist's reluctance to police his yard, and to dispose neatly of his refuse, is a boon to the archaeologist, who gains much from the trash left behind by these untidy husbandmen. The plantation has excavated eight Colonial sites in the area, and these have produced approximately ten thousand bone fragments, which are now being studied for information on animal use, butchering techniques, and diet.

Although the study is not complete, there are already a few surprises evident. One is of sentimental interest: as yet, not a single turkey bone has come to light. Turkeys were consumed at the first Thanksgiving; while they may have been frequently hunted by the colonists, by mid-century—from which the earliest sites date—turkeys may well have become quite scarce. Even more unusual are the small numbers of wild mammalian bone

from these sites. By mid-century the colonists were relying almost entirely on domesticated animals for their meat supply. How much earlier this pattern exists is not yet known, but it is possible that hunting never did contribute greatly to the table. Of the domesticated animals, the commonest is pig—not surprising when one considers the ease of keeping pigs, and the variety of easily preserved meat that these animals furnish. Cattle, sheep, and goats are also common, and one site even produced horse bones in its domestic refuse. Until mid-century, Plymouth relied heavily on cattle as a basis for its economy, trading them to the Massachusetts Bay Colony for other commodities, but of course this use of cattle would never be reflected in faunal analysis of archaeological materials. Wild ducks are fairly common; in the inventories, fowling pieces far outnumber muskets. Unlike a solitary deer, a flock of sitting ducks is easily bagged by firing into its midst with a weapon that will scatter shot over a broad area.

Other common artifacts from these sites tell us of the life ways of their former occupants. Spoons occur in large numbers and knives are common. As yet no forks have come to light, and it is doubtful that they will. During the seventeenth century, the fork was a recent arrival from Italy, thought of as something only fops and dandies used. The common eating implement of the Pilgrims was the hand, and knives were used to cut food into manageable, easily handled pieces. The different types of ceramic ware found at various seventeenth-century sites dramatize the initial Americanization of the Pilgrims. Only two sites have produced significant amounts of pre-

The reality of women's work: making rope.—
Photo: Plimoth Plantation

1650 pottery; one was dug by the plantation; the other, unfortunately bulldozed away during construction of a parking lot. The early ceramics are all imported and have a strong medieval look about them—plain green—and brown-glazed pottery. English ceramic styles changed rapidly in the seventeenth century, marked by a proliferation of decorated earthenware and the tin-glazed earthenware commonly called ''delft.'' These wares occur in Plymouth Colony archaeological sites of the later half of the century and are joined by large quantities of locally produced redware. Thus an early site will have pottery that gives an impression of late-medieval England, while ceramics from sites of the later half of the century give a feeling of more of the simple, but competent, products of local craftsmen.

Archaeology not only provides us with insights into the daily lives of the Plymouth colonists, but also lends support to certain aspects of this history. A small incident in Plymouth during King Philip's War (1675-76) was the so-called Eel River Massacre, at the Clark Garrison house south of Plymouth. The facts of the episode are few and simple. In the spring of 1676 a group of Indians attacked a garrison house belonging to William Clark,

Trencher mates at Plimoth Plantation.—*Photo: George Chapman*

located on the Eel River. The attack took place on Sunday, while some of the occupants were at church. Eleven lives were lost, and the building was set afire; the Indians responsible were apprehended and executed. In 1941, archaeologists excavated a homesite not far from the locale traditionally identified with the Eel River incident. While not so much as a brick had ever been turned up at the later location, the excavated site turned out to be that of a house that stood until ca. 1675, and was then burned. The artifacts from the site included the normal domestic artifacts of the period and a variety of objects that indicate some special function for the building. Large quantities of shot, as well as lead scrap and lead lumps that had cooled in the bottoms of melting ladles, were recovered. Gun flints were also manufactured on the site, as indicated by massive amounts of waste flakes of English flint. Parts of a military uniform, a fragment of an epaulet, and a boot tap were found. The conclusion in this case seems quite obvious and provides further documentation of a historical event.

A totally pragmatic approach added another dimension to the village presentation, when several of the houses were used experimentally in a genuine living situation. In the house furnished according to the Wright inventory, for example, a family of eight lived for a week according to seventeenth-century ground rules. The project was an experiment in determining whether this method would provide any greater insights into how to present all the houses in the village. It has succeeded to the extent that the plantation staff is now convinced that a much greater amount of this kind of investigation should be pursued. One striking result was the pattern of clutter and debris that comes from full-time living, day and night, over a sustained period of time. It is very difficult to simulate clutter, unless it is done by actually engaging in the activities that produce it. After carrying water, chopping wood, and preparing the food necessary to sustain eight people, certain patterns of use became apparent. The constant supply of water needed at the hearth ensured a rather damp area in the line from door to fire. Problems of disposal of purely natural refuse became very obvious; one must do something with all the corn-husks, bone scraps, onion peels, and clamshells that accumulate. Taking note of the archaeological evidence for dumping refuse in the yard, it was tried, and while a certain amount of debris did remain, the ever-present chickens consumed a surprising amount. Were pigs to be added to the roster of live dispose-alls, the problem would be even less serious.

At a time when man has just set foot upon the moon, and technology promises to dominate our society, it is somehow reassuring to look back to another era, when problems, although just as serious, were at least somewhat more at one's immediate disposal. There is a strong feeling in the nation today of a loss of individuality, of control over one's social destiny. Attempts are being made, some successful, some not, to return to earlier standards—to an earlier style of living. In placing our

Colonial ancestors in their proper perspective, at least one can hope to learn if the lost world we are mourning did once exist. It is strange, indeed, that many Americans invoke values in the name of the country's founding fathers, including the Pilgrims, that these men of the past would find somewhat peculiar. Some of the dissent that has recently disturbed much of the nation is not essentially dissimilar from that which caused our first settlers to remove themselves from familiar ways and set out into an unknown world. It matters little, in fact, whether Myles Standish ever spoke more than three words to Priscilla Mullins—he may not have—but it matters greatly if the Pilgrims are considered to have established religious freedom in the New World—they did not. But there is much to respect, admire, and appreciate, from our three-century perspective, in what and who these people truly were, and it is through Plimoth Plantation's efforts, along with those of historians and anthropologists concerned with seventeenth-century America, that the story of the Pilgrims and their fellow colonists can be told "like it was."

Old Sturbridge Village Introduces Social Conflict into Its Interpretive Story

15

Andrew H. Baker and Warren Leon

The March 1986 issue of History News *published two important articles dealing with the potential of historical simulation to interpret conflict within a community. The first by Andrew H. Baker and Warren Leon describe two innovative programs developed at Old Sturbridge Village: the town meeting and 1840 presidential election campaign. The authors note the success of these programs at bringing to the visitor's attention such significant nineteenth-century social issues as abolition, temperance, educational reform, and relief for the poor. The importance of dealing with these issues at outdoor museums should not be minimized. "As we take up the challenge of incorporating conflict and the public sphere into the interpretation at our museums, we will not only enrich our historical presentations, but we will remain in the forefront of historical investigation as well. During the past twenty years, rising public and scholarly interest in social history has given living-history museums both popularity and growing academic respectability."*

The townspeople were gathered in the large white meeting house facing the town common. A mill owner stood up to speak. "I move," he proclaimed, "that school district number 12 be divided so that the textile manufacturing village can provide its own school for the citizen's children. This will ensure a better education for our children."

"But what about my children?" complained a farmer. "We live in a rural part of the district. If the factory area is set off, we will lose the mill's tax base. Our district will be poorer, and we won't be able to provide adequate schooling."

"Bah!" interjected another irate farmer, scornfully. "These manufacturers don't care about education. They just want to control the school, so the children will conform to their work schedule in the mills."

"That's not the case, sir."

"Yes, it is, and your dams flood farmers' fields as well."

"Hear! Hear!"

"Order! Order, gentlemen!" roared the moderator over the increasing din. "This is a divisive issue, but let us deal with it as gentlemen."

Visitors to Old Sturbridge Village, in Sturbridge, Massachusetts, witnessed this heated argument during a recreated town meeting last fall. At first glance, you may think that OSV has gone too far—staff interpreters actually yelling at each other in front of visitors. But this

scene and others just as vituperative are part of the OSV's new two-prong interpretive thrust to show the conflicts, tensions, and instabilities within early American communities and to emphasize the way Americans interacted in the public sphere. Although both approaches are rare in living-history museums, we believe they are central to a full interpretation of the past.

Living-history museums have difficulty integrating conflict or politics into their presentations. Up to now, such museums have concentrated on the physical settings and everyday activities of past societies. The farmer plants a crop, the school mistress teaches a lesson, the blacksmith forges a tool, the miller grinds grain, and the householder cooks a meal.

The object and process approaches at living-history museums most closely match the social history themes of work and family. The full development of living-history museums over the past two decades has coincided with an increased academic interest in these themes. The actual and potential connections between history museums and academic historians have thereby increased, particularly as academic historians have begun to appreciate the importance of material culture analysis.

But other themes derive from social history as well—themes that living-history museums can illuminate. Too often visitors do not make the connections among the various demonstrations at living-history sites. For this reason, several living history museums have recently gone beyond portrayals of work and family life to uncover and interpret the relationships among community members. At Old Sturbridge Village, for example, where we show a rural New England town of the 1830s, we concentrate on a complex web of economic and social relationships. Rather than depict the potter in isolation, we identify his customers by placing in his shop a facsimile of his 1830's account book and items he would have sold. We also have on hand some of the goods the potter would have received in trade.

By interpreting the interaction among the individuals and groups within our historical community, we face the challenge of showing not only cooperation, but conflict as well. Many relationships, like the potter's with his customers, may have been comfortable and amicable, but nineteenth-century communities often split into antagonistic groups along religious, economic, and geographic lines. Living-history museums that attempt to portray convincingly the resulting conflicts may find that while costumed museum interpreters talk about the issues that caused Americans to disagree, the visitors' sensory experience leaves a different impression—one of contented, friendly residents going about their daily work and family activities. Museum staff members, ever-courteous and open toward visitors, convey a sense of harmony and stability at the site.

So, a more explicit approach is necessary. At Old Sturbridge Village, we have introduced conflict and community tensions into our interpretation by re-creating aspects of public life—both the political and governmental process and private groups' consideration of public issues. Political rallies, town meetings, lyceum debates, and meetings of voluntary associations, such as temperance and abolition societies, provided an arena for nineteenth-century Americans to express their differing opinions. Activities in the public sphere reveal to our twentieth-century audience how at least some New Englanders viewed their society and how they reacted to the changes taking place in it. Issues that produced significant conflict and debate reveal most fully people's feelings, emotions, and beliefs.

New England Town Meetings

Conflicts of many types beset early nineteenth-century town governments in New England. At Old Sturbridge Village, we capture the spirit of a nineteenth-century community with its numerous officials and open decision-making through town meetings. This form of local government provides an excellent vehicle for portraying competing philosophies of the community, of progress, and of the government's responsibility. Through twice-yearly re-created town meetings, we examine such diverse and divisive issues as relief for the poor, temperance, educational reform, and economic growth, while portraying governmental structures and processes.

Preparing the Script

For the historical data needed for our presentations, we turned to an analysis of state and town records by researcher Caroline Sloat. These records helped us set the parameters for the official actions to be taken in our re-created meetings, but other primary sources, including diaries, tracts, newspapers, and personal accounts, enabled us to flesh out the discussion of the issues. Because we change the content of the meetings each time we present them, interpretation department staff members Andrew Baker, Robert Olson, and Dennis Picard re-examine the historical sources every spring and fall

A reading of the Declaration of Independence on the fourth of July at Old Sturbridge Village.—*Photo: Robert S. Arnold, Old Sturbridge Village*

before drawing up the warrants and writing the scripts. Whenever we re-introduce an issue in a new context, we review the documentation to ensure accuracy. Just as in the 1830s, some issues are carried over from one meeting to the next. Our hypothetical establishment of a poor farm, for example, took six town meetings and three years to cover. By carrying over the discussions in this way, we give returning visitors a sense of passing time. We also deal with physical changes in the village itself, such as new roads, and one town meeting even spurred us to make historically appropriate changes to the site by adding signposts.

Once the script is ready, staff members take on roles reflecting the different social, religious, and economic divisions within the community, so all possible points of view are represented. We allow time for the staff members to review the script, get more information about the issues if they need it, and practice reacting in character. We conduct the meeting itself as a sort of readers' theatre, which allows the role-players to use scripts. As staff members participate in successive meetings, they become more familiar with the issues, and using their knowledge of their particular characters' views, they begin to improvise on the script.

The issue of temperance is a good example of how we present various points of view within the community. The temperance movement had achieved prominence by the 1830s. Its advocates had moved beyond moral suasion to a more active approach. They exhorted town governments and the state of Massachusetts to restrict or ban the consumption of ardent spirits. Communities split over these attempts at regulation, and town meetings became temperance battlegrounds.

In town meetings, the temperance issue was dealt with in a variety of ways. The town could order the selectmen—the town executive authority—to cease licensing retailers of ardent spirits, or it could order its representatives to vote for changes or repeals of licensing laws. To prevent consumption at public expense, the town could forbid the purchase of alcohol as an expense for road maintenance or for the poor farm. Occasionally, the selectmen discussed poor relief and the ways in which they believed alcohol consumption caused poverty. Because the county commissioners had ultimate power over licensing, the election of commissioners, held during the town meetings, often hinged on the candidates' temperance credentials.

In our re-created town meetings, various characters present their opinions on temperance. An old farmer, who has drunk rum all his life, sees no reason to prohibit spirits for men working on the roads. A young artisan, concerned with taxation, complains about drunkards who are now a public burden at the poor farm. A progressive market-oriented farmer claims that his farm's productivity increased after the elimination of ardent spirits. Other residents note that drinking at the tavern provides their primary recreation and relief from hard labor. A mill agent argues, however, that a sober, work-

ing populace is more productive and easily controlled. And then the ministers always remind the townspeople of the need for moral improvement. As the citizens discuss temperance, they also express their differing views of community responsibility and future directions for their society.

We ask the visitors present at these discussions to consider the various arguments and then vote as if they lived in the 1830's community. Some are persuaded by the ministers' moral pleas, others by the desire of the old farmer to leave things as they are. Some see that there is no easy answer, and they begin to understand the pros and cons of temperance. Visitors often realize that, despite the way conflicts are couched in terms of good and evil, divisive issues are complex. Our goal through all of this is to give visitors some understanding of the social, economic, and religious factors generating these community divisions along with an understanding of the methods town governments used to resolve conflicts.

Voluntary Organizations

Not all issues were debated in town meetings, so we have also re-created other settings where public issues were considered. We are specially interested in the meetings of the numerous voluntary organizations nineteenth-century New Englanders formed for the purposes of self-help, reform, and political action. As French traveler Alexis de Tocqueville observed in the 1830s, "Nothing is more deserving of our attention than the intellectual and moral associations of America . . . Americans of all ages, all conditions, and all dispositions constantly form associations."

To illuminate this important phenomenon, the staff created the Sturbridge Charitable Society, which holds its monthly meetings in several houses in our village. This group of women re-creates a representative rural organization that aided the sick and destitute by providing clothing and household textiles. Like nineteenth-century society members, our interpreters drew up a constitution and elected officers, including a first directress who conducts the meetings. Behind-the-scenes, under the direction of Margaret Piatt, assistant director of interpretation, and Betty Few, lead interpreter, the interpreters develop an outline for each meeting and then role-play improvisationally in front of the public. Our research into the structure of the meetings, as well as the interpreters' careful consideration of their characters, make informal role-playing effective and historically accurate.

Last year, however, we changed the format of our regular charitable society meetings when we introduced a particularly controversial subject—slavery and its abolition. To ensure that we presented accurately the range of rural New England views on this complex issue, we wrote out the script of the entire meeting and presented a dramatization that was more akin to a formal theatre presentation. Chief Historian Jack Larkin and Consultant Robert McDonald of the University of Connecticut Theater Arts Department prepared a thirty-minute dramatization based on period documents. Into the meeting of our town's charitable society, they introduced the formidable presence of Abigail Kelley, an important abolitionist speaker and organizer active in the New England countryside in the late 1830s.

In our script, Kelley was brought to the charitable society meeting by a member who had become a fervent abolitionist and hoped, with Kelley's help, to convert her colleagues to the cause. The ensuing discussion exhibited grave differences of opinion in the society's membership as the participants discussed colonization, the status of free blacks in New England, the right to petition, and the Constitution as the symbol and vehicle of national unity. The script not only conveyed what the various women believed but how their socio-economic backgrounds influenced their beliefs.

The twelve staff members with parts in the dramatization memorized their lines and rehearsed periodically for several weeks. McDonald helped train them in the difficult and important task of expressing the views of the characters convincingly. It was specially difficult because the interpreters would be expressing views sharply at odds with their own beliefs and those of most twentieth-century Americans. The resulting dramatization drew a capacity crowd, and during the provocative follow-up session, audience members discussed and weighed alternative ways to resolve the antislavery conflict and suggested parallels to contemporary problems.

Tippecanoe and Tyler, Too!

Issues like abolition and temperance initially concerned only a particular segment of the community but often later grew into major divisive factors in state and national elections. To deal with the sort of national and statewide issues traditionally considered by political historians, Old Sturbridge Village presents every four years a re-enactment of the 1840 presidential election. Visitors see these larger conflicts through a unique lens—the view and activities of the members of a local community. As the first modern presidential campaign, the 1840 election, with the Democrats under Martin Van Buren, the Whigs under William Henry Harrison, and the Liberty party under James Birney, was particularly well suited to our goal because the election spurred more local activity than most others.

We introduce visitors to the issues of 1840 and then show why a rural population like ours disagreed on these issues, as well as how they were affected and involved in the campaign. One issue that caused the community to split was economic growth. Should the state spend tax revenue to buy stock and give loans to private corporations for the construction of the railroad? Should a tariff be imposed to protect American industry from foreign competition? Other issues, as well, mobilized voters to go to the polls. Should the militia system be revised, abolished, or superseded by a national standing army? Should the state try to restrict the consumption of alcoholic beverages?

The local citizenry, even those segments of the population that were not allowed to vote, became politically active not only because of their concerns over the issues but because of the mobilizing efforts of each political party. Paralleling their historical counterparts, the interpreters get involved in the 1840 campaign early in the year when the town meeting splits along party lines. Through the summer, the parties organize meetings and sponsor speeches, and each major party holds its own Fourth of July celebration. Before the Whig celebration, participants roll an eight-foot "Harrison Ball," which is covered with canvas and painted campaign slogans, from Boston to Sturbridge. By drawing up local party constitutions and resolutions to express local opinion on national issues, we are able to show the importance of the party organization as a means of mobilization. Our interpreters make banners in the houses, and women discuss the issues as they gather for tea. The intensive media aspects of the campaign, which we re-create with songs and parades, especially appeal to visitors.

Careful research provided details about small town campaign activities and suggested how our museum community could be divided over issues. We assigned to each of the village households and many of the tradespeople political views and issues on which to focus. For example, the printer and his household actively support the Whigs by printing political materials in the printing office and by hosting ladies' gatherings to discuss the issues from a Whig point of view. The outlying Freeman farm is the focal household for the Democrats.

We try to educate visitors not only about the issues of the day but also about the electoral process. We encourage visitors to participate in several ways. Through a printed folder highlighting several campaign issues, we ask visitors to compare their own views with those of the period parties. We also invite visitors to vote whenever we consider issues in political association meetings or in the town meetings. During the final voting on election day, visitors use reproduction period ballots to cast their votes.

Politics as Staff Development

Staff members who vote in nineteenth-century manner with open paper ballots also learn from the experience. Our charitable society meetings and town government activities have played an important role in staff development. Just as an interpreter can better understand and discuss spinning after having engaged in the process, so can that person better interpret conflict after having participated in it. Our public issues programs have awakened many staff members to interpretive themes they had never considered and have given these staff members confidence that their understanding of the past is now more sophisticated and complete. These days interpreters regularly talk to visitors about slavery, temperance, and poor relief, and they use their firsthand experience to dispel the myth of stable, conflict-free communities.

Many of our programs have generated spinoffs, just as the monthly charitable society meeting developed from a Whig ladies' meeting during our 1980 re-creation of the 1840 election. Soon we will add a temperance society, an antislavery society, and a debating society. Using a grant from the National Endowment for the Humanities, we will dramatize the way New Englanders during the early nineteenth century understood and debated the implications of the Constitution—implications such as the meaning of "freedom of religion." Continued extensive training will enable us to improve our programs and will help interpreters expand and refine their repertoire of interpretive techniques.

Can our experience be applied to other institutions? After all, other parts of the country did not have town meetings with their wide community involvement, and museums focusing on other time periods cannot necessarily re-create an election like that of 1840, with its high public participation, or meetings of an organization like the charitable society. Yet every community has some arena in which conflict and controversy appear; every society has a public sphere in which political issues are considered and government is carried out. Old Sturbridge Village re-creates a unique society, but there are ways to focus on conflict as a historical concept in any museum.

As we take up the challenge of incorporating conflict and the public sphere into the interpretation at our museums, we will not only enrich our historical presentations, but we will remain in the forefront of historical investigation as well. During the past twenty years, rising public and scholarly interest in social history has given living-history museums both popularity and growing academic respectability.

Social historians in academia are beginning to realize that they must incorporate conflict and public life into their presentations of the past. New York University's Thomas Bender has recently called for a new synthesis of American history that, while retaining the current interest in social history, would "reclaim the public realm." Living-history museums can help shape this reconceptualization by incorporating public issues into their already strong presentations of work and family life. In fact, our ability to integrate these subjects in a three-dimensional environment gives us a unique role to play in shaping the synthesis.

Connor Prairie Refocuses Its Interpretive Message to Include Controversial Subjects

16

John Patterson

In the second of two articles on conflict and community which ran in the March 1986 issue of History News, *John Patterson discusses how Indiana's Connor Prairie developed programs that interpret important nineteenth-century themes such as slavery, temperance, religion, and death. These issues often tore apart frontier communities in the 1830's and were as controversial then as they are now. Given our concern with the teaching of "values" in the public schools, the experience of living history museums is indeed useful and thought provoking. Patterson concludes that "None of us can portray the past exactly; the source materials have not survived, and no one would pay to walk through raw sewage on Main Street." Nevertheless, he argues, "At Connor Prairie, presentations of conflict have made our village more human and realistic and have added to the ability of our visitors to relate to our programs."*

In the historical profession, we perpetuate the American ideal. We like, and are comfortable with, our idealized past—from Thomas Jefferson's yeoman farmer to Walt Disney's version of Davy Crockett. These visions are simply not true.

How do we dispel the image of a generic past—a past filled with quaint village greens, sleepy Midwestern towns where nothing much seemed to happen, or a gold strike in every California settlement—from the public's mind? Recently, museums have begun to sensitize their publics to the differences among people, as museum boards and staffs see that ignoring the disagreements and conflicts that compose our heritage paints a distorted picture. Our past is not bland. There is no generic pioneer settlement. The past the public is beginning to see in museums across the country is rich and diverse and full of conflicts that give it human perspective and scale.

Conner Prairie is a major, outdoor, living history museum located approximately ten minutes north of Indianapolis. The museum contains three separate areas: The William Connor Estate, with the 1823 Conner house and five outbuildings, where we use traditional third-person interpretive techniques; the Pioneer Adventure Center, an area with six buildings, where we use second-person interpretive techniques such as hands-on participation; and the village of Prairietown, where it is always 1836, and the interpreters use only first-person interpretation. The buildings that form the village of Prairietown

have all been relocated from elsewhere, and while "residents" are fictitious, they are all based on solid historical research.

Recently Conner Prairie reviewed its interpretive programs in light of the museum's purpose to depict the life, times, attitudes, and values of the first generation of Indiana settlers. Through our review, we found that we were presenting the first generation of Hoosiers as a cohesive, even generic, group. The past we presented was boring.

We are now refocusing parts of our interpretation to portray the different backgrounds of the people in the historical village. These differences often translate into sometimes subtle, sometimes not so subtle, social conflicts.

The People of Prairietown

Prairietown's story emphasizes several issues that faced early 19th-century settlers. One is the problem caused by the death of the head-of-household of a pioneer family. We tell the story of Mrs. Zimmerman and her husband Johann who arrived in Indiana in the spring of 1835. Of German descent and from western Pennsylvania, Johann brought his family West to manage the Campbell farm and the newly completed Golden Eagle Inn. Johann died just a few months after arriving in Prairietown. Rather than give up and return home, Mrs. Zimmerman and her sons fulfill their contract to Campbell. Her grown sons, John and Martin, manage the farm, while she runs the inn. Several local people think it isn't proper for a woman to work as an innkeeper, but she does a good job, and the travelers are all pleased with the accommodations, especially the food.

Old age and retirement are other issues we examine. Mr. Fenton, originally from South Carolina, has been a farmer and seasonal weaver most of his life. Now that he is in his 60s, he has turned the farm over to his children and moved to town, where he spends time doing what pleases him most—working at the loom.

We deal with the issue of manufacturing progress through the Baker family. Originally from England, Jonathon Baker brought his family to Prairietown by way of Virginia and Tennessee. Potters by trade, the Baker sons continued manufacturing redware after their father's death until 1834, when they built a new kiln and switched to stoneware. Generally, the sons would rather hunt, fish, trap, swim, and otherwise enjoy their surroundings than work. They see no need for education, or even for the ability to read or write beyond the level necessary to keep their accounts.

We try to help visitors understand how communities historically dealt with the poor by introducing them to Mr. Hasting, a 67-year-old veteran of the American Revolution and the Battle of Tippecanoe. He has petitioned Congress for an army pension and hopes to hear about it soon. In the interim, Mr. McClure purchased a "contract for the poor" for Mr. Hastings. He is on welfare, and the first week in May he is "sold" to the lowest bidder for the year. His character allows us to discuss not only welfare but the general condition of old people in American society.

Another cultural difference we interpret, centers around the Curtis family, who arrived in Prairietown in 1833. They came from Canadaigua, New York, and purchased their property—the house, the blacksmith shop, and 160 acres—through correspondence with Lucas Wainscott. Mrs. Curtis has dreamed of living in a new brick farmhouse but has realized that she'll probably never have one. To lessen her homesickness, she persuaded her husband to paint the parlor floor and stencil the walls. Her home has become the talk of the town as other residents note the "oddities" in its appearance.

Through these people and the physical material of their homes and lives, we show that then, as now, the individuals who make up communities were not all alike. We point out that, in every community, differing cultural backgrounds often caused low-level community conflict and strife. In Prairietown, the different physical appearances of the homes provide the residents with fodder for the gossip circuit. Our efforts go a long way toward making the community more realistic and believable.

Dealing with Death

Another addition to Conner Prairie's historical village is a cemetery. In March 1985, headstones, modeled after 19th-century stones, were hand-carved and put in place. In the 22-year history of Conner Prairie and the 14-year history of Prairietown, we had never dealt with the subject of death.

Last year, we performed an 1836 funeral at Conner Prairie. The staff had discussed the possibility for years but had decided against it because of fears of a negative public reaction. Last year, we discussed the possibility again. We knew of two other outdoor museums that had funeral programs—Old Bethpage Village Restoration and Plimoth Plantation. To test the waters, we talked to their staff members, who informed us that there were no public backlashes, and in fact, that the public seemed to respond favorably. They also said they advised visitors at the ticket desk that a funeral was being presented, so those who did not wish to deal with death could avoid the performance. We took their advice and did the same thing.

Because the "residents" of Conner Prairie's village are based on extensive historical research and all add to our interpretive message, we did not want to let one of our "residents" die. We chose, instead, Isaiah Fairbanks, a traveling salesman, as our victim. According to our story, Fairbanks was traveling in the West to explore farmers' needs before deciding whether or not to invest in patent rights for a new reaper. During his journey, he caught influenza and died during the early morning hours of September 15. The funeral service followed the Methodist Episcopalian rites and was held at three o'clock that afternoon.

We received excellent media coverage of the event—40 inches of feature copy and a photograph in the Sunday *Indianapolis Star*. A crowd of 641 visitors, an increase of 17.2 percent over the same day the year before, came to see the funeral.

What was most interesting was the interaction among the visitors. As a grave digger, I saw first-hand many exchanges between visitors. Children, with their natural curiosity, asked questions about death and American funeral customs, and the answers they received from accompanying adults were sometimes odd. One grandmother could not explain why we bury the dead. Two or three visitors cried at the graveside.

More than 250 visitors were waiting at the Golden Eagle Inn, where the coffin sat, when we arrived to move it to the cemetery. After four interpreters carried the coffin to a wagon, the entire crowd formed a procession and followed the wagon to the cemetery where another 200-plus visitors were waiting.

Public Reaction

Overall, we believed the day was a success. We heard no negative comments, and after conducting an informal survey of the visitors, we concluded that they found the funeral educational and sensitively handled. The majority also thought we should do it again the following year. More importantly, we showed a part of life that we had consciously avoided before. At Conner Prairie, as at other museums, staff members are concerned about the public's reaction to such programs. All of us in the history museum profession want to show life as it was, but none of us desire to insult or irritate the public in the process. Sometimes these concerns stop good programs, as our concerns caused us to delay the funeral program. Not only were our public relations fears unfounded, but the public seemed to appreciate our efforts in handling the subject.

Camp Meetings and Temperance

In the last few years, Conner Prairie has added other programs or expanded existing ones, which, on the surface, might cause negative repercussions from the public. Before embarking on such programs, we try to anticipate problems and think through ways to minimize them.

One recent addition is our camp meeting. Using the character of a Methodist-Episcopalian circuit rider, we re-create a 19th-century camp meeting each August. Obviously, the camp meeting is condensed, so it can be completed in about 20 minutes. Even though religion is one of those difficult topics, the program has been well received.

The same circuit rider also helps some of the local citizens organize a temperance meeting. This program was added in 1985 to illustrate a significant social issue of 1830's America. Ezra Higbee, who lives just outside town and can usually be found at the Golden Eagle Inn, has a tendency to imbibe—frequently. Thus, the program often

revolves around the temperance faction, headed by the minister and the Curtis family, and Ezra and one or two of his supporters, who maintain that a man should be allowed to have a drink when the urge strikes, without all this fuss.

What is interesting about this program is the level of sympathy on the part of the public for the temperance cause. Because of the modern-day connection with efforts against alcohol abuse by such groups as Mothers Against Drunk Drivers (MADD), the media coverage of this program was exceptional.

Even our Christmas celebration—"Conner Prairie by Candlelight"—revolves around a theme that includes low-level community conflict. The town's residents share their individual thoughts about Christmas with visitors, and since these settlers have come from different parts of the country and have different religious beliefs and values, their feelings about the day also differ. Their discussion revolves around Dr. and Mrs. Campbell's Christmas party, a very new and radical idea in town. In fact, residents who are used to Christmas being just another day are not pleased with the Campbell's party.

Tampering with the public's concept of Christmas can be as risky as portraying an 1830's funeral. The public likes its notion of Christmas, and the images most of us carry around in our minds of a 19th-century Christmas come from the 1880's and 1890's. Our program attempts to make people aware of how Christmas has evolved

Death and poverty in Victorian America: a funeral at Old Bethpage Village.—*Photo: Nassau County Department of Parks and Recreation, Division of Museum Services*

since the 1830s. Between 6,000 and 8,000 people have visited our site each of the last three years during our 20-day Christmas season.

Indiana's Black Heritage

The next major program we plan to add is the interpretation of the role of blacks in the 1830's Indiana. An important theme in American history for more than 350 years, the subject of race relations is seldom addressed by living history museums. Trying to design a program that remains true to the past, while not offending the public, can be a challenge.

Conner Prairie is probably ideally suited to portray this aspect of history. Slavery was a major issue in Indiana's early years, and the state borders Kentucky, a former slave state. While there were some black residents in the state before, the early 1830's saw a large increase in the black population. Many came from North Carolina and settled in the central part of the state. To some extent these settlers followed the same migration path as the Quakers who settled in Indiana.

To accomplish our program goals, we will add a first-person black interpreter to our village who will discuss some of the social and intellectual issues involved in slavery. One of Indianapolis' most respected black historians is researching and developing the character for the project. So far, the research is not complete, but unless the historical evidence indicates otherwise, our interpreter will play the role of a free black who has left the South on the heels of the Nat Turner Rebellion in 1831. As a free black, he will relate black views of Southern society, especially the institution of slavery, and will discuss various aspects of black life without being typecast as an extreme radical or an Uncle Tom.

Also critical to this program's success will be the involvement of a task force of black community leaders. When the research is completed and the character sketch is developed, the task force will examine what we are attempting to accomplish.

We think that this approach, which specifically includes the involvement of members of our public who are not museum professionals, will improve the program's presentation. Perhaps we can finally show part of

The village pauper is sold to the lowest bidder for his yearly "care" at Connor Prairie.—*Photo: Jim Phillips*

the important role that blacks played in early Indiana. If so, then our story will be more complete and more historically correct than it was before.

None of us can portray the past exactly; the source materials have not survived, and no one would pay to walk through raw sewage on Main Street. At Conner Prairie, presentations of conflict have made our village more human and realistic and have added to the ability of our visitors to relate to our programs.

A Sense of Another World
History Museums and Cultural Change

17

James Deetz

This is one of the first articles to identify the interpretive potential of "full-scale community re-creations, such as Colonial Williamsburg, Old Sturbridge Village, Conner Prairie, and Plimoth Plantation." It was published in the May-June 1980 issue of Museum News. *Deetz argues that "a community re-creation can immerse the visitor in the entire world of the past, or at least some approximation of it." He suggests that re-created "communities have the potential of conveying the strongest sense of change in America since its early years, but, at the same time, the highest possibility of failure if not done with skill and a feeling for the time that is being represented."*

History museums of all kinds and sizes, from the Smithsonian's Museum of History and Technology to the smallest, most modest historic house, are assuming an increasingly significant role in telling Americans about their past. This past is ever subject to interpretation, and we will never be able to re-create it completely, with all of its subtleties and texture, or to know the past as a participant in it might have done. It is the task of the museum to choose those aspects of an earlier time that are worthy of interpretation and to devise effective methods to make that interpretation work.

American culture has been characterized by both continuity and change over nearly four centuries. Whether we are exhibiting a collection of delftware in a formally labeled case or creating a living context in which delftware can be understood as part of a larger cultural system, the problem remains the same. Is a delft plate to be interpreted as a simple analog to a piece of modern dinnerware—modern culture projected unchanged into the past—or should it be interpreted more in terms of the period and circumstances of its use? Both approaches have merit. To understand the longer traditions of a culture provides a valuable perspective on continuity, but to interpret differences in the functions of commonplace items at different times addresses the question of cultural change more directly. Such change has indeed been profound since early Colonial times, but history museums often do not acknowledge the changes as much as they might. While continuity seems to be emphasized more than change, a consideration of difference might well provide a different and more sophisticated kind of interpretation. To discern the differences, one must not look at material culture—the built environment—merely as a simpler version of what we have today.

Fortunately, museums deal with one of the most eloquent legacies from the past, the actual objects used by people to organize and expedite their lives. Far more than documents, things have a special kind of immediacy. It takes little imagination to picture a smoke-blackened cooking pot in its original place over the fire in the huge fireplace of a seventeenth-century house. After all, it once was there, and it forms a powerful link between then and now in a way a written account cannot. Likewise, an old timber-framed house can place the visitor in the same space used by the original inhabitants, a space that reflects their attitudes about social living. Properly interpreted, the hall of a seventeenth-century house can convey a sense of another world, one very different from that which we inhabit.

The basic building block of any exhibit, whether in a small table case or in a full re-creation of an early community, is the individual artifact. The term "artifact" is somewhat vague, and while a house can be thought of as an artifact as well as a thimble can, normal usage restricts "artifact" to smaller objects, usually portable; furniture, ceramics, firearms, toys, clothing, books, and tools, for example. The artifact is the material correlate of the individual. An artifact is often made by a single person and used at any given time for a specific purpose. Thus, artifacts are useful indicators of individual behavior and can be used to interpret that behavior. Exceptions to the individuality of artifacts are also informative and shed light on important aspects of the way in which people functioned together. For example, if a seventeenth-century wooden trencher is simply interpreted as a container from which food was taken, its obvious relationship to a modern dinner plate is apparent. Such an interpretation emphasizes the continuity between the seventeenth century and the twentieth century. However, fundamental differences can also be interpreted, and an important statement of the change in culture over three centuries may be made. Contemporary descriptions of seventeenth-century food customs and probate inventory evidence made it clear that trenchers were used corporately. More than one person ate from a single container; such persons were known as trencher-mates. This fact highlights differences, but it also serves as an example of the corporate nature of seventeenth-century society. Sharing trenchers was not an isolated practice, but rather a reflection of a larger pattern of shared living space and burial space, as well as attitudes and responsibilities.

The corporate nature of seventeenth-century society contrasts with American culture during the later eighteenth century. Accordingly, the interpretation of a dinner place in the context of the first decades of the nineteenth century can better be done from the perspective of culture change. By that time, every person had his or her own dinner plate, cutlery, chair, and, to a greater degree than before, private living space. Rather than simply view this individualization as similar to our use of artifacts today, it is better to bring it into relief by contrasting it with an earlier, quite different pattern.

Another way in which the interpretation of historical artifacts can focus attention on culture change is through a consideration of their function. The most obvious, and most interpreted, function of artifacts is their technical function, their practical use in everyday life. Axes cut, needles sew, beds are slept in, and plates hold food. Yet, beyond their technical uses, artifacts served other functions. Objects that appear, from twentieth-century perspective, to have had only technical functions had social functions as well. Large delft plates called "chargers" probably served an almost exclusively social function in the earlier years of the seventeenth century in America. Their rarity in most households as indicated by probate data and archaeological excavations shows that they were not used for serving food, even on a shared basis. When these plates are analyzed, again through the use of inventories, on a room-by-room basis, they are most commonly located in the parlor, a room which served a highly social function. The parlor was a place where important visitors might be received, where bodies were laid out before funerals, and where objects of visible wealth were publicly displayed. Large delft chargers were such objects, and they often served the social function of making a statement to the community about the means of their owners. It was not until late in the seventeenth century, and then only among

people of higher than average means, that delft plates seem to have been standard equipment for food consumption. Any interpretation of such artifacts, whether through passive museum labels or active live interpretation, should take these differences into account. Merely to describe the object in terms of its physical attributes and a function derived from a twentieth-century analog not only masks important differences that reflect culture change, but also is incorrect.

What is true of plates and chargers is true of all the other material aspects of early American life. We can perceive differences in individuality of use or of social function only if we resist the tendency to describe earlier, different cultural patterns in terms of our own modern ones. Historical museums can deal effectively with culture change only when interpretation is freed, at least in part, from the imposition of twentieth-century categories and values. This can be a difficult task; it requires considerable research and probably can never be done completely. Yet it must be attempted, since even a few perspectives of change over time can be very powerful aids in communicating an understanding of cultural differences and the changes that brought them about.

If single artifacts tend to mirror individuals and their behavior, collections of them organized into systematic and functional groupings mirror the behavior of groups of people. The commonest such grouping of artifacts is the so-called "period room." Properly created, such an exhibit can be very useful in interpreting familiar roles, division of labor, and the integrated relationship of a wide variety of artifacts. Modern period rooms tend to concentrate a careful selection of artifacts from a single place and a very brief period of time. The period rooms at the Winterthur Museum are examples of this kind of exhibit. They show the viewer a selection of furnishings that have primarily aesthetic appeal, and their interpretation tends heavily to an art history perspective. Yet the earliest period rooms installed in this country seem not to have been made with this end in mind, but rather were groupings of artifacts designed to help the viewer better appreciate the interior environment in which early Americans lived. Charles P. Wilcomb was responsible for these assemblages, installing the first of a series he was to create in the New England Hall of the Golden Gate Park Museum in San Francisco in 1895. Later, Wilcomb installed such rooms in the Hall Museum of Anthropology in Pittsburgh and the Oakland Public Museum. All were very similar, and Wilcomb did not call them period rooms, but "Colonial kitchens" and "Colonial bedrooms." His stated intent was to convey to the viewer what such an interior looked like, and he emphasized the commonplace over the finer quality pieces. After Wilcomb's death, his successor at the Oakland Museum, John Rowley, wrote:

> Group installation methods lend themselves to many classes of objects. . . A good example of a historical group, for instance, is the colonial kitchen installed in the Oakland Museum by the late C. P. Wilcomb. . .

How much better this is than simply to have arranged all the articles displayed in these rooms in a glass case. No matter how carefully and artistically they might have been arranged, nor how explicitly the descriptive labels might be gotten up, the average visitor would not carry away with him the details of the mental pictures of those rooms and the purpose and character of the objects displayed therein. (John Rowley, *Taxidermy and Museum Exhibition*, 1925).

Rowley's statement describes the advantages to be gained from a well-executed interior re-creation. As with the exhibition of individual artifacts, such an exhibit can contribute to a better understanding of culture change in America. When the function of a room is at least somewhat clear, critical omissions can be dealt with.

It is known that even people who left sizeable estates in seventeenth-century New England often did not own bedsteads. Beds, the seventeenth-century term for what we would today call "mattresses," were laid directly on the floor. With a room exhibit, this difference can be illustrated and interpreted. The difference is related to what the people themselves felt had value, and clearly bedsteads were rather low on such a scale. If this fact is not taken into account, and a twentieth-century view is taken, most if not all re-created bedrooms would include a bedstead, since they did exist in quantities at the time.

Wilcomb's pioneering period rooms had an element to them, however unwittingly arrived at, that would serve as a good model for museum curators of the late twentieth century. Since he collected widely and included objects of a broad range of time, his rooms were a wonderful mixture of the new and the old. Adherence to a strict time limitation in a period room's furnishings overlooks the obvious fact that in the past, as today, people had both heirlooms and articles that were brand new. Inventories show this in many cases. Probate records also shed light on the clutter that marked living spaces in earlier times, a clutter that few if any period rooms replicate. Not only does the close adherence to probate records help us to put the right things in the right places, but the variety of objects attests to the different activities carried on in a single area then and now. In his introductory chapter to *A Guide to the Artifacts of Colonial America*, Ivor Noel Hume comments on a Virginia inventory that lists several axes in a lady's bedchamber, and he goes on to remark, quite correctly, that no curator would ever dream of including them in a bedchamber re-creation. Yet, if inventories are followed closely and combined with period graphics (paintings, woodcuts and engravings), re-creations can be achieved that strike the viewer with a sense of the exotic. Such re-creations say, "This is a different world; these people did things differently than people today." This realization is a first critical step to an awareness that our national culture has changed profoundly since its beginnings centuries ago.

A number of "period rooms" placed together under a single roof make up a historic house. Historic houses are perhaps the commonest type of historic museum in America today. Nearly every community has one, and it is not unusual to find many in a town of modest size. Unlike period rooms and static, glass-encased exhibits in formal museums, historic houses are often explained by interpreters. Live interpretation is a mixed blessing. Done well, it allows flexibility and positive interaction with the visitor. Done badly, it can be repetitive, stale and uninspiring (even wrong). An affliction that is more apparent in live interpretation than in written text is what might be called "misplaced quaintness." The symptom is a tendency to see everything in the past as quaint or very ingenious. This is but one more case of a twentieth-century view being imposed on an earlier time. What is "quaint" to us was commonplace to those who did it. To complicate matters, much of the perceived quaintness is a nineteenth-century legacy. Large numbers of seventeenth-century historic houses in New England have "borning rooms," where, visitors are told, expectant mothers repaired to give birth. Yet no such term appears in any room-by-room inventory or any other seventeenth-century primary source. In fact, the idea of such use of space is from a later time. Such semantic and factual distortions work directly against an appreciation of the changes that were worked on society as a whole. In a more subtle way, the use of period dress for interpreters of historic house museums creates a similar distortion. It is confusing to hear a person dressed in eighteenth-century costume speaking in modern colloquial idiom about what "they" did in the past. (First-person interpretation has its problems as well, but that approach works better in "living-history" programs, under certain special conditions.)

Interpreted well, historic houses can achieve a level of explanation not possible with period rooms. Since the entire house, or a large portion of it, is the subject of interpretation, it provides an ideal opportunity to explore changes in building and social space over time. As recent studies of the social and psychological aspects of folk housing, such as Henry Glassie's *Folk Housing in Middle Virginia* (University of Tennessee Press, 1975), make clear, the historic houses can become an ideal tool for exploring dramatic changes in the American mind and American society from the seventeenth century onwards. A hall-and-parlor house addresses the corporate nature of seventeenth-century America just as a wooden trencher does, and for the same reasons. The rise of Georgian-inspired central-hall houses during the eighteenth century parallels the appearance of individual dinner plates. These two house types, and variants of them, probably account for the majority of historic house museums in America. Viewing them as containers for people whose ideas about the world shaped them in turn opens an exciting avenue of interpretation.

Explaining a central-hall house from this perspective would involve calling attention to the way in which the hall separates the people in the house from the world beyond. This withdrawal by the inhabitants from the community contrasts with the practice, typical of houses in an earlier time, of having direct access into the hall, or main working room of the house. The trend again is toward privacy, and central-hall houses no larger than their hall-and-parlor antecedents were usually more divided within, producing both specialized and private spaces.

Earlier hall-and-parlor houses can also be interpreted in terms of room function. If probate inventories are consulted, the furnishings of each room will probably look quite different, and the parlor's role as a social and quasi-ceremonial room can be stressed. By comparison, the furnishings of the hall (usually a room that housed a number of functions, mostly of a technical nature) can create a strong contrast. While some of this space use resembles that of today—parlors have only recently vanished from the American house—the strict separation of functions tended to be more distinctive of seventeenth- and early eighteenth-century building use. Both of these examples of interpretation stress cultural change and transformation, and both use a combination of houses and furnishings to impress the dimension of this change upon the visitor.

The most ambitious of America's historic museums are the full-scale community re-creations, such as Colonial Williamsburg, Old Sturbridge Village, Conner Prairie, and Plimoth Plantation. All that has been suggested relating to artifacts, room re-creations, and house interpretation applies to these museums as well. Another dimension is added, however—that of exterior space and the relations between structures. Such re-created communities have the potential of conveying the strongest sense of change in America since its early years, but, at the same time, the highest possibility of failure if not done with skill and a feeling for the time that is being represented. A community re-creation can immerse the visitor in the entire world of the past, or at least some approximation of it. In truth, the possibility of any such simulation being true to what it is attempting to re-create is exceedingly slim. There are just too many variables that are beyond control. If Myles Standish were to reappear in modern Plimoth Plantation, it is certain that he would not quite know where he was, any more than James Geddy would recognize resurrected Williamsburg as the town where he had worked. But in each case, one would like to think, and with good reason, that such time travelers would feel at home. Again, the differences that centuries of change have worked on the American physical and social world are more important to convey to the public than the way earlier American communities were similar to ours of today.

Creating this kind of ambience is a difficult task. In the case of full-scale community re-creations, a whole slice of the world is being simulated. Unlike traditional museums and their period rooms, or historic houses, the exhibit statement is no longer being made within walls. This difference requires that the space surrounding the buildings in the community be made to appear as we know such areas did in the past. Once again, in many cases, twentieth-century landscaping concepts are ap-

plied, including carefully mowed grass, foundation plantings around houses, and small garden plots, which seem to grow little more than an assortment of herbs and flowers. Such a treatment of grounds conveys a false sense of the past—prettified and clutter-free. Anyone who has done archaeological excavation around a seventeenth- or eighteenth-century house knows well that the amount of exterior clutter must have been far more than we are usually shown in "living-history" communities.

Interpretation in a community re-creation also has its special problems. The problem of interpreters clothed in period dress while speaking in third person applies here as well. One approach that seems to correct the paradox is to involve the interpretive staff in as many tasks as possible in a genuinely productive way. If the interpreters have done most of the things they are supposed to discuss, they will automatically employ first-person interpretation in a natural way. After all, if one has been driving shingles to attach to the roof of a house, it is more natural to say "we do it this way" than "they did it that way." The shift from third-person past to first-person present, if done well, goes a long way toward making the interpretation convincing to the visitor. After all, if the visitor is given to believe that the houses are the way they were, why shouldn't the interpreters also fit into this plan? Such considerations naturally lead to first-person interpretation in a systematic format, or "role-playing." That approach has been in use at Plimoth Plantation for several years, and the effect has been excellent. It requires that interpreters keep actively busy at all of the tasks that life in the community required in the past. Interpreters actually build houses and outbuildings as an interpretive activity (thus, exhibits are built more economically); they cook food and even eat it in period fashion. They often get dirty and touseled in their work in the fields and house lots, but the sense of reality is truly impressive. It is significant that demonstrations do not work in this context, if demonstration is taken in its usual sense as the constant repetition of a single process. Such repetitive action, whether dipping candles only to melt them again for the next turn, or splitting hundreds of rails, none ever to be used, is damaging to morale. Much better to involve the interpeters in productive activities when needed. It is much more faithful to the real world as it was, since early Americans did not demonstrate crafts in their houses.

All of these considerations lead to the conclusion that effective "living history" must be just that. Every effort must be made to create a world so convincing that the visitor comes to it much as an anthropologist would come to a community that he wanted to study. Only then can a historical re-creation on the scale of a whole community be used effectively to convey a sense of cultural change. All of the pieces must fit systematically. A re-creation community is far more than a collection of historical houses, each interpreted on its own. The community is a single exhibit and must be treated as such. Live animals and their droppings, dusty streets, the smell of wood smoke and cooking, and the sound of active workers all contribute to the reality that we who work with such re-creations wish to achieve. Done well, such an exhibit has no equal in placing visitors in another time and giving them a sense of the great and complex change that has marked the progress of American culture.

Part VI
Experimental Programs

Immaterial Material Culture

The Implications of Experimental Research for Folklife Museums

Jay Anderson

The author, who at the time of writing was chief of research and interpretation at Living History Farms in Des Moines, Iowa, suggests that experimental archaeology as practiced at Butser Hill and Lejre might be used by living history museums. He argues that, in addition to "correcting our perception of the past, experimental archaeology can also teach us much about contemporary postindustrial cultural behavior and the mental and physical distance we have put between our forefathers and ourselves." Museums such as Plimoth Plantation and the Colonial Pennsylvania Plantation are not only "repositories for the material culture of the past, but also catalysts for questioning one's own culture. . . they have the potential to become powerful mediums for encouraging in visitors the habit of disciplined self-analysis." This article originally appeared in Keystone Folklore *21 (1976).*

Folklife museums and centers are playing an increasing role in preserving and interpreting our nation's cultural history. Colonial Williamsburg, Old Sturbridge Village, Mystic Seaport, and Greenfield Village, for example, host millions of visitors annually and have become significant tourist attractions and educational centers serving both a national and regional audience. In addition to these four giants, there are at least 3,500 smaller regional cultural history museums in operation (Burcaw, pp. 26-27). A good number of these, such as Plimoth Plantation, the Farmers' Museum in Cooperstown, New York, and Living History Farms in Des Moines, Iowa, number their visitors and students in the hundreds of thousands. Many Americans are looking in museums, especially open-air folklife[1] museums like these, for their images of how their counterparts once lived (Sidford, pp. 30-34). Visitors, it seems have accepted Henry Ford's dictum: By looking at things people used and that show the way they lived, a better and truer impression can be gained than could be had in a month of reading (Lowenthal, p. 27).

Unfortunately, the images presented at many museums are bowdlerized, with an emphasis on elitist culture (Lowenthal, pp. 27-32; Flitch, pp. 45-46). Critics of cultural history museums, frequently museum professionals themselves, clearly understand this fault and the need for greater accuracy in research and interpretation (Ronsheim, pp. 16-19). They have identified many of the problems that inhibit a realistic presentation of the realities of life in the past, especially the failure to understand fully and communicate the cultural context within which historical artifacts, Henry Ford's "things," functioned. Since museums are essentially institutions which collect "things" and make sense of them to visitors, this is strong criticism indeed (Jenkins, pp. 502, 508). Without an appreciation for the culture frame of reference of artifacts, a museum's material culture becomes for visitors and students alike simply "immaterial," lacking significant relevance to serve as a bridge to better relate past and present realities. Central questions that must be asked of any artifact—milk dish or hoe, long house or barn—are too frequently ignored or glossed over: How can it be exhibited so as to reasonably convey an impression of the setting and system in which this object lived?

The subject of this paper is a method of material culture research and interpretation which should, if used carefully, help answer more successfully these crucial questions. This method is now generally called "experimental archaeology" (Asher, pp. 793-816; Coles), although the more inclusive designation "experimental ethnography" perhaps describes it more accurately.

Initially, experimental archaeology was developed as a means of (1) practically testing theories of past cultural behavior, especially technology processes involving the use of tools and (2) obtaining data not readily available from more traditional artifactual analysis and historical sources. The resulting data could then be used to formulate new theories about historical economic and sociocultural systems. Because the researcher sought to "imitate" or "replicate" the original process as nearly as possible, the method has also been called "imitative" archaeology, or ethnography. Folklorists and folklife researchers familiar with Kenneth Goldstein's induced natural context will readily note the similarity between

Interpreting the context of woodworking on the Indiana frontier: Dave Heighway in the carpenter's shop at Connor Prairie.—*Photo: LaVonne Heighway*

the two methods. Goldstein, working with living cultures, suggests the induction of a natural context in which a true folkloric performance could be sustained and studied (Goldstein) while experimental ethnographers seek to recreate a reasonable facsimile of a limited historical milieu and then use it as an historic laboratory for carrying out circumscribed experiments. The goals of theory testing and data generation are the same for both methods.

The history of experimental archaeology has been summarized by Robert Asher in "Experimental Archaeology" (1961) and elaborated by John Coles in *Archaeology by Experiment* (1973). Examples described by Asher and Coles include imitative experiments with prehistoric and historic forest clearing, crop planting, harvesting and storage, ploughing, cooking, house building and usage (including natural and accidental destruction), construction of earthworks and roads, boat building and voyaging, stone and wood working, manufacturing of weapons and musical instruments, antler and steel craft, metal processing, leather and textile production, pottery, paint, paper manufacture, and animal and plant breeding. Given its due is the most spectacular and publicized experiment to date, the Kon Tiki expedition, in which Thor Heyerdahl sought to prove that people could have sailed the 4,000 miles between South America and the Polynesian Islands, transplanting themselves and their culture before 1100 A.D. (Heyerdahl). Heyerdahl didn't claim that they actually did make the voyage, he only proposed to generate new data that could prove that such a voyage was feasible and therefore must be considered as evidence in all further considerations of the cultural history of the Pacific and South America. His experiment attained its goal. Many other experimental research projects, more modest in scope, have contributed similarly useful data on theories relating to past cultural behavior.

Asher and Coles, after evaluating a number of such projects, suggest a series of procedural rules applicable to all experiments that will aid the scholar in achieving valid data. For example, Coles reviews eight basic rules that he notes are observed in most experiments, although they may be unacknowleged as such, because they are basically common sense (Coles, p. 15). These include analyzing the scope of the experiment beforehand, thereby keeping the number of variable factors to a minimum; using only historically accurate materials and methods; limiting modern technology so as not to interfere with the experiment's results; documenting the process carefully enough so that it could be repeated later by another researcher; improvising new methods if feasible; assessing the experiment in terms of its reliabilty; and never claiming absolute proof, just the degree of probability that the process is indeed historically accurate. For as Coles cautions, experimental archaeology or ethnography does not prove anything. It is a tool by which some of the basic economic activities of ancient man, those concerned with subsistence and technology, can be assessed for their development and competence (Coles, p. 18).

Recently, many of the most innovative experimental research projects have been undertaken at European folklife museums by research, educational, and folk museum staff people. Two, especially, are worth careful regard: The Lejre Historical-Archaeological Research and Educational Center thirty miles west of Copenhagen, Denmark; and the Butser Hill project, near Petersfield, Hampshire, about seventy-five miles southwest of London.

Lejre, the world's first center for experimental archaeology and enthnography, has since 1964 been the setting for a wide variety of extremely careful experiments in preindustrial Danish technology and folklife. Under the direction of Hans-Ole Hansen, the center's staff has sought to "re-invent and perpetuate" traditional processes using accurate reproductions of historic material culture. They have been conducting tests with upright warp-weighted looms, textiles, and tailoring, pottery making, pit and kiln baked earthen-ware, bog iron smelting and forging, Neolithic and medieval housing and usage, animal and plant breeding, slash and burn agriculture, ploughing and field preparation, food processing, preservation and storage, tool construction, saddle and horse gear, and household and domestic activities. Hansen is cautious when making claims about the ultimate significance of experimental research, and he prefers to say that its chief value is in augmenting archaeological and anthropological sources by testing theories suggested by them. But he also notes its educational potential: The idea behind this work is that besides yielding valuable experimental information, these reconstructions have great value for modern man's impression of the living environments in which his ancestors should be imagined as living in through the ages (Hansen, p. 7). Hansen warns that the method's usefulness as an interpretive medium can easily be undermined if the results of the experiments are not arrived at scientifically and are not capable of being verified through duplicate tests. Recently, experimentation at Lejre has included tests not only of Neolithic Danish culture, but of medieval and recent peasant economic systems; for example, flax production and linen processing and the interior arrangements and working of seventeenth-, eighteenth- and nineteenth-century farmhouses. The high standard of previous experimentation has been maintained for these studies in historic archaeology despite increasing pressure to exploit the center more fully for large number of tourists and students intereted in Danish folklife.

The Butser Hill Project, under the direction of Peter Reynolds, a classical scholar and archaeologist, has been sponsored since 1964 by the Ancient Agriculture Research Committee of the British Association and the Council for British Archaeology. Located in a 525-acre county park, it is divided into two sites: a fifty-seven-acre Iron Age farm serves as a historical laboratory for experimental research and a smaller, similar farm nearby is open to students and the general public as an open-air museum. On the basis of experiments by Reynolds and his staff on the folklife of Roman Britain, new theories have been postulated on Neolithic population, settlement patterns, land use, agriculture, food storage, vernacular architecture, and other aspects of culture. Many of these suppositions, quietly advanced in Reynold's *Farming in the Iron Age* conflict with the popular stereotypes of pre-medieval England. For example, because of new data yielded by experiments with the ard plow and wicker caches, Reynolds suggests that far more land was under cultivation far earlier, that grain storage pits had been perfected to preserve the additional wheat, oats, barley, and vetches grown, that the rural populations was considerably larger than previously belived, and that the Romans invaded Britain because it was a potential bread-basket for their empire. Such theorizing on the basis of experimental research and the re-evaluation of historical sources is forcing a complete reconsideration of British folklife and cultural history. Reynolds, like Hansen, is cautious: Perhaps the story of Iron Age farming as told in *Farming in the Iron Age* is almost right, perhaps it is largely wrong. As more excavations take place and more evidence is discovered we shall need to revise the story in places. In ten years time we may even have to rewrite the whole story (Reynolds, p. 4).

Reynolds and his colleagues have not had the level of financial support that would allow them to follow Lejre's lead and undertake research on more recent folklife problems; e.g., medieval and post-medieval heavy plows or grain yields before and after the introduction of the eighteenth-century crop rotation systems. Assistance may come in the near future when the British public realizes the educational and symbolic value of the project to the nation. As Keith Spence pointed out in a *Country Life* article:

> When Butser gets under way, its combination of accessibility and technical interest should give vast numbers of people an entirely new idea of what "Ancient Britain" was really like. When Julius Caesar sailed across the Channel in 55 B.C. he was not confronted merely by parties of capering wood-painted savages. The Celtic farmers of the Iron Age were skilled operators, admittedly not concentered in towns, but with farming techniques of a high order. And the crowds who will flock to Butser from the cities at weekends will, perhaps subconsciously, feel a kinship with their ancestors who tilled the chalk downs 2,000 years ago (Spence, p. 693).

The pioneering work being done by Hansen and Reynolds has been paralleled in America by Errett Callahan of the Department of Anthropology, Virginia Commonwealth University. His *The Old Rag Report: A Practical Guide to Living Archaeology* (1973), *Experimental Archaeological Papers (APE)* (1974), *Living Archaeology Projects in Subsistence Living* (1975), and three volumes of *Living Archaeology Newsletter* (1973-1975) constitute the most thorough introduction in English to the potential of experimental projects, and the problems of implementing research programs. Callahan's recommendations are based on his experience directing three projects, each consisting of a variety of specific experiments with tool manufacture, architecture, foodways and daily living. Callahan summarized his approach in 1975:

> There exists in archaeology the problems of interpreting the archaeological record. This record consists for the most part of artifacts, objects used by a people for obtaining and/or maintaining their cultural and/or biological objectives. An artifact would therefore seem to reflect at least a part of a person's behavior in response to a need. . . With the advent of W. W. Taylor's treaties, "A Study of Archaeology" in 1948, archaeologists began looking at the archaeological record in a newer and more comprehensive light than before. This new outlook, the "new archaeology" as it has come to be known, called for more creative and comprehensive ways of viewing the archaeological record. . . Foremost among the objectives of the new trend was the need to view archaeological sites and components as wholes, as interacting systems and subsystems, rather than as isolated islands of culture. . . It is our contention that only by re-creating, as closely as we are able, the original environmental and behavioral conditions, can we reduce the skewing of data to a minimum. Of course, we will never be able to re-create *exactly* all facets of a tool's creation and utilization or of a people's life-style because of non-evident cultural influences that have vanished without a trace. We may not be able to reconstruct prehistorical political, religious, or social behavior with much accuracy in most cases. . . . But it is our contention that we can ascribe considerably more information than is possible with sterile laboratory tests. This re-creation is no less than essential to the accurate interpretation of the archaeological record. Such a recreation is a major aim of subsistence projects in experimental archaeology (Callahan, 1975: 2-3).

So far, there is no American counterpart of Lejre, where extensive research of the standard achieved by Hansen, Reynolds, and Callahan could be carried out and interpreted to the general public. Experimental research has been carried out and interpreted at a number of open-air museums, notably Plimoth Plantation in Plymouth, Massachusetts, and the Colonial Pennsylvania Plantation outside Philadelphia. At Plimoth, Roger Welsch and I conducted a limited experiment in traditional brewing in the spring of 1972 before and after the folk museum opened to the public. We were able to thereby first use the folk museum as an accurate historic laboratory and then, once our experiments were completed, to interpret folk brewing utensils and processes to interested visitors (Welsch, 1974: 356-357). Later in 1972, I undertook a series of experiments in Plimoth on food procurement, processing, and preparation following the basic rules, which Coles would be recommending the following year (Anderson, 1975: 21-23; Welsch, 1975: 23-26). Similar tests were also instituted at the Colonial Pennsylvania Plantation from 1974-1976. Supervised by the plantation research director, Don Callender, Jr.,

these experiments included the traditional reconstruction and use of a spring house, eighteenth-century farming, monitoring of trash pits, energy used in agricultural activities such as rail splitting and hoe weeding, and the building and functioning of a 1770's wooden mold board plow (Callender, pp. 173-177). These experiments at Plimoth and the Colonial Pennsylvania Plantation confirmed for those involved the conclusion already reached in Europe: folk museums need to develop experimental research projects to understand fully the original functions of the collections and to communicate accurately to visitors historic environmental contexts and technological processes. The basic research and general interpretive potential of the method for American institutions was recommended at a symposium on "Experimental Research and Living History," held in Philadelphia, January 1976, as part of the Annual Meeting for the Society for Historic Archaeology.

Since then, four other reasons for embarking on experimental projects have come into mind. Experimental research, in addition to correcting our picture of the past (as Reynolds' work at Butser Hill has shown), can also teach us much about contemporary postindustrial cultural behavior and the mental and physical distance we have put between our forebears and ourselves. This lesson was brought home to Roger Welsch and me during our brewing experiments at Plimoth Plantation in 1972. We had anticipated that living and working in an early seventeenth-century village would be enlightening—and it was. What we had not expected was the stupifying effects of being confined within the narrow, drab (to us) village in a small one-room hut for even a short period of time (Welsch, pp. 357-358). After a week of sleeping on an itchy straw-filled mattress, of being chilled to the marrow by damp nor'easters off Cape Cod Bay, of unremitting physical work punctuated by meals of boiled salt fish and sour beer, we were worn down in body and mind. It was obvious that neither of us was prepared either mentally or physically for seventeenth-century Colonial living. Our conversations turned increasingly from the brewing experiments we had undertaken to how the realities of life had changed in 350 years.

Exactly the same point was made by Errett Callahan's students in 1974. Cut off from all twentieth-century contact, they found that the sudden comparison of prehistoric mid-Atlantic Woodland Indian life with their own modern one heightened their own cultural self-consciousness, often raising more questions about their folklife than giving answers about precontact Indian cultures. Obviously, open-air folklife museums can serve not only as repositories for the material culture of the past but also as catalysts for questioning one's own culture. They have the potential to become powerful mediums for encouraging in visitors the habit of disciplined cultural self-analysis. Too often folklorists are rightfully accused of being at best antiquarians interested in "folksy" survivals, of living in the never-never land of the "good old days," of beckoning visitors to folk museums to leave the cares of the modern world behind and stroll into a simpler, quieter past. Experimental research projects can help us re-evaluate the validity of our knowledge of the folklife of particular regions and periods through personal experience and use this experience as a stimulus to question the assumptions of our modern culture today and in the future. The folk museum can and should become an effective medium for humanistic education.

Another value of experimental research is to help us evaluate our own enthnograpahic methods. For example, Roger Welsch and I had both done extensive work on folk brewing processes before we conducted our experimental research in Plimoth. We felt we had a clear idea of the technology involved in making small beer in Jacobean England and early New England. Only when we actually tried to simulate these processes in an accurate historical context did we realize the extent of our (and other scholars) ignorance. In even the best of recipes from primary sources, basic steps were omitted. Experimental research with historical technological processes rapidly indicated the data that can't be obtained from the traditional written material and oral sources. Fortunately, it is precisely this kind of data that experimentation generates. However, Hansen cautions,

> It is imperative that every single experiment should be observed and recorded to such a degree that it is possible for another researcher, without performing an extensive trial series, could use these results as a foundation for further research. . . The need for the detailed recording of work processes might be surprising to some people: "But can't these work processes be obtained through still living traditions?" The answer, unfortunately, is no. Very little of the information in ethnographical studies is sufficiently detailed to be used as work descriptions and as the basis for initiation of the work. Therefore, every notation about

an almost extinct work process, a disappearing house-building technique, and other preindustrial skills, should be recorded from the viewpoint of the possibility of future imitation. . . imitative experiments may make an essential contribution to general anthropological research: the development of a way describing the work process so that the process could be repeated not only by the observer but also by someone unfamiliar with the original work (Hansen, pp. 11-12).

A third reason for beginning an experimental program in a folk museum is the method's educational value. It can be an effective means of teaching how history's artifacts were once used. For example, once the researcher has carried out a series of experiments with natural dyes and rediscovers the materials and processes which give a duplicate of the color found in a piece of historic cloth, the experiment could be demonstrated for students, allowing them to encounter the same problems, account for the same variables, and arrive at the same conclusion. The goal of this exercise would be to allow the students to learn by experience not only the principles behind a historical process but also the methods of historical and scientific research. The emphasis is on historiography as well as history. The strength of this approach is obvious. The point of view taken is a questioning, modest one: What don't we know about the work and the lives of our ancestors? How shall we find out? Learning to answer questions by step-by-step experimentation is recognized by educational psychologists as one of the best ways to master and retain material. The practice can be carried over into other disciplines and real life situations. Such learning is experimental. It involves all the senses and leaves a deeper impression on the memory. By rediscovering how to make a simple tool, such as a broom, by trial and error following a sketchy

Rebekah Allen making apple cider at Utah State University's Ronald V. Jensen Living Historical Farm.—*Photo: Tom Allen*

word description gleaned from an oral history source or old "receipt" book, the experience will have a deeper effect on the student than watching a documentary film or reading a *Foxfire*-like description of the craft.

Finally, experimental research may help to create what Alvin Toffler calls enclaves of the past, specialized centers of living which will increase the chances that someone will be there to pick up the pieces in case of massive calamity (Toffler, pp. 390-391). He writes:

> Such communities not only should not be derided, they should be subsidized by the larger society as a form of mental and social insurance. In times of extremely rapid change, it is possible for the larger society to make some irreversible, catastrophic error. Imagine, for instance, the widespread diffusion a food additive that accidentally turns out to have Thalidomide-like effects. One can conceive of accidents capable of sterilizing or even killing a whole population (Toffler, p. 391).

For example, at Living History Farms, Iowa's open air agricultural museum, we face this challenge daily. Here, outside Des Moines on a 550-acre tract bounded by interstate highways, industrial parks, and suburban developments, we are re-creating two accurate central Iowa farmsteads, circa 1840 and 1900. These "historic laboratories" serve as the setting for many of the experiments and educational programs described in the paper. However, we are also developing a "farm of the future," embodying many of the brightest new ideas from the various agricultural colleges at nearby Iowa State University. Our prototypes, as well as many of the ideas underlying it, rely on the expectation of a continued supply of inexpensive energy. We naturally worry about a Toffler-esque catastrophe, possibly a sudden elimination of conventional energy sources before newer reservoirs (e.g., solar, thermal, wind) are rendered easily usable for farming. Perhaps, the "farm of the future" will draw more heavily on our 1840's subsistence homestead with its twelve acres worked intensively and our 1900's farm with its root cellar, storage cave, and windmill than we had previously planned.

In conclusion, experimental archaeology or ethnography has already played an important research and educational role in European folklife museums and historical centers. Its potential as a supplement to other more conventional research has already been demonstrated. Some parallel work has been undertaken in America with modest success. Hopefully, folklife researchers in this country will examine more carefully the experience of European and American scholars and museum professionals using this method and consider initiating pilot programs in folk museums and living-history centers here with a goal of developing their potential as historical laboratories. The study and interpretation of material culture can, utilizing experimental techniques, have a very "material" effect on our society and culture. There will be problems (Anderson, 1976) but the potential results certainly justify the effort.

Notes

[1] I am using the definition of folklife commonly used in Europe and recently put forth by Ward Goodenough: Folklife refers to the study of one's own national cultural heritage (Goodenough, p. 20).

[2] This paper is an extended and revised version of one presented at the American Folklore Society Meeting on November 12, 1976.

References Cited

Anderson, Jay. "Foodways Programs on Living Historical Farms." Association for Living Historical Farms and Agriculture Museums, *Annual* 1 (1975): 21-23.

————."On the Horns of a Dilemma: Research, Interpretation, and Fund Raising in Folk Museums." Association for Living Historical Farms and Agricultural Museums, *Annual* 2 (1976): 18-19.

Asher, Robert. "Experimental Archaeology." *American Anthropologist* 63 (1961): 793-816.

Burcaw, G. Ellis. *Introduction to Museum Work*. Nashville: American Association for State and Local History, 1976.

Callender, Donald W. "Reliving the Past: Experimental Archaeology in Pennsylvania". *Archaeology* 29 (1976): 173-178.

Callahan, Errett. *The Old Rag Report: A Practical Guide to Living Archaeology*. Richmond, Va: Department of Sociology/Anthropology, Virginia Commonwealth University, 1973.

————.*Living Archaeology: Projects in Subsistence Living*. Richmond, Va.: Virginia Commonwealth University, 1975.

Callahan, Errett, ed. *Experimental Archaeological Papers (APE)*. Richmond, Va.: Department of Sociology/Anthropology, Virginia Commonwealth University, 1974.

Coles, John. *Archaeology by Experiment*. New York: Charles Scribners' Sons, 1973.

Flitch, James Marston. "Uses of the Artistic Past," in *American Folklife*, ed. by Don Yoder. Austin, Texas: University of Texas Press, 1976.

Goldstein, Kenneth S. "The Induced Natural Context: An Ethnographic Folklore Field Technique," in *Essays in the Verbal and Visual Arts*, ed. by June Helm. Seattle: University of Washington Press, 1976.

Goodenough, Ward. "Folklife Study and Social Change," in *American Folklife*, ed. by Don Yoder. Austin, Texas: University of Texas Press, 1976.

Hansen, Hans-Ole. *Some Main Trends in the Development of the Lejre Center*. Lejre, Roshilta, Denmark: Internal Publications, 1973.

Heyerdahl, Thor. *Kon-Tiki*. Trans. by X.F.H. Lyon. New York: Rand McNally, 1950. Reprint. New York: Pocket Books, 1973.

Jenkins, J. Geraint. "The Use of Artifact and Folk Art in the Folk Museums," in *Folklore and Folklife: An Introduction*, ed. by Richard Dorson. Chicago: University of Chicago Press, 1972.

Lowenthal, David. "The American Way of History." *Columbia University Forum*, (Summer 1966): 21-32.

Reynolds, Peter J. *Farming in the Iron Age*. Cambridge: Cambridge University Press, 1976.

Ronsheim, Robert D. "Is the Past Dead?" *Museum News* 53 (1974): 10-19.

Sidford, Holly. "Stepping Into History." *Museum News* 53 (1974): 28-36.

Spence, Keith. "The Iron Age Brought to Life." *Country Life* 17 (September 1970): 692-3.

Toffler, Alvin. *Future Shock*. New York: Random House, Inc, 1970. Paperback edition, New York: Bantam Books, 1971.

Welsch, Roger. "Very Didactic Simulation." *American History Teacher*, (Spring 1974): 356-364.

———— "Sowbelly and Seedbanks." Association for Living Historical Farms and Agricultural Museums *Annual* 1 (1975): 23-26.

Reliving the Past
Experimental Archaeology in Pennsylvania

19

Don W. Callender, Jr.

Don W. Callender, Jr., was research director of the Colonial Pennsylvania Plantation, a 1770's living-historical farm outside Philadelphia. In this important article first published in the July 1976 issue of Archaeology, *he wrote: "The Plantation is not conceived as an open-air museum (such as Colonial Williamsburg, Old Sturbridge Village, or Plimoth Plantation), but as a laboratory in which serious investigators are testing their understanding of a Colonial farm by seeking to re-create its original environment. . . using the kinds of tools and techniques that were standard in the eighteenth century and are doing many of the daily tasks which were performed by Colonial husbandmen. . . In many cases this leads to more questions than answers." Callender goes on to document a number of "imitative experiments" carried out at the plantation during 1974-1975.*

July 2, 1776 First Day [Sunday] flying Clouds & hot, Hannah Jeffreies here last night; I went to Meeting PM; Wm. Trimble & Phebe came to Visit us.

July 3, 1776 Second Day Coll. Plowing [Dolan, a part-time worker?]

July 4, 1776 Third Day Draw'd Some Dung; bot [bought] of Trimble 2/6 [2 shillings 6 pence]; paid Richard Webb for my Shoes 9s & for Jan Marshall a pair 7s, Total 16s; [owes] Jane [for] 26 weeks, she [owes him indentured time]

July 5, 1776 Fourth Day Hazy & cool, Paid & laid out since the 20th of last month 7L [pound] .05S [shillings] .06D [pence]; Ballance by me 76 L. 14 S. 03 D; I went to monthly meeting.

July 6, 1776 Fifth Day fog & Some Clouds. Plowing & make Rakehead & pitch fork handle.

July 7, 1776 Sixth Day, Some few Drops of rain; Draw'd Wood & Dung; Went to Town; Expences 3 [pound]; Rachel Seal came.

July 8, 1776 Seventh Day Went to Town; bot of Wall [a part-time entrepreneur] Sundries 22s 7 1/2 pence; paid Son Wm for Corn 4/6 pence; plowing fallows.

July 9, 1776 First Day Warm I went to meeting.

From the diary of Benjamin Hawley.
Manuscript in the Chester County Historical Society; transcribed by the Bishop's Mill Historical Institute.

The above entries appear in the diary of an independent farmer named Benjamin Hawley of East Bradford Township, Chester County, Pennsylvania. The time was the week of July 2, 1776. The momentous events occurring in Philadelphia, the second largest city in the British Empire, some twenty-five miles away, go unrecorded by this Quaker farmer as he faced the daily task of running a farmstead in southeastern Pennsylvania.

What was Hawley's life really like? What skills did he need? What tools did he use? How much time did he have for each necessary task? The answering of these and similar questions is the aim of research currently being done at the Colonial Pennsylvania Plantation in Ridley Creek State Park, Delaware County, Pennsylvania. The project is supported by the Bishop's Mill Historical Institute, a nonprofit corporation formed to investigate and conserve the remains of rural southeastern Pennsylvania. The plantation is not conceived as an open-air museum (such as Colonial Williamsburg, Old Sturbridge Village, or Plimoth Plantation), but as a laboratory in which serious investigators are testing their understanding of a Colonial farm by seeking to re-create its original environment. Based on archaeological and historical research, this interdisciplinary endeavor employs specialists from various backgrounds: folklore, archaeology, anthropology, historic agriculture, and American studies. The researchers, using the kinds of tools and techniques that were standard in the eighteenth century, are doing many of the daily tasks which were performed by Colonial husbandmen.

The translation of data and artifacts into actual processes has been given a number of titles: action archaeology, living archaeology, imitative research, experimental research, replication research and so on. At the Colonial

Example of experimental archaeology: Jim Phillips living in a reconstructed pioneer's dugout at Farmamerica in Waseca, Minnesota.—
Photo: Jim Phillips

Pennyslvania Plantation the investigators are continually testing and refining their understanding of documents and artifacts by replicating Colonial plantation life. In many cases this leads to more questions than answers. Yet there are those infrequent times when test results make a strong inference for or against a particular interpretation, such as the type of plow that was used, the kinds of food that were stored or the amount of trash that was discarded by a family during the period of the American Revolution.

This type of experimental method has been used by various researchers since the beginning of archaeology as a science. Probably the best known example is the Kon-Tiki voyage by Thor Heyerdahl in which a theory about Pacific oceanic migrations was given new impetus. Most experimental replications, however, have not been as spectacular or controversial as Kon-Tiki, yet hundreds of imitative experiments have enabled prehistorians to better understand artifacts and their cultural contexts.

The work done in this new yet old sub-discipline of ar-

chaeology and history falls into three major categories: (1) the laboratory experiment in which a particular process, such as firing a pot, is taken out of context in order to study its particular phases; (2) the field experiment in which a pot is made in its original context, from local material by a technology inferred from archaeological remains; and (3) the total subsistence experiment in which the pot is not only made and fired using the original technology, but is used as an interrelated part of a recreated living situation.

In their definitive summaries two archaeologists working in this area, Robert Ascher of Cornell University and John Coles of Cambridge University, indicate that the majority of imitative experiments fall into the first and second categories. The work of Errett Callahan (Virginia Commonwealth University) belongs in the third category. His series of Middle Woodland subsistence experiments in Virginia has generated the most prolific results of such experimentation in the United States. In Europe pioneering efforts in experimental subsistence living at the Butser Ancient Farm Project in England and at the Lejre Research Center in Denmark are also demonstrating the viable application of this third kind of imitative research for understanding the past.

As director of research for the Bishop's Mill Historical Institute, I am responsible for the program of experimental archaeology at the Colonial Pennsylvania Plantation. So far the imitative research falls into the first two categories. This is due to the present intensive development for the Bicentennial celebration. During this summer, once the plantation is fully operational, we hope to begin conducting live-in experiments.

Among the experiments already completed at the plantation are the reconstruction of a springhouse and the analysis of its functioning, the comparison of eighteenth-century farming techniques with modern ones and the monitoring of several trash pits, a subject so dear to the hearts of most archaeologists. The purpose of the trash-pit experiment was to see how nonorganic waste accumulates—at what rate such pits grow and what factors effect that rate. From July 1, 1974, to June 30, 1975, almost 182 pounds of material, the disposal from an operating "Colonial" kitchen, was collected in pit 1. The refuse was gathered during 76.6 days of use—230 meals for an average of ten to fifteen people with two persons preparing the food. Since it is clearly impossible to know what relationship this amount of material has to the annual debris accumulating in an actual Colonial kitchen, we are currently looking for a historic trash pit of the same period and locality. Trash pit 1 did allow us to gain some insight into what affects the rate of accumulation. Our inexperience clearly increased the rate of breakage and discard. This became especially clear with our second trash pit, July 1, 1975 to June 30, 1976, which grew at a markedly increased rate after we lost our experienced housewife. Pit 2 also has a faster rate of accumulation because of extraordinary rodent activity, a circumstance due to temporarily opened doors and windows resulting from the reconstruction of the farm house. No doubt similar animal activity plagued colonial households at times of construction. On July 1, 1976, a third experimental pit was begun. The plantation house is complete, the inventory for the kitchen being developed, and our expertise improved to the point that breakage should be nominalized.

Some of our most interesting experiments deal with the reconstruction of buildings. Here we use preindustrial techniques and keep a careful log on the details of each structure—the types of woods, the methods of joinery, the tools necessary for each task, the constituents of the sand lime mortar, the formulas for oil-oxide paints, and the amount of time necessary for each task. Written sources on Colonial construction are full of gaps, and many times the researchers who were acting as carpenters and masons had to experiment with a tool or a method in search of a technology that is now lost. Each successful solution can only suggest, not verify, its use in historic times. For this reason we try different solutions employing the tools and the known technical skills of the period.

In the process of reconstructing an eighteenth-century springhouse, preliminary exploration of the still-standing building showed that the large roof beams known as "plates" had been cut from felled trees, hewn with a broad ax, and then pit-sawn to the correct size. Evidently, the other timbers used in the structure had been sawn in a mill, probably a local water-powered one known to be operational at the time. We then reconstructed the springhouse using the processes and materials indicated by these architectural features. It soon became apparent why the plate beams had not been

Mary Anne Stewart Andru's experimenting with World-War-One-period Mormon cooking in Cache valley, Utah.—*Photo: Jeannie Thomas*

The wood fired kiln at Living History Farm's 1875 Walnut Hill pottery.—*Photo: Living History Farms*

sawn in a mill. Their weight, four hundred pounds, and their size, ten feet by ten feet by twenty-five feet, prohibited their being transported any great distance. The rough-hewn logs that supplied these beams weighed three quarters of a ton. When they were hoisted into position on the sawing platform, smoke could be seen coming from the blocks and tackle, a clear indication of stress of the load. The smaller roof rafters, flooring, and framing could have been moved by cart or wagon down the muddy roads but the largest timbers would have had to have been made on the plantation by hand.

We were also interested in how the springhouse functioned. Once the structure was completed and was ready for use, an experiment was set up to test the range in temperature of both the air and water of the interior room. A springhouse, used by the Colonials to store food, works because the constantly flowing ground water passes through the enclosed spring room keeping the items cool in the summer and preventing them from freezing in the winter. A temperature profile taken between April 1, 1975, and April 1, 1976, showed that the temperature in the room never exceeded 56 degrees fahrenheit in the summer nor went below 46 degrees in the winter. In other words, a good temperature for storage was maintained all year long.

The principles of experimental research are also being applied to the agricultural development of the plantation. The farm manager, Ross Fullam, maintains that it isn't enough to be able to split rails, weed with a hoe, milk a cow, or plow a field. These skills, like the building and household skills, must be developed to a high enough level of expertise that the energy put into such tasks is used efficiently. In that way strength and time will be left over to carry out all the demands of a preindustrial farm, thus simulating the actual work load of the Colonial farmer. Fortunately, broken plows and harnesses, ruined tools, and overly tired bodies are becoming less and less prevalent.

The efficiency between a modern plow and two wooden replicas of a 1770's plow of local origin was compared. Results were as expected. The modern plow required less energy—approximately 1.7 pounds per square inch less than the replicas, for furrows seventy-five feet in length. The modern form also turned over 30 percent more ground with each pass. Comparisons were made between a constant source of energy, a tractor and a depreciating source, a team of horses. Results are confusing because the horses refused to pull normally with the dynometer to measure the work load hitched between them and the plow. An important result, however, is the determination of the quantitative difference between two types of plows that are separated by two hundred years of development. We also now have some idea of the limits of plow technology in the 1770's in southeastern Pennsylvania. Our next step is to test these limits against the insights gained from the historic record. Can our farmer with a team of horses and a somewhat inefficient but historically correct plow keep twenty acres of ground under cultivation on an annual basis and still have enough time and energy to operate the entire farm?

It will be years before the Colonial Pennsylvania Plantation is running at a level that in any way approximates

Drying codfish at New Brunswick's Acadien village.—*Photo: Acadien Historical Village*

its historic prototypes, but the steps via living archaeology open new vistas for both observer and participant alike. This type of research, although still in its infancy, is adding new dimensions to historical and archaeological methodology. The possibilities of substantiating conjecture and establishing lifestyles by actual controlled experience are endless.

Further Reading

Robert Ascher, "Experimental Archaeology," *American Anthropologist* 63 (1961) 793-816

Errett Callahan, *Old Rag Report, A Practical Guide to Living Archaeology* (Richmond, Va.: Virginia Commonwealth University, 1973).

John Coles, *Archaeology by Experiment* (New York: Charles Scribners' Sons, 1973).

Thor Heyerdahl, *Kon-Tiki* (New York: Rand McNally, 1950).

Very Didactic Simulation Workshops in the Plains Pioneer Experience at the Stuhr Museum

20

Roger L. Welsch

During the summers of 1973 and 1974, Roger L. Welsch taught adult workshops in Great Plains folklife at the Stuhr Museum in Grand Island, Nebraska. His classes consisted primarily of secondary school teachers and college students interested in the history and literature of the Great Plains. Welsch argued in this article, which appeared in the May 1974 issue of History Teacher, *that the realistic late-nineteenth-century atmosphere of Stuhr, with its re-created railroad town and cottonwood log farm was more 'didactically stimulating' than an air-conditioned classroom in Lincoln. Long hours were spent not only in talking about the Plains pioneer experience, about which Willa Cather and other people had so eloquently written, but also in reliving it—cooking biscuits over a corncob fire, sleeping in the open, getting the feel of a sod house. The living-history movement now has many fine adult live-ins. Roger Welsch's Stuhr workshops were some of the first and are happily among the best documented.*

During the summers of 1973 and 1974, Nebraska Wesleyan University, the University of Nebraska at Lincoln, the Stuhr Museum of the Prairie Pioneer, and the Nebraska American Revolution Bicentennial Commission worked cooperatively in an effort to use the Stuhr Museum complex effectively as a learning laboratory, a massive piece of total-environment audio-visual equipment. At every level the participants—from student to faculty, from the museum staff to commission representatives—are enthusiastic about the effectiveness of the concept. Many of the teachers who participated in the first workshops are now using the museum to simulate pioneer environments for their own classes. Stuhr will continue to offer the workshops in the coming years, with the possibility of extensions and expansions of the concept, and I am hoping to transfer the idea to other times and environments.

My own enthusiasm for the technique is boundless and almost evangelistic. Perhaps the best way to explain that enthusiasm is to trace its development, which started, strangely enough, not on the Plains but at the Plimoth Plantation Museum within view of the Atlantic Ocean.

The Plimoth Plantation Museum in Plymouth, Massachusetts, is the result of efforts to reconstruct the environment and life of the Pilgrims of 1627. In March and April of 1972, I was invited by Plimoth Plantation foods consultant Jay Anderson of Pennsylvania State University (Capitol Campus) to serve as a consultant in the area of traditional brewing, a craft pursued by both the Pilgrims and me.

My interests in folklore and history have been very parochial, centering totally within the North-Central Plains region, and so my grammar school knowledge about this country's Pilgrim heritage was blurred and dimmed by a distance of years, a cloud of disinterest, and the conventional rose-colored (or perhaps black-and-white colored) lens through which grade school teachers all too often view the squalid Pilgrim experiment. To bolster my understanding of the Pilgrims' life, I augmented my specific readings in seventeenth-century food and beverage ways with other texts like Bradford's *Of Plymouth Plantation* and Syndey James' *Three Visitors to Early Plymouth*. A certain intensity was lent to my reading because I knew that I would actually be visiting and working on the sites mentioned in the books, but ultimately it must be admitted that such cultural, temporal, and spatial gulfs cannot be bridged intellectually.

Anderson and I had access to modern housing on Cape Cod, but we decided that it would be at best clumsy, at worst disabling to our research, to commute to the Museum grounds. With the permission, therefore, of Jim

Deetz, director of the Plimoth Plantation Museum, we moved into the village's Brewster House, a home set up and furnished as precisely as possible as it was in 1627. In keeping with the spirit both of the museum and of our work, Anderson and I also resolved to adopt authentic modes and so dressed, ate, and worked in the clothes, with the implements, and in the manner of 1627.

It was not a lark. The same muscles that trembled with the cold at night trembled with unaccustomed exertion by early afternoon. Accommodations and compromises were continually necessary because physically and intellectually neither of us was capable of sustaining seventeenth-century life for very long—a stern lesson in itself.

But we expected that. The surprising and exciting element involved the "cultural, temporal, and spatial" gulf that "cannot be bridged intellectually." It quickly became evident that even though we had anticipated sore backs from carrying water in wooden buckets, we had not anticipated the stupifying effects of being confined within the narrow, drab village and in a small one-room hut for even a short period of time. We understood that it would be messy eating boiled fish with our fingers, Pilgrim-style, but we had not anticipated the mental effects of being dirty virtually all of the time with little respite. We were prepared for the inconvenience of leaving our car and hence our American "civilization" outside the village walls, but we were not at all ready for the staggering despondency felt on the evening of April 5, as we stood in the center of the dark, dreary village in a light snow, looking out on a stormy sea, listening to its roar, overcome by the realization that some 350 years before the Plimoth villagers had watched their last real contact with the world they had known, the *Mayflower*, sail eastward on this very night, leaving them alone—perhaps the word is "abandoned"—on these hostile shores.

In short, Anderson and I found that by immersing ourselves in a simulated environment, we made great strides toward understanding the depression, antagonism, and despair that had characterized the original Plimoth. To be sure, the requisites for a productive experience like this include a romantic heart and a rigorously accurate re-creation of the environment in question; anything less could more mislead than educate.

Upon my returning to the Plains and the twentieth century, I considered the pedagogical lesson I had learned and tried to analyze its implications for my own teaching in the area of Plains folklore. For years I had been trying in my research and writing, and in my classes, to teach the lesson of the great American desert—that while today we can point with derision at early Plains visitors who called the region a desert, we must remember that for them, against the backdrop of their previous experience and the contemporary conditions of the Plains, what they had seen was indeed a great wasteland.

Clearly, two barriers hinder intellectual bridging. The Plains have changed, so that there is now water and trees where before there were none, while interstate highways have reduced a week's wagon journey to an hour's drive by automobile. The second factor is far more subtle and difficult to grasp: the eyes that see the Plains have changed. The European eyes that saw the Plains had never before seen such distances, for example, nor prairie fires, rattlesnakes, Indians, grasshopper storms, blizzards, extreme temperatures, drought, thunder and lightning, and duststorms like those on the Plains. Even settlers from the eastern states were unprepared for the total absence of rocks and trees, the immensity of the mountains, and the violence of Plains weather.

It is, of course, very difficult to re-create a mental attitude by unlearning experiences but, given an appropriate environment, as I found at Plimoth, a willing mind can approach that ideal far closer than it might by purely intellectual effort. It followed, I felt, that given a nineteenth-century Plains environment, I could better describe and communicate the life and ways of the nineteenth-century Plains Indian, homesteader, cowboy, and railroad worker to my students.

While doing research on Plains folklore and history, I had frequently used the library and collections of the Stuhr Museum of the Prairie Pioneer in Grand Island, Nebraska, and it came immediately to mind in this connection. The Stuhr Museum offers a remarkable contrast. Its central building is a stunningly magnificent structure designed by the eminent architect Edward Durell Stone. The second part of the museum, however, spoke more to my needs—some sixty buildings, including a complete and accurate re-creation of an 1890 Plains railroad town.

Stuhr offers, in addition to the immediate physical environment, a historical and spiritual environment that for my purposes profoundly enhances its suitability for a re-creation of Plains frontier living. It lies within a few miles of two great Pawnee earth-lodge villages and directly on Indian and buffalo migration routes. It is within calling distance of the Oregon and Mormon Trails, the early stage lines, freighting trails, and Texas cattle trails. From our log cabins we would hear the whistle of trains still traveling the transcontinental road completed at Promontory Point, Utah, in 1869. Pony Express stations still stand within easy driving distance. Fort Hartsuff, meant to keep the Sioux literally out of the hair of the Pawnee and homesteaders, still stands and Fort Kearney has been reconstructed—again within an easy hour's drive from Stuhr. Finally, Stuhr lies at the heart of a complex of museums and monuments within a 90-minute radius that considerably enchances its educational usefulness: the House of Yesterday (Hastings; 25 minutes), Pioneer Village (Minden; 60 minutes), Fort Kearney Museum (Kearney; 45 minutes), Buffalo Bill's Scout's Rest Ranch (North Platte; 2 hours), Nebraska State Historical Society Museum (Lincoln; 90 minutes), Willa Cather Memorial Museum (Red Cloud; 60 minutes). In short, it became increasingly clear to me that Stuhr might prove to be the perfect site for a didactic simulation of the Plains pioneer experience, not only by virtue of its own facilities but also because of the complex of museums and historical sites that surround it.

I approached Jack Learned, the director of the Stuhr Museum, and Harold Holoun, its educational director, about the museum's potential as an educational laboratory and both agreed enthusiastically that the concept was worth trying.

We decided to offer two such programs during July, 1973, which for the lack of a better term we called "workshops," a label that ultimately proved exhaustingly accurate. Moreover, we agreed that while we would use all the facilities the museum had to offer, our principal location would be a set of 1857 log cabins clustered in a small copse about a quarter mile from the 1890 village and within watermelon-seed-spitting distance of the Wood River.

There followed several months of activities seldom enjoyed by professors and educational directors: rechinking log cabins, digging an ice pit, locating sources of cobs, raw milk, and sowbelly, and squeezing mulberries for cider. By July 9, the date of the first workshop, preparations were completed. The main log cabin—with two rooms and a loft—was outfitted with a complete pioneer kitchen. The second room was reserved as a rainy day sitting room, while the loft was used for storage and sleeping, exactly as had been the case when it was built in 1857. A second one-room log house was used for sleeping quarters. A smoke house was used for storage, while another small log building, the original use of which is uncertain, served as the location for our ice pit. A small cob and grass burning stove was put under a tree, and as it turned out, our use of the facilities paralleled pioneer custom, for we spent the hot hours of the day outside in the breeze, using the inside kitchen only on cooler days.

The thirteen participants in the first session ranged in age from about twenty to over sixty. Most were teachers, some were students, and one simply took the course out of interest. Few, I could see when I first met them, really understood the nature of our experiment, even though I had sent out repeated letters and warnings; their attire ranged from white pants-suits to light-colored summer dresses. All quickly learned that the rigors of pioneer life demand rugged clothes that will not be embarrassed by ashes, mud, biscuit dough, or buttermilk slipped from the churn. We spent long hours intellectualizing about the Plains pioneer experience but, even as we talked corn mush was being mixed in the kitchen, cast-iron pots were being scoured with cob, or the handle was being turned on the churn of the ice-cream freezer. While we had originally planned on providing only three meals on the workshop site, we eventually decided to intensify the experience by preparing almost all our meals at the cabins, which we did, eating typical Plains pioneer or Indian fare (excepting two special evenings dinners when we enjoyed typical migrant dinners of the period in this locale, one Polish and another German, prepared by outside parties, one served at the cabin site).

Because of the harsh conditions at the frontier cabins and the variance in ages and strengths of the participants, living arrangements were also varied. Three participants eventually joined me in living full time on the nineteenth-century site, while others commuted between the centuries. (It must be noted, however, that all students agreed that those who actually lived on the grounds profited most from the workshop experience, especially in regard to the wildlife—coyotes, muskrats, fire-flies, and deer—that were evident only at night or in the early morning hours.)

In spite of the highly restricted nature of the workshop—we did no plowing or harvesting, had no farm animals on the site, faced no real physical threats—we learned a wealth of lessons: The amazing efficiency of an ice pit, the frustration of trying to maintain a cob cooking fire, and the profound veracity of pioneer folksongs, like "Little Old Sod Shanty on the Claim," which goes, "My clothes are plastered o'er with dough, I'm looking like a fright, and everything is scattered round the room."

In order to evaluate our efforts and provide a basis for improvements in the 1974 program, we distributed an evaluation questionnaire and requested an anonymous response. A few suggestions were made, mostly regrets that we did not have the chance, for example, to make soap or dress out a deer, but the evaluations were unanimously enthusiastic in their approval of the workshop program.

In this context the costs and tangible benefits of the workshop should perhaps be noted. The museum and instructional cost for five and one-half days were $95. Most students made arrangements with their schools to earn credit for the workshop, ranging from three hours of graduate credit to four hours of undergraduate credit, which added a tuition cost of from $50 to $85, for a total of $145 to $180, with some participants paying additional sums for housing. All participants assured us that the session was worth whatever they had spent for it.

The Stuhr Plains pioneer workshops had begun, you will recall, as a pedagogical experiment. Our results, therefore, offer two separate sets of conclusions—the ones regarding pioneer life itself, already suggested above, and a second set about using such methodology for teaching history. We—Jack Learned, Harold Holoun, and I—are unanimous in our enthusiasm about this methodology. Never have museum facilities been put to a more effective use. Never in the many years of teaching pioneer and Indian folkways have I felt the lessons so easily taught or so well learned. But, as should always be true with any carefully done experiment, the conclusions provoke more questions than they answer. Would the workshops have to be modified for particular groups? We would now like to try operating the workshops for a group of German or French nationals, or a group of high school students, or an exclusively urban group. We would also like to expand our facilities for students remaining full time on the museum grounds, and perhaps broaden the nature of that housing—one night, for example, in the 1890 hotel, another in a Pullman rail-car (the Stuhr Museum has two full sets of railroad rolling stocks), a third at the log cabins.

A project endorsed by the Nebraska American Revolution Bicentennial Commission will provide yet another living experience and will also profoundly enrich the entire scope of the workshops. The commission has granted the Stuhr Museum $5,000, to be matched by another $5,000 from the museum, to re-create a living farm for 1876, and the key word in that description is "living." The farm will not be a set of sterile exhibits but a genuine operation complete with people, animals, machinery, crops, and equipment, and all the appropriate smells, sights, and sounds of 1876. This will carry food production one step further, giving us the opportunity in the workshops to get our milk from the cows, our eggs from the hens, and our corn from the stalk. Because the farm must be operated by interpreters in the costume of the period, all workshop participants who are involved with the living farm will also have to dress in accurate costumes, thereby further approaching the ideal of my Plimoth experience and further enhancing the effectiveness of the workshop.

In conclusion, I feel that my experiences at Plimoth and Stuhr are of more than passing or anecdotal value to teachers, especially in the field of history. Plimoth and Stuhr are particularly excellent museums, but they are not unique in their concept. Outdoor museums, living-history museums, folk museums, and other reconstructions and preservations of this type exist in nearly every state (varying, it must be admitted, in the quality and quantity of the environment attempted).[1]

Wherever these museums are to be found, it would be worth the while of history teachers to consider visiting the museum grounds not merely to view its holdings as an exhibit but with the intention of using the museum's holdings and environment as massive and intense audio-visual (and for that matter, tacticle, gustatory, and generally sensual) devices. Obviously, those museums that are preserving rare, valuable, ancient, or venerable holdings cannot risk them to fire, breakage, or general wear and tear, but perhaps, given the opportunity, they would be willing to construct or develop a more expendable reconstruction, specifically for such educational purposes.

Like schools, museums are themselves going through transition. More and more of them are moving from sterile exhibits of items behind glass or chicken wire to living exhibits of processes. No longer do museums, for example, tack up exhibit boards of horseshoes, with a printed or recorded description of how they were made or used. Even the simple display of the process of smithing or shoeing is fading. The historical museums of the future will demonstrate such processes in an accurate working environment, the blacksmith in a smithy, the ferrier in the stable, or, better yet, in the larger context of a working village, making shoes and putting them on a horse not just as a demonstration exercise but as a part

Reece Summers harnessing a Belgian work horse as part of his graduate studies in outdoor museum work at Utah State University.— *Photo: Tom Allen*

of the actual operation of the functioning organism of the village—in other words, not because patrons are at the forge but because a horse in the reconstructed village needs shoes.

The participatory historical workshop is certainly appropriate to the rapidly converging concepts of experiential learning and living museums. I offer our Stuhr Plains pioneer workshops as a case study of an effort to develop precisely this kind of educational experience.[2]

Notes

1. If there are questions about the locations of such museums in the United States, excellent guidance can be obtained from two sources: Nicholas Zook, *Museum Villages USA* (Barre, Mass.: Barre Publishers, 1971), where it might be noted that Stuhr is discussed on pages 65-66 and 131 and the Plimoth Plantation Museum on pages 32-34; and John T. Schlebecker and Gale E. Peterson, *Living Historical Farms Handbook* (Washington, D.C.: Smithsonian Institution Press, 1972), noting especially the indices "State Directory of Historic Farms and Museums" on pages 59-79. In this volume Plimoth is mentioned on pages 41, 42, 48, 63, and 72, while Stuhr is covered on pages 25, 50, and 76.

2. Current plans call for the workshops to be offered twice during the summer of 1974 through the English Department of the University of Nebraska. The new arrangements with a major educational institution will provide greater services, credit, and opportunities for out students, while at the same time simplifying the registration and financial arrangements.

Retreat into History

Tracey Linton Craig

21

Washburn-Norlands Living History Center in Livermore Falls, Maine, has been operating a superb adult live-in for over a decade. The child of Billie Gammon, this successful program takes place on a 430-acre historic site, a farm that in the 1870s belonged to the politically powerful Washburn family. Tracey Linton Craig's article appeared in the June 1983 issue of History News. *The program was begun in 1977 and is held on ten weekends each year. Fifteen participants adopt the personae of two families and a collection of Maine villagers who actually lived in the community in 1870. Gammon notes that people today want to "experience another period in time," not a vacation or nostalgic trip to Grandma's but a realistic, authentic version of "Fantasy Island."*

Cast of Characters

The Waters Family
    Simeon
    Emeretta
    Almira
    Brooksie
    Clarendon
The Pray Family
    Eliza
    Otis
    Albert
    Pitt
    Fessenden
    Rosetta
    Bethiah
Aunt Clara Howard, the widow woman
Miz Lovejoy, the pauper
Emeline Hilton, the farmhouse cook
Julia Chase, the schoolteacher
Eunice Chenery, another schoolteacher
Brother Stevens, the preacher
Nathan Barnett, the blacksmith
Assorted villagers, balladeers, farmhands, cousins and hired help

The Setting

On the road to nowhere, on a windswept hill in Livermore, Maine, five nineteenth-century buildings nestle on the east side of a country road. There is a school, a library, a church, the Washburn house with its attached farmer's cottage and a barn. To the west, there is nothing but gently rolling hills in the distance, fields and forests in the foreground. In the aggregate, with all of its 430 acres, the place is known as "Washburn-Norlands." It is a working farm, a living-history center where visitors travel back to an earlier age to take part in the daily round of toil on a nineteenth-century Maine farm.

The Time

It is 1870, and Ulysses S. Grant is president. All the seceded states are back in the Union. The United States has just purchased Alaska, much to the dismay of downeasters, who think it sheer folly to waste money on a natural icebox.

Act 1

In the early shadows of twilight, a group of adults and children come walking through the backyard of the Washburn house, headed for the kitchen of the attached farmer's cottage. Of the dozen or so, several are Maine schoolteachers, and there is one family with a boy, nine, and a girl, twelve. Each has left behind twentieth-century accoutrements. No one wears a wristwatch, no one carries a flashlight or cigarette lighter. Many of the men wear flannel shirts and work boots; the women are clad in calicos, and some wear pokebonnets. The hand luggage and eyeglasses a few sport provide the only visible anachronisms—if you don't look too closely. They have all come to participate in a Washburn-Norlands "live-in" experience.

After settling in, dividing up the three upstairs bedrooms—choosing which cornhusk mattress to hunker down on and noting the chamber pots underneath—they regroup in the farmhouse kitchen.

These twentieth-century players in nineteenth-century garb first play a guessing game with an array of common nineteenth-century tools and household items—apple parers, pot scrubbers, soap savers, and calf muzzles. Many items—such as the skirt lifter, a device that allowed women to raise their hems on muddy days without bending over—need explanation. Emeline, the cook, and Billie Gammon—not yet in character—are there to provide those explanations.

Gammon directs this orientation period and heads Washburn-Norlands as well. It is Gammon, with assistance from her nearly all-volunteer staff, who will create the atmosphere necessary to take the group back in time. Each participant in the "live-in" has paid $155 for the privilege of spending three days sans twentieth-century amenities—electricity, indoor plumbing, central heat. And they will soon take on new identities in which they will be expected to interact as members of the two Maine families who once lived here at Norlands.

Back at the Beginning

Washburn-Norlands is a living-history center, located some sixty miles west of Augusta and nearly ten miles from the nearest hamlet, Livermore Falls, a town of 3,800. The adult live-in is only one of the programs it offers, but it is the live-in that seems to fascinate people most. The in-depth experience is billed as a "total involvement experience of rural life as it was lived in northern New England a century and more ago." According to its creator, Mrs. Alfred Q. Gammon—better known as Billie—the live-in's goal is to help adults establish an identity with the past and an appreciation of the present. The program carries three teacher recertification credits through the Maine Department of Education and graduate-level college credits through the University of Maine at Farmingham.

Museum educators throughout the country have been intrigued with the teaching methods Washburn-Norlands uses. Thomas Schlereth, author of several AASLH books, including *Artifacts and the American Past*, is one. A professor of American Studies at the University of Notre Dame, Schlereth has written to Gammon to compliment her on "the range of your historical interpretation of the period. Whether you realize it or not, you are very much in tune with the current trends in research and scholarship in American social history. This is especially the case since you tastefully and accurately have researched and interpreted numerous activities of human behavior so often left out of history books and history classrooms.... You involve your audience in thinking about eighteenth- and nineteenth-century attitudes toward senility, poverty, sex, old age, welfare, and death." Others have praised the role playing and participatory first-person history techniques that Washburn-Norlands features.

Though the roles participants assume during the live-in at Norlands are based on the lives of the Pray and Waters families, during the weekend the group also learns the story of the Washburn family, owner of the Maine homestead. The Washburns, a nineteenth-century equivalent of the Kennedys of Massachusetts, called Norlands home. One Washburn son became a congressman and governor of Maine, another a businessman and bank president. The third son left the hard-scrabble farm to serve first in Congress and then as U. S. Secretary of State; another founded the Gold Medal Flour Company and also served as a congressman, brigadier general, and governor of Wisconsin. The fifth struck it rich in the California gold rush and became U. S. ambassador to Paraguay, a novelist, and an inventor. Yet another became a sea captain and Civil War hero, and the seventh became a

wealthy railroad magnate, a congressman, and senator from Minnesota. One nineteenth-century political wag is said to have remarked, "Every male member of the Washburn family is born with 'member of congress' franked across his broadest part." The Washburn brothers spent fifty years in Congress, a total never since equaled by any family.

It was with the story of the Washburn brothers that Billie Gammon began her journey some thirty years ago as a young schoolteacher new to the area. Upon first hearing the story, Gammon was amazed. The Washburn estate had fallen into disrepair, the family's story had been lost to history. In 1953, at the request of one of the Washburn descendants, Gammon began opening the family's library one day a week. Only twenty-seven people came that first summer, but Gammon started researching the journals and other primary sources among the library's dust-covered tomes and began what she calls her "love affair" with the Washburn story.

A Place for Living History

Officially, she was working as chair of the American Baptist Convention's ministry for youth from 1962-1972, but she spent a good deal of her time in the library, researching and learning more about the family, trying to find a way to share its story with others.

"I would sit in the library and when I got tired of reading, I'd look up and dream about what this place could be," Gammon remembers. "I always had a wild imagination. I could look over to the schoolhouse and see schoolchildren in the late afternoon sun. Though the building was smothered by bushes, I could see it with smoke coming out its chimney." It reminded her of her own childhood. "I lived in Nova Scotia as a child and went to a one-room schoolhouse, wrote on a slate board. The teacher used to leave to have her lunch where she boarded, and I remember being terrified by the bigger boys at noon. Later on, I taught at a one-room school too."

In December of 1971, Gammon chanced upon an article in "Musings," the newsletter of the Maine State Humanities Commission, that was to have a profound effect.

She read: "New Hampshire has its Strawbery Banke, Massachusetts its Sturbridge Village—surely, somewhere in the state of Maine there is a site for living history." Gammon knew exactly what to do. She wrote a long letter, "spilling my dream," as she puts it, to describe the site and a little about its history to the journal's editor. She closed with the line, "Please try to get a little bit excited."

The letter found its way into the hands of the article's author, Ron Kley, then head of research and collections at the Maine State Museum and active in the Association of Living Historical Farms and Agricultural Museums. Kley wrote back, telling Gammon: "To say we are excited is the understatement of the year." Within a couple of weeks, Kley was on his way to the Norlands site.

"He came to visit, and the schoolhouse was all shuttered up," Gammon recalls. "The snowbanks were as high as your head. But Kley was the first person who listened to my dream—and approved. You know, twelve years ago, people didn't listen to women. To have a man listen and approve meant a lot."

Kley says he "damn near froze to death" that frigid February day—but he was excited. The Washburn heirs were interested too. They had heard there was grant money available for restoration work. "And they had heard I had a good track record," says Kley. "The Washburns wanted to know if I could help. I was fairly brutal. I told them there was no more possibility of their getting grants than of my getting federal money to re-roof my house. You have to turn it over, I told them."

On the advice of Kley, and with the assistance of a local lawyer named Ben Butler, 136 Washburn heirs "signed off" their rights to the property and created the Washburn-Norlands Foundation in 1973. Gammon was project director.

Kley wrote the first grant proposal himself and succeeded in getting $15,500 under the Elementary and Secondary Education Act, (ESEA) Title IVC. Gammon, an educator with her MA from the University of Maine at Portland, knew that the state education department needed development opportunities for history teachers. She had been shocked to read in the newsletter of the Organization of American Historians the results of a survey by OAH's president Richard Kirkendall on the status of history in the nation's schools. He had discovered "that history was the most hated subject from cradle to grave, and he called for innovation on the part of teachers to make history come alive," remembers Gammon. "It was a needs assessment I didn't have to perform."

With the ESEA grant, restoration of the schoolhouse at Washburn-Norlands began. Gammon hired two certified Maine schoolteachers: one young woman for the summer (her daughter-in-law) and another recent male graduate for the winter months—in keeping with how it would have been done in 1870. She trained them, and the two were paid through the school system. In 1974, the program opened to high praise from local educators. Students came from neighboring county schools to spend a day as nineteenth-century scholars. After a bevy of consultants had approved the program, the University of Maine granted Gammon adjunct faculty status. Washburn-Norlands held special teacher-training sessions at the schoolhouse as well. Because it was working with ESEA money, each step required testing, proof that

Adult students at one of Norland's live-in weekends, beginning the first stage of a quilt on the farm kitchen table.—*Photo: Washburn Norlands*

the students were indeed learning something. Pretest, post-tests, and constant evaluation even beyond what the grant stipulated, says Gammon, proved that indeed students were "engaging in a significant learning experience."

Seat-of-the-pants History

One member of the educational assessment team encouraged Gammon to go after additional grants. She remembers that he asked her a question that took her quite by surprise. "He asked me, 'What is your over-arching goal?' " She felt rather like Miss America, she says, hit with one of those on-the-spot questions. "I looked out the window at the schoolchildren playing in the schoolyard. I thought about how, when these children attend the Washburn-Norlands school in mid-winter, it's icy. They go to the outhouse, and it's icy. Those kids were feeling history right in the seat of their pants," she laughs. Finally, she told the consultant, "I want to help people establish an identity with the past. . . and an appreciation of the present."

The next step, Gammon decided, was to restore the farm cottage. Participants had seen what a day at school in 1870 was like; now they would see what their home lives would have been like. In 1975-1976, the foundation requested and received $21,000, also from ESEA, to restore the cottage. To comply with regulations, they had to put in a furnace and a small stove for a Russian fireplace (similar to a brick oven). The cottage already had electricity.

None of this fitted very well with Gammon's plans for exact replication of what the home would have been like. "Old-fashioned ways don't meet with modern sanitation requirements. So we cover up the faucets, hang things over the switch-plates . . . when people are involved in what they are doing, they don't notice," Gammon insists.

"I have the ability to brainwash people," she says with pride. "They told me that when I worked for the American Baptist Convention," and they tell her that now, too. "Any good teacher knows that drama is one of the best ways of teaching anything," Gammon continues, "and any teacher worth her salt can make people do what she wants them to, make them think it's their own idea . . . and have fun doing it."

Gammon was hard at work hatching another idea, a more intensive experience that would be primarily for adults. She drew up initial plans for the three-day live-in, an outline of sorts.

Others, such as Plimoth Plantation in Massachusetts, had abandoned similar programs, or handled them in a non-period way. Ron Kley, author of the first grant proposal and now a trustee of the foundation, remembers that in researching other living-history programs, he found that the few places that had tried "live-ins" had encountered problems because of their generally large flocks of visitors.

"We wanted to and thought we could do it," says Kley. "We didn't have and didn't want a great crush of visitors. We wanted to reach teachers, because of the ripple effect that would have. If you deal with a teacher, you can touch every kid he or she teaches. It's the method [of living history] we were concerned with more than the specific message."

Gammon listened to what others told her about her plan; she, Kley, and the "resident fanatics" held several brainstorming sessions and discussed a variety of possibilities. But in the end, she says, it was a good thing she wasn't drawing any salary. "I wasn't being paid, so I didn't have to do what people told me. They kept saying, 'You can't do this.' I figured I knew more about how people learned. I did it my way. If I'd done it theirs, it would have been a pretty strange live-in experience."

Her instincts were confirmed, even saluted, when in 1981 a group of nine consultants, brought in through the Museum Assessment Program and NEH grants, all praised her fresh, new approach. "They said it was a benefit that I hadn't been previously concerned with the museum field," she says.

In 1977, Washburn-Norlands held two live-ins for a total of twenty-six people. The second and third years, there were five. In 1980, Washburn-Norlands held six and in recent years Gammon has scheduled ten per year, involving a total of about 140 people. Each year, there are two or three unscheduled live-ins as well, such as when Nyack College or Outward Bound schedule their own live-ins at the site. Gammon figures that slightly more than 500 people have traveled back in time to 1870 since the program first began.

A "Fantasy Island"?

Participants at first were almost exclusively Maine schoolteachers, who used the weekend to qualify for recertification. But in the last several years, Norland's fame has spread, and it is not unusual to find museum professionals, teachers and their families, and just people who crave the experience Washburn-Norlands offers for the weekend.

Gammon thinks, "This is a lot of people's secret dream. They want to experience another period in time. It's a Fantasy Island, a respite from the pressures of the 1980s, for them." But she warns participants that the experience is not a vacation, a visit to grandma's house, or a nostalgic trip. When people write to inquire about the program, perhaps having read the articles that have appeared in *Yankee* magazine, *The New York Times* or the *Boston Globe,* or having seen the documentary Maine's public television station has prepared on Washburn-Norlands, Gammon sends them what she terms an "Is-Is Not" sheet.

No showers for three days

"I warn them, you won't take a shower for three days, you'll sleep on a cornhusk mattress in the dead of winter. There are no private rooms and no electricity. This is real." Usually, she admits, the more you tell them, the more they want to come. But the program does make two concessions: "Window screens in summer and toilet paper year round," she laughs.

Two weeks prior to the live-in experience, Gammon

sends the participants—no more than fifteen or so allowed per weekend—a chatty letter. "It is 1870," she writes. "Ulysses Simpkins Grant is president, the United States has just purchased Alaska. . . . Julia is back now, teaching in the school." She sends a fourteen-page booklet as well, including sections she asks them to study on what a farmhouse is like, what books are being read, what women and men do on the farm, the role of religion in their lives.

Based on this information, participants first engage in the role-playing characteristic of the weekend. Gammon plays teacher, asking her new class of scholars to answer her questions in full and complete sentences. They fall naturally right into the role every time, she says. "I ask them, 'Who is president of the United States?' Someone will say, 'Ulysses S. Grant is president, ma'am.' " She asks the class to repeat the answer.

Then she asks, "But what is Grant's middle name?" Usually, no one remembers, and she scolds the class, which acts properly contrite. "When I get them to play scholars, they do it instantly. . . William Garland of William and Mary College was ever the skeptic; he came and couldn't believe it," she says. "At first we're obviously playing, laughing. . . but each activity is calculated to give them practice in role playing. It can't fail." She then prepares the class for the next step by telling them that each will receive a new name and identity for the weekend.

After the guessing game with kitchen implements—played without learning each other's real-life names—the group receives its new identities. They line up along the north and south walls of the dining room and kitchen. Emeline Hilton, the cook and farm wife, tells those on the north that they will be the Waters family, and the ones on the south, the Prays. Going down the short line, she gives each person his or her new name, at the same time giving just a tidbit of information. "How's the saddle business?" she'll ask the Pray patriarch. To Brooksie, the Waters' daughter: "I've been hearing terrible things about you, but I don't believe them." While the room roars with laughter, curious about just what flagrant behavior Emeline has observed, to Brooksie's sister, she says, "But just in case, you keep an eye on her, hear?"

Gammon says that throughout the weekend "there's laughter and lots of it. Sometimes after a live-in, my cheeks ache. We're in the happiness business . . . what makes you feel good at the end of the day is to be able to say, "Today people learned something and had fun doing it."

After the "christening," the two families sit down together to a hearty Maine supper with great platters of food: hot breads, chicken and dumplings, and apple pie. Sometimes it's smoked ham or another product of the working farm. "That dinner," says Kley, "is really a celebration of American nostalgia. . . but by the last night, they're saying, 'My god, it's apples again.' " And, too, by the last night, they have also helped make the food they

are to eat, kneading bread, killing a chicken or churning butter. ("I had no idea it took so long to get just a tiny pat of butter," grumbled one participant.)

During that first meal, several visitors may drop by, possibly the local minister, and always Miz Lovejoy (played by Billie Gammon), a pauper dressed in rags who constantly wipes her runny nose. At the meal, remembers Lynn Lowlby, a teacher from Wyndham, New Hampshire, who brought her family, "We only knew each other as characters. I'm not sure my little boy [nine-years-old] knew quite what to make of Miz Lovejoy. . . . At some point in the meal, you suddenly realize that it is 1870. Conversation is no longer based in the present. We were totally unaware that we had made the transition."

Gammon, who plays several characters throughout the weekend, particularly enjoys the role of pauper Lovejoy. She loses herself in the character. "It's as if your body is given over to that character," she tries to explain. "The minute I put on those pauper's rags, my nose begins to run. I become that person. I hear her say things I never would have thought of."

Aided by the informative banter of the volunteers who run the weekend—two men who run the farming operations, two women who instruct participants in farmer's cottage activities, the woman who teaches school on Monday, the preacher on Sunday morning and the assorted residents and musicians who sometimes drop in-participants learn to respond in character, some even with classic downeast country accents. They are encouraged—but not required—to step completely away from their twentieth-century personas. The volunteers who staff the program do not step out of character, nor does Gammon once the brief orientation is finished. Three volunteers, the ones Gammon calls her "think tank," have been at Norlands since the live-in program began. Glenda Richards, who plays Emeline, Willi Irish, who plays the widow Aunt Clara, and Norma Boothby, who plays schoolteacher Eunice Chenery, are her "main strength and support."

The "busy cradle"

It is Gammon who tells the "busy cradle" story that is about the Washburn brothers' lives and which participants act out under her tutelage as she tells it. Gammon is the one who leads the participants the first night past their "own" homesteads and to the cemetery where they discover "their" graves.

Many participants say that it is at the cemetery where there is that first "click" of how real their play-acting is.

"Wandering through an old country graveyard at twilight is a spooky experience at the best of times, but if you expect to stumble over your own grave at any moment, it becomes positively goose-bump-producing," wrote journalist William A. Davis in the *Boston Globe* Sunday magazine, after having taken part in a live-in.

The inexplicable

The second night after dinner the group takes a candle-light tour of the Washburn mansion. That, too, is a "click," a point at which people question where reality

Norland's farmer, Curt Bonney, harvesting a field of wheat with his reaper-binder.— *Photo: Washburn Norlands*

ends and play-acting begins. Sangamon University history professor Ed Hawes, one of the consultants who back in 1981 took part in an evaluatory live-in, remembers: "We toured the ghostly house, with all the Washburn furniture still there. You imagine that the eyes in the portraits are following you. In a sense, their spirits are still there. You really get into the skins of those people. There is a sense of mystery and play, and you are never quite sure if Billie believes in spirits, or if she's just playing." Others who have taken part say certain rooms are inexplicably cold, that there are peculiar gusts of chilly air and that one encounters a "Twilight Zone" confusion.

"You really do forget about the twentieth century," says Jim Dachos, a Lewiston schoolteacher who took part in a live-in nearly a year ago and has since recommended it to several colleagues and students. "I was skeptical, but after a day, I felt so close to the others. We had to cooperate because of the responsibilities. And it was so encompassing that we did talk and joke based on the real routines of farm work. You think you are living in that period."

Bowlby, the teacher who brought her family along to participate, remembers that it took them awhile to get into the role-playing—her own son played her character's son, but it seemed strange having her real-life husband as her father, she says. "We didn't know what was coming next. We did wonder from time to time, where do we wash? What will we eat?" She wanted her kids to experience it. "No one appreciates what went on before. Today it's all TV, video games. I knew I wanted to do this. You learn something from getting out and shoveling manure, churning butter, discovering how long it takes to make a quilt . . . you appreciate what people did back then, how hard life was."

Her kids loved it, she says, and the family has been back several times since. "My daughter will say, 'I think it's time to go home to the farm.' She really liked being out there in the barn, waiting for a warm egg."

Coming home

No one ever seems to want to leave, according to Gammon. In the letters she receives from past participants, almost all speak of wanting to "come home" again. Some even sign their notes by the name of the character they took on a year or two or five years ago.

Many do come back again and again. Some send Christmas cards. Others write to tell Gammon of how they've adopted her methods in their own classrooms. Bowlby has taken up the craft of spinning to teach her fourth-grade students a little about how hard making clothing was, how much a pair of socks would have been worth. Dachos is using primary sources with his eighth-graders in the class he teaches on Maine history. Both are working on programs designed to incorporate the role-playing into other classroom history situation. Dachos says, "Kids like personal experience. They remember more that way than if they read it in a book. And kids have trouble making [historical] connections. By doing it themselves, they get a lot more out of it."

Throughout the live-in weekend, participants work with real nineteenth-century artifacts to prepare food, cut ice, or perform other farm tasks. As Kley puts it, "Preserving objects is not our primary function. We are not geared to perpetual preservation. We work with artifacts of the period where possible, with generic artifacts. We don't use Washburn pieces or documented pieces, but why use replicas when we can buy a kitchen chair of the period for $15 or $20 instead of $150 for a replica?" There are a few exceptions, for example, with farm equipment. If the plow the farmer uses dates from a later period, the farmer will explain just how it is different to his "student farmers."

In the course of the weekend, particpant also do some primary research, based on the journals left in the Washburn library, and take part in typical seasonal social events, perhaps a husking bee, a barn dance or quilting party. They prepare—and in the case of the chickens, kill—all the food they eat, all of which is grown on the premises. They build wood fires from wood they have chopped. They rise early on Sunday to attend the Universalist church and spend some time as a character of the opposite sex to discover more about the differences in men's and women's work. On Monday, all attend school where they use original hornbooks to learn their lessons.

In 1981, consultant Hawes encouraged Billie Gammon to add a last segment to the weekend, a time where participants could meet each other in their real life roles and get ready to return to the twentieth century.

"Ed Hawes scolded me when he came here," Gammon says. "He said, 'You have to help get participants back to the 1980s.' I had thought the live-ins would teach people how to teach history, but it's also a profoundly emotional experience. You put them under a spell, and you must bring them out again. So we changed that. At the end, now, they meet each other, and talk about who they really are."

Other living-history programs

The live-in, while undoubtedly the most "complete" immersion experience, is only a direct outgrowth of the other programs Norlands offers. Throughout the year, it hosts school groups from throughout the New England area for one-night versions of the live-in. It charges young students $25, and high school and college students $35 each. Marcie Cohen, hired just over a year ago as curator, takes a large part in those student programs. She says the kids "have good imaginations, they throw off conventions readily and start 'playing.' It's a game of pretend."

Teachers who have taken their classes to the mini-live-in say that the kids love it, that it facilitates a different quality of learning. "There is a remarkable qualitative difference in children's learning when, rather than relying solely on lessons (however creative or exciting) for information, children have a safe and structured opportunity to use their knowledge and actually become people of another time or culture," wrote Maine schoolteachers Kristen Kaiser and Jackie Reizes, who both went through the adult live-in and later brought their classes to take part in the one-day version.

Cohen says when she first visited Norlands several years ago that "Billie absolutely wowed me. I told her I'd do volunteer work, anything," she says. Once hired, she did some conservation work, got the library program together, organized archival materials. She now runs Washburn-Norlands when Billie Gammon takes her infrequent sailing vacations in summertime.

Cohen is also in charge of the Washburn-Norlands internship program. There are currently two interns working at Norlands, one from Southeast Missouri State and one from the University of Michigan. Each receives a minimal stipend of $25 per week, and each met the criteria Cohen looks for in an intern: specific interest in living history, flexibility, genuine enjoyment of the isolated Maine lifestyle, and enthusiasm. After receiving two weeks of training, the interns help run the program, including the live-ins.

Another special event held each year at Norlands, one that Gammon is particularly proud of, is a living-history program where high school students re-enact "the journey westward." History teacher Jon Rice from Winnacunnet High School in Livermore wanted a way to get students to understand the dangers and hardships of the pioneers' journey west. Too many knew only the stereotypical view of the trip, a view based on old movies and romantic novels. Rice wanted them to understand what it was really like.

He went to Gammon, and together they planned a four- to five-day experience for the students. Each year now, his students raise the money necessary for the trip, purchase the supplies they will need to make the journey west. The exercise starts back in the Livermore classroom with a year of reading and research. Then the students come to Washburn-Norlands to really "do it." They come in the rainy season, camping out for a day and a half in Norland's soggy field. With the assistance of Washburn-Norlands volunteers, they make their own soap for the journey and engage thee services of blacksmith Nathan Barnett to accompany them to take care of the oxen hooves and wagon wheels. After a big send-off party, the class starts the trip that will wipe all the Hollywood glamour out of the journey westward.

They take off slowly, and before long, the first wagons are stuck. They go another few hundred years and again the wagons stick in the muck and mire. During the course of two days, the group travels approximately twelve miles, down the oldest roads in the county. Outlining the journey was a problem, Gammon admits. Rice and Gammon's husband mapped out the circuitous path, and in order to use roads appropriate for the 1850's journey, they needed to direct the students along roads that actually headed east. So far, says Gammon, "No one has caught on to that yet."

This summer, for the first time, Washburn-Norlands will offer a six-credit course, accredited by the University of Maine. Gammon wrote the course curriculum, which combines archaeology, research and writing. During the two-week course, scheduled to be offered twice this first summer, students will meet daily from 8:30 to 5:00. The archaeological dig will zero in on the Otis Pray homesite, explains Gammon, and historical archaeologist Robert Bradley from the Maine Historic Preservation Commission will conduct the course.

Gammon hopes the research will turn up new information she can use in her interpretive programs. She's fascinated with Otis Pray. 'He was a bad man," she says. "He bought his morning ration of rum one day and was never again seen in Livermore. Much later his wife received a lock of his hair and his ring, along with a note saying he had died at sea. "But later," she says, her voice dropping to an almost conspiratorial whisper, "someone from Livermore was way out west and saw him in a little town. This man called his name—'Otis Pray'—and the man turned and ran."

Washburn-Norlands also offers a variety of outreach programs, and Billie Gammon or a representative will visit schools as far away as Boston, bringing along the requisite props of slates and original schoolbooks. Gammon does outreach programs for adults too, for a variety of civic and historical groups. Recently she presented the Washburn brothers' story at a lawyers' convention. How does she get them involved so quickly in role-playing?

"I'll ask for the ten handsomest men to come forward," she explains, "and then I'll get them to sit in ten chairs facing the audience. I'll select one to be the father and choose another with long hands—he gets to be the brother who was the inventor. I'll ask if one rides a horse or has military experience . . . and if there's one who was a spoiled brat." She says both the audience and the "actors" have a lot of fun. "The presentation is filled with humor, and with suspense," and, she says, it's a memora-ble experience. "I'll meet people three years later, and they never forget the role they played. You know, twenty-eight years ago, I told the Washburn story straight, with slides. . . you'd go to sleep. There is no earthly point in doing a program no one needs and no one wants." Gammon believes that "if you just look around, you'll find out what's needed."

Another Time-machine Trip

Right now Gammon thinks Washburn-Norlands needs live-in experience "number two." Based on the letters she's received from past participants, she knows what she wants to do next. She has in mind the first and oldest house in Livermore, Deacon Elijah Livermore's home: "You can't drive to it except during certain seasons of the year. The deacon was a key member in the foundation of this community."

For this live-in, Gammon wants to have participants do more research with primary sources and to get a sense of what went into founding a community. She plans to start participants back at Norlands and have them walk to the deacon's house. "It's only three miles, but they'll be walking back in time almost 100 years, from 1870 back to 1779."

So far, the foundation's trustees aren't especially excited about her plans.

Experience in History
A Museum Time Machine for Teaching History

22

Robert J. McQuarie

Bob McQuarie describes an intensive summer program for children which was developed at Littleton Historical Museum in Littleton, Colorado. "Is it really possible for a seven-, nine-, or eleven-year-old child to assume the role of an adult in the late nineteenth century and actually become skilled enough to hammer out a weather vane, set type for a newspaper, build a baby cradle, or place a dozen bales of hay in the second-story loft of a barn? And can a museum be used to teach the whys of history instead of just who, how, what, where, and when?" His answer, based on the experience of the children using the museum's seven-acre living history farm, log schoolhouse, and blacksmith as an outdoor classroom, is "Yes, it is possible." This article which appeared in the January 1981 issue of Social Education *analyzes the program's development by his interpretation staff. While there are similar living-history programs for children in many American and Canadian museums, few have been described as carefully.*

They fled the crowded, industrial Maryland town and the tobacco fields of Virginia, hoping that settling west of the Mississippi River, on land secured under the Homestead Act, would bring them good fortune.

In 1879, they raced across the country on the ironhorse—the speedy transportation provided by the railroad company—hoping for new settlers and users of the company line. Twenty-seven set out on the journey. The group was made up of brothers and sisters, friends and strangers of varying ages, all eager to build a new community in the American West.

Many persons before them had set out to build a town, a home. They learned the trades of carpenter, blacksmith, printer, and gained new experiences in farming, tending livestock, and weaving cloth or rugs to ward off the cold of the winter. Each member of the new community left much behind. But they were also excited, sometimes unsure, and, most importantly, willing to share and learn in the hard times, frustrations, and fun of building their own community.

In reality, the time was the summer of 1980, and the setting was the seven-acre site of the Littleton Historical Museum in Littleton, Colorado. The new settlers were, in fact, twenty-three elementary-age children and four museum staff members who would work together for a week in the museum's ten-week summer education program, "Experiences in History."

The Littleton Historical Museum is located in the south end of the Denver metropolitan area. It opened in 1970 as a new department of the City of Littleton. Littleton was settled in the 1860s and remained a small agricultural town until the rapid growth of the last twenty years increased the population in the area to 90,000 residents. The museum's goal when it opened was to be a center for the collection and interpretation of the community's past and present. Today the museum consists of the main exhibit, a research and office building, and adjacent nineteenth-century living-history farm, log schoolhouse, and blacksmith shop. Most of the museum's programs are those commonly associated with a local historical museum. However, since the summer of 1972, the museum has offered Littleton children the opportunity to enroll in one of ten week-long sessions. It is hoped that they will learn that the museum is a place that belongs to them and where they can touch, hear, use, and learn from history in a different form than often experienced in the classroom.

The program was conceived with the idea that the museum could offer more than tours for classes during the school year. Using all the museum's resources, the programmers developed a comparatively new approach to teaching that would enable children to have a prolonged chance to experience the joys of learning history directly. There were questions about dealing with children ranging in age from seven to eleven and about having them spend Monday through Friday from 9 a.m. to 3 p.m.

at the Littleton Historical Museum concentrating on learning when they had just finished the school year. Would they do it? Could the staff maintain a high level of commitment and enthusiasm for ten weeks with any assurance that children in the tenth week would receive the same attention as those during the first week? A museum might be a fun place for a short visit, but six hours every day for a week?

If registration day for the 1980 summer series was any indication, then the museum was fulfilling its goal. Parents began lining up for registration at 4:30 a.m. Such interest is no absolute guarantee of the success of "Experiences in History," but there are numerous other factors that point to the success of using the museum in this approach to an educational center.

How does the program work? Is it really possible for a seven-, nine-, or eleven-year old child to assume the role of an adult in the late nineteenth century and actually become skilled enough to hammer out a weather vane, set type for a newspaper, build a baby cradle, or place several dozen bales of hay in the second-story loft of a barn? And can a museum be used to teach the whys of history instead of just who, how, what, where, and when? Yes, it is possible, and all without ever saying, "We are going to pretend to live in the pioneer days."

Monday of each week begins by staff members greeting the children in the parking lot. After the children say goodbye to their parents, the newcomers are led to a gathering spot beneath a large cottonwood tree amidst the grass entry to the museum. Each child is given an apron with his or her name on it, and a few minutes after nine the orientation begins. The group of children and costumed staff members sit in a circle, and, after introductions and a few basic instructions, the challenge begins. One staff member begins by asking the children where they were born. With Littleton's growing population, there are many newcomers. Consequently, several children respond that their birthplace was New York, Indiana, Georgia, or some other distant state.

"Why did you move to Littleton?" "A change in jobs," "Wanted to be closer to relatives," and many other answers are given. The answers are often the same reasons why people moved and settled the West in the last century. "How long does it take to build a community and how many people does it take to do the job?" More answers and more questions lead to the exclamation by one staff member, "I've got an itchy foot, and it's an itch no scratching can help!" That statement is followed by another, "I read in the *Baltimore Times* that there is land still available west of the Mississippi River and the government will help you get it under the Homestead Act."

The orientation continues and soon all participants begin to wonder about a more personal question, "Would you be willing to pull up stakes, move West, and join me in building a new town?" Some children are not sure; but the process continues until the group leader judges that the questions have reached a peak and asks for a show of hands of how many want to join the group

and leave their homes in the East to build a new town in the West. It's unanimous and the transition from twentieth-century Littleton to nineteenth-century America has begun without the staff ever having said, "We are going to pretend to be adults and talk about pioneer days."

Some might contend that children cannot grasp the meaning of time and events of a hundred years ago. But they do understand and quickly respond to the chance to play the role of an adult in America's past.

The orientation process continues with the group breaking into four small units, each under the direction of one staff member. The groups plan the journey, and decide on the food, tools, livestock, and all the other necessities for building a new town. The groups intervene to report to each other of all the plans, including where they will settle. The site selected might be in the Dakotas, Kansas, Texas, or some other area revealed in the reproduction maps of nineteenth-century America, which lay before them. The group has been purposely steered away from settling in Colorado so their minds and imaginations can be challenged for the rest of the week without the intrusion of knowledge about their twentieth-century resident state.

In the next part of the orientation, we concentrate on getting some experience before moving on. Each staff member has found time during the earlier discussion to identify himself or herself as a master weaver, carpenter, blacksmith, or printer. Now it is time to visit the shops and plan the packing for the trip. At the shops the children receive their first exposure to the trades they will have to learn once settled in their new town. Each shop is visited by the whole group for forty-five minutes, during which time the master tradesman covers the workings of the trade. No detail is spared.

The orientation on Monday is vital to the success of the week. Each child, or "community member" as the children are called, will work with a large variety of tools, equipment, and livestock, so a carefully planned process takes place. The shared experiences in the shops, barn, and surrounding grounds are planned to give the children the opportunity to work together and to learn that teamwork, perseverance, success, frustrations, mistakes, and fun are all part of building a town and growing up.

Safety is stressed in each shop. The blacksmith introduces his trade by explaining what he makes and the importance of the products. Several children are selected to help build a fire in the forge. While waiting for the coal fire to reach forging temperature, the blacksmith names his tools and their uses. The anvil and its parts—face, table, horn, heel, pritchel hole, and hardie hole—are described. All participants repeat the names several times and then move on to tongs, sweages, and other tools. This process is followed by a brief demonstration during which several children assist in making a tool—maybe a candle holder or hay hook. The demonstration provides the group with a direct encounter of how to hold and swing a two-pound sledge hammer, and how to gauge when the steel in the fire is ready to forge. This also reassures everyone that a child can do the job and not get burned. The group is introduced to the philosophy that no tool by itself is dangerous. "Can a hammer smash your finger? Can a 2,000 degree fire burn you?" "No! Only careless people hurt themselves!"

The blacksmith shop is hot, and all participants show signs of the heat. The blacksmiths ask if there are any carpenters around who could repair the bed of a wagon. The master carpenter is thus introduced and invites the group to the carpenter shop, where a similar orientation takes place.

Two hours of intensive orientation have elapsed, and on the way to the carpenter shop the group pauses to "wet their whistles" just enough to sustain them until lunch. Following the work in the carpenter shop, everyone pitches in and carries tables, benches, and food to a shady spot for lunch, during which time the conversation about planning for the trip West continues.

After lunch it's off to the garden, chicken coop, hog pen, and barn. How do you clean a horse's hoof or put a work harness on him when he weighs 2,000 pounds and you weigh only seventy? It's all part of a new experience. The remainder of the afternoon is spent in the print shop learning how to print a newspaper and at the farm house for an introduction to spinning wool, operating three different looms, making a quilt, and learning how the noonday meals for the whole community will be prepared on a wood-burning stove.

The children have now finished their first day of the program. Just prior to their departure there is a brief discussion about the ensuing journey and the importance of packing all their belongings tightly because of the limited space on the train. What are the children thinking? Are they really going to move West? The children depart the museum for home where most share their first day's experiences with their family.

The staff reconvenes to assess the day and to divide the children into four equal groups for Tuesday's work. Because the children will encounter various tasks requiring manual dexterity, strength, reading and mathematics skills, and the ability to share and help, they are divided with a near equal number of girls and boys of various ages and abilities as determined by the staff after close observation during the day-long orientation. At the end of each daily session, the staff also judges the children's progress and how well the goal of building a community is being met. The children are assigned to a different shop each day, so they all work as apprentice blacksmiths, carpenters, weavers, and printers with new partners. Throughout the week there are chores in the garden to be tended to, stalls in the barn and hog pen to be cleaned, and hay, which must be brought in from a nearby field and hoisted into the barn.

On Tuesday morning, the children return to the museum and to their roles of community builders. Another transition point has been passed when the children arrive. They are now in their new town in the West and the work begins. After a few morning chores, each group goes to one of the four shops to begin its apprenticeship.

What will the carpenters or blacksmiths make for the community? What are the printers going to do? And how will the weavers have enough time to spin, weave, work on a quilt, and prepare a stew, salad, biscuits, and beverage by high noon? Teamwork and hard work. But fun too! There are also all the regular museum visitors that are often greeted as travelers passing through. The "community members" have the added role of being interpreters for all the visitors. Imagine visiting the Littleton Historical Museum and walking out to the print shop to be greeted at the doorway by a ten-year-old child who says, "Good morning, welcome to our print shop," and then proceeds to tell you about printing a newspaper—how type is set, how the press is inked, how the mechanism works—and, oh yes, who adds, "We're building a town."

The experience is rewarding for all. It's one thing to sit in a classroom and see a film about printing a newspaper when all the type was set by hand. But it is another kind of learning experience to set type if you are seven-years old and just barely learning to read. The challenge and reward for the staff is to teach without being thought of as a teacher, but rather as one of the townspeople and a friend who will share in success and failure.

There is much sharing in the program. During one session the weavers decided they needed a wooden chest for blankets. An order was sent to the carpenters, who drew up a plan for the chest and after they conferred with the weavers, the project was begun. Metal hinges and handles were needed, so the weavers visited the blacksmith shop to discuss their plan with the blacksmith and his apprentices. Work on the hinges and handles was begun. The weavers did not give up. They visited the printers and asked them to print a fancy paper liner for the blanket chest. In a matter of days the project was finished and there was a certain sparkle in everyone's eyes.

Toward the end of each program day, all the children and staff gather in the farmhouse to report on what has been accomplished. If the apprentices have completed a project, they bring it to the "town meeting" and explain how it was done. Each item is marked with an appropriate tag and price as determined by the markers—"One boot scraper, $6 hard cash or two chickens." During the Wednesday town meeting, names are voted on for the community and the newspaper. There is also a daily discussion about the progress of the community. On Friday it is determined that the group has succeeded in building a town and that it is each person's responsibility to see that his or her community—real or imagined—continues to prosper. Just prior to departing, a suggestion is made that there should be a community gathering at the end of the summer to check on the crops and the progress of the town. As the children leave the museum, the printers hand each person a copy of the community newspaper.

On the last Saturday of the summer there is a "gathering of the communities." On that day all the children who have participated in the summer program are invited to return to the museum with their families to share with their parents and other kinfolk their experiences of building a town.

For ten weeks each summer, children assume the roles of adults building a community some place in the American West in the later part of the nineteenth century. The Littleton Historical Museum, it is hoped, has taught the children to look at history in a different way.

Part VII
Concerns

The American Way of History

23

David Lowenthal

A Professor Emeritus of geography at University College, London, Lowenthal was one of the first scholars to examine critically the American way of "imaginatively creating" history at outdoor museums or "History Lands." In this article, which appeared in Columbia University Forum *9 (1966), he challenges Americans with the observation that "What is old is looked at as special, 'historic,' different. Not wanting to be different, Americans anathematize the past. In the process, they became conscious of antiquity as a separate realm. And as the past was cut away from the present, history emerged as an isolated object of reverence and pleasure. For all its deliberate relevance, History Land remains detached, remote, and essentially lifeless."*

"**H**istory is bunk" was Henry Ford's vivid and infamous dictum. He had no idea of dismissng the past as useless. It was only written history that roused his dander. No visitor to Greenfield Village in Detroit can fail to be aware of Ford's wholehearted devotion to the physical remains of the past; and his statement of purpose in the official guidebook drives the point home: "By looking at things people used and that show the way they lived, a better and truer impression can be gained than could be had in a month of reading." This bent toward visual presentation seems to me largely responsible for the character of historical landscape in the United States.

The place of the past in any landscape is as much the product of present attitudes as of past history. The visible effects of human enterprise, great and small, deliberate and unintended, agricultural and architectural, tend to fade and finally vanish at a fairly uniform pace, except as man retards or acceleratess the process of decay. The degree to which the past depends on our idea of it is beautifully suggested in Jorge Luis Borge's mythical Lion, where things all tend "to efface themselves, to lose their detail when people forget them."

In America, most memories are short, the relics of history are often unrecognized, and few deplore their passing; so rare an element is the past that when it is appreciated it becomes the Past, a Historic Heritage—not a natural part of the landscape, but a special feature fenced off in a preserve called History. It may be touched, handled, tasted, even participated in, as at Wiliamsburg; but it is not a part of everyday life. Either neglected or put in museums, the American past is not permitted to coexist with the present. It is always in quotation marks and fancy dress. In Boston, a marked "Freedom Trail" leads blinkered tourists from one historical monument to another. The scrupulous separation of treasured yesterdays from nasty today may also be seen on Boston's street signs, each bearing the present street name and beneath, in a small green rectangle, the "Olde Name." The temporal topography of the town consists of two parallel but segregated dimensions.

True historical landscapes, however, are the creations not of isolated epochs, but of the cumulative activities of generation upon generation, clearing, farming, building, destroying. The absence of such landscapes in northern America impressed—and often appalled—Colonial settlers and travelers. To be sure, untold generations of Indians had inhabited America, but their relics were few and ephemeral, their impact on the early American landscape difficult to distinguish from natural processes. Compared with Europe, America was a land hardly lived in, and American landscapes conveyed little sense of depth in human time.

With the American Revolution, it became essential to find and venerate an American past. And theorists of beauty and esthetics considered historical associations a prime factor in landscape and architecture as well as in painting and poetry. "What are the most esteemed paintings?" students were asked in a typical reader of 1806—and the correct answer was "Those representing historical events." Home from visits to Europe, sensitive Americans frequently expressed dismay at the raw, unfinished look of America; the works of man seemed here to be brash and inadequate, the uprooting of nature harsh and ugly. "Oh, that we could have ivy in America!" lamented Hawthorne in England.

Most Americans, however, reconciled themselves somehow to landscapes pretty much devoid of evidence of antiquity. "The conversion of a wilderness into a de-

Three examples of the American way of history: the presidential election campaign at Harper's Ferry.—*Photo:* Living History Magazine

sirable residence for man," averred Timothy Dwight in 1832, "may compensate the want of ancient castles, ruined abbeys, and fine pictures." The physical character of America seemed to many others a sufficient substitute for historical relics; American scenery fired the imagination with its unlimited potentialities for future development.

By the 1830s Americans were viewing wilderness scenery as morally preferable to the stage sets of history. Fenno Hoffman considered the "hoary oak" superior to the "mouldering column" and contrasted Europe's "temples which Roman robbers have reared" unfavorably with "the deep forests which the eye of God has alone pervaded." Mistrust of antiquity reached its apogee in Thoreau, who thought all relics of the past should be destroyed: America must disown the pattern of England, "an old gentleman who is travelling with a great deal of baggage, trumpery which has accumulated from long housekeeping, which he has not had the courage to burn." Periodic purification was the explicit program of the reformer Holgrave, in Hawthorne's *House of Seven Gables:*

> Our public edifices—our capitols, statehouses, courthouses, city-halls and churches—ought [not] to be built of such permanent materials as stone or brick. It were better that they should crumble to ruin once in twenty years, or thereabouts, as a hint to the people to examine and reform the institutions which they symbolize.

Much of America has in fact been dealt with as Holgrave prescribed. Newness is continuously pursued, obsolescence is planned, and the latest edifices vanish unmourned overnight.

Americans also continue to condemn antiquities on moral and nationalistic grounds. Ever since Mark Twain's *Innocents Abroad,* tourists have been rebuked for looking at ruins and castles. In a tirade against "cobwebs, cobblestones, mustiness and decay" reminiscent of Fenno Hoffman, R. L. Duffus inveighs against chateaux and other remains "of an idiotic class system": the "quaintness" prized by tourists "is usually another name for inefficiency and poverty." "Let us," he urges, "inspect today's—not yesterday's, not ruined, not medieval—farms and shops."

Those who disapprove of the past often seem to have equally little use for the present. "The Americans love their country, not, indeed, as it is," wrote a German traveler in the 1830s, "but as it will be. They do not love the land of their fathers; but they are sincerely attached to that which their children are destined to inherit. They live in the future, and make their country as they go on." The futurist strain remains powerful today. Even those who celebrate the past frequently see it mainly as a highway to the future—as in Bruce Catton's apothegm that "America is full of milestones on the road from yesterday to tomorrow." In like spirit, the inscription, "What's Past is Prologue," derived from a different Shakespearean context, disposes National Archives visitors to think of the past as something to get through in a hurry.

What use has history, then, if it is not bunk? Why have Ford and other philanthropists taken it on themselves to "paint a vivid and nostalgic picture of America's full, rich past"?

The prime rationale of history is pedagogy. "That the Future May Learn from the Past" is the official motto of Colonial Williamsburg. We preserve and view historical sites, houses, and artifacts in order to learn about the past—how our ancestors lived, what the landscape looked like, what techniques were used for taming it, and so on. Salesmen of history from Williamsburg to Freedomland assert that education is their chief end. Seeing all the children there, who can doubt them? This pedagogy of the past is overwhelmingly patriotic. History in the landscape is no bald summary, but an explicit expression of the genesis of American virtues. Cultural nationalism is the hallmark of the historical site. Such sites, are, indeed, called "historic" rather than "historical," to signify their unique and enormous importance.

The lesson of practically all historical sites is the American heritage of liberty. "Visit King's Mountain — where the mountainmen made you free," a gasoline company urges motorists. "Out of mountains they came with hunting knives, Kentucky rifles and freedom blazing white-hot in their eyes." The past that historians purvey is no less momentous. *The American Heritage Book of Great Historic Places* steers people "to those sites where American history took on the haunting gleam of everlasting significance." Colonial Williamsburg aims to reproduce the "authentic setting in which the Virginia patriots strove to establish the rights of the people"; as the official guide puts it, the visitor should "see Williamsburg as an affirmation of the spiritual vigor which must underlie any strong democratic society." "Concepts" to be applauded in this cradle of American history include the integrity of the individual, responsible leadership, self government, individual liberties, and economic opportunity.

The message does come through. Recalling the "rare pleasure" of being "in the same church where Washington prayed. . . the same chamber where Patrick Henry shouted. . . the same classroom where Thomas Jefferson studied law," one wartime visitor declared that Williamsburg "made me realize the heritage and rich gifts of our country. Of all the sights I have seen, and the books I have read, and the speeches I have heard, none ever made me see the greatness of this country with more force and clearness."

Candlemaking at Philipsburg Manor.—*Photo: Sleepy Hollow Restorations*

Such lessons, however, are less relevant to the actual past than to today's idealization of it. The Lexington Minute Men, portrayed as "farmers ready to exchange hoes for rifles, at a minute's notice, in the struggle against the colonialist aggressors," recall the American past less than they conjure up distant struggles against contemporary imperialism. But history in the form of narcissistic nostalgia conveys a further message: the past is fun. State-coach rides, paddle-wheeler tours, fife-and-drum marches, automated Abraham Lincolns, real printing presses manufacturing facsimiles of ancient gossip, costumes to dress up in, stocks for make-believe transgressions—no opportunity for visitor participation is neglected. History is a play, in both senses of the word, and the customer is the actor. Visitors at Freedomland enjoyed putting out the Chicago fire with pseudo-hoses pointed at the pseudo-blaze while the jets were turned down behind scenes. *American Heritage* offers "an American History Game" to sweeten the perusal of "the faces, facts, battles, and dreams that make up the story of our country." It is no use complaining, as one visitor did, that Plymouth is "a patriotic Disneyland"; this is history as Americans like it. Tourists in the Southwest come not to see the archaeological remains, J. B. Jackson reports, but to participate in make-believe gold-panning and rodeos. They know very well these are make-believe but enjoy them all the same.

With pleasure goes business. Freedomland was a financial flop, but other representations of the past reap amazing returns. Williamsburg's turnstiles admit close to a million visitors and $11 million a year; though the founders never dreamed it would pay its way, receipts now make it almost self-sustaining. Other history lands reap comparable profits with less investment. Sightseers in California's ghost mining towns have yielded more gold than the Forty-niners ever saw, and no less than 53 "official" ghost towns in New Mexico are now alive enough to rate Zip Code numbers.

The zeal for progress has never precluded nostalgia for the homely relics of an idealized agrarian yesterday. The old arm chair, the old oaken bucket, the old homestead, the old barn, and scenes of haying, of going to fetch the cows, and of other farm chores 'a la Currier & Ives still retain their popularity on calendars and magazine covers. The current vogue for antiques suggests that we require not mere contemplation but actual possesion of the past; the public demand for antiques has already outrun the supply of both the genuinely and the spuriously old. And following the lead of "Colonial craftsmen" in "historic" villages, manufacturers have begun to produce new matchboxes and telephones, doorknockers and kitchen gadgets, with the shape and even the patina of age.

In this history-conscious age, every locality must have its heritage; no less than twenty-five historical markers within two blocks in Lincoln, New Mexico, commemorate the deeds of Billy the Kid. Nothing is too inconsequential to merit notice; Nashville, Tennessee, vaunts "the oldest and longest continual Saturday night program on radio" at its Grand Ole Opry House (built in 1891 as the Union Gospel Tabernacle). Any place with a genuine past becomes "history-drenched" and sets itself up as a tourist resort, complete with cobblestones, pewter tankards, and native candle dippers.

History is most frequently found not where it occurred, but where it is least in the way—that is, very seldom *in situ.* High land values in built-up areas militate against the retention of historic structures there; when relics of the past on valuable real estate are saved from demolition, they are as a rule moved elsewhere. The severing of structures from their local associations does violence to history and landscape alike. Yet such moves are quite taken for granted. Daniel Webster's old home, *The New York Times* reports, "is, of course, being moved from its original site elsewhere in Portsmouth to the spe-

cial Strawbery Banke project," an enclave of restored Colonial houses. The significant term is "of course"; it means that the furnishing of the historical museum that will be Strawbery Banke takes precedence over geographical and historical truth and the dignity of the remainder of Portsmouth. Indeed, history is readily redone anywhere. Old Sturbridge Village, an agglomeration of reconstructed buildings advertising "the environment of that spirit and enterprise which is our native heritage," occupies a place where no real village ever existed.

Museumization alters what history is, as well as where it is. American historical areas tend toward a highly elective display of the past—selective as to epochs, contents, events and personalities. The most familiar truncation of historical landscapes is their restriction to one period of time. Now standard treatment for real as well as fabricated historical areas, this practice was inaugurated at "Colonial" Williamsburg in the 1930s. Williamsburg's restorers chose an arbitrary cut-off date of 1800, removed all later structures, stripped away nineteenth- and twentieth-century additions to earlier buildings, and replaced them with Colonial buildings from elsewhere, together with reconstruction of eighteenth-century buildings that had since vanished. "To maintain this superbly executed vacuum," Ada Louise Huxtable notes, "nothing else is permitted to exist within the project's didactic limits; a Greek Revival house or other later structure, good or bad, on a spot that once held a colonial building, must go, and a newly created colonial substitute, constructed with exquisite taste, painstaking accuracy, and alarming artificiality, is put up instead." As a result, Williamsburg lacks vitality, reality, and historical continuity. Selective preservation and restoration not only prevent the integration of past and present, they denigrate excluded epochs as inferior and unworthy of attention. A British delegate at a Williamsburg preservation conference confessed that after two days of being immured in Colonial architecture, "I sneaked off, like a man to a saloon, for a good look at some very nice 1840 houses."

For all its scholarly verisimilitude, moreover, Williamsburg has the flavor of a well-kept contemporary suburb. One historian argues that Colonial folk themselves would have liked fresh paint if they could have gotten it—but after all it is the reality and not the dreams of the past that Williamsburg supposedly portrays. In fact it is the sanitary needs of the present that prevail: eighteenth-century odors would be such a shock to twentieth-century noses that every other impression might be blotted out. And without paved streets, visitors would keep Williamsburg in perpetual dust or soil their clothing in mud. Cleanliness itself is the prime consideration; people feel that just because a thing is old is no reason for it to look dirty. Nashville's Centennial Park boasts "the only full-size replica of the Parthenon in the world! 'And what is more,'" Tennesseans told Alex Atkinson, "'this one's cleaner.'"

The stage coach at Upper Canada Village.—
*Photo: Upper Canada Village, Morrisburg,
Ontario*

Sanitation aside, most Americans prefer history parcelled out in segments because it is easy to describe, thematic, and represents no threat to the present. The Colonial is by no means the only "period" thus elevated to an exclusive cage in the American historical zoo. The new grandstand at the Saratoga racecourse "has been built to fit in with the old architecture" of the town—that is, nineteenth century—even to the gables on the roof. And Cape May, which claims "the largest collection of Victorian buildings in the nation," plans restoration to the gingerbread era; "houses that do not fit into the Victorian scheme will be moved or torn down."

The static quality of single-epoch sites might be expected to pull on Americans. But entrepreneurs in Wisconsin have come up with a gimmick to make history dynamic as well as homogenous. Stonefield Village, near Cassville, is designed always to appear seventy-five years old—an age "within the context of 'tales my father told me.'" Built from scratch only a few years ago, Stonefield is already changing according to plan: the local newspaper has abandoned its hand-operated Washington press for a Monoma flat-bed press, a telephone exchange will shortly be installed, and "gradually, the horse and wagon will give way to the automobile, and the kerosene lamps will be replaced by electric lights... In 2040, [Stoneville] will look like a town of today."

It will be interesting to see how people react to the destruction of Stoneville's "past"; they may insist on preserving bits of it while the rest of the town moves ahead; or, impatient with the slow pace of "progress," they may insist on more rapid modernization, at a rate of two or a dozen "Stoneville years" to one real year. For many Americans, time is not duration but a commodity. Will they not prefer the jumbo size with speedy action, that washes the past so white?

History homogenized, cleaned up, and expurgated usually ends as an entirely artificial re-creation of an imaginary past. Civil War battlefields now foster the illusion that the struggle between the Blue and the Gray was merely a trial of strength between high-minded and gallant brethren divided by no serious issues. The Walk of Fame at Rollins College, Winter Park, Florida, is paved with stones "taken from the birthplaces of 600 bona fide World Personalities"; Rollins is thereby endowed with an aura of age, like a new convertible impregnated with a special concoction to make it smell of very old leather and spaniels. The past is the product of the present, and the usual aim is restoration, not preservation. In the process the line between "old" and "restored" is often blurred, and the visitor does not know or care whether he is seeing real or fake relics. As a promoter of Lincoln's supposed birthplace remarked in the 1890s, "Lincoln was born in a log cabin, weren't he? Well, one cabin is as good as another." The White House guide who said of a piece of furniture, "This is considered a very authentic reproduction," was telling people what they wanted to know. An advertisement for cuff links reproduced from "the original dies of official state uniform buttons in an old New England factory [representing]... each of the fifty States" shows how far history can safely be stretched. Critics may gibe, but "instant Stonehenge" is the American way.

Although hundreds of historical reconstructions, more or less artificial, more or less imaginary, festoon the face of the nation, they are not sufficient to satisfy American desires for a place in time, for the hallowing of antiquity. "For any self-respecting people," an English scholar once commented, "it must be an embarrassment to possess a national history less than five centuries old. (This deprivation may partly account for the zeal with which Leif Ericson advocates insist on the authenticity of Viking relics.) Possessing little human history, Americans early adopted natural history. The sheer immensity of the Blue Ridge mountains led Jefferson to speculate on the eons required to form them. The palms on Lake Worth reminded Henry James of the Nile, but the Florida lake seemed older, as if America were "previous" to everything. The pre-election comment that Senator Goldwater's house was built of Arizona sandstone 160,000,000 years old conveyed the message that, although the construction was modern, these ancient materials symbolized the Senator's attachment to eternal changeless values.

No matter how old they are, however, rocks have a limited appeal; the most popular historical surrogate in America is a species of extinct vertebrates. At Dinosaur National Monument, a visitor reports, fossilized footprints "are roped off and treated with the respect reserved in Britain for Roman mosaics and Iron Age burials." As a gasoline trademark, the dinosaur connotes both antiquity and abundance. Replicas of dinosaurs lumber across the country in all sizes from World's Fair mammoth to dime store midget. The dinosaur is focus and attraction for natural history study in American schools, occupies pride of place in American museums, and is frequently assumed to be essentially, if not exclusively, American. And as with sequoias and redwoods, the extreme age of dinosaurs is hallowed by their enormous size.

Like other biggest, oldest things, dinosaurs strike many foreigners as too improbable to be authentic. "I personally believe that they are made in New Jersey," was one Englishman's reaction, "and shipped out in crates with packets of screws and assembly instructions and a mimeographed line of spiel for official guides." What is absent in America's pursuit of the past, he pointed out, is the familiarity of constant association. "With a thing like Westminster Abbey. . . it's a different matter. You know where you are with Westminster Abbey."

With the Abbey you are, presumably, at ease; in the Abbey, past merges into present with scarcely a break. But in America the discontinuity is profound; what is old is looked at as special, "historic," different. Not wanting to be dominated by "antiquity," Americans anathematized the past. In the process, they became conscious of antiquity as a separate realm. And as the past was cut away from the present, history emerged as an isolated object of reverence and pleasure. For all its deliberate relevance, Historyland remains detached, remote, and essentially lifeless.

It Wasn't That Simple

Thomas J. Schlereth

24

Thomas J. Schlereth, head of the American Studies Program at Notre Dame, compares history texts with outdoor museums and finds both lacking. Museums often present "wrong-headed accounts of the past" that are elitist, chauvinistic, rigidly periodized, sexist, and naive. "Historical museum villages are still, with a few exceptions, remarkably peaceable kingdoms, planned communities with over-manicured landscapes or idyllic small towns where the entire populace lives in harmony. . . . The visitor. . . comes away from the museum village with a romanticized, even utopian perspective of the popularly acclaimed 'good old days'." Schlereth is particularly bothered by the "homogeneity" of museum villages. He notes that "villages are still largely populated by white, Anglo-Saxon, nondenominational Protestant males." Schlereth suggests at the least that museum curators should become better historians. His article appeared in the January-February 1981 issue of Museum News.

Edward P. Alexander once called the historical museum village "a huge textbook of three-dimensional American history." Outdoor historical museums, like history textbooks, have proliferated in almost a geometric progression in the past three decades. Despite competition from numerous other forms of popular history—historical novels, films, television programs—historical texts and historical villages continue to exert an enormous influence on the average American's perception of the national past and on his understanding of history as a way of knowing.

An analysis of a typical outdoor historical museum as a "textbook" of American history demonstrates the obstacles that curators must overcome when using this museum format to interpret historical knowledge. It also partially accounts for the traditional indifference that most professional historians have had toward museums as potential reserach and teaching resources. To some academic historians, the "museumization" of American history produces many of the same distortions, inaccuracies, and oversimplifications that result from history textbooks. . . .

Authors of history texts generally follow a chronology of the American past based primarily on the events of political or military history. Despite an excess of artifactual survivals that should force an extensive study of social, economic, and cultural history, historical museums are prone to similar time-line interpretations that define all their activities as being either before or after the Revolutionary War or the Civil War. . . .

Modern history textbooks, moreover, often betray a second chronological fallacy to which historical museums also succumb: the assumption that American history is singularly progressive. Since their origins in the nationalistic fervor of the early nineteenth century, American textbooks have been the histories of winners, of individuals who succeeded in *The March of America, The Victory of Freedom* or *The Triumph of Democracy* (current text titles). Given their origins in the isolationism of two post-world war eras, the 1920s and the 1950s, it is not surprising that historical museum villages have been equally addicted to what Walter Muir Whitehill calls the "celebration rather than the cerebration of the American past." Villages, perhaps biased by the associational aura of the houses of the "great white men" that often form the nucleus of their sites, tend to champion an inevitable evolution of democratic principles, a glorious series of technological advancements, and a continual rise in the American standard of living. Museum villages are not highly populated with Loyalists or Luddites, Anti-Federalists or Knights of Labor, Molly Maguires or Copperheads.

Various observers naturally accuse both textbooks and museum villages of being overly patriotic. . . . Of course, sophisticated curators are aware that cultural nationalism is probably endemic to their sites.

They might also consider their installations as evidence of what Robert Bellah and other sociologists define as the "American civil religion." Outdoor museums are historical shrines to which visitors are beckoned to make pilgrimages, particularly on national holy days (Memorial Day, Independence Day, Thanksgiving) when the American democratic faith is reiterated in numerous secular homilies. Historical villages often inculcate, in ritual and symbol, a worship of the national scriptures (the Declaration of Independence, the Constitution) as

163

Scalding a hog at Philipsburg Manor: Interpreting the reality of life in the past.—*Photo: Sleepy Hollow Restorations*

well as the Republic's civic saints, prophets, and martyrs (Revolutionary and Civil War heroes). The folk religion that Will Herberg summarized as "the American way of life" pervades many exhibits and much interpretation. . . .

When Williamsburg's restorers decided in the 1930s that Colonial history terminated in 1800, and all structures or additions built thereafter had to be stripped away, a museological practice of enormous influence was inaugurated. Selective preservation, restoration, and reconstruction in a museum village, like selective ar-

rangement of chapters and the number of pages alloted in a textbook, promote a discontinuous perspective on the past. Moreover, this practice often deliberately denigrates the excluded historical epochs as inferior and unworthy of study and understanding. Consider, for instance, how little attention is given, either in textbooks or in historical museum villages, to the era 1660-1730, the so-called "glacial age" of American history.

Plotting change across time—the historian's *raison d'etre*—is done in textbooks and historical museums with a dogmatic certainty that unnerves the professional historian. Textbook authors rely on the simple linear order of their chapters to show change across time; museum curators resort to simplistic, single-factor explanations in exhibitions designed to demonstrate historical change. Both historical genres are methodologically prejudiced to show only development, not decline; neither is informed by the abundant literature on the difficulties of explaining and communicating historical change currently surfacing among historiographers and philosophers of history. . . .

Curators rely too heavily on craft demonstrations to give a visitor some sense of change, of history as process. Unfortunately, such demonstrations are often themselves static, providing the viewer with little awareness of shifts in technology, materials or what Page Talbott calls the changing "ethnography of the artisan. . . ."

Change in history is often caused by conflict. Yet textbooks and museums remain lodged in the "consensus" historiography of the 1950s. Historical museum villages are still, with a few exceptions, remarkably peaceable kingdoms, planned communities with over manicured landscapes or idyllic small towns where the entire populace lives in harmony. The visitor to such sites, who usually does not see the artifacts of convict laborers, domestic servants, hired hands, or slaves in the statistical proportion in which such material culture would have cluttered most communities, comes away from the museum village with a romanticized, even utopian perspective of the popularly acclaimed "good old days."

Deliberate utopian ventures constitute an inordinately large proportion of American outdoor history museums. There are more Shaker villages in the United States than there are Shakers. Unfortunately, the acute social and religious radicalism (and ostracism) of these and other dissenters (now ironically organized into a National Historic Communal Societies Association) is never adequately portrayed in the twentieth-century restorations of their lifestyles. In fact, more often than not, the once bitterly maligned countercultures of earlier years have been homogenized into respectable middle-class cultural establishments.

Homogeneity pervades American history textbooks, in part because of pressure from school boards, in part because their authors tend to plagiarize from one another, but particularly because they have traditionally omitted large, usually documentarily inarticulate, components of the population in their historical surveys. The same holds true for museum villages. Despite the increased scholarship and availability of materials on racial and ethnic minorities, both historical texts and villages are still largely populated by White, Anglo-Saxon, nondenominational Protestant males. . . .

Similarly, trends in American religious history have not been translated into museum village installations that, while they invariably have a single Georgian or Federal white clapboard church, are hardly suggestive of the extensive religious pluralism and conflict that existed in most American communities.

To be sure, women's work has been depicted, but only that centering around the home and hearth, particularly in kitchens furnished with more equipment than any cook could ever have used. . . . If it is any comfort to musuem curators, textbooks have been even more resistant to women's studies. . . .

Museum curators, like textbook writers, do not have access to a highly developed scholarly appartus of systematic, collective research procedures common to most profesional disciplines. Primary research is ongoing in museum villages with research divisions and in museum-university related graduate programs. Unpublished inventories, correspondence, account books, and other manuscript materials are now used frequently in museum interpretation. Unfortunately, those who do this research do not always mount the exhibit or determine how much of their research is to be used and in what fashion. Nor is this research sufficiently shared. There is no national network for collecting, cataloguing,

Preparing "sweet scents" begins with careful blending of herbs and dried flowers—a complex task.—*Photo: Sleep Hollow Restorations*

publishing and distributing it; there is no abstracting service to condense it to manageable format, convenient to distribute and to retrieve. Since most studies in American material culture are masters' degree papers , the extensive graduate research done in programs like those at Winterthur, Cooperstown, or Hagley is not listed in *Dissertation Abstracts* and consequently is not available in either microfilm or photocopy. . . .

Historical museum villages and textbooks lack both footnotes and bibliographies. Neither the historical scholar nor the curator, much less the interested museum visitor, is encouraged in most outdoor museums to consult the elaborate (and generally unavailable) staff research reports, laboratory analyses of artifacts, minutes of curator-designer meetings, or the registrar's records that are the documentation on which the interpretation of a historical environment is based. . . .

There are still no regular scholarly mechanisms whereby individuals can get behind the facade of an exhibit, restoration, or reconstruction. The credibility and

Demonstrating the difficult use of the broadaxe.—*Photo: Sleep Hollow Restorations*

A complex, difficult craft, here recreated at Ontario's Black Creek.—*Photo: Black Creek Pioneer Village*

historical authenticity of such background research cannot be adjudicated by professional peers; it cannot be a base on which other scholars might build further research; it cannot be a cross-reference to parallel work in the field. Although historical museum village installations are indeed curatorial publications, they have no footnotes and are never used as footnotes to other publications.

Curators may argue that their guidebooks, research studies, or craft demonstration leaflets perform this function. Although some local research studies and craft series do have bibliographical leads, there is no comprehensive, documented catalogue or interpretive analysis of a major historical museum village and its study collections. At best, most guidebooks are mementos rather than monographs, souvenirs rather than reference and interpretive works for the library shelf.

Historical museum villages, like most textbooks, do not have prefaces, forewords, or introductory statements. In fact, for all the public knows, historical museum installations are self-generating, since curators are usually never credited with authorship. No standard vehicle exists that allows textbook historians or historical curators to explain their objectives, delineate their hypotheses, or articulate the problems they may have encountered in researching the data, organizing it, and communicating it to a wider audience. Neither textbook historians nor historical curators have an appropriate public forum in which to admit their reservations about certain aspects of their interpretation or to explain the documentation that supports controversial judgments or unfamiliar facts. Consequently, village visitors, as well as their volunteer guide interpreters, have no clues as to the methodological difficulties or evidential gaps in an exhibition, and almost inevitably regard the published result as the definitive study on the subject.

Professional historians, of course, are not as easily convinced. In their work, they depend on peer review in order to appraise completed scholarship and stimulate further research through constructive criticism. . . . If the historical museum profession were to follow suit, it would escape another of the critical comparisons made her with history textbooks, which do not usually receive professional peer review. . . .

Peer review prompts interpretation revision. . . . Without such revisionism, museums and textbooks lack both a historical tradition and a tradition of historical analysis. . . . Both genres of historical interpretation . . . would profit if their practitioners thought more seriously about their philosophical assumptions and professional practices. If museum curators took more time to explore the epistemological questions of chronology, causation, periodization, and generalization, the quality of interpretation in historical villages would be more sophisticated, but still comprehensible to the average visitor. . . .

As curators can learn from the methods of academic historians, teaching historians can profit from the scholarship of museum professionals.

Before both professions is what American historian William Hesseltine, in *The Present World of History* (1958), called "the challenge of the artifact." "[How can] artifacts be made into historical facts? By what method can they be examined? What internal evidence can they produce to aid in the search for historical truth?" For, as Hesseltine rightly saw, "until artifacts can be subjected to internal criticism and made to bear their witness, the task of historical methodology is unfinished."

Afterword, 1984

I wrote the preceding essay in the wake of the American Bicentennial. I prepare this brief coda in the early years of a decade devoted to the 200th anniversary of the American Constitution. Anticipating some of the chauvinistic manifestations that the next bicentennial will

An interpreter demonstrating the art of broom-making.—*Photo: Black Creek Village*

undoubtedly elicit, I again find myself wondering how history museums and history textbooks will portray the Constitutional era in particular, and American history in general, during the decade of the 1980s.

I am persuaded that history museums will do their work with increasing sophistication. Not so textbooks. Their authors seem almost forever doomed, much like Sisyphus, to roll their hard little rock of historical dogma up and down the minds of bored students everywhere. Many history museums, on the other hand, are venturing forth onto new interpretive frontiers and demonstrating the intellectual openness and methodological savvy that I called for in 1978.

How and why is this happening? In brief, many history museums are now seriously re-examining both their professional activities and the philosophical assumptions involved in their conceptualization and communication of the past. In professional terms, new forums such as the *Museum Studies Journal* have appeared, joining the ranks of publications such as *Museum News* and *History News* in a common aspiration to publish more rigorous museological research and more analytical museum history. In addition to this growing liveliness in professional literature, exhibit catalogues are occasionally evolving into major research publications. The Boston Museum of Fine Arts' three-volume catalogue, *New England Begins: The Seventeenth Century* (1982), is an example. History museums still need, however, more critical peer review of their publications in all forms—exhibits, monographs, catalogues. My hope for a regular exhibition review section in each major museum journal has yet to be realized. Only *Technology and Culture* provides the history museum profession with exhibition reviews containing a critical edge.

Re-evaluation of philosophical premises, I suppose, has been largely a result of the social history juggernaut. In fact, many institutions are becoming as deeply committed to the social history gospel as they once were to a political history ideology. Colonial Williamsburg, for example, an institution of which I was critical in 1978, now contends to be the major museum research center for the interpretation of eighteenth-century colonial society. At nineteenth-century sites such as Sturbridge, Greenfield Village, and Old World Wisconsin, we now see a perspective on the past that is more diverse in human motivation, more representative of actual human populations, and more complex in its explanation of human behavior.

Despite these achievements, interpreting certain dimensions of the American experience is still problematic for many history museums. The complicated and often controversial role of religion, for instance, is not researched or communicated in ways appropriate to its importance. The presentation of difficult historical issues such as conflict, failure, dissent, or prejudice also continue as interpretive challenges that we have not adequately met. And questions perennial to the historian's craft—the nature of causation, the rationale for periodization, the differing velocities of change, or the limits of historical explanation—still haunt our best efforts.

Finally, I think my earlier insistence that one of the most urgent tasks of contemporary historical scholarship is to explore, both in the museum and in the academy, the full potential of material culture evidence, remains as demanding an imperative now as it was six years ago. If museum and academic historians, with American history museums as research laboratories, can join in expanding historical understanding through a sensitive and systematic study of the past's objects, this may be the history museum's most vital contribution to historical methodology in the remaining decades of this century. However, I should add that just as we have come to realize that the past wasn't that simple, we can be certain that the effort to comprehend the measure and the meaning of its material universe won't be easy.

Is the Past Dead?

Robert Ronsheim

25

The November 1974 issue of Museum News *is a benchmark for the living history movement. With this issue of the journal of the American Association of Museums, historical simulation became respectable as a medium of museum interpretation. In a series of articles by William Alderson ("Answering the Challenge"), Peter Cook ("The Craft of Demonstration"), Holly Sidford ("Stepping into History"), and Robert Ronsheim's "Is the Past Dead?" which is reprinted here,* Museum News *presented the strengths and weaknesses of living-history interpretation. Ronsheim, a veteran of Plimoth Plantation's experimental years, advanced a cautionary essay that was especially prophetic in the Bicentennial years that witnessed many ill thoughtout, almost faddish living-history programs. Those years are, thankfully, over but Ronsheim's wise words remain.*

It is not enough to be busy . . . the question is: what are we busy about?

Trying to bring the past alive: French marines at Fort Niagara.—
Photo: Old Fort Niagara

Thoreau's question has as sharp a cutting edge today as it did when he raised it. I wish to use it to examine some aspects of living-history programs, aspects that reflect only too well that we still frequently answer Thoreau's question as though busyness were its own justification.

Living history has undoubtedly been generally successful in increasing the interest and enjoyment of many museum visitors. It is a valuable tool for historical interpretation. However, when it is used without careful thought about its purpose and without sufficient control, it is a proper target for Thoreau's inquiry. The goal of a living-history program should be to help visitors understand the culture of a particular period and place and to educate the public in the problems and pitfalls of studying a past culture.

Perhaps some life can be breathed into these bromides by a brief examination of some living history we have recently experienced: the impeachment process against former President Nixon. The interpreters were real and their costumes, words and actions, authentic. The evidence surpassed the wildest dream of a historian: the voices and facial expressions of the actors. Moreover, these were people of our time and culture, and we were aware of the beliefs, assumptions and patterns of thought that gave strength, a sense of stability and sanity to their lives. Yet, who, watching the proceedings, could believe that he understood the thought processes or could plumb the psychological state of any participant? We responded, but empathy is not understanding. If it was difficult to get inside the actors, it was in part because we could approach that task from many different directions, and many of those approaches were overlooked because they were so familiar as to be unconscious. The sources or reasons for those actions were many and tangled, and we separated them and focused on a few for analysis, only at our peril.

Historians at some future time will probably understand some actions in the impeachment process better than we do, for they will have evidence now unobtainable. Even so, they will not be able to re-create completely what happened and, being of another time, will probably be less able to understand the thoughts and feelings of the actors.

What is the relevance of this living-history lesson for living-history programs in museums? Just this—if their goal is to help visitors understand the past, three things need to be kept in mind. First, the visitors need to perceive something of the complexity and unity of the culture the museum is attempting to recreate. Second, the visitors must be made aware that the re-creation is not complete, not authentic. Third, visitors should be helped to perceive the difficulty of understanding what life was truly like in the past. There are a number of characteristics of living-history programs that make it difficult for them to achieve these goals.

Making History 'Come Alive'

Living history "makes history come alive" or so we are assured. Perhaps such phrases reflect a disenchantment with history as a field of study or a low opinion of the intelligence of visitors. So museums offer living history, something almost not of the past. This presumed unity of past and present is confirmed by values visitors bring to museums. Some features of living history programs, especially the activities and crafts, the realistic look and the visual references to rural life and self-sufficiency, at the least, reflect, and, at the worst, play upon the current yearning for a return to a better life, to nature and natural things, to self-mades rather than ready-mades, to community, togetherness, love and granola. The visitors' late 20th-century values and feelings guide and shape their perception of life 100, 200, or 300 years ago. They admire the skill of the potter, the blacksmith, the farmer, the cook and envy the people of the past their opportunity for self-expression while earning a living. Although this is inevitable, the likelihood of misunderstanding the past is promoted and multiplied by the sense of involvement and approval given by the living-history program. The visitors are told that they are reacting to the way it was and thus feel assured that they know "what it was really like." Responding to costumed individuals carrying out roles from the past, the visitors also gain a sense of knowing how individuals in the culture that has been re-created "really felt."

I wonder what the craftsmen and women of the past would have thought of such perceptions. Did a potter feel creative in his production of jars and bowls day after day? What of the cook or the candlemaker? True, the potter and the cook probably had pride in their skills, if they actually were skillful, but there is a distinction between skill and self-expression and creativity.

Stuffing chickens at Old Sturbridge Village's Richardson Parsonage.—*Photo: Robert S. Arnold, Old Sturbridge Village*

Perhaps one reason we undervalue contemporary skills that are essential to our culture (to the point of not viewing them as crafts)—the ability to drive in rush hour traffic for example—and romanticize the skills and crafts of the past, is that we do not view the culture of either the past or the present as a whole. The unity of a society and the fact that segments of a culture—a craft, the family, political institutions, religious and scientific beliefs—must not be ripped out of their context should be perceived by visitors at historic museums that promise to make history live.

Although "living history" was nurtured in the dissatisfaction with the narrowness that many involved in historic interpretation found in an emphasis on presidents and wars, and in fine buildings and expensive furnishings in historic museums, programs of living history do have an inherent bias. The visitors' strong reactions to crafts and a rustic scene not only distort their interpretations of what they see but also tend to block their vision of the whole. To test this, let us assume that someone visits a dozen museums, which, taken together, depict American history from its European beginnings through much of the 19th-century. In each of these museums our visitor watches a practitioner of living history bake bread and observes a costumed carpenter at work. Will the visitor realize that the societies he visited at the beginning of his trip differed radically from those studied at the end? It is even less likely that he would note the great changes from 1800 to 1860.

The test could be conducted at a number of museums that deal with the same period but with different locations. Would the visitor perceive the difference in the role and life of a craftsman in a small eastern town, a small southern town, a city, a newly settled farm area and at a frontier fort? Or that the potter, the cooper, the weaver and the blacksmith had different roles in the same community and that his role and the way the craftsman thought of himself would vary with the individual?

An imbalance and incomplete picture of the past also results from the emphasis on re-creation of buildings and productive activities inherent in a living-history program. It is very difficult to represent, let alone explain, concepts and beliefs, through buildings and work. If a church and a town house are part of the scene, the buildings indicate that religion and government and the beliefs, attitudes and actions associated with them had a very restricted area of impact. It is nearly impossible to represent visually the larger economic system of which the re-created area is but a small and not necessarily representative part. It is hard to show by material means the impact of the economic system on other institutions or on individuals.

The very concreteness of living history tends to disguise the difficulty of understanding the past. The fact that there was frequently a proper and an improper way to use a tool or perform a process and the almost mystical belief in the skill of all those who lived in the past give an unnatural sharpness of focus and power to the highly selective and limited knowledge that has survived. The visitor is frequently oblivious of the blurred and missing portions. Many living-history programs try

A difficult lesson at Black Creek's school house. The date is September 13, 1866.—*Photo: Black Creek Village*

to involve the visitor even more intimately in the process. He is encouraged to touch and to handle, to take part in the past by using all his senses. Perhaps this is an unconscious confession that, despite the efforts at realism and all the activity, the past has not come alive. So the visitor is invited to sit in the chair, to sample the food, to lie on the bed, to hear the sounds and to smell the odors—or some of them. This direct confrontation, however, can also operate, consciously and unconsciously, to cut off questions the visitor or staff may have about the nonmaterial aspects of the past. The chance to experience with the senses is an inviting path that leads away from harder questions.

What does the visitor learn about the past by using his senses? How soft is a feather bed? How hot a job is it to cook at a fireplace? How good a tool was a 17th-century axe? The bed is soft, the fire hot, the axe well-balanced—compared to what?

The only standard the visitor has against which to measure his museum experience is his own past. Nor is the visitor able to bring earlier nonmaterial criteria of judgement to bear. Perhaps this was the first feather bed the family owned, perhaps a servant usually cooked the meals, perhaps the axe was a special gift from father. The material objects of the past do not contain the inner life of the past.

"Live-in" programs are a very popular extension of living-history programs. Overlooking the questions of the accuracy and completeness of the re-creation, even the best of "live-ins" have their limits. Those enjoying the learning experience might shiver with cold and object to the new foods, but they know their trials will soon end. At a deeper and more important level they know that a serious illness or accident will probably not mean death and that a drought will not bring economic disaster or hunger.

Learning mid-nineteenth century dances at Sunnyside. This couple enjoys a polka.—
Photo: Sleep Hollow Restorations

Living-history programs have some problems that especially involve the responsibilities of the professional staff. Two of these deserve brief attention. First, a living-history program places a heavy interpretive burden on the craftsmen involved: They should be historical interpreters in the broadest sense. This is especially true for those museums with an exaggerated emphasis on crafts. Craftsmen are not always trained for this work, and this creates a difficult and continuous training problem. It is the other interpreters, however, who will probably determine the success of the program; they have greater freedom and opportunity to address the nonmaterial side of the re-creation. This means another training burden, one that is never finished and sometimes is not fully recognized, perhaps because it is difficult to assess how well the living-history program is helping visitors achieve a better understanding. As in a war, the battle is decided at the front lines. Unlike a war in which the generals can measure the gains and count the costs, in a living-history program, it is the privates who have the best sense of how the battle is going.

A second problem is that of supplying the interpreters with the necessary ammunition: relevant information about the particular culture being interpreted. Demographic studies are basic, and of the few that have been done there is little to fill the needs of specific re-creations. The study of the beliefs and attitudes of a society largely composed of the inarticulate is difficult and only beginning. The study of the life and feelings of ordinary individuals is even more difficult. These problems are multiplied for museums that do not represent a specific time and place from the past, for their re-creation and costumed practitioners of living history represent generalized concepts of a place and people who never existed.

History Is an Art

The past is dead, and it cannot be brought back to life. Those beliefs and attitudes, conscious and unconscious, rational and irrational that provided a foundation for institutions, governed conduct and controlled behavior cannot mean to us what they meant to those who lived by them. Some of the elements are missing; others have a different color and shape when viewed from our pattern of beliefs. So, too, with the affective life of individuals and families. Nor can any material re-creation ever be complete or authentic.

Any historian, social scientist or curator dealing with the past must tell his student, the museum visitor, that the past cannot be recovered. The message is, however, a positive one: The past has a unity and needs to be considered as a whole. This is something many historians who write books or give lectures have been able to avoid by dealing with specific portions of the past; most historical museums cannot avoid the issue.

A living-history program is an important, even an essential tool, to be used in capitalizing on that opportunity. Properly used, the interest and involvement it can generate can be used to aid the visitor to a clearer perception of the past. That will not happen unless the goals are deliberately chosen and there is the discipline needed to direct efforts toward achieving them.

History is an art. The pianist preparing a Beethoven sonata must, if he is to gain some understanding of the composer's intention, study the rest of Beethoven's works, have a knowledge of the musical culture of his time and of his inner life. It is not enough to practice one sonata on the piano used by the master. Which would you choose to hear if you wanted to know how Beethoven might have approached the sonata: a costumed pianist giving a note-perfect performance on a period piano, but without the benefit of much study of Beethoven and his music, or a performance on a modern piano by someone who had devoted himself to Beethoven and his music? A more realistic choice and precise analogy is between expending the bulk of limited time, money and thought on reproduction of costume, piano, Beethoven's mannerisms and practice of the one piece, or on the broader study of Beethoven's intent.

The Relationship Between Artifacts and the Public in Outdoor History Museums

26

Mark Leone

Mark Leone, an archaeologist at the University of Maryland who often applies Marxist interpretation to contemporary museums, visited Shakertown at Pleasant Hill, Kentucky, and used the experience to suggest that our history museums could be evaluated as complex artifacts that promote a particular ideology. "For instead of being warehouses of artifacts needing further analysis or as neutral masses of potential information, such museum presentations can be seen as fully operating parts of modern American culture. . . . [museums] can be a clue to the ideological part of our own society, in this case our conception and use of the past and its relationship to the present." This original article first appeared in the New York Academy of Science Annals in 1981.

Let me tell you what a visitor sees when he visits Shakertown at Pleasant Hill, near Lexington, Kentucky. I relate the following impressions after a brief visit to this outdoor living-history museum in December 1980. My impressions were formed as a tourist and, of course, as an anthropologist. They are useful because of the theory about the tie between past and present that I am interested in. My impressions do not represent consistent fieldwork at Shakertown, Kentucky, any discussions with the professional staff there, or a permanent commitment to the impressions' accuracy. They represent an effort at exploring a hunch about museum collections and their tie to the assumptions that link past and present for us in America. Nothing here is intended to be critical of this engaging and successful presentation of the Shakers' history.

There are two dozen original buildings laid out along a straight main street in Shakertown. The buildings vary in size, some being quite large; in material, some limestone, some brick, or wood; and in age, but most fall between the 1820s and 1850s. During the 1970s all standing structures along the main street were restored. A visitor to this living history museum buys a ticket for $3.50 and gets a map to guide himself on a walking tour. There are two initial impressions formed on this tour which provide a clue that one is in a museum, not in an original setting: The place is very beautiful, even perfect, and the place seems like other outdoor museums, for example, Colonial Williamsburg. Nothing needs to be fixed, raked, painted; there is no dung, no puddles, no weeds; it is all on display just for you. Since few people can bring them-

selves to believe for long that a place has been readied just for them, the feeling remaining is: Where did they live? What's back stage? The absence of inhabitants constitutes an invitation to seek them and so, as in similar museum settings, the visitor is invited to search for those who are gone.

This initial feeling, or perhaps inquiry, is addressed by the museum in two ways. The visitor guides himself, asking questions of costumed workers in the buildings, and, second, visitors discuss with each other the displays of artifacts presented in the many rooms throughout the site. In the course of these many conversations, the visitor comes to know Shakertown and achieves some understanding of what went on there. There are in general two domains on which information is offered: religious life and agricultural affairs. One is told that the Shakers lived in three large families, that they were celibate, that children came in only through conversion, that men and women lived separately, were not to touch each other, and worked apart at sex-specific duties. In the Meeting House one learns that the Shakers danced in rows, men and women apart; sang, having written hundreds of songs; and invited guests to observe them in Sunday ritual, being careful to exclude anyone who ridiculed their worship. All along one hears of the sobriety, solemnity, and deliberateness of their way of life. In their workshops and kitchens one sees the famous Shaker utensils, stoves, machinery, and, in some cases, the revitalized production of barrels, buckets, quilts, and the inevitable candles.

Along the way one learns that here at the settlement at

A young member of the public relating to a draw-knife.—*Photo: Black Creek Pioneer Village*

Pleasant Hill the major exporting industry was packaging seeds. These were sent all over the country and to England. The Shakers were the first to sell garden seeds in packets, one learns; they shipped half-a-ton of them annually and, on view, are some of the shipping boxes stacked casually in a corner with old labels on them. The equipment for seed production on display, all original, is arranged in a bedroom of one of the common family houses; the same is true for the weaving equipment, shoe-making equipment, and the pharmacy, which in addition to the tools of medicine-making, includes artificial limbs, crutches, and walking frames for the more disabled. The material on display is simple, normally easy to identify, and not turned into art by method of display. Although Shakertown at Pleasant Hill is too neat and clean by the standards of contemporary photographs of the same village, which are also on display, the materials shown maintain some of the integrity of their

original function through the context of presentation. One does learn something of how the items were used by the Shakers by the time one is finished looking.

The houses, workshops, and outbuildings are each used to display a particular part of Shaker life and as one tours each, Williamsburg fashion, one learns about sleeping and cooking, worship and furniture, a bit of history, some dates, laundry and seeds, water works and bathing. All information is accurate, although somewhat fragmented because the displays are by nature limited to rooms and buildings and it is up to you to walk between them all. It is fair to say that one gets the overall impression that the Shakers were admirable but must have believed in some quite peculiar things. This minor conflict is resolved in favor of Shaker efficiency.

The resolution comes in many ways. The best illustration of it is connected with the Herb House. This house is a small two-story wooden building near the end of the main street. Inside it is hung with bunches of dried plant materials. There is some furniture, including a piece or two, as is usual in these buildings, so beautiful you want to take it off with you. The costumed worker there, one of the more outgoing, asks if you would like to hear about the Herb House. Since you have closed the door behind you and find yourself in a little fenced-in rectangle, you can either say yes or leave. Then comes the story. The Shakers farmed over 5000 acres at their peak, many of them in herbs, which they processed and packaged like the garden seeds and shipped virtually everywhere. The lady in costume then takes a wooden rack with two bars on it from which are tied 18 or 20 bunches of dried herbs. Identifying each, she says

This is wormwood, a natural moth repellant, it was mixed with this next bunch, lavender, and packaged to protect woolens; this is foxglove, or digitalis, a natural heart medicine; "also used were sage which is useful for coughs and colds; hoarhound for coughs, colds, and asthma; lobelia or wild tobacco which helps with epilepsy and, used in a poultice, helps with sprains and bruises; catnep for upset stomachs; and thyme which is good for flatulence, colic, and headache."[1]

The recitation goes on naming each plant, its properties, and use. A clear picture emerges of how practical, inventive, and industrious the Shakers were. There is the very clear notion that the Shakers with their labor-saving devices and medicines were working for the greater good of mankind. I learned subsequently that this is a view duplicated in the literature, which presents Shaker industries from herbs[2] to carpentry, tanning, food processing, cloth, and utensils as practical, skillful, ingenious, and instructive for our own betterment.

The Shakers produced 50 tons of food a year for their own use at this settlement, built and ran "a saw mill, a grist mill, a fulling mill and an oil mill. They also had a printing office. Broom-making was a specialty. They made their own implements and wagons and turned out the hundred and one things needed in daily life. They made butter and cheese...and canned vegetables. They even made wine. . . ."[3] The Shakers, who numbered 500 at their height at this settlement, fed all these and at times hundreds of visitors. Furthermore, all this activity required 200 buildings, of which the remaining two dozen are a residential remnant. All the mills are gone, and there is no way to gain a sense of the size of the agrarian industries that must have existed to back up an exporting business that "made money hand over fist...allowing always for their generosity and philanthropic work which were note worthy."[4]

Eventually one reaches two impressions at Shakertown upon which to build an analysis of how museum collections on public display are used to instruct the public. The first is that Shaker life and thought, which we can rightly call a culture, is so broken up and fragmented by the presentation that it cannot be seen as a whole. It must be emphasized that this is not only not

deliberate, it is likely to be contrary to the intention of the curators of the museum. One can also see that the meaning of some of the museum's more interesting facets is likely to stem from modern American ideology.[5] By this I mean that an unseen assumption within the American world view, one essential to modern day life, has been fixed on an aspect of Shaker culture and in being fixed there is given objective existence while simultaneously hiding Shaker history.

The aspect of modern American ideology that is fixed on Shaker life is best labeled and most fully described by Marshall Sahlins as Culture and Practical Reason.[6]

The reasonableness of institutions, and above all their utility, is the principal way we explain ourselves to ourselves. Rationality is our rationalization. Boas gives the telling example of the incest tabu, which once we were content to ascribe to religious reasons, but now "a utilitarian concept, the fear of unhealthy offspring due to intermarriage of close relations, is brought forward as the reason for our feelings."[7]

Given this, Sahlins concludes that, the derivation of organization from practical activity, and of consciousness from the relations of persons, ignores the constituted symbolic quality of our own institutions... [which] is the self-conception of capitalism."[8]

In identifying Shaker efficiency, rationality, innovation in labor-saving devices, export, profit, philanthropy, and the logic connecting wormwood with preserving woolens or foxglove with preventing heart trouble is to misunderstand their world, and to misunderstand it systematically in terms idiosyncratic to our own, particularly the world of capitalism. To see Shaker industry as efficient, profitable, logical, and ingenious is to see it with accuracy devoid of analysis. It is to see culture as rising from function, behavior from efficiency, and thought from material necessity. That is of course American thought; that is, just as obviously, how everyone has always thought and probably not how the Shakers thought.

It is likely that an otherwise accurate portrayal of Shaker life at Pleasant Hill forms an imposition of the present on the past when it renders "the conventional as useful, it also becomes for us 'natural,' in the double sense of inherent in nature and normal in culture... [that is] the appropriation of the meaningful realities of other people's lives by the secondary rationalizations of our own."[9]

This appropriation has two parts which make visiting Shakertown a dual process. The first event is the hiding of Shaker history. Shaker culture is fragmented, reduced to isolated items like work, worship, celibacy, and some dates. The unintended hiding of their history is achieved, not avoided, by the premium put on accuracy and authenticity in the museum presentation. The second part of the ideological process is the imposition of meaning from the present onto Shaker material. Efficiency, practicality, and wholesome materialism are the values we are allowed to come away feeling best capture the society we have seen. This is at best only partially true and is an inevitable imposition which can occur effectively only through the first half of the process, which is the masking of Shaker history by presenting it as organized into parts like our own society.

The dual process is what Marx called ideology and, when operating in an outdoor history or archaeological museum, creates an ideotechnic artifact. Lewis Binford[9] defined but never isolated this class of artifacts. He never found them because his theory of culture, use of sociocultural levels of integration, and emphasis on culture process show an underdeveloped concept of ideology, a problem that could be corrected by a more thorough integration of Marxist theory into the new archaeology.

Once outdoor presentations that use archaeological knowledge and collections are seen as ideotechnic, the way to treat them becomes substantially more clear. For instead of being warehouses of artifacts needing further analysis or as neutral masses of potential information, such museum presentations can be seen as fully operating parts of modern American culture, and when we see the presentations of the artifacts as the true artifacts, then we, as archaeologists, can treat the ideotechnic item the way we would any item. It can be a clue to the ideological part of our own society, in this case our conception and use of the past and its relationship to the present.

In the face of all these possibilities, the proper role of the anthropologically trained archaeologist, and particularly but not exclusively the historical archaeologist, becomes clear for the first time. Most obvious, an archaeologist, working at Shakertown would find the mills, tanyards, waterworks, machinery, quarries, and associated written material. Once an archaeologist, who was a materialist, looked through the fragmentary picture of Shaker life presented today and realized the ab-

A lesson in marketing.—*Photo: Black Creek Pioneer Village*

sence of a subsistence base, he would excavate the remains of the means of production. At Shakertown the mills and industrial sites are all ruins; there is some archaeological work going on, but it is at this point not open to the public. A visitor realizes that whole industrial areas existed because shoe-making, seed packaging, and herb processing did not take place in bedrooms or little buildings where the remaining artifacts are now stored. Present displays often make the work look like hobbies, but true agrarian industries housed these leftovers and it was not merely subsistence but industry. For the Shakers were not farmers, they were escapees from early industrial capitalism and created agrarian industrialism as an alternative to it.

The Shaker history at Pleasant Hill that is hidden unintentionally is the commentary the Shakers made on industrial capitalism. Mother Ann Lee, the English founder of Shakerism, had a series of wrenching experiences with factory life, marriage, and childbearing, during the mid-18th century in Great Britain. She founded a religious group, which claimed for her after her death that she had been the Second Coming. Ann Lee and a few followers came to the United States in the late 1700s, settled in New York near Troy where the group caught on, came to be known as Shakers from the dancing and ecstasy in worship, and reached a peak of 6000 members scattered in a dozen communities over the eastern United States by the 1850s.[10]

Shakerism, like related utopian socialist communities, reacted to the rise of industrialism by turning to agrarianism and communalism as a cure for enforced poverty, the destruction of the extended family, the reduction of social relations to the individual, the evaluation of all behavior as efficiency, and the debasing of emotion in religion that occurred in the established churches. Early industrial capitalism altered life so completely for those involved in it that its effects have been made famous in literature by people like Dickens and Sinclair Lewis, in scholarship by Marx, and in religion by the Shakers, the Mormons, the Christian Scientists, and the Spiritualists. These are a few of the religious groups in this country which responded to early industrial capitalism. Each produced a critique of society, a plan for action, and a social experiment.

It is more misleading than accurate to see the Shakers as farmers and as a utopian movement that sought out Jeffersonian agrarianism as a cure for social and economic ills. First, the farming was industrialized; second, the communities produced virtually all goods and therefore had to have industries at every level from hand crafts to mass production including heavy machinery; and third, they intended to turn a profit." The profit however, was owned in common. So, it is inappropriate to envision a social isolate and more appropriate to see a group that was actively engaged in the renovation of industrial society and missionized actively in order to proclaim its success and recruit accordingly in the parent society. The Shakers saw what their museum does not

allow us to see: Their active engagement in the renovation of the worst aspects of the society that gave them birth. Further, of course, we do not see that Shakerism was destroyed as much by industrialism as by its members' celibacy. The process was twofold. Because their products were so excellent, the demand for them caused a shortage of labor, forced them to hire hands, and to turn out products at a rate dictated more by demand than religion. This process began to occur with the Civil War and later, some products like cloth, became so inexpensive when purchased in the outside world, that the Shakers closed down many of their own industries as ineffective.

The Shakers were subject to industrialization and its other side, obsolescence. This weakened them substantially and points out the difficulty the Shakers had in avoiding the very social forces they were trying to escape. Mechanization, standardization, obsolescence, or the governing of life by production crushed them by the end of the Civil War. Whether developed from within or introduced from outside, a change in the means of production (subsistence) meant a change in the mode of production, i.e., the social relations accompanying subsistence. Once this happened, the relations of production were altered. Since Shakerism's major innovation was to place work in the context of kinship and worship, as it had been before the Industrial Revolution, this relationship of producing, once violated, left its members with little more than a set of aesthetic values. They and their commentary on their parenting capitalism were overcome by the forces they were trying to escape. Their analysis of capitalism was too weak for them to cancel its effects for more than a generation or two.[14] Almost all of this background is taken away when their life is presented as a museum exhibit.

The Shakers were produced by economic and social forces endemic to early American industrialism; they attempted to remedy the worst effects and to preach and convert on that basis. They intended to be humane industrialists, not the isolated celibate farmers we often make of them. They were always engaged in society, knowing that they were produced by it. They failed in their effort and were overcome by what they tried to correct. None of this remains intact of Shakertown at Pleasant Hill. Intact is peculiarity, bucolic beauty, neatness, and isolated oddments.

The proper job of the archaeologist, especially the materialist, is to recapture the relations of production, which is the means (mills, barns, fields, technology, machinery, amounts, prices, numbers) and the mode as well (sexual division of labor, hours, compensation, promotion, training, assessment of need, adequacy of reward, definition of children, old age, sickness, infirmity). These relations of production can be established by excavation and use of period texts.

Mode of production for the Shakers contained a radical realignment of sexuality, work, family, and thought. We know we tend to see Shakers as peculiar, which has the function of isolating them from us. This occurs when we see them as celibate and do not connect celibacy with a political statement, or when we see their dancing as ecstasy and sublimated sexuality as opposed to an effort to keep emotions out of destructive competition between workers. Mode of production is all these and when connected to mills, machines, and agrarian industrialism in a socialist context, produced a different way of life, which an archaeologist could retrieve.

An archaeologist attached to a museum involving the use of materials like these to reach the public may consider going further by seeing that the interpretive process is ideological. It is neither a neutral process nor is it wicked just because it is ideological. In other words, the use of materials on Shaker history and archaeology in a museum interpretation is the process of creating an ideotechnic artifact. The point is not to find Shaker ideotechnic artifacts; I doubt they had any. The point is that the use of a museum collection of Shaker artifacts, or similar displays of analogous material at Colonial Williamsburg, or at St. Mary's City, Maryland, or any of the hundreds of living-history museums and farms in this country may be considered the creation of such an artifact category. Binford's term is useful because it helps us see that there probably are no ideotechnic items among our collections, rather it is those collections in public use with modern meaning that forms the ideotechnic item. And that item, let us be clear, is not to be understood in Leslie White's[15] or Lewis Binford's definition but in Louis Althusser's.[5] For him ideology is composed of the givens, taken-for-granteds, and obviousnesses of a culture. Ideology is the hidden assumptions not the acknowledged beliefs and philosophies of a group. They can be found in the ideas of person, time, change, object, and history of a people. This definition, which contradicts nothing in Binford, moves him a little closer to his true roots in Marx and archaeologists closer to understanding what the relationship is between the artifact, the past, and the viewing present.

That relationship is neither given or invariant. It certainly is not neutral. Casting back to a visitor's impressions at Shakertown, artifacts are used to illustrate the past, which is taken in some way to be instructive to the present. But the museum is the artifact, and in fact is an ideotechnic artifact serving (1) to make the Shakers illustrate culture as practical reason, (2) thereby validating and reproducing in history this particular piece of ideology, and (3) hiding, without any such intention on the museum's part, Shaker culture as a commentary on our own. Naturalizing the present by imposing some part of it on the past is, as all historiographers know, inevitable and unavoidable. There is nothing wrong with it; the difficulty comes when archaeologists working in settings involving public interpretation do not realize it and thereby are controlled by the process.

Once the process is visible, then the composition of the ideotechnic artifact can be at our disposal, if we want it

to be. And it is at that point that the museum collection offers a dual option paralleling the dual process that creates it. It can illustrate, in the cases I have mentioned, the cultural processes in early capitalism and industrialism that formed the matrix of modern American society. Second, a museum can illustrate the misinterpretive or masking process, the ideological process wherein society appropriates the history and culture of others to ground its own in what seems to be the natural state of things. This second option creates consciousness of history and is probably the only way to save history and keep the remnants of it housed in our museums from seeming useless.

The process by which this might be done is aptly described by George Lukas when clarifying the role of consciousness in relation to history.

> The succession and internal order of the categories [in which a history is written or told] constitute neither a purely logical sequence, nor are they organized merely in accordance with the facts of history. "Their sequence is rather determined by the relation which they bear to one another in modern bourgeois society, and which is the exact opposite of what seems to be their natural order or the order of their historical development."[16]

Linking tools, herbs, efficiency, merchandizing, and religion as we do with the Shakers is no more than telling ourselves that the Shakers used labor-saving devices for farming pursuits that were carried out on a scale big enough to produce a profit useful for philanthropy.

Insofar as that can be called our interpretation, it is inaccurate. Shaker life itself can be glimpsed through a series of quotations. This first is from a journal kept at Pleasant Hill recording the herb industry and collected by Miller.

> July 25, 1850 Gathered sage and other herbs in the garden. The largest cutting ever known. Gathered blackberries at the Cove spring.
> Sept. 29th, Gathered hops, grapes and walnut roots for dye. Went after herb roots with Joel and three sisters and all the boys, but got none.
> May 1, 1849 Trimmed off the thyme and tanzy in John's garden. May 1-8th. Cut herbs in the garden, burned caterpillars, gathered hoarhound, tanzy, bulgeweed in the hen lot, cleaned herb house and press house.
> June 16-19th. Gathered and shipped off catnep, gathered sage, thyme and other garden herbs.
> June 31st. Gathered blackberries and mint.
> August 6th. The whole society of sisters went out after supper and cut sage. Williams went to Harrodsburg after roots.
> August 24th The young sisters set up the night previous and cut peaches and apples to fill the dry house and press herbs. The sisters generally took a walk to the Cliffs with the North Union Visitors [another group of Shakers.][2]

There is little here to lead us to see how these actions fit into Shaker life or how that life was enacted through these activities. But there is no efficiency, practicality, or materialism either.

The sweet smell of success: baking gingerbread men and oatmeal cookies in Victorian Ontario.—*Photo: Black Creek Pioneer Village*

The following quote does introduce us to Shaker perspective and, if it could be taken metaphorically (and there is no way to know whether it should be), would advertise more than patent medicine in 1877.

> Pure and Reliable medicines: Manufactured and for Sale by the Shakers, Pleasant Hill. We append to our catalogue of Preparations our Remedies, with the methods of the U.S.P. (Pharmacopaea) 1877 so that all parties concerned may compare the results of each and in this way may draw their own conclusions as to which method is the best to Secure Pure and Reliable Medicines of full strength in acts of principle and menstrums. N. B. Spurious and fraudulent imitations may be sold for much less than the Real and Pure, but are vastly more costly in the end.[12]

Here the Shakers proclaim their integrity against universal standards saying clearly they are different and better, at least in making medicine.

But what made them different and better? The efficiency and practical reason we see today at Pleasant Hill? I do not know all the parts to the answer but one part consists of their definition of the body including sex, and action's (work's) relationship to thought. These are drawn out in the following quotation.

> Writing about the character of Baudelaire, Jean-Paul Sartre said that "in general, the poet considered sin to be a form of eroticism." The psychological experiences forming the background of the Millennial Church seem to presuppose a tacit adoption of the principle as stated by Baudelaire himself, when he affirmed "that the sole and supreme pleasure in the act of love lies in the certain knowledge that one is doing something evil, and that, from the time of their birth, both men and women are aware that evil is the source of all physical delight." This sounds like what Mother Ann experienced or like what she labored, through her confessional techniques, to bring to the light of consciousness in her disciples, for without this personal experience of evil as "the source of all physical delight," how can a reflective person accept the principle that in physical pleasure all evil is to be found? But from this point on, Baudelaire's po-

A boy's first lesson in woodworking at Plimoth Plantation.—*Photo: George Chapman*

sition and the Shaker attitude lead to very different patterns of behavior. Baudelaire, as Sartre tells us, "chose the path of evil, and this meant that he had chosen to feel guilty." One can imagine Sartre saying of the Shakers that "since they chose the path of goodness, this meant that they had chosen to feel justified and perfect." And, in fact, the Shaker elders admitted that they were no longer able to sin. In the Testimonies we read that when inquirers asked them, "Are you perfect? Do you live without sin?" the elders answered, "The power of God, revealed in this day, does enable souls to cease from sin; and we have received that power, we have actually left of committing sin."[13]

Shaker asceticism, not an aesthetic temper, formed the remains left to us which are celebrated in their village museums.

Mother Ann...favored the life of hardship. She condemned the Shaker sisters for huddling around the fire. She forbade idle conversation as time lost from work. In matters of dress, furniture, and table settings she required her people to be simple, practical, and modest. No silver tableware, no jewels, no table cloths were permitted. The Shakers lived standing up. Laziness, play, and self-

indulgence were rigorously proscribed. Shaker furniture will long testify to this inspiration.[14]

From these quotations we can see that the Shakers were not like ourselves at all. They labored to avoid sin, not for a profit; they had no economy, but an elaborate system of penance; the only efficiency they knew was the kind created between self-mortification and a hair shirt. If pleasure was sin, practical reason is the last idea we should find ourselves discovering at Pleasant Hill.

Lukas and Marx allow us to see that the Shakers are different by discovering that we have tended to make them like ourselves. We can only do the first by assuming the second, because by assuming that the categories of our own relations of production have been imposed on theirs, we can see the breaks or separations that the two cultures make in ordering their respective worlds. But Lukas and Marx do not let us off with these realizations, for they insist that contemplation of differences in history is not enough to achieve knowledge of the present.[15] Self-knowledge of our own social situation may be achieved

...if two conditions are fulfilled. On the one hand, all the categories in which human existence is constructed must appear as the determinants of that existence itself (and not merely of the description of that existence). On the other hand, their succession, their coherence and their connections must appear as aspects of the historical process itself, as the structural components of the present.[16]

The first move, which is one that comes in knowing the Shakers through our distortion of them, if successful, will achieve some sense of the differences between thought and action in the two societies. The second move is one which asks us how our own (and perhaps Shaker) thought and life came to be constructed as they are. In other words, how the categories we imposed initially on Shaker life came into existence in the first place. The two moves amount to asking: How do we view the world and how did the view come about?

This second question could only be answered by a more detailed picture of early American industrialism before it was tied to capitalism. A museum like Shakertown must be counted successful in the terms set here if it fulfills the first part of the dual process and leaves the visitor with the question: If they were that different and we both come from the American past, how did we get to be so different from them?

ACKNOWLEDGMENTS

I am grateful to Russell G. Handsman for a careful reading of this paper and for pointing out that Shaker culture needed to be "put back together again." M. Alison Wylie, Ann Palkovich, and JoAnn Magdoff made helpful observations on the paper and suggested changes.

1. Miller, A.B. 1976. *Shaker Herbs: A History and a Compendium.* Clarkson N. Potter. New York. pp. 105-108; 125-256. Permission granted by Shakertown at Pleasant Hill, Kentucky, Inc.
2. Miller, p. 107.

3. Andrews, E. D. 1933. *The Community Industries of the Shakers.* Facsimile Reprint of New York State Handbook Number 15. Emporium Publications. Charlestown, MA.
4. Hutton, D.M. 1936. *Old Shakertown and the Shakers.* Harrodsburg Herald Press. Harrodsburg, KY. pp. 28-29.
5. Althusser, L. 1971. Ideology and ideological apparatuses. In *Lenin and Philosophy.* Monthly Review Press. New York, pp. 127-186.
6. Sahlins, N. 1976. *Culture and Practical Reason.* University of Chicago Press. Chicago. Permission granted by the University of Chicago Press.
7. Sahlins, (4) pp. 72-73.
8. Sahlins, p. 54.
9. Binford, L. R. 1962. Archaeology as anthropology. *American Antiquity* 28: 217-225.
10. Desroche, H. 1971. *The American Shakers: From Neo-Christianity to Pre-Socialism.* University of Massachusetts Press. Amherst, MA. Permission granted by the University of Massachusetts Press. Copyright by The Shaker Community, Inc., 1971.
11. Desroche, (10) pp. 144-145.
12. Desroche, (10) p. 228.
13. Kanter, R. M. 1972, *Commitment and Community.* Harvard University Press. Cambridge, MA.
14. Marx, Karl. 1972, *Manifesto of the Communist Party.* pp. 72-73. Foreign Languages Press. Peking.
15. Lukas, G. 1971. *History and Class Consciousness.* MIT Press. Cambridge, MA. p. 159.
16. White, L. 1959. *The Evolution of Culture.* McGraw-Hill. New York. pp. 261-274.

Visiting the Past
History Museums in the United States

27

Michael Wallace

A revisionist historian, Wallace seeks to demonstrate in this article first published in Radical History Review *25 (1981) that from "the mid-nineteenth century on, most history museums were constructed by members of dominant classes, and embodied interpretations that supported their sponsors' privileged positions." Wallace argues that although most living-history museums had abandoned the "American Heritage" notion of history for a "more pluralistic conception of the U.S. past," still they "shied away from politics and struggle: slave culture was one thing, slave revolts another." Wallace feels museums have failed "to explore the ways the present evolved out of the past." Williamsburg, he believes, fails to "explain the connections between eighteenth-century slavery and twentieth-century racism (or black nationalism). Admitting the realities of exploitation contradicted the ideals of liberty was only a first step." Wallace sees hope in the living historical farms movement developed by a "new generation of historians and educators concerned to explore work and family life with even higher standards of accuracy, and in some cases, with an eye to modern parallels."*

On any given summer afternoon, a considerable number of Americans go to visit the past. They drive to Greenfield Village, or Colonial Williamsburg, or Old Sturbridge. They stroll through old houses, admire antique cars, or watch colonial farmers and shoemakers at work. They might also see a movie, read a guidebook, or listen to costumed interpreters explain the way things used to be. Hundreds of these history museums dot the U.S. landscape; millions of people visit them each year; and it seems reasonable to suppose that they help shape popular perspectives on the past.

In this article I intend to discuss the kinds of perspectives the museums promote. This can best be done by looking at their history. I will try to demonstrate that from the mid-nineteenth century on, most history museums were constructed by members of dominant classes and embodied interpretations that supported their sponsors' privileged positions. I do not contend that those who established museums were Machiavellina plotters; the museum builders simply embedded in their efforts versions of history that were commonplaces of their class's culture. From the 1930s onward, elite control of these markers of the public memory came under increasing challenge. This survey will examine how the museums responded and conclude with some speculations on their future.

Antebellum Americans were not sentimental about saving old buildings. In the midst of the War of 1812, the state of Pennsylvania tried to tear down Independence Hall and sell the land to commercial developers. Protests saved the building, but not before two wings had been demolished and the woodwork stripped from the room in which the Declaration of Independence had been signed. Most other venerable buildings situated on valuable real estate fared less well. This exuberant and cavalier demolition of the remains of the past reflected partly a booming land market and partly the antihistorical bent captured in Thoreau's contemptuous dismissal of England as "an old gentleman who is travelling with a great deal of baggage, trumpery which accumulated from long housekeeping, which he has not had the courage to burn."[1] It was not until the approach of civil war in the 1850s that a small segment of the patriciate, frightened that the Republic seemed to be coming apart and persuaded that a memorialization of the nation's founders might serve as an antidote, began to reconsider this position. In 1850 Governor Hamilton Fish asked the New York State Legislature to save George Washington's revolutionary headquarters in Newburgh from impending demolition. The legislators agreed, noting, "It will be good for our citizens in these days when we hear the sound of disunion reiterated from every part of the country...to chasten their minds by reviewing the history of our revolutionary struggle." On July 4, 1850, the flag was raised over the first historic house in the United States— as much a shrine as a museum.[2]

Three years later a group of businessmen tried to buy Mount Vernon and turn it into a hotel. This provoked another and far more significant preservation effort. The governor of Virginia asked John Washington, the current occupant, to sell it to the state. Washington agreed, but asked a stiff $200,000. The price, he noted somewhat defensively, "may appear to be extravagant, yet I have good reason to believe it is not more than could be readily obtained for the property were it in the Public market." The governor asked the Virginia legislature to appropriate the funds, arguing that although the figure might be "exorbitant," if considered as an "ordinary transaction of business...dollars become as dust when compared with the inestimable patriotism inspired by a visit to the tomb." The outraged legislators balked, and the movement to preserve Mount Vernon shifted to private hands.[3]

Ann Pamela Cunningham, daughter of a wealthy South Carolina planter, announced a crusade to save the homesite. She, too, wanted to create a rallying point for nationalist forces, but was perhaps even more worried by the disintegrating effort of a commercial and capitalist political economy, of which the attempt by "soulless speculators" to disturb "the shades of the dead" was yet another symptom. Because it was thought to be Woman's special role to preserve the frail bonds of social solidarity against threatening Commerce, she turned for help to wealthy, socially prominent women who had family connections to the revolutionary generation. Cunningham and her new colleagues formed the Mount Vernon Ladies' Association (MVA) and set out to create a "shrine where at least the mothers of the land and their innocent children might make their offering in the cause of the greatness, goodness and prosperity of their country." The MVLA campaign soon attracted members of the middle and upper classes, North and South, who were working to preserve the Union. Edward Everett, a former Massachusetts senator and secretary of state, gave an immensely popular oration on the life of Washington to 139 gatherings across the country and contributed the proceeds to the MVLA. He hoped that Mount Vernon would offer 'a common heritage for the estranged children of a common father, the spell of whose memory will yet have the power to reunite them around his hallowed sepulchre."[4]

Mount Vernon was saved in 1850, but the Washington cult failed to spark a pro-Union revival. Nor did it inaugurate a widespread change in attitude to the past. John Hancock's house was demolished during the Civil War; he had been an exemplary revolutionary hero, but when the market value of the land reached $120,000, his birthplace was turned over to the wreckers. In the postwar Gilded Age, it was definitely business as usual, and even the Centennial celebrations of 1876 looked more to the dynamos of the future than the inheritance of the past.[5]

Still, the crusaders of the 1850s had blazed a trail to the past. Their legacy included an insistence that private gain be subordinated to larger concerns, a demonstration that it was possible to appropriate the aura that Washington's presence had invested in particular buildings and put it to work, and a certification that it was proper for upper-class women to preserve and present history to the public.

In the 1880s the dominant classes' attitude toward history began to change. By the 1890s it had undergone a remarkable transformation. Upper and middle-class men and women established ancestral societies and historical associations in great numbers. They also set about rescuing old buildings and displaying them to the public, preserving battlefield sites, and erecting shrines and monuments. By 1895 there were twenty house museums; by 1910 there were one hundred.[6] How are we to account for this?

These were, of course, years of triumph and consolidation for corporate capitalism in the United States. But the masters of the new order—the industrial magnates, the financiers, the old patrician families, and the powerful middle class of managers and professionals—found their position contested by social classes who had also been summoned into being by the new order of things. The battles with immigrant workers, discontented artisans, and disgruntled small farmers were often brutal and direct trials of military, political, and economic strength. But the combat had cultural dimensions as well, and it was in this area that new attitudes toward history were generated.

The Haymarket affair and the great strikes of the 1880s appear to have been the events that galvanized the bourgeoisie into reconsidering its disregard for tradition. Convinced that immigrant aliens with subversive ideologies were destroying the Republic, elites fashioned a new collective identity for themselves that had at its core the belief that there was such a thing as the American inheritance, and that they were its legitimate custodians. Class struggle was transmuted into defense of "American values" against outside agitators.[7]

The progenitors of this class culture were chiefly the older patrician elite—those who had inherited landed, mercantile, or early industrial wealth. They found long-standing cultural and political authority suddenly being challenged; the Adams family's turn to the past accelerated markedly after the Knights of Labor captured the Quincy town meeting in 1887. Nor were they pleased with the rawboned plutocrats whose command of immense concentrations of capital had catapulted them to political prominence. Patricians discovered in their historical pedigrees a source of cultural and psychic self-confidence and took the lead in forming a host of new institutions. Some were exclusive ancestral societies like the Sons of the American Revolution (1889), the Daughters of the American Revolution (1890), and the Mayflower Descendants (1897). They also took part in establishing historical societies and preservation groups, like the Association for the Preservation of Virginia Antiquities (1888), the Native Sons of the Golden West (1888), the American Scenic and Historic Preservation Society (1895), and the Society for the Preservation of New England Antiquities (1910).[8]

Patricians formed the vanguard of these groups, but the rank and file often included middle-class professionals, small business men, and civic and political leaders. Some big capitalists followed their lead, either as members (John D. Rockefeller joined the SAR) or as fiscal underwriters (Jay Gould supported the still-flourishing MVLA and C. F. Crocker, California's first millionaire, aided the Golden Sons), but the center of gravity of the movement lay in the ranks of the old monied.[9]

A central and enthusiastically pursued activity of these groups was the construction of shrines and memorials, including finding and marking the graves of old soldiers.[10] The MVLA was the model; many of the leaders of the new organizations were daughters of MVLA members. They sought out, bought up, restored, and displayed the houses in which famous men had lived. These projects enabled the elite to associate themselves and their class with the virtuous and glorious dead. In the process they also constructed and cultivated a class aesthetic: seventeenth- and eighteenth-century architecture became something of a cultural emblem. Some groups (like the Society for the Preservation of New England Antiquities, founded by William Sumner Appleton, the grandson of Nathan Appleton, one of the first textile magnates) were consequently willing to preserve buildings hallowed by association with the entire pre-immigrant social order, even if not connected with any particularly distinguished patriot. This class aesthetic tastefully demarcated them from both immigrants and vulgar nouveaux riches—the railroad barons, mine owners, and streetcar magnates then transporting disman-

Visiting the past: Harvesting herbs in 1620s Plymouth.—*Photo: Plimoth Plantation*

tled European castles to the United States in order to live in "simulated feudal grandeur."[11]

The house museums also served a didactic function in the patricians' cultural offensive. Along with campaigns for patriotic and military education and drives to foster a cult of flag and Constitution, the museums sought to Americanize the immigrant working class. The shrines were thought magically to transform aliens brought within their walls. Mrs. J. V. R. Townsend, Colonial Dame, vice-regent of the MVLA, and chairwoman of the Van Cortlandt House Committee in New York City, explained in 1900 that the "Americanizing of the children—by enlisting their interest in historical sites and characters has a great significance to any thinking mind—the making of good citizens of these many foreign youths." Good citizenship meant accepting bourgeois rules of political action and abandoning radicalism. The working classes, one speaker told the Sons of the American Revolution, must be educated "out of all these crass and crazy notions of popular rights...into a true understanding of American liberty as handed down by our Fathers." The past, including the revolutionary tradition, had been transformed into an abstract symbol of Order.[12]

It is difficult to assess the impact of this Americanizing campaign. A rich literature shows that working-class communities fought to preserve their various national customs, traditions, and communal cultures. Sometimes their efforts took defensive, conservative, and ethnocentric forms; at other times they offered a base for revolutionary fervor. But always the community provided a self-identity that aided resistance.[13]

It seems likely that the Americanization campaigns had the greatest impact on those who organized them. The Bourgeoisie buckled History around themselves like moral armor. The more they felt threatened, the more they grew convinced of their inherent, because inherited, legitimacy. Finally, what had been a relatively benevolent, if patronizing and provincial, mentality turned nasty and belligerent. Groups like the Immigration Restriction League (IRL)—bankers and professor driven to the point of hysteria by strikers and socialists—began to argue, with ever-greater racism and religious bigotry, that, in the words of IRL member John Fiske (the ancestral societies' favorite historian), "the antidote to the bane of foreign immigration" was "the enforcement of those American ideas inherited from the Revolution."[14] This tendency reached its peak in 1917-19 when the U.S. bourgeoisie, terrified first by the Bolshevik victory and then by the postwar strike wave, transmuted Americanization into a zenophobic and antileft demand for 100 percent Americanism. The viciousness of the time—the crushing of strikes, the raids on radical parties, the incarceration or deportation of critics, the support for lynch mobs and vigilantism—was fueled in large measure by the bourgeoisie's self-righteous conviction that it was defending not simply class privilege but a historic legacy.

After the war corporate capital moved to the forefront of the return to the past.[15] With labor and the left set back severely, business leaders bagan to exude a smug assurance that they were the sole and legitimate heirs of the American tradition. The president of the National Association of Manufacturers was sure that the citizens were "tired of chasing the will-o-wisps of radicalism in government, in religion, in art, and in social life, and are about ready to return to the god, the Bible, and the fundamental principles of their forefathers"[16]

Increasingly in the 1920s, businessmen became involved in bringing history to the masses. Some of these interventions into public history followed the patterns developed earlier. In 1923, for example, a group of New York lawyers and financiers directed a drive to save Thomas Jefferson's Monticello. But though Wall Streeters, not patrician women, were in charge, the outcome was the same: another shrine.[17] The really decisive transformations in the history museum genre came at the hands of Henry Ford and John D. Rockefeller, Jr.

Before the war Henry Ford had been the very model of the ebullient, go ahead capitalist; the mood of the 1880s and 1890s barely touched him. He had dabbled in Americanism, albeit of a forward-looking sort. At the Ford Company's's English School (compulsory for all non-English speaking employees), students acted out a pantomine in which some, dressed in national costume and carrying signs denoting their country of origin, entered a giant "Melting Pot"; simultaneously, prosperous-looking students streamed out of the pot dressed in business suits and waving little U.S. flags. In 1916, convinced that he and his class were revolutionizing the world, Ford made his most famous pronouncement: "History is more or less bunk. It's tradition. We don't want tradition. We want to live in the present and the only history that is worth a tinker's dam is the history we make today." Lampooned as an ignoramus, he stuck to his guns. "I don't want to live in the past," he told John Reed, "I want to live in the Now."[18]

The war years badly shook Ford, a committed pacifist, and the postwar labor upheavals unsettled his conviction that American capitalism could transcend class struggle via such devices as the five-dollar day. By 1919 he had discovered a new respect for the past.[19] In that year Ford began excavating and restoring his own history. He fixed up the old family farm, a schoolhouse he had attended, an inn he had danced in. He and his friends dressed up in old costumes and held nostalgic parties.[20]

In 1923 he intervened in a more traditional preservation effort. A drive was on to save the Wayside Inn, a Sudbury, Massachusetts, hostelry built in 1702 and celebrated in a Longfellow poem. Ford bought the place outright and single-handedly restored it, added on a new wing and a ballroom, purchased 2,667 surrounding acres, built a special highway to detour auto traffic away from it, and transported there a gristmill, a sawmill, a blacksmith's shop, and a little red schoolhouse allegedly once attended by the Mary of "Mary Had a Little Lamb." When he had finished, he had created one of the first museum villages in the United States at a cost of somewhere between three and five million dollars. "I'm trying," he said, "in a small way to help America take a step, even if it is a little one, toward the saner and sweeter idea of life that prevailed in prewar days."[21]

Little steps soon grew to giant strides. Ford reformulated his position on history: only history as traditionally taught in schools was bunk. It concentrated too much on wars, politics, and great men (perhaps he had the ancestral societies in mind) and not enough on the material reality of everyday life for commonfolk. It also relied too heavily on book learning. "The only way," he thought, "to show how our forefathers lived and to bring to mind what kind of people they were is to reconstruct, as nearly as possible, the exact conditions under which they lived." This required assembling "the things that people used." "Get everything you can find!" he ordered the 35,000 Ford dealers across the United States. He wanted "a complete series of every article ever used or made in America from the days of the first settlers down to the present time." As Ford was the richest man in the world, offers to sell poured in, and in short order he had become the world's greatest collector of Americana. Carloads of relics were dumped into the tractor plant warehouse in Dearborn. In 1927 Ford announced that he would open an Industrial Museum to display his now immense horde of objects. By 1929 he had constructed a fourteen-acre building (with a replica of Independence Hall for an entrance facade) that housed exhibits recording the mechanization of agriculture and industry, the evolution of lighting, communications, and transportation, and the development of objects used in domestic life.[22]

In 1928 Ford announced that he would construct an early American Village next to the museum and had trucked in a windmill from Cape Cod, the courthouse where Lincoln practiced law, two slave cabins, which went behind the Lincoln courthouse, a country store, an old inn, a New Hampshire firehouse, a Massachusetts shoeshop, several assorted buildings associated with his own youth, and the entire Menlo park "invention factory" in which his good friend Thomas Edison had invented the light bulb.[23]

Ford's museum village—popularly known as Greenfield Village—was inaugurated in 1929 in the grandest possible manner. The Ford Motor Company teamed up with General Electric to reenact Edison's discovery of the electric light bulb in a ceremony presided over by President Hoover and attended by such titans as Charles M. Schwab, Gerard Swope, Otto H. Kahn, Owen D. Young, Henry Morgenthau, and John D. Rockefeller, Jr. History had arrived. Greenfield Village also became a popular success, with attendance figures dwarfing those compiled at the shrines. In 1934, the first year records were kept, 243,000 visited; in 1940, 633,000 stopped by.[24]

Most historians of the Ford phenomenon believe that Greenfield Village lacks any "clear central idea." Keith Sward finds it a "hodge-podge, despite its core of excellent restorations. It has the appearance of an Old Curiosity Shop, magnified 10,000 fold." But there are, I believe, some clear messages embedded in Ford's construction.[25]

The first is that life was better in the "saner and sweeter" Good Old Days of the rural republic. The vehicle to prove this assertion was the early American Village. Perhaps unwittingly, the Village drew upon a well-established European genre—the open-air museum. A brief sketch of that earlier movement will help illuminate Ford's vision.

Back in 1891 Dr. Artur Hazelius had opened Skansen, a seventy-five acre outdoor museum on a site overlooking Stockholm harbor. There he assembled farm buildings from various parts of Sweden and soon added an iron-master's house, a manor house, a log church, windmills, stocks and whipping posts, and a series of craft shops. He staffed the museum with guides dressed in folk costumes, stocked it with farm animals, and threw in strolling musicians and folk dancers. It became quite popular. Similar enterprises soon opened in Norway, Finland, Russia, Germany, Belgium, Wales, and the Netherlands. The Skansen movement blended romantic nostalgia with dismay at the emergence of capitalist social relations. As the new order had introduced mechanized mass production, a burgeoning working class, and class conflict, these museums, often organized by aristocrats and professionals, set out to preserve and celebrate fast-disappearing craft and rural traditions. What they commemorated, and in some degree fabricated, was the life of "the folk," visualized as a harmonious population of peasants and craft workers.[26]

Ford's Greenfield Village can best be understood as an Americanized Skansen. Ford celebrated not "the folk" but the Common Man. He rejected the DAR's approach of exalting famous patriots and patrician elites. Indeed, he banished rich men's homes, lawyers' offices, and banks from his village. This museum-hamlet paid homage to blacksmiths, machinists, and frontier farmers, celebrated craft skills and domestic labor, recalled old social customs like square dancing and folk fiddling, and praised the "timeless and dateless" pioneer virtues of hard work, discipline, frugality, and self-reliance. It was a precapitalist Eden immune to modern ills, peopled with men and women of character. As Ford's friend and collaborator William Symonds wrote during the Depression, a "significant lesson of the Village" was that in the old days, when Americans "looked to themselves for a means of livelihood rather than to an employer," there had been "no destitution such as is seen today in large industrial centers during slack periods."[27]

Ford's village was a static utopia. There was no conflict, no trouble within its grounds. Ford had banished war and politics. He had also—by excluding banks, lawyers, and the upper class—precluded discussions of foreclosure, depressions, and unemployment. That, in turn, obviated the need to refer to farmers' movements,

Candlemaking at Williamsburg Colonial Fair.—*Photo: Colonial Williamsburg Foundation*

strikes, and radical political parties. Ford's thrifty and self-reliant common folk (if only his assembly-line workers had been half so virtuous!) acted as individuals; square dancing was about as close as they got to collective action. There was no hint that nineteenth-century shoemakers and blacksmiths had possessed a vibrant alternative, and often anticapitalist, culture.

Ford did not leave Greenfield Village trapped in an idyllic past. In the Industrial Museum he supplied the motor force of history. The serried ranks of machines, arranged in developmental order, and the tributes to inventors and entrepreneurs like Edison (and himself) conveyed the other unmistakable message of Greenfield Village: life had been getting better and better since the good old days. Progress—as evidenced by ever-improved machines and commodities—had been made not by the farmers and craft workers, but by the mental labor of men of genius and rare vision.

The two messages together—life had been better in the old days and it had been getting better ever since—added up to a corporate employer's vision of history. From the vantage point of the village a gentle criticism of the current order was permitted; the declension in virtue from the times when men were men (and women were women)

could be bemoaned. Still, one would not really want to turn the clock back to those primitive times, so it was best to get on with life, perhaps inspired to emulate not George Washington but the sturdy pioneers. Greenfield Village distorted the past, mystified the way the present had emerged, and thus helped to inhibit effective political action in the future.

But why would the billionaire master of mass production indulge in a vision that contained even a smidgeon of anticapitalist nostalgia? Why would the man who presided, in the 1920s, over a plant regarded as one of the worst sweatshops in Detroit, laud even a fictionalized and gutted old order of farmers and craftsmen? Part of the answer is that by the 1920s Ford had become a most atypical capitalist. Ford Motor, though gigantic, was still a family firm. He hated the newer forms of organization and the initiation of competition through models and colors, instituted by Alfred P. Sloan over at General Motors. He also despised financiers and considered Chrysler a plot by Wall Street bankers to do him in. It was precisely when Ford began to lose out to these new forces, as his biographer, James Brough, notes, that he sought to underline the closer connections of his own business approaches to traditional ways. Greenfield Village took shape at just the time that the Model T was forced into retirement. More broadly, Ford was something of a utopian and really believed that mass production/mass consumption capitalism could be made to work. The upheavals of 1919 had disturbed him, and so he spent the 1920s oscillating between past and future. When it all collapsed in 1929, he turned sour and ugly, bitter toward the bankers he held responsible, and vicious toward his protesting employees. In the 1930s he spent more and more time at Greenfield Village. It became for him a retreat from which he could criticize contemporary society without having to examine too closely the part he had played in creating it.[28]

Greenfield Village departed dramatically from the DAR formula. The other great enterprise of the twenties, John D. Rockefeller, Jr's Colonial Williamsburg, was more rooted in the traditional house museum mode but in the end proved equally revolutionary. Unlike Ford, Rockefeller, Jr. was quite comfortable with the new world of corporate capitalism; he had, after all, been born into it. But what really engaged his mind and spirit was not business, but buildings.[29] In 1923 he embarked on his long career in historic restoration. Attending a June fete at Versailles, he was disturbed to find the walls crumbling and water coming through the roof. He discovered to his dismay that Fontainebleu and Rheims were in a similarly deplorable condition. He immediately sent off a check for a million dollars to the French government to help repair the structures: he added another $1.85 million in 1927. His donations enabled the French to replace acres of roof. Rockefeller was particularly pleased that workers had also been able to revive the thatched houses and hedged lawns of Marie Antoinette's play peasant village, and to restore her marble-walled dairy to working order. It was, he thought, "a perfect dream of beauty and delight."[30]

From fixing up the abodes of French monarchs, Rockefeller turned next to the planter elite of eighteenth-century colonial Virgina. The original idea of resurrecting Williamsburg belonged to W.A.R. Goodwin, a local minister. He had first written to Henry Ford, heatedly insisting that the Motor King underwrite the cost of restoring the town the automobile culture was destroying, the town where Washington, Jefferson, and Patrick Henry had once walked. Ford never answered. But Rockefeller, to whom Goodwin next approached the idea, was hooked. He authorized Goodwin to buy up property in the town anonymously, sending him money under the name of "David's Father." When, in 1928, Goodwin disclosed who was behind the massive purchases, some old southern families were outraged at this intrusion of Yankee gold (as of 1980 a Mrs. Armistead was still refusing to sell). But the majority waved such reservations aside, and restoration began.

Rockefeller and a host of supporting experts selected the 1790s as a cut-off decade and proceeded to demolish all 720 buildings constructed after that and to remove as many traces of modernity as possible, even rerouting the Chesapeake and Ohio railroad. Then they restored 82 surviving eighteenth-century buildings and, after meticulous research, reconstructed 341 buildings of which only the foundations remained. Rockefeller took to spending two months each year in Williamsburg. Ruler in hand, he was all over the site, insisting on scrupulous accuracy, regardless of cost. When architects discovered that they had reconstructed a house six feet from where new research showed it had actually stood, he immediately provided the money to move it. "No scholar," he said, "must ever be able to come to us and say we have made a mistake."[31]

When the bulk of the work had been completed, in the mid-1930s, Rockefeller, at a cost of $79 million, had built an exquisite little eighteenth-century town, clean, tidy, and tasteful. He was delighted. So was Virginia. In 1942 the commonwealth made him an honorary citizen, the first person so honored since the Marquis de Lafayette in 1785.[32]

Williamsburg, however, was far more than simply a personal indulgence a la Antoinette. Nor was it a Greenfield Village. Perhaps Ford's project had whetted Rockefeller's competitive appetite a little. But though there would be craft shops and costumed guides at Colonial Williamsburg, Rockefeller was not the least bit interested in recapturing the culture of "the folk." There were precious few "folk" in evidence, and there was absolutely no reference to the fact that half of eighteenth-century Williamsburg's population had been black slaves. This town commemorated the planter elite, presented as the progenitors of timeless ideals and values, the cradle of that Americanism of which Rockefeller and the corporate elite were the inheritors and custodians. Rockefeller had suggested such a connection as early as 1914. A member of a congressional committee investigating the Ludlow massacre, perpetrated by the Rockefeller family's Colorado Fuel and Iron Company, asked whether he would continue to fight unionization "if that costs all your property and kills all your employees?" Rockefeller responded that he would do whatever was necessary to defend the "great principle" of the open shop: "It was upon a similar principle that the War of the Revolution was carried on."[33]

But Colonial Williamsburg was more than simply the DAR approach writ large. The ancestral societies had saved isolated houses. In a 1937 statement about his motives in building Williamsburg, Rockefeller wrote that "to undertake to preserve a single building when its environment has changed and is no longer in keeping, has always seemed to me unsatisfactory—much less worthwhile." What had attracted him about Williamsburg was that it "offered an opportunity to restore a complete area and free it entirely from alien or inharmonious surroundings." A similar concern for an all-encompassing approach characterized his other projects in the 1920s and 1930s. While he was staking his claim to the past at Williamsburg, he was building Rockefeller Center, his notion of the future, in midtown Manhattan. Tearing down 228 brownstones and stores, he raised in their stead a mammoth entertainment-business complex in which, for the first time, skyscrapers became constituent parts of an integral order. He applied a similar logic and practice to land conservation. Touring western national parks in the mid-twenties, he was appalled to find that Jackson Hole, a valley in the Grand Tetons, was being developed in a hodge-podge, piecemeal fashion. His response was to buy out every single private owner in a 33,000-acre area—ranchers, farmers, lumbering industries, everybody—and deed the land to the U.S. government as a park. Like his father, who had made his fortune by overcoming the anarchy of production by a multitude of individual entrepreneurs in the Pennsylvania coal fields, Rockefeller, Jr. was interested in totalities.[34]

Colonial Williamsburg flows from this perspective. It does not simply borrow and display a historical aura; it embodies a vision of a total social order. Unlike Greenfield Village, Williamsburg's order flows from the top down. It is a corporate world: planned, orderly, tidy, with no dirt, no smell, no visible signs of exploitation. Intelligent and genteel partician elites preside over it; respectable craftsmen run production paternalistically and harmoniously; ladies run well-ordered households with well-ordered families in homes filled with tasteful precious objects. The rest of the population—the 90 percent who create the wealth—are nowhere to be seen. The only whiff of conflict appears in recollections of the stirring anti—British speeches in which the Founders enunciated the timeless principles since passsed down, like heirlooms, to the Rockfellers and their kind. Colonial Williamsburg and Rockfeller Center formed a matching set. Ford, at least, had grappled with history in the course of mystifying it; Rockfeller denied that history had ever happened.

A sleigh ride in Victorian Ontario.—*Photo: Black Creek Pioneer Village*

The crash, Depression, and revival of working-class movements brought the decade of complacent capitalist supremacy to a sudden end. The great corporate and genealogical museum projects would grind on through the thirties, but as the balance of class forces shifted, so did the nature of public history.

Franklin Roosevelt's administration supported new approaches to the past. Partly this was a matter of symbolic politics. He attacked—by mocking—the DAR, reminding them that they were descendants of immigrants and revolutionaries; when they denied Marian Anderson access to Constitution Hall, he supported Eleanor's arranging the famous concert in the Lincloln Memorial.[35] Apart from such cultural signals that elite claims to exclusive possession of the past were now open to question, Roosevelt and his advisors embedded within the federal government an approach to public history that expanded the definition of the historic. Several bureaucratic agencies demonstrated that the state could compete with private capital as guardian of the public memory.

In 1933 a National Park Service architect proposed to Secretary of the Interiror Harold Ickes that unemployed architects be set to work surveying and recording all "historic" buildings in the United States. Within two weeks 1,200 were employed by the Historic American Building Survey (HABS): by 1938, they had produced 24,000 measured drawing and 26,000 photographs of 6,389 historical structures. This campaign was remarkable in that many of the buildings surveyed had no connection whatever to famous men; their historical importance was rooted in local memories and traditions. Similarly, the Works Progress Administration (WPA) set writers and historians to work in the Federal Writers' Project. The WPA state guidebooks and collections of local lore reflected a populist shift away from the approach fostered by traditional and corporate elites, uncovering legacies of struggle and redefining American history as something that included common people as historical actors.

In 1933 the Civilian Conservation Corps began actual restoration projects, and in 1935 the Historical Records Survey hired thousands to inventory public records in every U.S. county.[36] In the same year the Historic Sites Act authorized the Department of the Interior, acting through the National Park Service, to undertake an extraordinary range of preservation activities, including the actual acquisition of property, the preservation and operation of privately owned historic sites, the construction of museums, the development of educational programs, the placement of commemorative tablets, and the perpetuation of survey programs similar to HABS. Almost overnight, a massive federal presence had been authorized. It was not, however, exercised. In a few years the forces of reaction and the onset of war put an end to the New Deal and its public history initiatives.[37]

In the postwar period labor gains were rolled back, left movements were suppressed, and multinationals and the military moved internationally to establish what they hoped would be the American Century. The cultural concomitant of capital's renewed supremacy was the thorough suffusion of cold war ideology, with stultifying effects on public presentations of history. The appropriators of past labor reappropriated labor's past. The populist openings of the thirties were checked and reversed, and the meaning of "historical" was narrowed once again, as the bourgeoisie set out to uproot "un-Americanism" and celebrate, with renewed complacency, "the American Way of Life." This revanchist movement took a variety of forms.

First there was what might be called the Corporate Roots movement. Boeing invested heavily in a new Museum of History and Industry in Seattle in 1952. The American Iron and Steel Institute spent $2,350,000 in 1954 to restore the seventeenth-century ironworks at Saugus, Massachusetts. R. J. Reynolds, Inc., donated substantial funds to restore the Miksch Tobacco Shop in Old Salem in 1957 and went on to pour large amounts into the restoration and "interpretation" of the old Moravian Community. The Stevens family and others in the textile industry sponsored the construction of the Merrimack Valley Textile Museum in the late fifties and early sixties. Most of these enterprises promoted a fetishized history, focusing on technological developments and ignoring social relations of production, to say nothing of class struggle. Visitors to Boeing's museum were not introduced to the Wobblies or the 1919 Seattle General Strike.[38]

Second, several Skansen-type villages were established. The Farmers' Museum at Cooperstown, New York, composed of buildings transported from nearby sites, were dedicated to chronicling the everyday life of pioneer farmers and craftsmen. The museum focused relentlessly on objects and work processes rather than social relations or politics (visitors learning nothing, for example, about the antirent wars in New York State). In the Ford manner, the Farmers' Museum projected a sentimentalized portrait of the past and celebrated the transcendence of primitive living conditions. It romanticized the drudgery of women's domestic labor—"here was a sense of contentment, and satisfaction with a long day's work well done, which we might well envy"—yet also praised the new textile mills as labor-saving devices without asking who worked in those mills or what crises in the country-side had forced women into them.[39]

Another example of this genre was Old Sturbridge Village, which opened in 1946 after a long oscillation between the Ford and Rockefeller approaches. Albert B. Wells, a wealthy businessman, had begun collecting a' la Ford in 1926. In 1936 Wells decided to build a museum village and called in the Williamsburg architectural firm of Perry, Shaw, and Hepburn. He soon fired them believing that they had no feel for the locality and were too much influenced by their collaboration with Rockefeller in a project where they "had all the money in the world." After a visit to the Scandinavian open-air museums in

1938, Wells settled on a plan of bringing together a few local buildings and adding local craftsmen plying the old trades. He wanted to demonstrate both the early new Englanders' "ingenuity and thrift" and the way that "modern industry assures a life far more abundant than what existed under a handicraft system."[40]

The third kind of postwar enterprise was the traditional patriotic shrine, now converted to cold war purposes. One million people visited Mount Vernon in 1948, and in the 1950s new shrines, like the Independence National Historical Park, were opened. But the flagship of the fifties fleet remained Colonial Williamsburg.[41]

In 1939 John D. Rockefeller III became the chairman of the board of Colonial Williamsburg and called for an aggressive educational and public relations campaign. During the war he arranged a liaison program with the armed forces, and troops were brought to Williamsburg for inspirational purposes.[42] The wartime effort proved to be the prelude to a massive cold war enterprise. Rockefeller III, Williamsburg's president, Kenneth Chorley, and the educational director, Edward P. Alexander, set out to make Colonial Williamsburg "a shrine of the American faith," a source of "spiritual strength and understanding" at a "historic time of trial, questioning, and danger." Thomas J. Wertenbaker, a Princeton historian who retired from teaching to work at Williamsburg, stressed in 1949 the political importance of the museum's mission:

> It would be difficult to exaggerate the educational value of historical restorations. At a time when the foundations of our country are under attack, when foreign nations are assailing our free institutions with all the misrepresentations which malice can suggest, when they are seconded by a powerful Fifth Column within our borders, when it has become a frequent practice to attribute selfish motives to Washington and Jefferson and Hancock and Samuel and John Adams...it is of prime importance that we live over again the glorious days which gave us our liberty.[43]

Chorley hoped that millions would come to Williamsburg and be reminded of the ancient heritage of contemporary ideals. John Edwin Pomfret, president of neighboring William and Mary College, suggested that such visits would help Americans "overlook those real or illusory differences of political or economic interest which ordinarily divide us. The flame of the patriots' passion welds us as nothing else can into a spiritual whole."[44]

Alexander, in his capacity as Williamsburg educational director, drew on the latest techniques to "create a historic mood through sensory perception." He wanted to generate a "moving inspiration of the American heritage" for visitors, and to inform them, through guidebooks, precisely what that heritage was. He taught that "eighteenth-century Williamsburg embodied concepts of lasting importance to all men everywhere." There were five such concepts: "opportunity," "individual liberties," "self government," "the integrity of the individual," and "responsible leadership." There was no mention of the concept—much less the reality—of slavery, nor of equally plausible revolutionary legacies like "equality" or "the right of revolution" or "anticolonialism." Williamsburg's concepts, though certainly capable of being invested with democratic meaning, were more often drafted into the service of the status quo. In the 1950s Chorley counseled the nation to follow its leaders as the young nation had harkened to the counsel of the Founding Fathers ("responsible leadership"), arguing that contemporary Americans should recognize that this "is becoming such a world as the Common Man cannot operate."[45]

Alexander's "concepts" could be bent to almost any purpose because they had been detached from the realities of eighteenth-century life. In the 1950s, as in the 1930s, Williamsburg was profoundly ahistorical. Fittingly, it received an accolade from the scholar most committed to the consensus history of the period, Daniel Boorstin. He applauded, as democratic and un-European, Williamsburg's attempt "to reconstruct the way of life of a whole past community." "Williamsburg," Boorstin said, was "an American kind of sacred document." It asserted a "continuity of past and present" and reminded us that "the past," rather than any "political ideology," was the living well-spring of contemporary ideals.[46]

Williamsburg launched aggressive programs to attract visitors. The Williamsburg staff initiated the Student Burgesses program, which brought together student leaders to discuss the nature of Freedom; International Assemblies for foreign students, at which they could learn about American ideals; and Democracy Workshops (co-sponsored by the U.S. Junior Chamber of Commerce and the Radio-Electronic-Television manufacturers Association) on freedom of expression. At the 1955 Democracy Workshop—co-moderated by the president of the American Committee for Liberation for Bolshevism—Vannevar Bush explained that preservation of the Bill of Rights would depend on a "natural aristocracy."[47]

With the arrival of the Eisenhower administration in 1953, Williamsburg became a semiofficial auxiliary of the state, a site of great bourgeois rituals and political ceremonies. Williamsburg served as the customary arrival point for heads of state on their way to Washington. Winthrop Rockefeller would greet the arriving dignitaries and ride them down Duke of Gloucester Street in an eighteenth-century carriage; the guests would make brief remarks; they might attend an evening's ball at the Governor's Palace; and the next day they would proceed to Washington. Over a hundred heads of state went through this Rockefeller rite. Nor were lesser luminaries ignored. Together with the Department of State and the United States Information Agency, Williamsburg worked out a foreign visit program for political and professional leaders, and hundreds came to town each year. (The trustees also made foreign visits themselves, as when they presented the Williamsburg Award to Win-

Recreating an 1870s Decoration Day in New England.—*Photo: Kenneth E. Mahler, Mystic Seaport*

ston Churchill at a glittering gathering at Drapers' Hall, London, in 1955. Churchill fondly recalled in mellow after-dinner remarks, that his 1946 Williamsburg visit had helped him recapture "the grace and the ease, the charm of by-gone colonial days.") By the late 1950s, Williamsburg required a staff of over 1,900 people to manage its booming affairs.[48]

In the 1960s there occurred another transformation in the museum field. Again it was closely connected to larger social and political developments. Since the late 1940s the highway and housing industries had been tearing up the material, cultural, and historical fabric of the country. State-backed developers rammed roads through cities, demolishing whole areas; urban renewal then devastated much of the remaining urban landscape. By 1966 fully one half of the properties recorded by HABS in the thirties had been torn down.[49]

By the early sixties the people most threatened with urban dislocation and disruption had begun to protest. Amid this ferment, a small band of social scientists, architectural critics, psychologists, and journalists began to fashion a compelling critique of the social and psychological consequences of the urban renewal and highway

programs. People like Jane Jacobs, Herbert Gans, Edward Hall, and Ada Louise Huxtable argued that the demolition shattered social networks and healthy urban communities, replacing them with bleak new high-rise projects and sterile suburbs. The new housing forms, they argued, denied human needs for historical connectedness; suburbs and projects alike undermined individual and social indentities by ripping people out of history.[50]

These social critics and others long involved with the historic preservation movement noted that the history museums exhibited a similar temporal one-dimensionality and historical disconnectedness. And so, in the course of criticizing the American present, they leveled their guns on the American past. Colonial Williamsburg, Huxtable thought, "pickled the past." It lacked "any sense of reality, vitality or historic continuity." David Lowenthal found this to be true of most of the museums: "The American past is not permitted to coexist with the present. It is always in quotation marks and fancy dress...an isolated object of reverence and pleasure...detached, remote, and essentially lifeless." The sterility of the museums now came under scrutiny. "Williamsburg," Walter Muir Whitehill thought, is a "fantasy in which the more pleasing aspects of colonial life are meticulously evoked, with the omission of smells, flies, pigs, dirt and slave quarters." It was "history homogenized, cleaned up, and expurgated...an entirely artificial recreation of an imaginary past."[51]

"Williamsburg," another critic noted, "has the flavor of a well-kept contemporary suburb." Others pointed out that the reverse was also true: postwar suburbs looked like Colonial Williamsburg. This was not mere coincidence. Banks and insurance companies had accepted "false colonial" as a sound style on which to base their lending programs, and so vast areas of the East and Midwest modeled themselves on the restoration. During the fifties the United Sates was "Williamsburgered": there were Williamsburg drive-ins, Williamsburg hotels, Williamsburg gas stations, Williamsburg A&Ps. Small wonder that Daniel Boorstin saw past and present as continuous: past and present looked remarkably alike.[52]

To this set of criticisms, rooted in resistance to wholesale devastation of historic properties and urban neighborhoods, was added another critique that came out of the political upheavals of the decade. Black, feminist, Native American, and antiwar (hence anti-national-chauvinist) activists began producing history in order to grasp the deep-rooted nature of the processes they were protesting against and to dismantle those readings of the past that provided powerful justifications for the status quo. In this climate of increasingly widespread awareness of the selective and distorted character of official history, the history museums' celebratory certainties became harder to sustain.

These various streams of thought and action produced a great ferment in the history museum field in the 1960s and 1970s. Grassroots museums sprang up around the country to preserve and commemorate local heritages. Many were amateur enterprises with an anticommercial ethic. "We are not out for the almighty buck," wrote one of the citizens of Russell Springs, Kansas, who saved their old courthouse and used it to display antiques, diaries, manuscripts, and memorabilia contributed by town residents. "We simply want to show people our past, of which we are rightly proud." Black residents in Bedford-Stuyvesant, New York, rallied in 1969 to block the demolition of four farmhouses that had been the nucleus of a nineteenth-century free black community and converted them into a black history museum. "One does not have to be a member of the Daughters of the American Revolution to be interested and concerned about their roots," insisted a black Kansas City preservationist: "It was good that we saved, and now maintain, Williamsburg, Virginia. And for the same reasons, we must save and maintain the slave cabins and some of the shotgun houses, little frame churches, jails and one-room school houses around the country that tell the story of black people in America."[53]

There were also instances of fruitful collaboration between community groups and younger historians whose work reflected a critical approach to the past. At Lowell, Massachusetts, community and university people produced a museum—housed in a still-working textile mill—that examined the history of the town from a perspective sensitive to working-class history and diverse ethnic cultures, and attuned as well to the nature of capitalist development in the nineteenth century.[54]

Many of the professional history museums changed with the times as well.[55] Some abandoned the filiopietistic approach (in some cases only after considerable internal conflict), insisted on rigorous standards of historical accuracy, and adopted the premises of the social historians then practicing in the academy. Many developed imaginative strategies for creating a more comprehensive portrait of past communities.

In the middle and late 1960s museologists unhappy with static reconstructions launched the Living Historical Farm movement. They sought to create a dynamic picture of farm life by organizing working farms that employed old agricultural processes. At some of these, like Plymouth, Massachusetts, interpreters lived in the old houses to accustom themselves to the furnishings and work practices. Structures developed a lived-in-look; chickens and sheep wandered in and out of the buildings, which consequently became (as they once had been) fly-ridden and smelly. Abandoning Howard Johnson standards of cleanliness allowed a marked gain in historical accuracy. Even where simulations were not taken so far, as at Old Sturbridge Village, the museums reflected the influence of a new generation of historians and educators concerned with exploring work and family life with ever-higher standards of accuracy and, in some cases, with an eye to modern parallels.[56]

The waves of change even beat against the walls of Williamsburg. Winthrop Rockefeller stayed at the helm until his death in 1973, when Supreme Court Justice Lewis Powell took over, and Rockefeller money continued to flow; so did the stream of domestic and foreign dignitaries (the Shah of Iran stopped by three times). Still, the pressures were intense. A series of blistering critiques lambasted Williamsburg's focus on elites, its pinched definition of the revolutionary legacy, its stopped-time quality, its genteel banishment of dirt, disarray, and disorder.[57] One of the few people who had anything good to say about Williamsburg during this period was Alvin Toffler, and he liked it precisely because it was so unreal. A future-shocked society, he argued, will "need enclaves of the past—communities in which turnover, novelty and choice are deliberately limited. These may be communities in which history is partially frozen....Unlike Williamsburg,...however,...tomorrow's enclaves of the past must be places where people faced with future shock can escape the pressures of overstimulation for weeks, months, even years, if they choose."[58]

Finally, in the 1970s, slavery was discovered at Williamsburg. The 1972 edition of the guidebook maintained Alexander's interpretive framework of the five concepts (he retired that year), but noted that, for example, the concept of individual integrity had been conspicuously limited in reality for slaves, women, debtors, and others. This trend was continued during that decade as a new, "modernizing" management team brought in a staff of young social historians who felt ill at ease with the traditional approach and who worked to transform the interpretive program. They consulted local black community groups and black historians on how to include the slave experience at Williamsburg and employed some imaginative street-theater techniques as a beginning. Alexander himself came to agree that the museums had been "too neat and clean, and [did] not pay enough attention to the darker side of human existence—to poverty, disease, ignorance and slavery," and he called for interpretations that would appeal "not only to the affluent and the elite, but also to the underprivileged and the discontented."[59]

But if the limits of the acceptable had been pushed back, limits remained nonetheless. Many museums abandoned "the American heritage" notion for a more pluralistic conception of the U.S. past: Williamsburg was now willing to set the story of the black slaves alongside the story of the planters. What they were less willing to tackle were the relations between those classes. Much in the manner of some of the "new social history," they shied away from politics and struggle: slave culture was one thing; slave revolts were another. Nor did the museums often explore how the present evolved out of the past. Williamsburg did not, for example, explain the economic connections between eighteenth-century slavery and twentieth-century sharecropping and debt peonage, or slavery's cultural legacies of racism and black nationalism. Admitting that the reality of exploitation contradicted the ideal of liberty was only a first step.

These limits were interconnected and reinforced each other. The refusal to confront internal conflicts lent a static and falsely harmonious quality to the projects, which in turn diminished their capacity to explain historical movement and bring their stories down to the present. Many of the farm museums concentrated on sowing and reaping; they balked at examining tenantry, foreclosures, world markets, commodity exchanges— the process of capitalist development at work in the countryside—and the agrarian movements that responded to these processes. They were therefore unlikely to help visitors understand how the old family farms (whose values many of the Living Museums enshrined) had succumbed to the corporate agri-businesses that today dominate American agriculture. Some industrial museums could now explore, often quite critically, the unfortunate living conditions of textile workers in the 1850s; the most advanced could even admit to historical memory the legacy of strikes. But it proved more difficult to locate the source of these problems in the dynamics of a capitalist political economy, dynamics that are still at work.

Alexander pointed to one crucial reason for the museums' reluctance to press beyond these limits when he noted, in his 1979 retrospective, that the museums were not interested in "securing social change." The disconnection of past from present and the separation of culture from politics was itself a political act. History was to be confined to providing entertainment, nostalgia, or interesting insights into vanished ways of life. It was not to be freed to become a powerful agent for understanding—and changing—the present.[60]

J. H. Plumb has noted that the "acquisition of the past by ruling and possessing classes and the exclusion of the mass of the peasantry and laboring class is a widespread phenomenon through recorded time."[61] I have argued that history museums were one way the dominant classes in the United States—wittingly or unwittingly— appropriated the past.

They did so, first, by presenting particular interpretations. Of course the museums cannot be faulted for having read the past selectively. There is, after all, no such thing as "the past." All history is a production—a deliberate selection, ordering, and evaluation of past events, experiences, and processes. The objection is rather that the museums incorporated selections and silences on such an order that they falsified reality and became instruments of class hegemony.[62] The museums generated conventional ways of seeing history that justified the historic mission of capitalists and lent a naturalism and inevitability to their authority. Perhaps more important, they generated ways of not seeing. By obscuring the origins and development of capitalist society, by eradicating exploitation, racism, sexism, and class struggle from the historical record, by covering up the existence of broad-based oppositional traditions and popular cultures, and by rendering the majority of the population invisible as shapers of history, the museums inhibited the capacity of visitors to imagine alternative social orders—past or future.

The museums served established power in a more indirect way as well. Quite apart from any particular message a museum suggested, its very structure promulgated a deeper one: history was irrelevant to present-day concerns. Recall here that the museums emerged in an inhospitable culture, one marked by a profound contempt for encrusted tradition. Businessmen had few qualms about demolishing the past in the interest of profit, and ruling groups took much longer to become attentive to the uses of the past than did their European counterparts. When patrician women and mugwumps turned to the past to legitimate their social order, their interventions necessarily took the form of rescuing isolated bits of the old order from the juggernaut of progress. The museums became preserves where the past, an endangered species, might be kept alive for visitors to see. The museums and other "genuine historical places" thus conveyed, by their very form, the idea that the past was something sharply separated from the present. History became antiquarianism—pleasant but irrelevant to present concerns. The museums did nothing to help visitors understand that a critical awareness of history, although not a sufficient guide to effective action in the present, was an indispensable precondition for it, and a potentially powerful tool for liberation.

If we now know a little about the museums' messages, we know a great deal less about how they are (and have been) received. Reception, in part, depends on who is listening, and we do not know who visits the museums. It is clear that there has been a steady increase in their popularity.[63] There is some evidence that current museumgoers are better-off and better educated than the average American; almost certainly they are overwhelmingly white, although schoolchildren are bussed in from inner-city ghettos in large numbers.[64]

Nor do we know why people go. One hypothesis often advanced is that increased attendance is simply a function of the spread of automobile culture and the increase in leisure time. There is clearly some truth to this, but vacationers could motor elsewhere. The museums have some obvious appeal: many are charming places that demonstrate interesting old craft techniques and exhibit quaint old objects; there are, after all, real pleasures in antiquarianism. The museums are also safe, well promoted, and one of the few available "family" experiences. Probing a bit deeper, some analysts suggest that the sterility of suburban life generates an attraction to places embodying a sense of authenticity and human scale.[65]

Perhaps advanced capitalism itself has fostered a desire to visit these mythic precapitalist enclaves. If there is indeed a human need for temporal connectedness, then capitalism's ruthless destruction of the old—its severing of people from one another across time as well as in space—may have created a desire to reestablish linkages to the past. The postwar years, after all, witnessed the breakup of tight local, ethnic, and regional communities, the fragmentation of families, the increasing segregation of the population into age ghettos, the devitalization of folk traditions, and the rise of corporate-dominated mass communications. It is conceivable that these concomitants of capitalist development made it more difficult for people to hand down their own history to the next generation and that citizens have been, in this as in other areas, partially transformed into consumers. Were tradition alive and vibrant, people might not be so willing to pay to visit these embalmed remnants of the past: zoos did not become popular until everyday familiarity with animals had become a thing of the past.[66]

Nor do we know what visitors come away with. Perhaps the well-off find their world ratified. Perhaps those not so well served by the status quo nevertheless prove susceptible to the museums' messages. But maybe they invest the messages with different meanings. There are, after all, truly radical dimensions to the U.S. tradition, and the shrines may serve to celebrate democratic as well as capitalist values.

Scholars have only just begun to investigate popular attitudes toward the past, so we are in no position to render definitive judgments. There are some heartening signs that popular memories of radical traditions are still intact, and we would do well to explore that possibility. Most Americans, however, know relatively little about their past and have an underdeveloped sense of how history happens. This is not a reflection on popular intelligence, but an estimate of the strength of our historicidal culture. People are clearly interested in the past, but when they seek understanding they are confronted with institutions (of which the museums are only one) that tend to diminish their capacity to situate themselves in time. The political consequences of this impoverished historical consciousness are profound, and it is a critical task for historians to contest those institutions which promote it.

If we are to take part in the history museum movement, it is important to assess what lies ahead for it. The burden of my argument has been that this question cannot be answered without considering the social and political state of the nation. The eighties are a period of right-wing offensives. Those who seek to repeal working-class, women's and black gains in the present are also working to reverse their gains in the field of history. It is necessary to resist these moves to reappropriate the past.[67]

One avenue is to work with the local museums created in recent years, many of which might survive because they are community-supported and not critically dependent on state funds. We should also support the more established museums in what I think will be their spirited resistance to any attempts to reimpose right-wing nostalgia. The social history movement, despite its limitations, was a decided advance, and should be defended. Critics have been too quick to dismiss the Williamsburgs out of hand. Despite their origins, there are splendid possibilities inherent in them for popularizing a meaningful and critical history.

More generally, as participants in the work, or as supportive critics, we should urge the museums to press ahead beyond social history to become places that deal with politics as well as culture; that reconstruct processes as well as events; that explain the social relations as well as the forces of production at work in the societies whose stories they seek to tell. The museums should give credit to historical actors where due, but stop short of inculcating an incapacitating awe. If their subjects were critics of their society, the museums should refuse to blunt the jagged edges of the original message. The museums should work to break down the distinctions between amateur and professional that stultify both. They should walk that difficult line between, on the one hand, fostering a defintion of the present solely in terms of the past, and, on the other, disconnecting the past so thoroughly from the present that we forget that people in the past produced the matrix of constraints and possibilities within which we act in the present. Above all, the museums should consider it their fundamental mission to assist people to become historically informed makers of history.

Acknowledgments

My thanks—as much for their patience as for their invaluable assistance—to Sue Benson, Steve Brier, Ted Burrows, Janet Corpus, Vicki de Grazia, Susan Henderson, Mike Merrill, Roy Rosenzweig, Alan Wolfe, and the New York MARHO Collective.

1. Cited in David Lowenthal, "The American Way of History," *Columbia University Forum*, 9:3 (Summer 1966), 28.

2. Charles B. Hosmer, Jr., *Presence of the Past: A History of the Preservation Movement in the United States Before Williamsburg* (New York, 1965), 35-37; Richard Caldwell, *A True History of the Acquisition of Washington's Headquarters at Newburgh by the State of New York* (Salisbury Mills, N.Y., 1887), 21.

3. Hosmer, *Presence*, 42-43.

4. Grace King, *Mount Vernon on the Potomac: History of the Mount Vernon Ladies' Association of The Union* (New York, 1919), 22; Mount Vernon Ladies Association, *Historical Sketch of Ann Pamela Cunningham, "The Southern Matron,"* Founder of the "Mount Vernon Ladies' Association" (Jamaica, N.Y., 1903), 20. On the Washington cult see Hosmer, *Presence*, 44-46; George B. Forgie, *Particide in the House Divided: A Psychological Interpretation of Lincoln and His Age* (New York, 1979), 168-99; Michael Kammen, *A Season of Youth: The American Revolution and the Historical Imagination* (New York, 1978), 252 and passim.

5. Hosmer, *Presence*, 39; Kammen, *A Sense of Youth*, 59-60.

6. Laurence Vail Coleman, *Historic House Museums* (Washington, D.C., 1933), 20.

7. John Higham, *Strangers in the Land: Patterns of American Nativism, 1860-1920* (New Brunswick, N.J., 1955), 45-63; Wallace Evans Davies, *Patriotism on Parade*, (Cambridge, Mass., 1955), 46.

8. Barbara Miller Solomon, *Ancestors and Immigrants: A Changing New England Tradition* (New York, 1956), 29-30; Hosmer, *Presence*, 55, 66-70, 73, 88-89, 122, 126-7; Davies, *Patriotism*, 44-73; Margaret Gibbs, *The DAR*, (New York, 1969), 32-76.

9. Hosmer, *Presence*, 55; Davies, *Patriotism*, 79-82.

10. Lewis Mumford, *Sticks and Stones: A Study of American Architecture and Civilization* (New York, 1924), 123-54.

11. Hosmer, *Presence*, 237-59; Matthew Josephson, *The Robber Barons: The Great American Capitalists, 1861-1901* (New York, 1934), 332-46.

12. Hosmer, *Presence*, 138-39; Kammen, *A Season of Youth*, 219.

13. See, for example, Herbert Gutman, *Work, Culture, and Society in Industrializing American* (New York, 1977).

14. Solomon, *Ancestors and Immigrants*, 87.

15. The ancestral societies continued their efforts, however. By 1930 there were over four hundred house museums, the bulk of them patriotic enterprises of the older sort. Coleman, *House of Museums*, 20.

16. James Warren Prothro, *The Dollar Decade: Business Ideas in the 1920s* (Baton Rouge, 1954), 4, 191.

17. Hosmer, *Presence*, 153-93.

18. Higham, *Strangers*, 248; John B. Rae, ed., *Henry Ford* (Englewood Cliffs, N.J., 1969), 5; William Greenleaf, *From These Beginnings: The Early Philanthropies of Henry and Edsel Ford, 1911-1936*, (Detroit, 1964), 96.

19. Walter Karp, "Greenfield Village," *American Heritage*, 32 (Dec. 1980), 101-2.

20. Ibid., 102-3; Geoffrey C. Upward, *A Home for Our Heritage: The Building and Growth of Greenfield Village and Henry Ford Museum, 1929-1979* (Dearborn, Mich., 1979), 1-21.

21. Roger Butterfield, "Henry Ford, the Wayside Inn, and the Problem of 'History is Bunk,' " *Proceedings of the Massachusetts Historical Society*, 76 (1965), 57-66; David L. Lewis, *The Public Image of Henry Ford: An American Folk Hero and His Company* (Detroit, 1976), 225-26; James Brough, *The Ford Dynasty: An American Story* (New York, 1977), 161; Karp, "Greenfield Village," 102.

22. Walter Muir Whitehill, *Independent Historical Societies* (Boston, 1962), 466; Greenleaf, *From These Beginnings*, 71-112; Karp, "Greenfield Village," 104.

23. Upward, *Home*, 21-58.

24. Lewis, *Public Image*, 278-81.

25. Keith Sward, *The Legend of Henry Ford* (New York, 1948), 259-75; Allan Nevins and Frank Ernest Hill, *Ford: Expansion and Challenge, 1915-1933* (New York, 1957), 504-5.

26. R. Douglas Hurt, "Agricultural Museums: A New Frontier for the Social Sciences,"*History Teacher*, 11:3 (May 1978), 368-69; Nathan

27. William Adams Symonds, *Henry Ford and Greenfield Village* (New York, 1938), 183.

28. See Karp, "Greenfield Village," for an alternative interpretation.

29. Raymond B. Fosdick, *John D. Rockefeller, Jr.: A Portrait* (New York, 1956); Alvin Moscow, *The Rockefeller Inheritance* (Garden City, N.Y., 1977).

30. Fosdick, *Rockefeller*, 356-57.

31. Cabell Phillips, "The Town That Stopped the Clock," *American Heritage*, 11 (Feb. 1960), 22-25; Fosdick, *Rockefeller*, 282-300; Rutherford Goodwin, *A Brief and True Report Concerning Williamsburg in Virginia* (Williamsburg, 1936); *Colonial Williamsburg: The First Twenty-Five Years, A Report by the President* (Williamsburg, 1951), 7-18.

32. Colonial Williamsburg, *The President's Report* (Williamsburg, 1962), 32. Hereafter, all presidents' reports will be cited as PR.

33. Testimony before the House Committee on Mines and Mining, in *New York Times*, April 7, 1914, 2; Graham Adams, *The Age of Industrial Violence, 1910-1915* (New York, 1966).

34. John D. Rockefeller, Jr., "The Genesis of the Williamsburg Restoration," *National Geographic Magazine*, April 1937, 401; Moscow, *Rockefeller*, 104-6; Manfredo Tafuri and Francesco Dal Co, *Modern Architecture* (New York, 1979), 232. See E. R. Chamberlain, *Preserving the Past* (London, 1979), 43-50.

35. *The Public Papers and Addresses of Franklin D. Roosevelt, 1938* vol. (New York, 1941), 158-61.

36. Thomas F. King, Patricia Parker Hickman, and Gary Berg, *Anthropology in Historic Preservation: Caring for Culture's Clutter* (New York, 1977), 22; Wolf Von Eckardt, "Federal Follies: The Mismanaging of Historic Preservation," *Historic Preservation* (Jan.-Feb. 1980), 2 (hereafter cited as *HP*); Weinberg, *Preservations*, 24; Edward Francis Barrese, "The Historical Records Survey: A Nation Acts to Save Its Memory" (Ph.D. diss., George Washington University, 1980).

37. King, Hickman, and Berg, *Anthropology*, 23, 202-4; Ronald F. Lee, "The Preservation of Historic and Architectural Monuments in the United States," *National Council for Historic Sites and Buildings Newsletter*, 1 (Dec. 1949), 2 (hereafter cited as *NCHSB Newsletter*).

38. Whitehill, *Independent Historical Societies*, 386-90, 469-70; Frank Stella, et al., *New Profits from Old Buildings; Private Enterprise Approaches to Making Preservation Pay* (New York, 1979), 247-48; Merrimack Valley Textile Museum, *The Housing of a Textile Collection, Occasional Report No. 1* (North Andover, Mass., 1968), 7-12.

39. My interpretation is based on a 1980 visit and an examination of old exhibits.

40. Richard M. Candee, "Old Sturbridge Village: From Model Village to Village Model," paper presented at Society of Architectural Historians, April 1975; A.B. Wells, *Old Quinabaug Village* (Sturbridge, Mass., 1941), 4.

41. Lee, "Preservation," 8.

42. CW News, *Fiftieth Anniversary Issue* (November 27, 1976), 4.

43. *Colonial Williamsburg: The First Twenty-five Years*, 10, 12, 18; Thomas Wertenbaker, "Historic Restorations in the United States," *NCHSB Newsletter*, 1 (Sept. 1949), 9.

44. Kenneth Chorley, "Historical Preservation—Issues and Problems, 1948," *NCHSB Quarterly Report*, 1 (March 1949), 2; Colonial Williamsburg and the College of William and Mary, *They Gave Us Freedom* (Williamsburg, 1951), 5.

45. Daniel J. Boorstin, "Past and Present in America: A Historian Visits Colonial Williamsburg," *Commentary*, Jan. 1958, 4; Edward P. Alexander, "Historical Restorations," in William B. Hesseltine and Donald R. McNeil, eds., *In Support of Clio: Essays in Memory of Herbert A. Kellar* (Madison, 1958), 195; Edward P. Alexander, *The Museum: A Living Book of History* (Detroit, 1959), 13; Kenneth Chorley, *The New Commonwealth of the Intellect* (London, 1958), 23-24.

46. Boorstin, "Past and Present," 3, 5-6. In 1969 Boorstin was appointed to the board of Colonial Williamsburg.

47. These developments are discussed in the presidents' reports of the 1950s. Bush is quoted in *PR* (1955), 14.

48. *PR* (1959), 37; *PR* (1955), 13; *CW News, Fiftieth Anniversary*, 10; *CW, Proceedings of the Presentation of the Williamsburg Award by*

the Trustees of Colonial Williamsburg to the Rt. Hon. Sir Winston Churchill at Drapers' Hall, London, December 7, 1955 (Williamsburg, 1957).

49. Weinberg, *Preservation*, 30.

50. Peirce F. Lewis, "The Future of the Past: Our Clouded Vision of Historic Preservation," *Pioneer America*, 7 (July 1975), 1-20.

51. Ada Louise Huxtable, "Dissent at Colonial Williamsburg," *New York Times*, Sept. 22, 1963; Ada Louise Huxtable, "Lively Original Versus Dead Copy," *New York Times* May 9, 1965; Lowenthal, "American Way," 31; Walter Muir Whitehill, "Promoted to Glory...": The Origin of Preservation in the United States," in Albert Rains, et al., eds., *With Heritage So Rich* (New York, 1966), 43.

52. Carl Feiss, "Preservation of Historic Areas in the United States," *HP*, 16:4 (1964), 145; Lowenthal, "American Way," 31.

53. America the Beautiful Fund, *Old Glory: A Pictorial Report on the Grass Roots History Movement and the First Hometown History Primer* (New York, 1973), 63; on the Society for the Preservation of Weeksville and Bedford-Stuyvesant History, see *HP*, 31 (March-April 1979), 23; Joe Louis Mattox, "Ghetto or Gold Mine—Hold On to That Old House," *American Preservationist*, 1 (Feb.-March 1978), 4.

54. Personal visit and interview with museum staff and university historians.

55. Not all did, however. See George L. Wrenn, III, "What Is a Historic House Museum?" *HP*, 23 (Jan.-March 1971), 55-57.

56. Hurt, "Agricultural Museums," 367-75; James Deetz, "The Changing Historic House Museum—Can It Live?" *HP*, 23 (Jan.-March 1971), 51-54; Darwin P. Kelsey, "Old Sturbridge Village Today," *Antiques* (1979), 826-43; G. Terry Sharrer, "Hitching History to the Plow," *HP*, 32 (Nov.-Dec. 1980), 42-49.

57. See, for example, Wrenn, "Historic House Museum," 55-56; David Lowenthal, "Past Time, Present Place: Landscape and Memory," *Georgraphical Review*, 65 (Jan. 1975), 1-36; Lewis, "Future of the Past," passim; Frank Barnes, "Living History: Clio—or Cliopatria," *History News*, 29 (Sept. 1974), 202. Thomas J. Schlereth's excellent survey presents the new consensus in summary form: "It Wasn't That Simple," *Museum News*, 56 (Jan.-Feb. 1978), 36-44.

58. Alvin Toffler, *Future Shock* (New York, 1970), 390-91.

59. CW, *Official Guidebook*, 7th ed. (Williamsburg, 1979), x-xi; Gary Carson, "From the Bottom Up," *History News*, 35 (Jan. 1980), 7-9; Shomer Zwelling "Social History Hits the Streets: Williamsburg Characters Come to Life," *History News*, 35 (Jan. 1980), 10-12; James R. Short, "Black History at Colonial Williamsburg," *Colonial Williamsburg Today*, 2 (Winter 1980), 10-11; Alexander, *Museums in Motion*, 210-11.

60. Alexander, *Museums in Motion*, 222. The disconnection of past and present generated peculiar but instructive difficulties. At Williamsburg, Rockefeller had stopped time just before that junction at which artisanal production succumbed to capitalist social relations. Williamsburg craft workers went through actual apprentice programs and had to have a masterpiece approved by other masters around the country and by Colonial Williamsburg, Inc. One problem with this system was that the craft workers could not, as the real ones did, develop their art; they had always to produce in the same style. This inhibition was enhanced by CW's desire to sell their pewter candlesticks and silver bowls as commodities. Indeed, when the old methods failed to keep up with demand, a modern factory was set up (not, of course, in the historic area), which churned these products out. And when the master silversmiths said that they wanted the profits from such sales—their forebears, after all, had owned their finished products—CW briskly reminded them of the facts of capitalist life: despite their wigs and shoppes, they were employees. The silversmiths departed from CW in a huff to set up their own company.

61. J. H. Plumb, *The Death of the Past* (Boston, 1970), 30.

62. See Raymond Williams' excellent discussion and deployment of this kind of analysis in *Politics and Letters* (London, 1979), 324-29, and *The Country and the City* (New York, 63, 1975), 22-34, 120-26.

63. Attendance at CW went from 166,251 in 1947, to 708,974 in 1967, to over 1,200,000 in 1976. Greenfield Village passed the 1,000,000 mark in 1960 and hit 1,701,559 in 1973; and Mount Vernon drew over a million visitors in 1975. William T. Alderson and Shirley Payne Low, *Interpretation of Historic Sites*, (Nashville, 1976), 22; Tony P. Wren, "The Tourist Industry and Promotional Publications," *HP*, 16 (May-June 1964), 111; Eleanor Thompson, "Mt. Vernon, America's Oldest Preservation Project: Past Accomplishments, Present Status, Future Prospects" (precis), *Journal of the Society of Architectural Historians*, 35 (Dec. 1976), 264; Lewis, *Public Image*, 280.

64. An unpublished 1979 Williamsburg survey found that 64 percent of their visitors had total family incomes over $25,000, and 17 percent had incomes over $50,000; 54 percent had some graduate credit or a graduate degree.

65. Wren, "Tourist Industry," 111, 112.

66. John Berger, *About Looking* (New York, 1980).

67. See Walter LaFeber, "The Last War, the Next War, and the New Revisionists," *Democracy*, 1 (Jan. 1981), 93-103; and Paul Berman, "Gas Chamber Games: Crackpot History and the Right to Life," *Village Voice*, (June 10-16, 1981), 1ff.

A Short Natural History of Nostalgia

28

Anthony Brandt

After outlining the history of nostalgia as a "disease," Brandt examines its impact on the development of "museum villages" and "historic restorations" in America. In this article which originally was published in the December 1978 issue of Atlantic Monthly *Brandt especially notes the motivation of Henry Ford in restoring the Wayside Inn and creating his Edison Institute. Colonial Williamsburg, Sleepy Hollow Restorations, Old Sturbridge Village, Mystic Seaport, and both Disneyland and Disney World are built on a foundation of nostalgia, Brandt argues. He does not mean that they are not needed; rather he contends that, "as islands of feeling in a largely unfeeling present, they provide a kind of relief we may need to keep our sanity. They represent values which, however unlikely it is that they were ever embodied in the actual past, at least attest to the endurance in us of a vision, a dream of an alternative way of life, quieter, more contented, in the fullest sense of the word, gentler."*

Except for a few acute cases, the nostalgia we see around us seems to be little more than a mild, sentimental longing for days gone by, a feeling which finds its most visible expression in television shows set in the 1950s, revivals of old Broadway musicals, a rage for the cheap oak furniture mass-produced in the early 1900s, clothing styles that veer back to the 1920s or 1940s, or whatever decade captures the designers' fancy, a run on Mickey Mouse watches, and so on. Perhaps aptly, nostalgia has been connected with a knowledge of trivia: the name of the drummer in Glen Miller's band, the year Pee Wee Reese retired, the name of the actor who played the guard in Jack Benny's vault. Who cares? Trivial facts for a trivial feeling. Was nostalgia ever anything but this superficial enthusiasm for the out-of-date?

We ought not to be fooled. The extent to which we are unaware of the depth of an emotion is the extent to which it controls us. In the case of nostalgia we are dealing not with a simple emotion such as fear, anger, or desire, which belongs to our evolutionary heritage, but with a complicated emotion, appearing in Western culture at a definite time, whose apparently trivial manifestations cover what was once, and may still be, genuine anguish. Nostalgia is an emotion with a history, in other words, and unless we know something about that history we can have little understanding of its impact on our lives.

Before nostalgia there was homesickness—what Ovid felt, exiled from his beloved Rome to the shores of the Black Sea, or what saddened the Crusaders in Palestine. With homesickness went its remedies, the Stoic ideal of cosmopolitanism, which held that a man should be at home anywhere, and the related Christian belief that life itself was a form of exile. Pope Urban II, urging the assembled dignitaries of the Council of Clermont to undertake the first Crusade, mentioned them both: "No love of native heath should delay you for in one sense the whole world is exile for a Christian, and in another the whole world is his country: so exile is our fatherland, our fatherland exile." This Christian Stoicism prevailed until the seventeenth century; it is the attitude we find in Robert Burton's encyclopedia *Anatomy of Melancholy*, published in 1621. Burton devotes less than a page to the homesickness of the exile. His remedies are the standard ones: "Every land is the brave man's land," and "All places are distant from Heaven alike."

By 1688 all this had changed; the sadness of the exile had become so intense that people were, some thought, actually dying of homesickness. In that year an Alsatian medical student named Johannes Hofer published a treatise on the subject and coined the word "nostalgia," from Greek roots meaning "home" and "pain." Hofer's was only the first of many medical treatises devoted to what had suddenly and inexplicably become a disease, often fatal in its consequences. At first the disease was confined almost exclusively to Swiss mercenaries to be known as "the Swiss disease." Typically one of these mercenaries would hear someone singing the "Ranz des vaches," a Swiss mountain song, and the longing for his homeland aroused by the song would plunge him into profound melancholy, which nothing could cure. He would grow pale and listless, lose his appetite, and at last take to his bed, where he would literally pine away. Eventually the disease spread to other countries; an English doctor reported a case of it in 1787, and in 1838 Balzac wrote to a friend: "Dear, I suffer homesickness. . . I come and go without any spirit, without being able to say what I have, and if I remained this way for two weeks, I should die." He was not speaking metaphorically. The disease was serious. People were afraid to travel too far from home; to travel was to risk death from nostalgia. A medical dissertation on nostalgia appeared as late as 1873. Not until the beginning of the twentieth century did nostalgia fade entirely out of medicine.

The history of nostalgia as a disease raises a number of interesting questions about the epidemiology of psychosomatic illness, but we cannot go into them here. Suffice it to say that other psychosomatic illnesses have appeared and disappeared in similar fashion. Hysteria was once a medical syndrome with a precise symptomatology, as anyone familiar with Freud's early work knows; the syndrome as Freud described it has more or less vanished, but many of us are likely to become hysterical from time to time. Perhaps it is inevitable that new feelings should be seen at first as aberrations. In any case, what concerns us now is the process by which nostalgia lost its character as exclusively a disease and spread into Western culture at large. This was not a process of simply domesticating the disease. The disease did not disappear with the development of nostalgic feeling. When we talk about the feeling of nostalgia we must keep in mind that for nearly two hundred years it existed beside its abnormal, dangerous counterpart, the disease.

Although the disease was born in the seventeenth century, no significant traces of the feeling of nostalgia appeared until the middle of the eighteenth, after the decline of the Augustan Age. This is not surprising, considering the attachment to a particular place—to home, the place where one was brought up—characteristic of nostalgia. The neoclassicism of the Augustan Age encouraged an attachment not to particular places, with their particular attributes, but to a generalized ideal: nature. Only nature in this Platonic sense, nature in the abstract, has dignity and deserves praise among Augustan writers. One's feeling for particular places—to some degree, feeling itself—was something one was supposed to control, to bring under the reign of reason.

In the second half of the eighteenth century, often called the Age of Sensibility, reaction to Augustan emotional austerity set in and a significant shift in attitude can be clearly discerned. Where in the first half of the century the passions were supposed to be subordinate to reason, a growing emphasis on and interest in subjectivity now reversed the priorities. Feeling came increasingly into repute; gardens became wilder, more "natural," more picturesque, reflecting an interest, foreign to the first half of the century, in the untamed. Poetry that celebrated particular places became popular. The most fashionable feeling of all during this period was undoubtedly melancholy. Thomas Warton pub-

lished his poem *The Pleasures of Melancholy* in 1747; this started a trend, and a host of poems praising melancholy and set in graveyards or the ruins of abbeys soon followed.

It was at this point that the feeling of nostalgia first appeared. It was, of course, one type of melancholy; quite rapidly it became a dominant type. Oliver Goldsmith, living in a garret in London and writing letters home to his family and friends in the Irish village where he was raised, is openly nostalgic. He tells them that he suffers from an "unaccountable fondness for country, this maladie du Pays, as the French call it." He confesses to sitting at the opera listening to "all the mazes of melody" and longing instead to hear "Johnny Armstrong's Last Good Night," a popular Irish song; to preferring the indifferent scenery of his home to the view from Flamstead Hill, "where nature never exhibited a more magnificent prospect." Other writers adopted these themes, and by the end of the eighteenth century the feeling of nostalgia had become thoroughly acceptable, even respectable, a bittersweet longing for one's distant home, a sad but rather pleasant sense of loss. Soldiers and travelers were still sickening and presumably pining away from the disease, but the poets were actively cultivating the feeling. Where the poets led, everyone else soon followed.

The nineteenth century witnessed a further development and generalization of the feeling. Now it was not simply a place, one's home, one had lost; one had lost as well one's past, both one's personal past and the historical past. We can see the development at work in a poet such as Wordsworth, who transformed an acute sense of loss for his childhood home into an even more acute nostalgia for childhood itself, or in the novels of Sir Walter Scott, who romanticized the medieval period and inspired a craze for Gothic architecture not only in Europe but in America. Both writers were extremely influential and set the style in these feelings for the rest of the century.

The end result was a profound change in people's relationship to the past. In the eighteenth century the past was something one studied for the lessons it had to teach about political conduct and morality. In the nineteenth century it had become something one felt. People went in pursuit of "impressions" and "associations"; from Washington Irving to Henry James, travelers made it their business, when abroad, to seek out castles and picturesque medieval ruins and describe what they felt there for the benefit of their American readers. The past had become subjective, a matter of feeling, of romantic aestheticism. History was valued no longer for its applicability to contemporary affairs but for the associations it aroused. George Bancroft, before writing his history of the United States, visited the historic places he was writing about. "I marked as near as I could the spot where Jacques Cartier may have landed," he reported in 1837, clearly believing that if he stood on that spot he could somehow recapture how Cartier himself had felt stand-

Nostalgia in the Rockies: cyclists at Colorado's White House Ranch.—*Photo: Eugene Smith, White House Ranch, Colorado*

ing there. If one could live in a Gothic revival house, one might feel Gothic; one might recapture the past. People's sense of history would never be the same.

The development of nostalgia does not stop here. In the twentieth century this emotion has become so widespread, so common, that it is difficult not to be nostalgic. People feel homeless, ill-at-ease in a world which has once more become a place of exile. Nostalgia has become the inescapable subjective complement to an objective alienation so pervasive as to seem a condition of life. The sociologist Dean MacCannell writes,

> For moderns, reality and authenticity are thought to be elsewhere: in other historical periods and other cultures, in purer, simpler life-styles. In other words, the concern of moderns for "naturalness," their nostalgia and their search for authenticity are not merely casual and somewhat decadent, though harmless, attachments to the souvenirs of destroyed cultures and dead epochs. They are also components of the conquering spirit of modernity—the grounds of its unifying consciousness.

Beneath the visible attachment to "souvenirs," to photographs, memorabilia, old movies, old furniture, old

styles in clothes, runs this sense that everything important is somewhere else, in another place or time. We have been set down between an ominous future and a vanished idealized past. We cling therefore to the things, the objects, that arouse associations in us of the purity and simplicity, the authenticity, we think we have lost. For us reality is indeed elsewhere. Life in the present is a dream of escape. We immerse ourselves in associations with better times; we cultivate a mood. It goes without saying that the result is an immense falsification of the actual past: the triumph, so to speak of nostalgia over history.

Nowhere in America is this triumph more evident than in the hundreds of "historic restorations" and "museum villages" that have appeared in the last fifty or sixty years. The restoration movement has its origins in the mid-nineteenth century nostalgia for the romanticized past. One of its first milestones was the long and ultimately successful effort to save Mount Vernon for posterity. The preservation of other places associated with George Washington followed, until "Washington Slept Here" became proverbial; the state of Tennessee bought and preserved Andrew Jackson's home, the Hermitage; entrepreneurs took a log cabin to the Columbian Exposition, advertised it as Abraham Lincoln's birthplace, and tried to sell tickets to visitors.

A corollary to the restoration movement was the revival of interest in Colonial architecture, which the architectural historian Vincent Scully dates to the 1870s and relates specifically to nostalgic feelings about the past. Scully quotes one writer who, in describing the town of Marblehead, Massachusetts, takes note of the presence of newer houses but says "they are very uninteresting in comparison with the houses that have tasted the salt air of the old town for two and three half centuries...[and] have a history...[and] associations." The Gothic revival of the early nineteenth century was an importation from abroad. Americans wanted their own romantic associations and were beginning to find them in Colonial houses.

Not until the early years of this century, however, did the movement find its true avatars: John D. Rockefeller, Jr., and Henry Ford. The junior Rockefeller's agreement to finance the restoration of Williamsburg in 1927 is generally thought to mark the real beginning of large-scale restoration in America. Less well known, but earlier and more interesting, was Henry Ford's interest in restoration, already in evidence in 1919. It is Ford who best reveals the nostalgia at the center of the restoration movement.

Ford's interest in restoration seems to have been an unexpected consequence of his statement that "history is more or less bunk," made when he was being interviewed by a reporter for the Chicago *Tribune* in 1916. At the time the remark attracted little attention. Three years later, however, Ford initiated a libel suit against the paper for calling him an "anarchist" and an "ignorant idealist." At the trial, the *Tribune's* lawyers cited the remark as evidence that Ford was indeed ignorant and had practically no knowledge of the history he was debunking. The newspapers played it up further, and the remark became famous.

Ford naturally resented this; what he had meant was that the history in books, the largely political history one studies in school, is bunk. Here is what he said in context:

> What do we care about what they did 500 or 1,000 years ago? I don't know whether Napoleon did or did not try to get across [the English Channel] and I don't care. it means nothing to me. History is more or less less bunk. It's tradition. We don't want tradition. We want to live in the present and the only history that is worth a tinker's dam is the history we make today.

The story goes that as he was riding home from the trial Ford told one of his subordinates, "You know, I'm going to prove that and give the people an idea of real history. I'm going to start a museum. We are going to show just what actually happened in years gone by."

The first fruit of this I'll-show-'em attitude was his restoration of the Wayside Inn in Sudbury, Massachusetts. Although it had been made famous by *Longfellow's Tales*

of a Wayside Inn, the place was closed and in disrepair when Ford bought it; he spent a total of $1.6 million restoring the inn, buying the land surrounding it, importing and reconstructing on this land other old buildings acquired elsewhere in New England, and protecting the atmosphere of the place by paying for the relocation of a highway that ran nearby. Ford's intention, according to his biographers, "was to restore an old American locality," not just a single building. It was the first such attempt in America.

The Wayside Inn was only practice for Ford. He had already set aside land in Dearborn, Michigan, near the Ford plant, for what became the Henry Ford Museum, and for a much larger "old American locality" named Greenfield Village. The village was restoration on a truly heroic scale. When it was finally opened to the public in 1933, it contained dozens of buildings which had been taken down, transported to Dearborn, and meticulously reconstructed on the village grounds. The list includes Thomas Edison's complete Menlo Park laboratory; the boarding housing near it, which was the first house in America to be electrified; a courthouse from Illinois in which Abraham Lincoln practiced law; Stephen Foster's supposed birthplace; Henry Ford's own boyhood home; a seventeenth-century house from Massachusetts; a Michigan inn built in 1831; the house from Vienna, Ontario, of Thomas Edison's grandfather; Wilbur and Orville Wright's bicycle shop; William Holmes McGuffey's birthplace; Luther Burbank's office; two of the schools Ford attended; the home of one of his first teachers; Noah Webster's house; numerous craft shops; a cottage from the Cotswolds in England; other assorted houses; a windmill from Cape Cod; a large number of industrial buildings; and so on. In all the village now contains over one hundred buildings, and more are being added.

In its details, the place carries to an extreme the search for "authenticity" common to restorations. When Ford imported the Edison complex from Menlo Park and rebuilt it on the grounds, he went so far as to bring along the soil that had surrounded the shops. The boarding house that Edison electrified stands at precisely the same distance from the main laboratory as it did originally in New Jersey. The plaster in the Lincoln courthouse was taken from the buildings in its original site, reground, and reapplied to the walls when the building was reassembled.

There are lapses, however, and the lapses are revealing. Stephen Foster may never have had any connection with the house exhibited as his birthplace. The machine tools in Henry Ford's first factory are all there, and are in working order, but the factory itself was reproduced on a scale smaller than the original. A jewelry shop with a charming tower containing a large clock and the figures of Gog and Magog, which strike the quarter hours, was brought from England, but the lower three stories of the original five-story building were left behind so that the building would not overpower the others in the village.

What all this reveals is an interest primarily in effect. Although he said his intentions were educational, Ford clearly wanted to move visitors more than he wanted to educate them. His biographers say that Ford "didn't really care" whether the Stephen Foster house was really the Stephen Foster house; "He wanted a memorial that would call the attention of visitors to the great song-writer." The reality of the association is unimportant; what matters is that one be touched by it. To emphasize the point, Foster's songs are piped into the house. the authenticity of the details, to which the guides constantly call attention, is also meant to be touching. These are the very walls that resounded to Abraham Lincoln's words. One has walked the same distance to the Edison boarding house that Edison himself once walked. This is the desk at which Noah Webster composed his *American Dictionary*. Here at last is the thrill of awe in the presence of the past that writers from James Fenimore Cooper on had found lacking in the American environment.

The village is obviously less an attempt to represent history than a record of what Ford himself found moving. His sense of what was historically important dominates the place. he seems to have thought jewelry shops were important, so the village contains three of them, not counting a "Swiss chalet" which Ford acquired as a "typical" example of a Swiss watchmaker's house. The reason is not far to seek: Ford spent most of his youth as a watch repairman. Ford was without question acutely nostalgic. He used to come down in the evening to the jewelry shops in the village and repair watches. The village contains not only his childhood home, but numerous other buildings out of his past: barns, houses, shops, sheds. Ford grew up on McGuffey readers; not only did he acquire McGuffey's birthplace, but he insisted on keeping a one-room school in operation on the grounds, and persuaded the Dearborn school system to supply children. He talked about the village as a "living museum" and brought the daughter of the woman who had run the Edison boarding house there to live in it. It is as if he was trying to reproduce a dream.

Perhaps the best way to understand the physical arrangement of the village, in fact, is by analogy to a dream. A seventeenth-century house from Maryland has been placed next to the seventeenth-century house from New England, which stands next to the windmill. These buildings are across from the Costwolds house, whose presence in the village is simply silly; Ford wanted it there to show what kind of house early American settlers emigrated from, as if they all emigrated from one kind of house. The Swiss chalet stands next to the putative Foster house. A log cabin faces the distinguished Noah Webster house. This village looks like no American village that ever existed. Things are juxtaposed that have no relation to one another. The village gives one no sense whatever of how actual villages developed, of the economic and social forces that shaped and organized them. Everything exists in isolation from everything else. Like a dream, the result is incoherent.

Ford wanted to move people, to inspire them with feelings; patriotism, a longing for the simple virtues of the past, and a rather complacent sense of satisfaction too, at how far we have come from our humble beginnings. This pursuit of feeling, of effect, is evident in other restorations as well. At Colonial Williamsburg one may sit in the stocks for a little while and experience what it felt like to be punished in the eighteenth century. To recreate the experience of what it was like to visit Washington Irving's house, Sunnyside, when he was alive, Sleepy Hollow Restorations razed the thirty-room Tudor mansion his heirs had built behind the house. Apparently, history must be personalized before it can have any meaning; if one cannot feel what it was like, somehow the past is not real. We have come very little distance from George Bancroft's searching for the exact spot where Jacques Cartier landed, from the "Washington Slept Here" mentality. We must see actual places and drink in their associations in order to get close to the past. In doing so, clearly, we are not trying to understand the past so much as to satisfy our nostalgia for it.

Inevitably, this leads to wholesale distortions of history. Both Disneyland and Disney World include a Main Street USA, modeled on a nineteenth-century small town. Each contains horse-drawn trolleys, a small village square, a host of stores, a movie theater, an ice cream parlor, and the other traditional accouterments of small-town America. Everything is scaled down, however, to five-eighths its normal size; the intention is, as one critic explains, to remind people "of trips back to childhood haunts; everything is so much smaller than one remembers." It is much cleaner too; horse droppings must be swept up within a minute of being deposited or the street sweeper loses his job. Nostalgia idealizes and isolates the past. The original Main Streets were muddy quagmires; telephone poles lined the streets, buildings were not necessarily pretty. Disney's Main Streets are both pretty and quaint. They come straight out of a movie set; we half expect Judy Garland to step from a doorway in a pinafore and sing a song.

How irrelevant these images are to New York or Los Angeles or the myriad shopping centers in between. On one side we have the generally bleak reality of modern America, on the other this dream of a paradise that never was, where Abraham Lincoln, Noah Webster, and Thomas Edison were neighbors; a world with no violence, no failure, no despair. Disneyland and Disney World are ghost towns. No one lives in them. The restorations, for all their seriousness, are only moderately less so. They stand hopelessly apart from us. No sense of continuity between past and present obtains in them. The reality of modern America must have emerged out of some past, but one finds no clue to it in the restorations. They belong to a world that never was. Old Sturbridge Village in Massachusetts stands on a spot where no actual village ever stood; its buildings have been collected from all over New England. The street lined with shops in Mystic Seaport never existed. While the the tourists stare, people dressed in "period costumes" make simulacra of wrought-iron toasters or pewter spoons, or print facsimiles of eighteenth-century newspapers (suitable for framing) on old hand presses. Dislocated in time and place, the past has become a kind of theater. We buy tickets to it. In every sense of the word, we patronize it.

In his book *The American Scene*, written after he returned to the United States in 1904 for an extended visit, Henry James said, "History is never, in any rich sense, the immediate crudity of what "happens," but the much finer complexity of what we read into it and think of in connection with it." He was writing before the restoration movement had achieved much popularity, but even then a number of historic places were being maintained as shrines. One of them was Washington Irving's house, Sunnyside. At that time the thirty-room Tudor mansion was still there, behind the house, and the property was still in the hands of Irving's descendants. At first James found the mansion regrettable—"The primitive cell has seen itself encompassed, in time, by a temple of many chambers"—but in the end he came to accept it. The original little house, he said, with its "small uncommodious study, the limited library, the 'dear' old portrait-prints of the first half of the century," offered an instructive contrast to the mansion; the older conditions represented by Sunnyside "encounter now on the spot the sharp reflection of our own increase of arrangement and loss of leisure."

James was himself capable of immense nostalgia; much of *The American Scene* is a lament for what has been lost. But he was also capable of precise discriminations; he could see through his own nostalgia, his regret at the accretion of the Tudor "temple" to Irving's "primitive cell," and read into the physical situation of Sunnyside the meaning of both the loss and the gain—the vanished leisure, the increased "arrangement." The visible record of change had not been wiped away. A sense of continuity could be read into the two buildings; one could see what had happened to the family after Irving's death: how they had grown, become rich enough for a thirty-room house, and had lost in the process the feel for quiet surroundings, for modest circumstances, that Irving himself, content with his cottage, evidently enjoyed.

Some restorations do preserve this sense of continuity. Many, however, do not. At Williamsburg every trace of physical change after the cutoff date of 1800 was rigorously expunged, and Williamsburg has set the standard in restorations for years. The word "restoration" is apt; the ideal is less to preserve the past than to restore it, to bring it back to its original state, as if nothing had happened in the interim. This hardly seems the way to understand the past. If history is what we "read into and think of in connection with" the immediate crudity" of

events, then we are one of its inescapable terms. The past cannot be known except in relation to ourselves. That clearly requires something more than knowing how people used to make candles or what kind of beds they slept in. It requires a sense of the persistence of the past, the manifold ways in which it penetrates our lives; which in turn requires a thorough understanding of our own attitudes to the past, including the extent to which our nostalgia blinds us to such complexities. Nostalgia does not liberate us from history; it only obscures the continuity of its operation.

If the history of nostalgia itself suggests anything, it is that people's attitudes and feelings do change over time. Attitudes and feelings are products of culture, which is not stable but dynamic. Since the horrors of the urban renewal program in the 1950s and early 1960s, when whole neighborhoods in the older portions of many cities were destroyed, a shift in attitude has become discernible; people are beginning to try to slow down the engine of change, or at least to control its movements. In nearly every major city attempts are being made to find new uses for dilapidated buildings, to save neighborhoods and to transform abandoned factories into office buildings or shopping centers, docks into residences, train stations into theaters. In Detroit, Seattle, Pittsburgh, and other cities, people have been elected to public office whose platforms included a commitment to the new preservationist policy. This policy is not, by and large, nostalgic; it is the product of an enlightened, shall we say postmodern, understanding of the necessity for a sense of continuity in change, for architectural variety, and for the economic use of existing resources. As a writer for the National Trust for Historic Preservation describes the trend, the traditional philosophy of restoration "is being side-stepped in favor of an approach that is geared to conserving the resources of the built environment in ways that make them consistent with contemporary needs and demands.

The continued development of this praiseworthy trend does not mean that the restorations will, or should, disappear. They are probably a permanent fixture on the American landscape, and perhaps they have a place there. As islands of feeling in a largely unfeeling present, they provide a kind of relief we may need to keep our sanity. They represent values which, however unlikely it is that they were ever embodied in the actual past, at least attest to the endurance in us of a vision, a dream of an alternative way of life, quieter, more contented, in the fullest sense of the word, gentler. The restored buildings are usually beautiful and they bespeak tranquility; there can never be too much tranquility in the world. We must not confuse the restorations with history, but once that caveat has been absorbed, perhaps we can enjoy them for what they are, emblems of paradise, reminders of a past which, although it may not have been real, is nonetheless sacred.

The Link from Object to Person to Concept

29

James Deetz

In this short article, Deetz relates living-history to contemporary anthropolocial theory in much the same way that Carson connects it with the new social history. Deetz notes that living-history museums have the potential to interpret not only material culture, but culture itself, the concepts underlying the objects. Visitors to such museums might be viewed as "anthropological fieldworkers going in to experience a community and elicit from it what they could." Museum interpreters then become "informants" who can share an insider's view of past cultures. Deetz's thoughts were first published in Museums, Adults, and the Humanities,, *AAM 1981.*

I am primarily an anthropologist, and we anthropologists fancy ourselves scientists (although much of what we do is very unscientific). My heart lies with the humanities, however; indeed, I have been accused of being a closet folklorist by many of my colleagues, and I will probably own up to it in a year or so. My museum experience has been in the unusual context of Plimoth Plantation, an outdoor folk museum in the east.

If we look at the way the human species has spaced the environment we can discern certain considerations that apply directly to the museum business. Any definition of the museum must include the three-dimensional object that is put out for public perusal and concern. Any consideration of how the humanities relate to museums must therefore depart from how the humanities related to things. Material culture is the core of our concern.

What are the humanities? They have to do with the entirety of the human condition. Public Law 94-201, establishing the American Folklife Center, gives us a listing of the kinds of concerns that constitute themes in the humanities: all forms of expressive culture shared by a group, whether the group is familial, ethnic, occupational, religious or regional. The forms of expression include a wide range of creative and symbolic forms, such as custom, belief, technical skill, language, literature, art, architecture, music, play, dance, drama, ritual, pageantry and handicraft.

All of these are legitimate themes in the humanities and can be related to the objects we all love, curate, catalog, mend, patch, exhibit, ship out, show to people and send to schools. These forms of expressive culture set humans apart from the rest of the world. So the humanities basically consider the human condition.

That comes close to a definition of what anthropologists call culture: what is carried in the minds of collective groups of people. Many of my colleagues believe culture is strictly in the mind, not out in the real world. It is a set of concepts and ideas, passed from person to person along nongenetic channels, that organize the world in systematic ways. The object is the hinge between concept and thought on the one hand and the museum that uses the object to communicate intangible concepts to the visiting public on the other hand.

In my book *In Small Things Forgotten,* I defined material culture as that part of the physical world that we have shaped according to a culturally dictated plan. In other words we are looking at how the human species, since the bottom of the Pleistocene epoch, has modified the environment in a wonderful diversity of ways. I hope that the definition is not too broad.

Anthropological studies, unfortunately, often treat material culture as synonymous with artifacts, things, objects, but the definition I just gave goes far beyond that. For example, it includes all of food. Food is not God-given or genetically determined; we structure foodstuffs according to rules in our heads. One aspect of material culture (though difficult to exhibit in a glass case) is cuts of meat. There are many ways to take an animal apart, all dictated by the rules of a given culture. From an archaeologist's perspective, butchering techniques have numerous implications. One can tell the kind of people involved from the technique used. From an interpretive point of view, even within the development of American culture there have been rather profound changes in the ways animals were taken apart. Around 1760 or 1770 people stopped chopping and started using saws. A chopped bone says something about what that culture was, what those people thought. In the simplest terms, it indicates that great big chunks of meat are being thrown into a pot, and the food is being consumed corporately. So the fact of chopping addresses the whole question of social structure, of community and familial interaction, and of how people laid food out on the table.

Today we all eat in a tripartite structure: meat, vegetables and potatoes. We are one of the few cultures of the world to do that. Most cuisines mix things up more; we set things apart. This is deeply reflective of an underlying psychological structure that insists on order and artificiality. It says worlds about our culture.

This three-part division is reflected in marvelous ways. Our paper plates are divided not into fours but into threes. Museums could exhibit a paper plate and explore what it means to us. It means we are probably the most compulsive, uptight culture that has ever existed. That same threefold structuring runs through everything we do. I recommend Alan Dundes's article on it, "The Magic Number Three in American Culture." It may go back to the Trinity, but I suspect most of it comes from the 18th century. We are completely and compulsively ordered by tripartite divisions—the three bears; the three billygoats; three wishes; three strikes and you're out; win, place and show. It is a subconscious, implicit little thing, but if you raise it into consciousness you can notice its impact when looking at objects of our culture.

The human physique is another example of material culture. Body language is a way of shaping the physical world. We are part of the physical world, and we shape ourselves.

One more example: Few people realize that most (but not all) Anglo-Americans like 16-foot squares in their architecture. The 16-foot square makes us feel warm and happy. This has been proved by constant measurement and remeasurement of folk structures the country over. The 16-foot square is the ideal architectural module for people of Northern European and Western culture.

Afro-American folk housing has a very different pattern. John Michael Vlach has written several very thoughtful papers on that housing tradition. Its standard dimension is an 11-foot square. That seems to be the comfortable proxemic shell for that society. (Proxemics is the study of normative social distances between people.) Spacing is part of material culture because it puts people in culturally dictated arrangements. The ratio of building modules for Afro-Americans and Anglo-Americans, about 12 to 16, matches almost exactly the ratio of proxemic distances for social interaction for the two cultures. Afro-American culture stresses intimacy and interaction more closely, and that is reflected in its buildings. Here we have buildings linked systematically with psychology and behavior.

Finally, I contend that even language is an expression of material culture. Language invests a substance, air, with attributes that are culturally determined. It is a very transitory material; you cannot pile words on tables or exhibit them for the viewing public. They are nonetheless patterned objects that reflect structured human

modification. Linguists, in fact, have taken the behavioral sciences further than other scholars in the direction of showing structure, order and predictability. They have given us the concepts of syntactic analysis, grammar and structural linguistics, which may be applied very usefully to the rest of the material world as well. We now see people turning up "grammars" of houses—the rules that make this house correct and that house not. Lila O'Neale wrote a very fine study of Yurok-Karok baskets in the late 1930s, developing the underlying, implicit, unconscious rules for correct baskets in the ideal concept. Henry Glassie, of the Folklore and Folklife Department at the University of Pennsylvania, has written a very articulate and accurate grammar of the folkhouse in the Piedmont area of Virginia, just west of Richmond. These grammars show how people conceptualize objects. In an interpretation we need to look at the object as it resides in the mind before the mind drives the muscles to create and produce it in the real world.

Objects, indeed all parts of material culture as I defined it, have several inherent dimensions. They can be measured, touched, scratched, lifted, weighed. Objects have a place in time, and they have a location in the world. Where an object rests on the dimensions of time and space can affect its form or, indeed, its significance.

Beyond these inherent dimensions, an object has a function. We often think only of the technical function of people's creations. But an object can function on a couple of other levels as well. It can have a social function, which may not be obvious from its physical attributes, and an ideological or philosophical function, reflective of world view or an attitude. Any time anything is exhibited, to get the maximum amount of humanistic or behavioral meaning out of it, consider at what functional level it is being seen. My favorite instance of this has to do with bathtubs. We take baths in bathtubs; that is their technical function. But during the Roaring Twenties the bathtub was also the center for social interaction. The term bathtub gin derives therefrom. In that instance, the bathtub was serving a social as well as a technical function. (I might point out that there is always a technological underpinning to other functions, but the other purpose transcends the technological purpose). Finally, there is a wonderful practice, in the upper midwest, of buying a bathtub, stood on end, halfway into the ground in your front yard, with a statue of the Blessed Virgin Mary inside, facing out at the world. It makes a little shrine. That is a bathtub functioning at an ideological, religious level.

I am going on about patterns, predictability, order, logic and system, but the one thing that endears all of my fellow people to me, and makes me very happy I had a chance to be a person, is that every once in awhile people do crazy things that defy logical organization and classification. I am always reminding my archaeological colleagues of this: You never know whether you have dug up a nut, rather than a typical representative of the species.

There is a whole wonderful area of what we might call

Another link from the object to person to concept: handwork in Victorian Ontario.—*Photo: Black Creek Pioneer Village*

folk monuments, all over the country. For example, Valley of the Moon in Tucson is a wonderful complex of tunnels and amphitheaters, built in the 1930s by one man. He filled it originally with little machines that were run by rabbits. Some walls have perspective paintings on them. He made it for the children of Tucson; it is a marvelous, loving, wonderful gesture. He built it out in the desert, but suburbia has moved out there now and swallowed it up. I think the man is still alive. Some young people were doing oral history with him. They had the place put on the state registry of historical places, and they are interpreting it to the public.

The Watts Towers are another example. An immigrant in Los Angeles wanted to do something to express that he was proud to be here, and he made these marvelous mosaic towers.

Let me give you an example with direct museum application. Suppose you took over a little museum in Duxbury, Massachusetts. You root in the back and you find a whole stack of blue-dash charger glazed Delft plates, those beautiful hand-painted ornamental plates loved by students of early America. If you do not do some research, you might make a dreadful error and give the wrong information in an exhibit of them. If you look only to the English literature to find out about those plates, you might conclude that they were part of the food service of a colonial family. Well, you would be wrong. If you were in England, you would be right, probably; but in America, more often than not, these plates had a social function, rather than a technical function: they were displayed in the parlor to impress visitors, and never were they used for eating. Probate analysis shows this very clearly. So, form can be misleading, and space can put a different interpretation on the very same plate-in England, by that time, the plates were being used for eating, while the artifact that took their place socially was, in most instances, pewter.

I have been applying some of the concepts of Henry

Glassie's book, *Folk Housing in Middle Virginia*, to the material world and found them quite helpful. If you look at the entire physical output of a culture across time, and you notice that all of a sudden a lot of changes begin to happen at the same time and in the same direction, you begin to wonder why. I spent years looking at three major material classes: dishes, houses and gravestones. They are three different expressions of one culture, but all of a sudden they begin behaving in a similar way.

Claude Levi-Strauss asserts that people think in binary terms, much as computers do. They set up oppositional structures and then mediate them in various ways. Here is an example: I was struck by the fact that, between 1760 and 1800, things begin to go white: houses (before that they were all different colors), dishes (before that they were all different colors), gravestones (before that they were pink, red, black, green, all kinds of earthy, natural shades). Even clothing tends to be more whitened than it was previously. (That is the same time, incidentally, when they stopped chopping bones and began sawing them.) What is causing this sudden trend toward whiteness? At least three different oppositional structures deep in the human subconscious appear to be mediated by the change. One is the opposition between complexity and simplicity. There seems to be a trend, throughout the 18th century, toward simplicity, and I do not think we can blame industrialism for it. If everything is white, it is a lot simpler than if we use various shades and colors. The second is the classic opposition between nature and culture. White is artificial. A white house out in a field says something very different from a brown or a red house. It says, "I am made by people. I am apart from the natural environment that is surrounding me." That kind of artificiality is more intellectual, less emotional— and that is the third opposition, between intellect and emotion. All of these things link together.

By the way, going back to the sawed bones, that is a beautiful example of the same intellect/emotion, culture/nature mediation: sawing is far more intellectual and artificial, and less natural. We can explain the shift in bone treatment by the same rubric, the same oppositional structures, as the whitening of dishes.

I want to discuss one particular bone, a long bone from the leg of a cow. It is sawed on one end and chopped on the other. That's all it looks like, unless we know several things. First, where was it from? That is the space consideration. It turns out that this bone came from Somersville, a coal mining town in northern California, occupied from 1856 to about 1910. next, why is the bone so weird? One would expect it to be either sawed or chopped on both ends. The answer to that says a great deal about what that town was about. It turns out, from voting and census and court records, that this town was very complexly multiethnic. It had at least six ethnic enclaves, each with its own traditional culture: Welsh, Cornish, Irish, Italian, Mexican and Chinese. From interviewing people who actually lived there, I discovered that a butcher wagon used to come up from the

town of Antioch every Tuesday to sell meat. At first this disappointed me, because I was hoping to uncover patterns of butchering that would reflect the residents' traditional life-styles. But I pursued the inquiry, anyway. The butcher was part of the culture in which sawing was the standard way to part a carcass. But he was selling the meat in great hunks, quarters, to different families. Some of these families were still following the older, more traditional, European pattern of chopping meat apart. Therefore, in that one bone, you could have an exhibit calling attention to an entire cultural shift.

Another example is a change that happened in gravestones in the 1730s and on into the 1750s in New England, out in country cemeteries. It coincided with the period of the Great Awakening, a time of religious revivalism and ferment—the final collapse of Puritan orthodoxy. The standard gravestone image of classic orthodoxy is a grim and grisly skull with wings sticking out of its ears, and an epitaph about worms and death. They were teaching devices; people would go out to the cemetery and read them. Starting in the early 18th century, these skulls begin to evolve in weird and wonderful ways. Their features slowly become—not human, but no longer faces of skulls. Peter Benes, in his book *Masks of Orthodoxy*, points out that this is a visual pun. These gravestones show up more often in parishes that were severely split, where part of the congregation wanted to hold to the old orthodox values and part wanted to go on to new, more progressive values. In the cities, an angel replaces the skull. But in the country gravestones the picture is sort of in between, a little bit angel, a little bit skull. A person in such a parish could look at this and choose to see it as a skull or as something invested with some humanity, some animation. Most writers on the subject call these "soul images."

What we have here is the old hiding behind the new. You could do an exhibit of rubbings or of castings to say what all of this means. You could make all those statements and then call attention to the fundamental structural similarities between that change and changes in houses. In the whole colonial world, at about the same time, we see the appearance of Georgian architectural order, which is severely tripartite and bilaterally symmetrical: five windows across the top; two windows, a door, two windows below. The older house in these areas was divided asymmetrically into a large hall, where most things happened, and a parlor, which was ritualized. With the introduction of the Georgian plan, we get a cross-passage injected between the two areas, so that, when you come in, you are no longer in the midst of all the activity. You are isolated from the people within by a barrier. This is a change again in the direction of privacy and artificiality.

When this change hit the folk building tradition of the area, houses from the front began to look Georgian, usually with three windows across the top and window, door, window below. But inside they are still only one room deep. So, hiding behind a newer architectural expression is still part of the old. I would suggest that the same phenomenon is being observed in two seemingly dissimilar categories: gravestones and houses.

A different set of considerations has to do with houses and with humanity, more than the humanities. I believe we should make every effort possible to invest what we show to visitors with a sense of human presence. I am speaking now specifically about museums that employ the "period room" concept in exhibits. That concept was invented by Charles Wilcomb, who used it in the Stanford Cameron House in Oakland. Period rooms are marvelous things, I wouldn't for a minute say we shouldn't have them, but I don't like them. Ivor Noel-Hume, the chief archaeologist at Colonial Williamsburg, takes what I feel is a long overdue swipe at period rooms, in a wonderful introductory essay, "Sign-posts to the Past," in his book *Guide to Artifacts of Colonial America.* He says the curators remind him of his wife: Every time you leave the room, she comes in, empties the ashtrays, fluffs up the pillows and makes it look as if no one was ever there. Period rooms, too, are pristinely perfect, straight, neat and utterly devoid of indications that a person came near them. They might just as well have been made on Mars. Really carried to the extreme, these rooms will have every single object made in the same year at the same place. Noel-Hume points out that real houses generally contain some things that are ancient, some that are new, some abused, some not. When I look at a period room, I always wish somebody would just scribble on a wall, to imply that there might have been a child nearby. Period rooms quickly give the impression that all Americans sprang into existence at the age of twenty-one and were very neat. Real rooms also have irrational things in them. Noel-Hume cites a property inventory list for probate for a family from colonial Virginia—it notes that one lady had several hatchets in her bedroom cupboard. Noel-Hume states that no curator in his or her right mind would put hatchets in a lady's bedroom closet, but nonetheless they were there.

I'd like to see, not only the accumulation of things from the past and the irrational materials that creep in, but also enough clutter and confusion to suggest that the people just stepped out for a minute.

Those of us involved in the creation of period environments would be well advised to look closely at probate data from the period under consideration, not for the totally unpredictable, like hatchets in a bedroom, but for things that were regularly present that we would never think to include form our 20th-century point of view.

This leads me to another point that I think is critical whenever anyone is interpreting the physical world of the past. We have to try to place ourselves within the minds of the people who lived then. We need what anthropologists call an emic perspective, which looks at the physical world in terms of the categories used by the people who lived in that world. Otherwise we make dreadful mistakes. When we were re-creating Plimoth Plantation, probate inventories were among the most

useful research tools for this kind of work. We put whole households together with re-created artifacts. From the probate inventories we discovered that fewer than half the houses had bedsteads. These people had considerable means, they owned several hundred acres of land, a number of cattle, lots of material goods; but, to that particular world view, their own emic perspective, a bedstead was not important. We had put bedsteads in all the houses, thinking, "Anybody with half an ounce of common sense knows that the first thing a person would do is get a bedstead to sleep on." We had to go pull them out.

It is easy to get fooled in a lot of ways. It happened to me with language. In refurnishing Plimoth Plantation, according to the inventory listings, we found a number of references to looking glasses. We went to great pains to re-create good 17th-century mirrors. We figured that, since these people had come over on those little sailing ships, they wouldn't have brought full-length mirrors; they probably had little table mirrors. So, we had carpenters build these, and we dotted them about in the exhibit where the inventories dictated that they should be.

At the same time, we noticed in the ceramics area that chamber pots were scarcely mentioned. We knew that they were used, but there were not as many in the inventories as one might have predicted. We had a few made up, and we stuck them under the beds, where the probate lists suggested they would be. Only then did I come to hear of the work of an English ceramic historian who had done a linguistic, historical and archaeological history of the chamber pot, pointing out that, from about 1600 to 1650, the standard folk term for chamber pot was looking glass.

That leads me to another point that comes out of my experience at Plimouth, which has a bearing on interpretive techniques and how to approach the people who come to view what you are doing.

It occurred to us that the live interpreters ought to be re-creations at Plimouth, too. We had them speak in period dialect, which we were able to research, in the first person. At that point the visitors became the interpreters, and we started calling the interpreters informants. It was as if the visitors coming into the exhibit were anthropology fieldworkers going in to experience a community and elicit from it what they could.

It worked very nicely. Our staff people were marvelous; they stuck with their roles even in situations that were not anticipated, and they could respond more often than not with great grace. In one of the houses was a family on its way to Virginia that had been shipwrecked on Cape Cod. It consisted of a fop, his Irish maidservant (who was pregnant), and his Irish manservant (her husband). When visitors walked in, what hit them full blast was a constant tirade of complaints, not only about not getting to the Virginia colony but also about the Ulster plantations, the whole English expansion into Northern Ireland, and a lot of wonderful, very organic interpretation. I recall one visitor asking the maidservant, "Are all of these things in here handmade?" She responded in

A link with the past: a Pilgrim housewife scraping sugar from a sugarloaf.—*Photo: Plimoth Plantation*

true preindustrial thinking, "Why, no, they are not handmade; we use tools."

I suspect that we are often too hesitant to place visitors in the role of interpreter and give only minimal guidance for looking at a physical configuration. For example, at the Lowie Museum in Berkeley, we are going to attempt an exhibit on a coal mining town in which we will shovel heaps of everything we have dug up into the exhibit cases. We will put up many photographs and extensive quotes from oral history. We will plaster one entire wall with documents about the things, but we will not give a single interpretive statement.

There is an implicit kind of interpretation in what we present, but there will not be any declarative statement from us about what it means. We will be interpreting in a far more open-ended way. For instance, we will have a picture of a wagon that says "Butcher Wagon," and a pile of bones, and we'll let people scratch their heads themselves.

One little section off in a corner will tell how we

started thinking about these objects to kind of give people a lead into the experience. If we had the money, I would also have an archaeologist there to interact with the visitors.

The garbage we dug up is so ugly that I would have been rather stupid to display it as great works—to put a busted piece of a lamp chimney on a pedestal. So we thought, "Since we cannot impress people with the intrisic beauty of what we are exhibiting, we can perhaps impress them with the sheer mass. We have something like 125,000 objects in one alcove. Unfortunately, people won't be allowed to touch the objects. I am a great believer in hands-on exhibits, but in this case we can't do that."

I have been talking about exhibiting objects created by people in humanistic terms, but I am mindful that many museums, such as natural history museums and observatories, really do not deal with things made by people. I suspect that just reversing the situation would work in the context of a natural history museum. In other words, there are aspects of the natural world upon which people impinge; also it is people who have created our perceptions of the natural world.

Folk science, folk taxonomies, the way certain societies classify the natural world—these are among the more interesting areas. A lot of good work has been done along these lines, primarily by linguists. A group from Berkeley is now working in Peru, looking at the way the Jivaro Indians perceive and organize the natural universe on which they depend. It is a beautiful mixture of natural sciences and anthropology. Consideration of the economic importance of the biological worlds lends it-

self very well to exhibits. At the Lowie Museum next spring we are going to install an exhibit on amber: how amber happens in a natural historical context and the human uses of amber. It is used not only in jewelry but also medicinally. Looking at both the cultural and the natural aspects of one category brings the two together in a nice way. It also lets us incorporate just about the entire known world, the whole range of natural, nonhuman phenomena as they relate to mythology, religion, art and other aspects of a culture.

If I have any conclusion, it relates to our duty as custodians of that which we, as a species, have stacked on this planet. We must not ony preserve it but also find reasonably imaginative and creative ways to share it with other people. That is what I think the museum business is all about.

REFERENCES

Benes, Peter. *Masks of Orthodoxy*. Amherst: University of Massachusetts Press, 1977.

Dundes, Alan. "The Magic Number Three in American Culture." In *Every Man His Way: Readings in Cultural Anthropology*, edited by Alan Dundes. Englewood Cliffs, NJ: Prentice-Hall, 1968.

Glassie, Henry H. *Folk Housing in Middle Virginia: Structural Analysis of Historic Artifacts*. Knoxville: University of Tennessee Press, 1976.

Levi-Strauss, Claude. *Structural Anthropology*. Translated by Monique Layton. 2 vols. New York: Basic Books, 1963, 1976.

Noel-Hume, Ivor. "Signposts to the Past." In *A Guide to the Artifacts of Colonial America*. New York: Alfred A. Knopf, 1970.

O'Neale, Lila M. *Yurok-Karok Basket Weavers*. University of California Publications in American Archaeology and Ethnology, vol. 32, no. 1. Berkeley: University of California, 1932.

Vlach, John M. *The Afro-American Tradition in Decorative Arts*. Bloomington: Indiana University Press, 1978.

Part VIII
Afterword

Serious Play

Jay Anderson

30

Originally published in 1985 as the conclusion to The Living History Sourcebook, *"Serious Play" argues that "the living history movement is a significant one that is here to stay." Based on a careful consideration of the field, I suggest that within the movement there is "an increasing dedication to quality—a widespread desire to simulate life in the past more truthfully." As a result of this move toward greater "authenticity," "historical accuracy," "realism," and "honesty," reenactors and museum interpreters are borrowing the tools and techniques of academic historians. In the future, I believe living-history activities will take on added significance. The dramatic, playful, experimental, and memorable characteristics of historic simulation will insure its continuation as a vital, positive mode of studying, interpreting, and celebrating the past.*

During three very foggy days in the summer of 1984, I visited the Fortress of Louisbourg on Nova Scotia's Cape Breton Island. To really get to know this massive living-history museum, three days is a minimum visit. Members of the staff showed me their mountains of archaeological artifacts, historic records, and research reports covering all aspects of culture in the French community during the first half of the eighteenth century. I also spent many hours wandering through the historic fortress, observing the variety of interpretive programs which simulate the life of Louisbourg's inhabitants in 1744. The visit was both exhilarating and exhausting.

Toward the end of my stay, I had dinner with William O'Shea, Louisbourg's acting director. We talked about the scope of the living-history movement and my field work for this sourcebook. Bill asked, "Do you think that living history has a real future? Or is it a fad? I think your new book needs to suggest an answer to that question." I hope that by now my answer is clear: the living-history movement is a significant one that is here to stay.

The number and variety of living-history activities are striking. A total of about ten thousand outdoor museums and historic sites, events, publications, organizations, suppliers, games, and films use historical simulation. Filing cabinets along my office wall are brimming with material for entries, many of which, sadly, I had to omit.

In short, the world of living history is not only kaleidoscopic but also continually growing. I have presented a stop-action portrait of this world in 1985. A decade from now, only a wide-angle lens will be able to capture the living history scene. I have no doubt that the movement will have doubled— surprising no one involved in it— and will cover aspects of life in North America's past that are currently neglected, such as the histories of minority groups. Insiders today take living history's popularity so much for granted that they are amazed to find articles in the popular press suggesting that an interest in history is on the wane. As far as living history is concerned, this assessment couldn't be farther from the truth. Living history is alive, well, and growing at a pace that often seems breakneck.

The movement manifests an increasing dedication to quality— a widespread desire to simulate life in the past more truthfully. Over and over as I talk with interpreters, reenactors, and history buffs, I hear the words "authenticity," "historical accuracy," "greater realism," and "honesty" used to describe their activities. Within the living-history movement, there is growing pressure to improve quality. Museums pride themselves on being historically accurate. Events are limited to "authentics." New sketchbooks are given tough reviews in reenactors' magazines. I recently saw a good example of this pressure in action. One winter evening I went over to Asgard, a model and gaming store near my home, to watch my son Coll "push micro" with some friends. The battle they refought was a post–D–day encounter in France between American and German armor and infantry units. There were about ten war gamers scattered around a large table in the shop's basement, each responsible for moving several tanks, cannon, infantry units, and so forth in and out of battle. The table looked like a model railroad setup, filled with miniature French buildings, farms, fields, and woods. When the battle had been raging for more than an hour, a German player asked, "Can I move my 75mm PAK 4 up this hill?" Everyone laughed. An older, more experienced player replied, "Of course not. Haven't you read the German manual on artillery of that kind?" I was astounded, but the players weren't. They seemed to take it for granted that a prerequisite for playing miniature war games well was a knowledge of history, especially battlefield tactics.

215

Serious play: Jim and Joy Phillips enjoying a spring rendezvous in Blacksmith Fork Canyon, Hyrum, Utah.—*Photo: Tom Allen*

To achieve greater historical accuracy, people active in the living-history movement are increasingly borrowing the tools and techniques of academic historians. This trend will certainly continue as more and more nonacademic historians within the movement recognize their need for quality control and realize that the academic has much to offer in historical theory, methodology, and knowledge of relevant primary sources. At one time we could speak of a gulf between academic historians and professionals and lay "living historians." To some extent this gap has been bridged. Living-history museums have hired hundreds of academically trained historians, curators, folklorists, and educational specialists. Internships and special educational programs have been developed specifically for undergraduate and graduate students. Articles by recognized historians lauding the interpretation at serious living-history museums such as the Fortress of Louisbourg or Plimoth Plantation are no longer unusual. But most important, the number of teachers and researchers who take part in living-history as a form of recreation has swelled. Professional historians have

increasingly realized that historical simulation can be a refreshing avocation. The participation of professional and lay historians alike has improved the quality of living-history activities.

Living history's most significant characteristic is its vitality, an energy which is the direct by-product of the movement's experimentation with historical simulation. The usefulness of simulation as a tool with which to research, interpret, and reenact life in the past is amply illustrated by the 361 entries in this sourcebook.

One of our generation's contributions to the field of history (and ultimately to society) is our experimentation with historical simulation. By breaking away from strictly written accounts of the past, we have developed a "living" history that is often successful because it is dramatic, playful, experimental, and memorable.

Historical simulation is dramatic. It unabashedly uses our society's traditional mediums of cultural expression: ritual, ceremony, pageant, theater (including film, radio, television), games, sports, festivals, and celebration. The power and popularity of these forms is obvious. I am certain that my own interest in Civil War reenacting germinated from my mother's continual and vocal devotion to the film *Gone with the Wind*. My own children's view of race relations was unquestionably influenced by the televised miniseries *Roots*. No doubt everyone in North America can point to a similar encounter with the past which came to them through the medium of theater, pageant, festival, or a related traditional dramatic form. I have met Scottish Americans whose interest in history was kindled by a "Burns Night Supper" or a "Highland Games," and in the South, hundreds of thousands of families troop off every summer to outdoor historical pageants. After spending a cool summer evening watching one local variant—*Shakertown Revisited*, in which the Shakers of South Union, Kentucky, are celebrated in song, dance, and story—I asked a native why historical pageants are so popular. He thought for a moment, then replied, "Part of it is an interest in old things, history. That's traditional around here. But like all people, we do enjoy a good show. *Shakertown's* not Broadway, but in the summer, it's the best show in town."

Much past criticism of living history focused on its theatricality. There was an underlying message: if history is entertaining, then something must be wrong. The truth must have been sacrificed somewhere; history must have been bowdlerized. You could almost sense the ancient puritan mindset behind this criticism—to grin is to sin. Some criticism of living history's account of life in the past (as too clean, neat, peaceful, male, white, and so forth), however, was and is right on target. Just as there are poor history books, there are poor living-history museums, events, films, games, and so on. Still, there are no dull historical simulations, and as the living-history movement matures and emphasizes programs and activities of higher quality, its role in purveying history to our society should become more significant.

For many people, historical simulations have an aura

The village mustering on Long Island.—*Photo: Nassau County Department of Parks and Recreation, Division of Museum Services*

of playfulness about them. Reenactors refer to living history as a "hobby." Games are considered a leisure time activity, and museum interpreters often describe their work as "fun and games." It would be wrong, however, to conclude that historical simulations are trivial. On the contrary, they are examples of "serious play." Tom Deakin, editor of *Living History Magazine*, once said to me, "Living history is one of the few hobbies that is intellectually demanding, that requires a commitment to historical research and plain old-fashioned book learning." After an encampment or battle reenactment, "you are bone weary but mentally invigorated." Living history synthesizes the mental challenges of the workplace with the physically and emotionally satisfying benefits of recreation. No wonder it has been described by people as "the participatory sport of the future." Recently a friend of mine who is a historian by profession and an "admitted closet buckskinner" wryly noted, "When the Yup-

pies get tired of all their running and exercising, you watch—they'll turn to living history." His point was, of course, that serious hardworking people will eventually be attracted to serious, intellectually strenuous play. And living history will be waiting in the form of a historical dramatization such as the television series *The Jewel in the Crown*, a demanding board game such as *Civilization*, or a place in the ranks of an authentic reenactment unit. In the mid-1970s a Dupont chemist and his wife, a computer programer, volunteered to work weekends at the Colonial Pennsylvania Plantation. One day I asked them why they were attracted to the rigors of historical interpretation. They agreed on one answer: "It's relaxing—but you never feel you've squandered your mind."

Living history is also experimental. Simulation is by definition an imitation of something real and so lends itself to experimentation. Rather than fight real wars, H.

An 1860s baseball game between the Mineola Washingtons and the Hempstead Eurekas.—*Photo: Wassau County Department of Parks and Recreation, Division of Museum Services*

A disagreement at Old Fort William: one of the historic site's many excellent vignettes.—*Photo: Ontario Ministry of Industry and Tourism*

G. Wells suggested in his 1913 classic *Little Wars*, people could use mock conflicts to simulate reality, as they now do in war gaming. Vicarious battles with miniature soldiers, Wells wrote, can provide the drama, excitement, and even mental exercise of warfare—without the tragic consequences. You can "experiment" with war without anyone's getting killed or maimed or suffering from shell shock. The loser's ego might suffer, but that's the price for a winner's glory—and both players can return to "fight" another day. Well's sensible book didn't end real wars, but it did start a popular, worldwide hobby for amateur military history buffs interested in testing their tactical skills. In the six decades since *Little Wars* was published, simulation has also become an acceptable research tool for professional experimental archaeologists. Scores of voyagers have sailed the high seas in the wake of Thor Heyerdahl; in Denmark and England significant research centers have been established to conduct "imitative experiments"; and experimental projects have been interpreted for the public in American living museums such as Plimoth Plantation, Sleepy Hollow, and Colonial Williamsburg.

Plimoth's experience perhaps best illustrates the experimental potential of historical simulation at museums. In the early 1970s, the museum made the courageous decision to remove its original Jacobean artifacts from the re-created village and to replace them with reproductions. In essence, Plimoth was transformed overnight from a museum of historic furniture to a living historical village. Freed from the curatorial restrictions involved in caring for valuable antiques, the interpretive staff could now devote its energy to present-

Hot air balloons on the fourth of July at Old Sturbridge Village.—*Photo by Robert S. Arnold, Old Sturbridge*

A chanteyman singing his heart out in nineteenth-century Connecticut.—*Photo: Mary Anne Stets, Mystic Seaport*

ing a realistic picture of Pilgrim life. The plantation rapidly established itself as an innovator in first-person interpretation and effective educational programming.

Finally, historical simulation is memorable. It involves a total sensory re-creation of life in the past. A realistic living-history museum or event can create the illusion that you have really traveled back in time and entered another world. Throughout my own involvement with living history, I have been struck by how often interpreters and reenactors talk about their experiences in almost bringing the past to life. The best you can do, of course, is authentically to simulate the past, but everyone seems to savor the moment when you actually feel as if you are part of a particular historical period or event. The memory of experiencing what it really must have been like is a reward that anyone seriously associated with living history prizes. I remember showing a well-known museum curator around Living History Farms in Des Moines, Iowa. He happened to be blind. He insisted on involving himself in the historical lifestyles we were

simulating at the three period farms. He wanted to touch the split rails of our pioneer fences, listen to the bells of the dairy cattle, smell the earthy aroma of a newly plowed field, and taste the full-flavored stew cooked over open wood fires. At the end of a long day of immersing himself in our facsimile of life in the nineteenth-century Midwest, he paid living history its highest compliment. "Thank you for the visit. You have brought the past to light. I'll see it forever in my mind's eye."

Endnote

Since this LIVING HISTORY READER was assembled in the spring of 1987, three excellent anthologies dealing with museums and interpretation have been published. The first was *Folklife and Museums: Selected Readings* by Patricia Hall and Charlie Seemann (1987, AASLH: Nashville). It contains fifteen articles on the realtionship between folklore and folklife studies and both indoor and outdoor musems. the second was Jo Blatti's *Past Meets Present: Essays about Historic Interpretation and Public Audiences* (1987, Smithsonian Institution Press: Washington, D.C.). Twelve new articles are included, focusing on innovative ways of interpreting a truthful account of the past. The third anthology was by Warren Leon and Roy Rosenzweig, *History Museums in the United States: A Critical Assessment* (1987, University of Illinois Press: Urbana). this anthology deals with all genres of the american history museum and includes a thought-provoking article on "Living-History Museums" by Warren Leon and Margaret Pratt.

Those who enjoy reading about living-history museums in this anthology certainly will find complimentary articles in these three first-rate books.

Contributors

Jay Anderson is professor of history and American studies and director of the graduate program in outdoor museum work and living history at Utah State University. He serves as director of the student-run Ronald V. Jensen Living Historical Farm, a 1917 Cache Valley dairy farm. He received his Ph.D. in folklore and folklife from the University of Pennsylvania and is the author of *Time Machines: The World of Living History* (1984) and *The Living History Sourcebook* (1985).

Andrew H. Baker is an agricultural historian at Lake Farm Park in Kirtland, Ohio. Formerly he worked at Old Sturbridge Village where he combined the duties of a lead interpreter and researcher. As lead interpreter he has been involved in developing and interpreting programs relating to agriculture and politics. He received an M.A. in history from the University of Connecticut in 1976 and is an active participant in the Association of Living Historical Farms and Agricultural Museums.

Anthony Brandt is a free-lance writer whose work has appeared in a number of national publications, including the *Atlantic Monthly, American Heritage, Esquire,* and the *New York Times Magazine.* He is the author of a book about the mental health system and is the nonfiction editor of the *Pushcart Prize* annual. He lives in Sag Harbor, New York, where he serves on the local board of historic preservation.

Don W. Callender, Jr. is a trained archaeologist. From 1966 to 1969, he worked at the Maya site of Tikal in Guatemala. During the bicentennial fo the American Revolution, he was director of research at the Colonial Pennsylvania Plantation, a Quaker colonial farm outside Philadelphia. There, he carried out a number of innovative projects in experimental archaeology. He now lives in Wilmington, Delaware, where he is director of the Historic Red Clay Valley Railroad Museum.

Cary Carson is vice president of research at the Colonial Williamsburg Foundation. He holds an M.A. from the Henry Francis du Pont Winterthur Museum Program in early American history and culture (1965) and a Ph.D. in history from Harvard University (1974). He has been Coordinator of Research at St. Mary's City, Maryland, and a research associate at the Smithsonian Institution. He has taught at Yale University, Carleton College, and the college of William and Mary, and has published a number of articles on the subject of historic site research and interpretation.

Tracey Linton Craig, former assistant editor of *History News,* is now associate editor of publications for the American Association of Museums in Washington, D.C. A graduate of Oberlin College, she holds a degree in history and has written a number of articles related to museums and cultural agency administration.

James Deetz is director of the Lowie Museum of Anthropology and professor of anthropology at the University of California, Berkeley. Formerly assistant director of Plimoth Plantation, he has written extensively on the subject of living history. He holds a Ph.D. in anthropology from Harvard and is the author of *Invitation to Archaeology* (1967) and *In Small Things Forgotten* (1977). He is the past president of the Society for Historical Archaeology and is in demand as a speaker, particularly on the subject of historical interpretation.

John Fortier is director of Historic Sites for Pennsylvania's Historical and Museum Commission and was formerly head of the Provincial Museum of Alberta. He holds an M.A. in history from the College of William and Mary, where he studied historical administration and interpretation in an advanced program conducted by Colonial Williamsburg. An enthusiastic reenactor since the Civil War Centennial, he has been Park Superintendent for the Fortress of Louisbourg National Historic Park and a historian with the Michigan Historical Commission. He has written numerous thoughtful articles on the theory and practice of living history and has consulted with historic sites in North America and Australia.

Mark L. Gardner holds an M.A. in American studies from the University of Wyoming. For almost ten years, he has been active in living history both as a reenactor and museum interpreter. He has worked at Bent's Old Fort National Historic Site and Harpers Ferry. As a member of the Missouri Civil War Reenactors Association, he has participated in numerous reenactments. Currently, he is site administrator for three Colorado historical Society sites in Trinidad, Colorado, where he also pursues his research in nineteenth-century photography and popular music.

Edward L. Hawes holds a Ph.D. in history from the University of Wisconsin. His doctoral dissertation dealt with central European agriculture and led to a serious interest in outdoor museums. He has worked with Sangamon State University's Clayville Rural Life Center and the Freeport Historical Society's intensive program for adults in Maine. A past president of the Association of Living Historical Farms and Agricultural Museums, he has published a variety of significant articles on museum theory and methods, especially historical simulation. Currently, he teaches courses on historical farmways and foodways, museum communication, and European and American folklife.

R. Douglas Hurt holds a Ph.D. in American history from Kansas State University. His research specialization is agricultural history and he is the author of *The Dust Bowl: An Agricultural and Social History* and *American Farm Tools: From Hand Power to Steam Power.*

Darwin P. Kelsey holds a Ph.D. in historical geography from Clark University and currently is director of Lake Farm Park in Kirtland, Ohio. He was formerly director of the Boy Scouts of America National Museum in Murray, Kentucky. He conceived and developed the first successful living historical farm while working at Old Sturbridge Village. A past president of the Association of Living Historical Farms and Agricultural Museums, his publications include *Farming in the New Nation: Interpreting American Agriculture 1790-1940* and numerous articles in journals such as *Historic Preservation, Agricultural History,* and *History News.*

Rod King currently works with Indiana and Michigan Electric Company in public relations. He graduated from Ohio University with a B.S. in journalism and has been a reporter with the *Fort Wayne News-Sentinel* and a free-lance writer. A history buff, King took on the role of Benjamin Franklin Stickney, Fort Wayne's Indian agent. His profile of Historic Fort Wayne developed out of his experiences as an interpreter.

Warren Leon works with the Union of Concerned Scientists in Cambridge, Massachusetts. Formerly he was director of interpretation at Old Sturbridge Village. His writings on museum education, history teaching, and community history have appeared in the *Journal of Family History, History News,* and other periodicals. He co-edited *Experiments in History Teaching* (1977) and recently completed editing (with Roy Rosenzweig) *History Museums in the United States: A Critical Assessment* (1988). He holds a Ph.D. in American history from Harvard University.

Mark Leone teaches archaeology at the University of Maryland. A prolific writer, he is the author of *Roots of Modern Mormonism,* which is based on his extensive enthnographic field work in the Mormon settlements along the Little Colorado River as well as a broad range of historical sources, including diaries, native histories, judicial records, and correspondence. His articles on historical interpretation have been published in journals such as *Museum News.*

David Lowenthal is professor emeritus in the Department of Geography, University College, London. He is one of the first scholars to examine the American way of 'imaginatively recreating the past at outdoor museums and historic sites.' A graduate of Harvard, he has been both a research associate and Secretary of the American Geographical Society. His recent book, *The Past Is a Foreign Country,* is a monumental study of the ways in which the *past* has been used in Europe and America from the Renaissance to today.

Robert J. McQuarie has been director of the Littleton Historical Museum for almost twenty years. He holds an M.A. in American history from New Mexico Highlands University. He has been the curator of the Historical Society of Colorado's educational department. He has consulted extensively throughout the United States and is respected as an expert on museum education.

John Patterson is executive director of Yuma Crossing Foundation, Yuma, Arizona. Formerly he was director of programs at Conner Prairie in Noblesville, Indiana. He holds an M.A. in history museum work from the University of Connecticut. He has worked at Old Sturbridge Village where he specialized in the interpretation of economic history.

Diane Spencer Pritchard is the former chief historian for the California Lands Commission and editor of *The Pacific Historian,* a quarterly journal of western history. She is the author of numerous articles on Californian history. She and her husband Bill helped organize the Fort Ross living history program in 1981. In 1985, the Pritchards were honored by the American Association for State and Local History with an Award of Merit for the body of their work on Fort Ross.

Robert Ronsheim studied American history at Wooster and Harvard. He has taught at Indiana, Northeastern, and Butler universities. A specialist in interpretation, he has worked at Plimoth Plantation and Conner Prairie and for the National Park Service at Hopewell Village and Minute Man National Historic Site. Ronsheim is considered an expert in developing interpretive programs that communicate the wholeness of historical periods. He currently lives in Dover, New Jersey.

Thomas J. Schlereth is professor of American studies at the University of Notre Dame, where he heads the graduate program in American studies and teaches courses on American culture; urban, landscape, and architectural history; and material culture. He is the author of nine books, including the landmark anthology *Material Culture Studies in America*. His numerous articles on outdoor museums have set a standard for other scholars. He is presently completing a full-scale study, *Everyday Life in America, 1876-1915*.

Paul Schullery is currently the associate editor of Country Journal. He has worked as a naturalist and historian for the National Park Service in Yellowstone. He is author, co-author, or editor of fourteen books, including *The Bears of Yellowstone, American Fly Fishing: A History*, and *Mountain Time*. He recently revised and enlarged Freeman Tilden's classic The National Parks.

Michael Wallace teaches history at John Jay College of Criminal Justice at the City University of New York. He is a co-editor of *Presenting the Past: Essays on the Public and History* (1986) and has written a number of thoughtful essays for *Radical History Review*. He is presently working on a history of New York City.

Roger Welsch was formerly professor of English and anthropology at the University of Nebraska, where he specialized in Great Plains folklore. He has published over fifteen books including *A Treasury of Nebraska Folklore, Shingling the Fog and Other Plains Lies*, and most recently *Cather's Kitchens: Foodways in Literature and Life*. In addition, he has published over fifty scholarly and popular articles on folklore, folklife, cultural history, humor, and foodways. He can be seen regularly on CBS's "Sunday Morning," sending his "Postcards from Nebraska" to Charles Kuralt.

Index